# HISTORY OF AMERICAN THOUGHT AND CULTURE

Paul S. Boyer, *General Editor*

# The Voice of America

PROPAGANDA AND DEMOCRACY,
1941–1945

Holly Cowan Shulman

*The University of Wisconsin Press*

The University of Wisconsin Press
114 North Murray Street
Madison, Wisconsin 53715

3 Henrietta Street
London WC2E 8LU, England

5  4  3  2  1

Printed in the United States of America

Library of Congress Cataloging-in-Publication Data
Shulman, Holly Cowan.
    The Voice of America: propaganda and democracy, 1941–1945
/ Holly Cowan Shulman.
    292 pp.        cm. – (History of American thought and culture)
    Includes bibliographical references and index.
    1. Voice of America (Organization)  2. World War, 1939–1945
–Propaganda.  3. Propaganda, American–History–20th century.
I. Title.  II. Series.
D810.P7U387        1990
940.54'88673-dc20        90-50098
ISBN 0-299-12620-X        CIP
ISBN 0-299-12624-2 (pbk.)

# Contents

# *Preface*

I BEGAN this book after my father's death.

Lou Cowan spent his war years in the Overseas Branch of the Office of War Information. First he was liaison to the OWI from the army. Next he became head of the Radio Program Bureau. Finally, he took charge of the New York office, directing operations to Europe, Africa, and the Middle East. He was a midwesterner from Chicago who had gone into publicity and radio production straight from college; the war, and the time he spent in New York and Washington, changed his life. He and my mother chose to stay in the East after 1945, reluctant to leave the excitement and the friends they had found there, and the expanding postwar world of television.

His belief in the power of ideas and the importance of propaganda pervaded our house, like the background sound of music. Our den, as family rooms were known in the fifties, was not called a den: it was the propaganda room, and the heart of our family gatherings. There my father repeatedly told me that the best way to present ideas was first to tell your audience what you were going to say, then say it, and finally tell them what you had said. That had been the structure of propaganda during the war, he reminisced, and it would serve me well in my student papers.

My father believed that ideas could transform people's lives, and that ideas were important to ordinary people, holding ordinary jobs, as well as to the nation's leaders. It was a creed he had developed as the son of an immigrant Jew from Lithuania, but his conviction took on a new intellectual respectability during the war.

He died, with my mother, in a fire that swept through their Madison Avenue apartment on November 18, 1976. I was looking for a dissertation topic, but I did not search through the remains of my father's life until three months after his death. I had gone to their memorial service in New York. There, inspired by a talk given by Michel Rapaport Gordey, a former writer for the French desk of the Voice of America, and encouraged by my brother Geoff, I began to think about writing a dissertation on the OWI. I finally decided to write about propaganda itself, and the Voice of America. This book has taken me many years to complete, but throughout the inevitable difficulties encountered in such an undertaking I have been sustained by the memory of my father, and by his conviction that ideas matter. It is with the greatest love and gratitude that I dedicate this book to him.

In the process of writing this book, I received willing aid from a large number of people. I would like to thank the many archivists and librarians who helped me find the material for this work, and especially Sally Marks, who patiently guided me through the holdings in the State Department documents of the National Archives. Monique Millholin helped me translate the directives and transcripts, and spent hours discussing French culture and the history of the Resistance with me. Angelene R. Terry indefatigably transcribed tapes and helped me sort through the dilemmas of word processing. I would like to thank the University of Maryland for its financial assistance, which allowed me to go to England and do research at the Public Record Office and the BBC Written Archives Centre. The Smithsonian Institution provided me with a year's fellowship, stimulating guidance, and archival resources. Elliot Sivowitch, in particular, helped me untangle the mysteries of the technical end of short-wave broadcasting. Forrest Pogue gave me great encouragement and insight into the workings of the military and diplomatic establishments in the 1930s and 1940s, and provided a model of enlightened scholarship. Many of the participants graciously allowed me to interview them. Some devoted whole days to the process of our interview and later wrote me letters in answer to further inquiries. I want especially to thank Connie Ernst Bessie, Michael Bessie, Wallace Carroll, John Houseman, Robert Newman, Oscar W. Riegel, Lord Ritchie-Calder, and Marie Pertchuk Whiteside. Michel Rapaport Gordey inspired this book and later reminisced with me and advised me on whom else I should contact from the French desk. Special thanks go to Leonard Miall, who spent many hours in conversation with me, opened up his personal papers to me, and helped me gain access to the BBC Sound Archives.

I would like to thank those who helped me with my writing. James Gilbert proved a superb dissertation adviser and thereafter continuing mentor and friend. He knew when to leave me to my own resources and when to step in to offer guidance. Many people read either all or part of the manuscript in some form and offered a variety of useful suggestions. For their aid I am grateful to Alexander Brummer, Wayne S. Cole, Marcia Feldman,

James Harris, Ronald Hoffman, Richard Kohn, Lawrence Lichty, and Susan Smulyan. Paul Boyer and Barbara Hanrahan at the University of Wisconsin Press have provided me with many insights and much support. I would like to thank, as well, the manuscript readers, Allan M. Winkler and Clayton R. Koppes. J. C. A. Stagg has read innumerable versions of this manuscript, invariably improving the product with his suggestions and criticisms. Finally, I would like to thank my family. My siblings, Geoff, Liza, and Paul Cowan, all read parts of this manuscript. Paul, especially, encouraged me throughout the last year of his life, despite the fact that he was stricken with leukemia. My husband, Seth, read many versions of the manuscript, supported me in the endeavor, and guided me through the thickets of computer technology. And finally, my children, Rebecca, Jonathan, and Polly, helped me retain my sanity and balance.

*THE VOICE OF AMERICA*

# Introduction

THE VOICE of America broadcast to Europe twenty-four hours a day throughout the Second World War from a building on West Fifty-Seventh Street, a former Chevrolet dealership with high ceilings, large rooms, and vast display windows. When not at their desks in glass cubicles, policy leaders divided their time between meetings in Washington, streams of official visitors, and endless staff sessions. In this cavernous building renowned but underpaid European writers translated propaganda policy into radio shows as they churned out stories on battles and American war production. Announcers retreated from the babble of languages into soundproof rooms where they enacted their scripts with an upbeat American sound. "This is New York," the Voice of America proclaimed, "the United States of America, calling the people of Europe." This was the Voice of America at war.[1]

International radio propaganda developed in Europe and Asia during the 1930s, and by September 1939, when Germany invaded Poland, every major power except the United States had its own international broadcasting service. America did not officially enter the world of international propaganda-over-the-air until 1942, but once launched, the Voice of America became a permanent instrument of international politics. This is a book about the wartime history of the Voice of America.

The art of political persuasion, or what one leading American propaganda theorist defined as "the control of opinion by significant symbols," has existed since the beginnings of recorded history. But popular democracy and the mass media transformed it from a minor activity into an instrument of total warfare.[2] The propaganda battles waged by the belligerent powers in the First World War had been prominent and frightening. Propagandists in every nation had projected ugly atrocity campaigns through words and images: posters, leaflets, speakers, and films. This newly visible weapon survived the war, at least in people's minds, as a weapon of terrifying potential.

3

During the next two decades, fears of propaganda merged with concerns about the hidden powers of radio. Professional broadcasting had not begun until after the Great War ended, but once on the air, radio's potential influence was quickly understood.[3] Words spoken into a radio microphone reached men and women sitting at home, listening to their radios. Within weeks of assuming office in 1933 President Roosevelt demonstrated how effectively he could use radio to reach ordinary citizens. His "fireside chats" became a milestone in politics and broadcasting. Until that March a single White House employee had handled all presidential mail, even during the First World War and the panic following the Wall Street crash in 1929. But following his first fireside chat unanswered letters piled up in Roosevelt's White House. Roosevelt established through radio a direct—an almost personal—relationship with the American electorate. The president had proven the political importance of radio.[4]

When it first began, broadcasting reached a strictly local audience. Programs could be heard only by those who could pick up a long- or medium-wave signal sent from a nearby transmitter. But in the early twenties the invention of short-wave broadcasting expanded the potential influence of broadcasting, and by extension of propaganda, because use of shortwaves allowed radio signals to be heard over a longer distance. Short-, medium-, and long-wave broadcasting are all characterized by amplitude modulation (AM). The shorter waves of the radio spectrum, however, are reflected off the upper layers of the ionosphere, bouncing around the globe like stones skipping across water and striking the earth at regular intervals. This "skip distance" effect allowed short-wave broadcasting across international boundaries. As early as 1924, low-powered, high-frequency transmissions could be received thousands of miles away from their points of origin.[5]

In the late twenties European governments seized on this new radio technology and began setting up short-wave broadcasting services. The first nation to do so was Holland, aiming to bind together the far-flung elements of the Dutch empire; it was soon followed by France, Belgium, Italy, and Great Britain. These early imperial stations were thinly disguised instruments of colonial policy, and they demonstrated the potential use of short-wave radio for international propaganda. When Adolf Hitler took over Germany, however, he converted radio into an aggressive weapon of foreign policy. By the end of the 1930s German radio was on the air over twenty-one hours a day, working to divide, confuse, and fragment the world.[6]

Then, in the spring of 1940, Germany overran western Europe. The Nazis not only used armored motorized vehicles; they employed propaganda to undermine their enemy's will to fight. The fall of France persuaded U.S.

government leaders such as John J. McCloy, and liberals outside the government such as Viking Press publisher Harold Guinzburg and newspaper columnist George Fielding Eliot, that a blitzkrieg of ideas was as effective as a blitzkrieg of tanks.[7]

These events reinforced American fears of propaganda. Americans had been deeply alarmed by the excessive emotions and hatred brought to the surface by George Creel's Committee on Public Information during World War I, and most of the nation, including President Roosevelt, rejected propaganda as a formal instrument of foreign policy. Yet political leaders and intellectuals were frightened by what they believed to be the might of Nazi propaganda. Roosevelt appointed a special committee to study the problem in late 1940.[8] Henry L. Stimson, the secretary of war, warned the committee that the Germans were undermining the American institutions of freedom of the press and freedom of discussion, and that the nation would have to fight back.[9] Stimson's assistant secretary, John J. McCloy, told the committee that the army needed to mobilize for propaganda warfare just as much as it needed to do so for ground and air warfare.[10] And the liberal playwright cum presidential speech writer, Robert E. Sherwood, boldly proclaimed that America had to fight Nazi propaganda with American propaganda. In July 1941, working under presidential orders, Sherwood created the Foreign Information Service (FIS), which in June 1942 became the Overseas Branch of the Office of War Information (OWI). The American government launched its war of words, and six months later the president authorized the Voice of America.

The Voice of America cannot be understood apart from the propaganda broadcast by the station. I have, therefore, retraced the trail of the broadcasts, month by month and year by year, in a single language. Because the French desk was the single largest language desk, I have focused on propaganda broadcast to France. In 1942 American propagandists believed they could influence the French, while they doubted that they could reach many Germans. Both the Occupied and Vichy French governments forbade their citizens from tuning in enemy stations, but the German government not only outlawed listening, it did so under penalty of death. Since 1940 the French had turned to the British Broadcasting Corporation (BBC), and American propagandists hoped the French would include the Voice of America in their listening habits. By 1944 propaganda to France had a special mission: to support the Allied liberation of western Europe.

The propaganda broadcast by the French desk changed dramatically over the course of the war. In 1942 the first director of the Voice of America,

John Houseman, created the initial broadcasting style of the Voice of America. Houseman came from the world of theater, radio drama, and film. He had, for example, produced "War of the Worlds," the radio science fiction program that in 1938 so alarmed listeners living near the supposed Martian invasion site in New Jersey that many packed their families and belongings into their cars and fled. He brought to the Voice his experience in experimental radio and his knowledge of drama-as-propaganda, or agitprop, and he used these techniques to originate a unique-sounding station whose very tones urged the French to rise up and resist the Nazis.

Following the American-led Allied invasion of North Africa in November 1942, however, the propaganda style of the Voice gradually altered. Increasingly it acquired a patina of calm and neutral news reporting, while its message shifted from encouragement of resistance to explanations of the coming Allied liberation of France. Between 1942 and 1944 the forms in which the Voice of America cast its propaganda moved from agitation to factual news reporting, a shift necessitated by the increasing American emphasis on Allied military victory.

These changes were part of a larger trend that had begun in the First World War, and that had taken place in all countries, both Allied and Axis. During the Great War, propagandists on both sides relied on the strength of moral argumentation. Themes of "our cause is right" and "the enemy's cause is wrong" predominated. World War I propaganda emphasized the brutality of the enemy, to the point of fabricating enemy actions in order to underline the moral righteousness of the propagandists' cause. During the Second World War—at least in Europe—Allied propaganda took a more sober and less emotional, moralistic, or didactic approach to the problem of persuasion, muting overt statements of ideology and dropping most allusions to enemy bestiality. Only the Nazis retained this style of propaganda. More and more, Allied propaganda relied on the presentation of facts and information. This trend was visible from the beginning of the war, but it became clearer the longer the war lasted.[11] By 1944 the shift to an informational format of propaganda was pronounced.[12]

All propaganda operates by taking cultural myths and symbols and reworking them in the service of nationally conceived aims. Nazi propaganda, for example, used and expanded on an important German myth and employed it at home and abroad. According to this myth, Germany was a young and pure nation, a nation of Siegfrieds, fighting evil schemers out to destroy the German people.[13] Throughout the war German propagandists drew on this myth; its power was so strong that even when, in 1944 and 1945, propagandists wanted to change course in the face of Allied victories and

Axis defeats, they could not do so; they could alter much of their style, but they could not escape the mythical universe they had constructed.

American propaganda also used national images, symbols, and myths: America was an innocent giant whose mission was to save war-tired Europe. This myth of innocence, with deep roots in American culture, prevailed throughout the war and colored and shaped propaganda's news and pronouncements on American foreign policy. This book studies the images used by the Voice of America: what they were and how they were projected; what prevailed and what changed; and how American propaganda achieved its emotional power.

My analysis of the actual propaganda of the Voice of America forms only one part of this study. What was said to the French was governed by committees convened to create directives and guidances issued daily, weekly, and monthly, for special events and for long-range campaigns. I have traced the process by which government representatives originated propaganda goals, how they turned these goals into guidances, and how propagandists translated political aims into broadcast shows.

I have, therefore, followed the history of the Voice of America within several contexts: those of foreign policy, domestic politics, and American culture. To comprehend the foreign policy goals of the French language programs I have examined American policy toward France. I have also looked at the complex, difficult, and often distant relationship between the State Department and the OWI.

Men from the Departments of State, War, and Navy met with the leaders of the Office of War Information at regular intervals. British propaganda leaders sent representatives to work in the OWI as well as political guidances to steer American propaganda toward British political goals. Congress reviewed the workings of the OWI and established limits beyond which the OWI was not to go. The Bureau of the Budget kept a watchful eye over the administration of the propaganda operation, and the Office of Strategic Services, the OSS, competed with the OWI for leadership in the field of propaganda. All this inevitably led to a second war, a domestic battle for control of overseas propaganda. The leaders of the OWI struggled with these conflicting pressures, which sapped their energies and eventually defeated the goals of the Overseas Branch itself.

Finally, the changes in propaganda over the course of the war were generated by a shifting intellectual and cultural climate. American culture during the war years traveled from the social realism and experimental modernism of the thirties to a conservative realism. The style of the propaganda radio programs had become increasingly factual and detailed rather than imaginative and experimental. It had moved, as it were, from the dramatic scripts of Norman Corwin to the seemingly straightforward news broadcasts of Edward R. Murrow, just as the poster propaganda of the OWI had altered from the social realism of Ben Shahn and the modernist abstractions of Jean Carlu to the conservative realism of Norman Rockwell and the photo posters cranked out to plaster the walls of the liberated streets of Europe. The propagandists also worked within the intellectual environment of changing social science theories on the achievable goals and potential influence of propaganda. Before the war social scientists believed that the thoughts and opinions of the radio listening audience could be moved through the conscious manipulation of a whole range of symbols and arguments. By the end of the war they no longer believed that propaganda could transform thought or provoke action.

The most important reasons why Voice of America propaganda changed between 1942 and 1944 lie with the war itself. The Second World War transformed America: its position in the world, its domestic politics, and its culture. By 1944 America had become a world power concerned with maintaining postwar stability and order. At home, the war had ended the Great Depression and with it the pressing need for reform and social experimentation. Postwar America would soon emerge as a more prosperous and conservative nation than it had been in the thirties. In short, the United States of 1946 was a very different place from the United States of 1939.

In February 1942, when the Voice of America first went on the air, the Allies were losing the war. By February 1944 it had become clear that the Allies had won and that the achievement of final victory was only a matter of time. The abundant resources of the United States, combined with the strength of the Soviet Union, had defeated the Axis. Equally important, throughout most of 1942, until the Allied invasion of North Africa on November 8, the United States had no troops in Europe: America did not go to war in Europe, except at sea, until the very end of 1942. For the first nine months of broadcasting by the Voice of America, therefore, the United States was not fighting the European war with soldiers, but with industrial supplies, military buildup, promises, hopes—and propaganda. In 1943 the Allies turned the tide of the war; in 1944 they invaded Normandy, liberated Paris, and in October freed all of France. The war slogged on in Europe for another seven months, and in the Pacific for another three months after that; but the war had been won.

American propagandists in 1942 thus had no good military news to tell their French audience; they had to work with continuing news of defeat and somehow create a positive image of an alliance that was on the defensive. They told the French about American war production and the U.S. commitment to the war, and they recounted battle news, both good and bad. Beyond this, American propagandists encouraged the French people under the regimes of both Occupied France and Vichy to resist the Nazis. The French Resistance was extremely small, far too small to have any military or political influence within France. But for the leaders of the OWI, the idea of resistance in France stemmed from their hope that a Popular Front Europe existed in which ordinary men and women were struggling to survive in their Axis-occupied nation and were engaging in total warfare against the Nazis.[14]

In part, this romanticized resistance, and what quickly became an attempt to enlarge it through moral persuasion, was a logical reaction to a situation of intense frustration. What could propagandists tell the French, and more to the point, how could propaganda, how could words alone, help win the war? The British had gone through the same set of agonizing questions in 1940 and 1941 and at the beginning of their propaganda war had created the *V* campaign. Over the winter and spring of 1941 the BBC had exhorted its listeners to paint the letter *V* across Nazi-dominated Europe and to show by this small symbol of resistance that they believed in freedom and were eager to fight for their own liberation.[15] Like the Americans, the British had initially turned to resistance when there was no good British war news to broadcast.

There was more to the encouragement of resistance than frustration and pragmatic decisions. Resistance, and with it support for European leaders of the Left, defined the politics of New Deal liberals as World War II propagandists. The leaders of the Overseas Branch of the OWI, and of the Voice of America, believed that the war was being fought to create a new world of peace, democracy, and freedom. They were New Deal liberals who, with a few exceptions, had held no government posts before the war. Even those leaders who had joined Roosevelt's government during the thirties had not been associated with the State Department and had had no role in diplomacy. The leaders of the OWI were part of a wave of New Deal liberals who with the coming of the war brought their political convictions to American foreign policy but did so outside the State Department, instead staffing new agencies such as the OWI or OSS, or joining the Treasury Department under Henry Morgenthau's liberal leadership.[16]

By the late thirties these men were obsessed with the need to defeat the Axis. During the war they poured their energies into the war effort. But by social status, education, and training, they could not comfortably join the ranks of the politically conservative and socially rigid State Department. In 1942, the special-for-war agencies such as the OWI and OSS seemed to offer a way for these liberals to join the government and perhaps even transform the hidebound foreign policy system. But by late 1943 their influence on foreign policy had clearly waned, and these outsiders-as-insiders found themselves politically stranded, alienated, and often angry at the State Department and the military, even if not consciously at war with President Roosevelt.

The leaders of the OWI were emphatically antifascist. For them, the rise of Fascism in Italy and National Socialism in Germany was connected with the breakdown of capitalism both abroad and within the United States. The price of failure in Europe had been the collapse of the old political systems and the rise of right-wing dictatorships. Hitler and Mussolini therefore had to be defeated in order to preserve the civilized world; the conquest of the Axis was intertwined with pruning the excesses of capitalism at home and rejuvenating democracy abroad. Sherwood and Houseman, for example, had supported the Republicans in Spain and the Popular Front in France.

The crusades of the thirties merged with the crisis of the war. When Hitler and Mussolini, and the Japanese in Asia, attacked the western democracies and the Soviet Union, they threatened the existence of everything in which liberal Americans believed. The war became a crusade against evil. And American liberals believed that just as they had fought the Depression with jobs they had to fight the Axis with democratic ideals.

As early as mid-1941, therefore, Sherwood and his colleagues set about using propaganda to defeat Hitler, Mussolini, and in France the Vichy government of Pétain, Laval, and Darlan, and to create a new world in which freedom and economic stability would flourish. Because they were deeply convinced that they were right, and because they believed that the president was on their side, they bypassed the stolid and conservative Departments of State, War, and Navy. They used propaganda to push on the edges of foreign policy in order to make American policy express what they believed was the true spirit of the United States. They ignored the State Department in 1942, taking political guidance instead from the British, and charged full steam ahead.

The American-led invasion of North Africa in November 1942 changed all this. General Eisenhower, and then President Roosevelt, decided that the United States should collaborate with a former Vichy minister of state, Admiral Jean Darlan. It was a devastating decision, one that undercut the wartime vision of liberal Americans. Recognition of Darlan emptied the liberal, Popular Front content from the rhetoric of the Voice of America.

Throughout 1943 great tension emerged between the liberal propagandists and the strategy of the American war effort. In 1943 the leaders of the OWI used propaganda to fight for what they believed American foreign policy should be. But in the end they had to fail, both because propaganda could not alter foreign policy and because, by late 1943, the propagandists were not only fighting the State Department but also the president. Roosevelt was determined to win the war with as few losses of American lives as possible, and in order to do that he not only postponed political decisions until after the war but also temporarily accepted fascist leaders in Europe as well as in North America. The propagandists found that they had been wrong about why America was at war and the goals for which the nation was fighting. Throughout 1943 they struggled against propaganda as information because they understood that a campaign of information meant support for a foreign policy they could not accept, let alone change.

By 1944 the liberal political vision of the early years of the war, of resistance and domestic revolution, no longer made sense. Moreover, in France General Charles de Gaulle had become the leader of the Resistance. Although he remained a symbol of armed combat against the Nazis, his leadership was of a nonideological alliance within France and with the Allies for liberation. By 1944 the French Resistance was no longer a revolutionary movement; it had instead aligned itself with the Allied powers, from whom it expected to achieve a peaceful transition to power, an expectation achieved in the fall of 1944.

Once U.S. leaders knew that the war would be won, despite the years of brutal fighting which still lay ahead, they had to face the question of what the political and economic goals for which they had been striving were. These questions had not been seriously raised inside the State Department or the White House in 1941 and 1942, and by 1944 the liberal vision of the thirties did not provide adequate answers to the issues of what America wanted from victory and of the nation's rise to world power. American foreign policy in 1944 and 1945 lacked clarity. The Soviet Union had not yet emerged as the dominant enemy; that would not happen until after the war had ended and Truman had become president. No political philosophy replaced the liberalism of the early war years. The men who led the OWI and the Voice of America in the last years of the war were not conservatives, but neither were they the firm New Deal liberals of the early days. They were men who were willing to work with the State Department and the military, men who were comfortable within a bureaucracy in which they lost as many fights as they won. They were committed internationalists, they accepted the Soviet Union as a staunch ally, and they wanted to create a democratic and prosperous postwar world without oppression or political tyranny. They understood that the Popular Front, revolutionary goals of the early OWI were no longer realistic, either as American foreign policy or as postwar French domestic politics. But they did not have a new vision to substitute for the old, and so they accepted the immediate American goals of military victory and political stability. They had, because of their politics, a different set of answers to the question of what the proper relationship of propaganda to foreign policy was than had their predecessors; they worked with American foreign policy instead of against it. In their hands the Voice of America became the Voice of Victory.[17]

# 1

# *Founding a Propaganda Agency*

PRESIDENT Roosevelt's speech writer and adviser Robert E. Sherwood gathered together a group of journalists, writers, and political activists in the summer of 1941 and mobilized them into a band of propagandists prepared to fight a war of words against the Axis. Throughout the first year and a half of their battle, the propagandists struggled to define their role, their aims, and their methods within a shifting and confusing environment. No authorized version of good, or even appropriate, propaganda existed. No department of the government or tradition of the government dictated what kind of message American propagandists should send the world: friend, foe, or neutral. The task of 1941 and 1942 was to establish a propaganda agency and define its goals and methods.

The story begins in 1940 with the creation of the Office of the Coordinator of Information and the Foreign Information Service. By the outbreak of war in Europe, President Roosevelt knew that his administration had to bolster morale at home and combat foreign propaganda. The president began discussing the problem over the spring and summer of 1940, and that fall he asked the secretary of the interior, Harold Ickes, to convene a sub-cabinet group "to meet and discuss the larger problems of propaganda, morale, and domestic information."[1] After three meetings, the majority concluded that the president should establish a government committee to work with private organizations.[2] The president did nothing.

That fall the State Department suggested to the president that the privately owned and operated short-wave radio broadcasting companies present the American viewpoint abroad, especially to France, to combat increasing Vichy French collaboration with Germany. If the U.S. government wanted to reach European audiences, the State Department reasoned, the only way to do so was through existing short-wave stations. The American radio industry—CBS, NBC, Westinghouse, and General Electric—had begun experimenting with short-wave technology in the mid-twenties, and by the early thirties had begun broadcasting abroad. In late 1940 the State Department went further with its plan and asked the British to retransmit American short-wave news broadcasts over BBC medium- and long-wave channels.

The British were intrigued with the idea. It presented an opportunity to supplement British propaganda to France with news from a still neutral nation, and they seriously listened to the American broadcasts for several weeks in January 1941 to assess their political value. Despite their initial enthusiasm, however, they concluded that these programs would not help the British war effort. But they were saved from having to reject the American offer on political grounds because the American signals proved too weak to be retransmitted.[3]

William J. Donovan forged the next link in the chain of events. In 1940 Donovan was a man in search of a mission. He was a distinguished New York lawyer who had seen active military service during the First World War and who had traveled extensively over the past twenty years. Through his journeys he had developed a passion for international politics, military affairs, and foreign intelligence. He was, moreover, both close to the president and a Republican. His presence in Roosevelt's government would lend credence to the president's efforts to create a bipartisan wartime government.

Donovan went to Europe twice that year. While in England he became friends with William Stephenson, the head of British Security Coordination and the spy popularly known as "Intrepid." Stephenson wanted Donovan to persuade Roosevelt to establish an American organization for intelligence and covert warfare, and Donovan soon became convinced that the United States would have to engage in propaganda as well.[4] He returned from his second trip in March 1941, eager to take up the twin causes of covert operations and psychological warfare.

Donovan's ideas about what propaganda should be were governed by his view of the political and military goals it should serve. For Donovan, propaganda was not a news service; it was a weapon that used news as guns fire bullets. He wanted to persuade listeners in Europe to fight the Axis, and he did not care whether propaganda carefully stuck to the truth or not.[5]

He outlined his theory of propaganda and its relationship to American foreign policy to Roosevelt. The specific role of propaganda, he wrote, was "to soften up the civilian population and make the job of the armed forces considerably easier."[6] Propaganda was the "arrow of initial penetration," after which espionage, guerrilla activities, and outright warfare would follow.[7] Donovan believed that propaganda could and should work toward such specific objectives as fomenting insurrection and directing political opposition. It aimed to demoralize the enemy before the sending in of troops. Propaganda, therefore, had to be woven together with a steady stream of intelligence about conditions in Europe, which in turn had to be studied and analyzed and then used for covert operations.[8]

In order to understand Donovan's goals it is important to view them within the context of contemporary British operations. The British, faced in 1940 with the prospect of invasion and defeat, had turned to unorthodox methods of war: intelligence, cryptography, subversion, and propaganda. They believed that the Germans had whipped through western Europe in part because they operated a successful fifth column that had destroyed morale and the will to fight back. Therefore the British decided to take the German idea and improve on it. By the middle of July Prime Minister Winston Churchill had given the go-ahead, christening the new organization the Special Operations Executive (SOE) and instructing the director "to set Europe ablaze."[9]

It was this idea that Donovan tried to replicate in America, and it explains why he believed that subversion, resistance, sabotage, and propaganda were linked. Donovan, in other words, supported resistance movements in Europe not because he advocated a revolutionary overhauling of the old order, but because resistance and revolution were tools with which to win a military war against the seemingly unbeatable Axis. The British had set a clear example for the type of propaganda which Donovan wanted to reproduce with the BBC's *V* campaign in the winter and spring of 1940–41. *V* was the first letter in the words for freedom in Flemish and victory in French and English, and the British exhorted Europeans to mark the letter *V* across the face of Nazi-dominated Europe. They were to paint it on walls, scrawl it over cars, and splash it across shop windows to show the Nazis that although Europeans might temporarily be conquered, they believed in freedom and would fight for victory. The British transmitted the spirit and the philosophy of the *V* campaign to Donovan, who tried to translate these goals into the objectives of American propaganda.[10]

Donovan had not counted on the deadlock of American foreign policy. But the differences between the foreign policy goals of the United States and Britain were paramount. British foreign policy supported SOE operations; American policy did not sustain the equivalent American actions. The British worked with resistance movements in Europe not because the British political establishment condoned communism or socialism or had any sympathy with the Popular Front. This was simply not the case. The British allied themselves with European resistance movements first of all to fight the war and later to win a peace in which the fulcrum for the balance of global power would remain in Europe with world leadership residing, at least in part, in Britain.[11]

Support for the French Resistance was a British operation. It was emphatically not American. In fact, the United States took a quite opposite tack by supporting Vichy France. Thus, no matter how cleverly Donovan learned his lessons from the British or how closely he recreated British operations in the United States, he was working in a context that undermined his goals of subversion and resistance. Ultimately, as we shall see, it made his vision of American propaganda unworkable.

But these events lay in the future. In the spring of 1941 Donovan poured his massive energies into creating an American counterpart to the SOE, meeting with Roosevelt and every influential civilian and military leader of whom he could get hold. By May he had persuaded presidential adviser Benjamin Cohen to work with him, and together they—and the Bureau of the Budget—wrote a military order for the president to sign.[12] This Roosevelt did on July 11. Six months before Pearl Harbor the Office of the Coordinator of Information, the COI, was born.[13]

The first person to join Donovan's new organization was the successful playwright turned presidential speech writer, Robert E. Sherwood. Sherwood had been in touch with Donovan that spring, and the day following the establishment of the COI he wrote Donovan that he was "appalled at the shortwave broadcasting, or lack of it" coming from American private stations. What the COI needed instead, he expanded, was "to set up a magnificent apparatus" to begin a real propaganda campaign. And that, he added, "cannot be done in the amateurish and uncoordinated way of the present time."[14]

That summer Sherwood created the Foreign Information Service, or FIS, which a year later was to become the Overseas Branch of the Office of War Information (OWI). In December 1942 he inaugurated the Voice of America. His beliefs permeated these institutions and gave them a distinct personality, atmosphere, and mode of operation.

Robert Emmett Sherwood was born in 1896 into an elite and politically conservative family that had long been prominent in American society. As a young man he was educated at Milton Academy and then at Harvard. His elite social and educational background gave Sherwood self-confidence and enabled him to move in circles of power and prestige.

He was a great raconteur who loved to pick up a hat and cane and entertain the party. But he was shy and often morose. He was plagued by a double tic douloureux that brought him great physical agony and would keep him up for hours, pacing the floor days and nights. At times he would leave his home in New York City in the middle of the night and go down to Grand Central Station, where he would board a train to Washington in order to cope with the intense pain inside his head.[15] His shyness was also intensified by his physical appearance and his speech. He was gaunt and exceptionally tall at six feet eight inches. He spoke painfully slowly and his conversation was often punctuated by uncomfortable gaps between brief utterances. Robert Bruce Lockhart, the wartime director of British overseas propaganda, remembered "having been placed next to him at a luncheon and had thought him speechless until he suddenly caught up with some question that had long drifted out of conversation and began to answer it." The listener had to wait for Sherwood's points, which came as victories of the tortoise over the hares.[16]

These personal characteristics affected him as a leader of propaganda. He was often depressed and introverted, a sensibility he hid under a veneer of playfulness and wit. He spoke slowly and earnestly, but at times he could not communicate in person as he could on paper. Some of his colleagues remembered great difficulty in getting political guidance from him, especially if they were abroad waiting on the end of a telephone line for immediate directions. But he also gave the Foreign Information Service, and later the Overseas Branch of the OWI, a very humane and civilized quality.[17]

Sherwood's politics were moral and naive. He had a knack of reflecting the nation's liberal political viewpoint just at its cutting edge. He supported Britain in World War I and fought in the Canadian army. In 1919 he favored President Wilson's League of Nations, but by 1920 he was an isolationist and a pacifist, casting his first presidential vote for Warren G. Harding.[18] He became a playwright of successful light comedies, but the events of the thirties turned him into an antifascist; by 1939 he had converted into an active interventionist. A year later he wrote the text for a full-page advertisement in the *New York Times* supporting all American efforts short of war to sustain Britain against the Axis, and in so doing he drew national attention to his political viewpoint.[19] Soon after the appearance of the ad Roosevelt asked Sherwood to take the job of presidential speech writer, and from then until Roosevelt's death it was Harry Hopkins, Sam Rosenman, and Bob Sherwood who wrote Roosevelt's major talks.[20]

Sherwood believed in the power of the word to influence people, and he wielded his words as weapons with sincerity and passion. He explained in the introduction to his interventionist play of 1940, *There Shall Be No*

*Night,* that "we have within ourselves the power to conquer bestiality, not with our muscles and our swords, but with the power of the light that is in our minds."[21] Again and again Sherwood reiterated this faith: "There is a new and decisive force in the human race," he wrote, "more powerful than all tyrants [and that] is the force of massed thought—thought which has been provoked by words, strongly spoken."[22]

An American voice, Sherwood believed, should be the voice of news about America and America's war effort. America's answers to Axis propaganda should emerge not through deftly created stage pieces, but from "the power of truth."[23] Speeches by government officials and real events about real people should form the substance of American propaganda. Sherwood wanted to shape this material into radio programs that would highlight Allied morale and disrupt the enemy's will to fight.[24] From the president's point of view Sherwood made a perfect choice for chief American propagandist: he was liberal, but not too left-wing; he had a national reputation and was well respected; he had no political enemies; and he was passionately committed to the president. As one of Sherwood's closest associates recalled, "there was nothing which Bob would not have done if he merely believed that Roosevelt wanted him to."[25]

Sherwood began by collecting a group of men who were comfortable with words and well acquainted with foreign languages and European governments. As a group they "believed deeply and almost in their bones that . . . wars are made in the minds of men and that wars are won in the minds of men."[26] He recruited men with three basic qualifications: knowledge of foreign affairs, aggressive support of Roosevelt's foreign policy, and willingness to work for very little money.[27]

Journalists dominated the early ranks of the FIS. Joseph F. Barnes, one of the very first men Sherwood asked to join the outfit, took over the New York office. Barnes was an extremely well-educated and experienced journalist. Something of a child prodigy, he had been admitted to Harvard at the age of fourteen. His parents decided instead to send him to England and there he lived for a year and a half on the outskirts of Oxford. He returned to the United States, went to Harvard (where he edited the school newspaper, the *Crimson*), and went back to England, to the London School of Economics. He soon became fascinated with the new Soviet Union, joined the American Socialist party, learned Russian, and left to study the country at first hand.

When Barnes came back to the United States he went into banking, perhaps an anomalous decision for a left-leaning young man. Whatever the reason, the Depression cut short his banking career and in 1934 Barnes joined the *New York Herald Tribune* and soon went to the Soviet Union as the *Tribune*'s Moscow correspondent. There he stayed, often intensely unhappy both with the limits the paper put on his copy and with Soviet censorship, until the *Tribune* sent him to Berlin at the end of 1938, a year he remembered as one of the unhappiest of his life.

He was in a Berlin tavern in 1939, drinking with fellow correspondent William L. Shirer of CBS News, when Barnes heard about the Stalin-Ribbentrop nonaggression pact between Germany and the Soviet Union. "Joe was absolutely stunned," Shirer recounted. "Everything he'd believed in about Russia went up in smoke. Till then he'd been very sympathetic to the Soviets and their aspirations." But Shirer recalled that Barnes continued to believe "that World War II had been ignited by capitalist interests."[28] Barnes soon came home to be the *Tribune*'s foreign news editor, where he earned a reputation as a first-rate foreign correspondent and editor. In the summer of 1941 he left the paper to join Sherwood and the FIS.

Throughout most of the twenties and thirties Barnes was a fellow traveler whose sympathies lay with the great Soviet experiment, the Spanish Republicans, and the French Popular Front. He was unquestionably and deeply loyal to the United States, but his well-known beliefs returned during the war—and even more so after the war—to plague him. George F. Kennan, who was in the Soviet Union as a member of the American embassy during the same years Barnes was there as a foreign correspondent, described him as "much more pro-Soviet than the rest of us—naively so, it seemed to me." He was "a warm, generous, if naive, idealistic [man], captivated, as so many had been in the early post-revolutionary period, by the excitement and the ostensibly progressive aims of the Soviet regime of that day."[29] The State Department and Congress were wary of a man with such warm-hearted left-leaning sentiments. But Barnes was firm in his conviction that the war was a crusade against fascism and for democracy, a war to end all oppression and bring about freedom. This belief infused his propaganda and gave him great dedication to his job.

Barnes was a man with enormous drive and great self-confidence. He believed in his own judgment and intelligence and was the sort of man to fight for what he believed in until he could fight no more, and then, if he had lost, to walk away knowing that he had played the game to the fullest, without regrets.[30] He was willing to fight higher authority, moreover, not only from political conviction, but out of his own sense of what made for good journalism. Papers, he believed, were shaped by editors, and not by publishers. They were the product of men who worked together, drank together, met in deskside huddles, flew past each other down a corridor, and had a thousand other daily encounters through which they developed shared values and a common outlook. Good journalism had little to do with politics, economics, or philosophy, and everything to do with craftsmanship and collegiality.[31] And good propaganda worked likewise: it could not be produced by the higher-ups in Washington; it had to result from daily New York operations. Barnes was a superb newspaperman. He threw himself into his work. And he was a man of the world. He led the New York office without throwing his weight around, and he very quickly became the driving force of the New York office.[32]

Barnes later described his own recruitment. "I had started as a newspaperman, equipped with languages to understand what the Axis was saying, and nothing but friendship with Sherwood to give advice as to the kind of devices of a propaganda nature to which we might turn. . . ."[33] But he had definite ideas about the proper relationship between news and propaganda. Like Sherwood, Barnes believed in telling the truth, but unlike his superior he wanted to "tell a true story to everyone, but to each one . . . the true story that will best serve our interests." He pushed American propaganda to support not only Britain and the Allies, but European resistance movements. As he recalled, "all stories must have a purpose in time of war."[34]

Sherwood brought Edd Johnson, a journalist by training from Winfield, Kansas, to supervise censorship over day-to-day policy and the analysis of foreign propaganda. Not much is known about Johnson's early life and work. He came directly from CBS's monitoring service. Before that he had been the managing editor of *Collier's* magazine and assistant editor of the *New York World Telegram*. Johnson's brother, Earl, worked for United Press and by 1941 was in charge of European news for the press service and well known to overseas journalists such as Barnes.

Like Barnes and Sherwood, Johnson believed in the effectiveness of hard news. He ran his organization with the speed of a daily news desk, and he instructed his staff to keep their analyses brief and concise. "He wanted reports to be short and he wanted them to be compiled very quickly," reported a member of his staff. He rejected academic methodologies such as content analysis; they were, he believed, too long to compile and too tedious to read, and he nicknamed them "sociological philly-phall."[35] "Mr. Johnson is a thoroughly competent man, with whom one could get on well," estimated one of the leaders of the British propaganda ministry.[36] And indeed, he got along famously within the FIS and early OWI, soon becoming, along with Barnes, one of the triumvirate below Sherwood who dominated the New York office and propaganda policy direction.

The third member of this troika was James Warburg, who became deputy director for policy planning in November 1941.[37] Of all the leaders of the FIS and OWI, Warburg was the most complex and protean. He was, to begin with, the only one of the original leaders of the FIS who was not a professional writer, although he wrote some thirty books over the span of his life. Whereas Sherwood felt he had roots in England and Barnes had spent part of his youth in Oxford and then London and lived as a young man in the Soviet Union, Warburg had shuttled throughout his childhood between Germany and the United States. He was a seventh-generation descendant of the international banking house of Warburg on his father's side, and a scion of a New York banking family of nearly equal importance, the firm of Kuhn and Loeb, on his mother's. Warburg grew up rich and talented with relations not only in Germany and America but in Britain as well. Like Sherwood he was a member of an elite, but unlike Sherwood, Barnes, or Johnson, Warburg was Jewish and could never fully belong to the American establishment. A high priest in his own world, his relationship to America was tinged with his sense of being an outsider.[38] He was warm, articulate, attractive, and charming, if also mercurial, and he brought enormous self-assurance and a strong sense of independence to his job with the OWI.

Like Sherwood and Barnes, Warburg had gone to Harvard; like Barnes he had edited the *Crimson*. After graduation he went into the family business, and over the next two decades became a financial leader. While achieving esteem in the banking world, Warburg also wrote poetry, books on finance, political tracts, and the lyrics to a successful Broadway musical. After the election of Roosevelt in 1932, Warburg became a political activist. He joined the early New Deal administration as a financial adviser until he quit Roosevelt's team in fury over the president's position on the gold standard, and then spent a full year fighting the president.[39] He wrote *Hell Bent for Election,* of which the Republicans distributed a million copies; unable to stomach Alf Landon as a candidate, he supported the Republican Frank Knox for the presidency—until he played double apostasy in an open letter to Secretary of State Cordell Hull, announcing that he would, after all, vote Democratic.[40]

Warburg was no man's minion, but much as he proved his commitment to his individual beliefs he lost his chance of ever attaining high office. Nevertheless, if he is to be categorized politically, it is important to note that in the early years of the New Deal Warburg was a conservative Democrat who accused Roosevelt of being a dictator and a socialist, and who proclaimed that he hated socialism "and even more its two misbegotten offspring, Communism and Fascism."[41] He railed against New Deal measures such as the

Agricultural Adjustment Act and argued that the improvement of people's lives did not lie in the province of the federal government whose role was more that of "a referee who sees that the rules are obeyed."[42]

It was not until 1937 that Warburg, preoccupied by events in Europe and deeply afraid of Hitler, became a domestic as well as a foreign policy liberal. After a trip to Hamburg to visit his uncle, Warburg saw that the world was headed for impending disaster, and that the United States had to regard any attack on the western democracies as an attack on America itself. By 1941 Warburg had directed his massive energies toward a campaign for intervention, and in the process abandoned his attacks on Roosevelt's domestic policies. Warburg founded the Fight for Freedom Committee, went on the radio where he delivered passionate speeches, organized mass rallies, and wrote more books.[43]

In these books, Warburg spelled out the political belief that dominated his tenure as chief of policy planning for the FIS and then the Overseas Branch of the OWI. The war, he wrote in *Foreign Policy Begins at Home,* was not just a military war against Germany and Japan for national survival; it was not just a war to prevent conquest; it was a war against fascism. Unlike the military war, the political war crossed all national frontiers. "It is a war between those who want freedom for mankind and those who want freedom for themselves at the expense of others; between those who believe in the equal rights of human beings regardless of race, creed, or color, and those who believe in the divine right of privilege and prerogative."[44] Warburg went on. The United States had supported fascism in the Spanish Civil War through nonintervention, and again in France through American recognition of Vichy. But in order to accomplish the true political ends of the war these policies must be changed, and the revolutionary nature of the war recognized.[45] The ultimate goal of the war, Warburg argued in *The Isolationist Illusion,* must be the establishment of an order "so permeated by justice that the majority of men will not be moved by violence."[46] And this, he wrote, meant that the energies of capitalism had to be harnessed to the ethical principles "in which we believe for the common good of society." America had to take the lead.[47]

Sherwood had linked his name to Roosevelt's New Deal and Barnes had achieved a reputation as a man of the left, but it is in the prewar and wartime writings of Warburg that we find the clearest statement of a Popular Front ideology that dominated the early propaganda effort. It was a radical vision, and so it was opposed by the Departments of State, War, and Navy and by Congress. But it was also very much an ideology of the late thirties and early forties, before the momentum of the war itself challenged this political vision and posed questions of the propagandists for which War-burg's answers were not wrong, but insufficient. But this was all to come after the end of 1942. For 1941 and 1942 Warburg's writings were a clarion call for the role of propaganda: to win the war and transform the world into a more just and peaceful place.

This cadre of men joined together in July 1941 to forge an organization prepared to fight the enemy by short-wave radio. They wanted to carry the American spirit directly to the Axis and to conquered peoples. "There is something more important than saving Europe," one of the early members of the FIS wrote, and that "is to make sure that . . . we do not lose our own souls."[48] These were men of passion and conviction who were not bogged down by bureaucratic traditions or constraints. They were free to act with the fresh vigor of a wartime agency, and they did.

Sherwood and Donovan concentrated on radio. Although they did not ex-clude the more traditional techniques of propaganda—leaflets, newspaper stories, films, posters—they assumed that these would have to come later as in 1941 radio offered by far the greatest hope of reaching Europeans. Leaf-lets could be dropped by the Royal Air Force, but the British were loath to risk their planes on such nonmilitary operations. It was hard to plant newspaper stories in Nazi-occupied Europe and impossible to show films or put up posters. Radio, however, could go behind enemy lines and reach directly into people's homes.[49] As one British commentator articulated, radio had become the "fourth fighting arm" of war. It was not simply that Euro-peans listened to radio as one source of news among many. They had in-creasingly come to rely exclusively on their radios for information as travel became difficult, governments censored all news reports, newspapers shrank in size, and curfews kept people at home.[50] Radio had become an indis-pensable weapon of political warfare.[51]

On August 1, 1941, Sherwood took a train to New York City and rented office space for the fledgling operation. There the FIS would be close to the radio industry and the press wire services of Associated Press, United Press, and International News Service. Sherwood put his policy staff in Wash-ington, but he hired writers, announcers, censors, and engineers in New York.[52]

Settling the operations of the Foreign Information Service in New York while leaving the planning staff in Washington had crucial ramifications not only for the FIS but later on for the Voice of America and the Overseas Branch of the OWI. From the very beginning the heart of overseas propa-ganda beat two hundred and fifty miles away from the president, the State

Department, the military, and Congress. Although Sherwood immediately established telephone links with the capital, the distance provided his organization with intellectual and political freedom while at the same time it generated a hostility increasingly felt and acted on by both sides. The separate locations enabled unhappy State Department officers and congressmen to charge the propagandists with excessive policy independence.[53] And in New York it created a sense of autonomy expressed as a stream of complaints about policy and control. Even between the two branches of the propaganda agency the geographic gap led to delays and misunderstandings. By the spring of 1942, less than a year into operations, the Voice of America staff resented what they saw as Washington's misunderstanding of the special problems inherent in radio writing and production. Johnson grumpily complained to Barnes that he had "the feeling that some members of the [Washington] Planning Board think we are saboteurs because we insist on making the plan suit the medium instead of changing the medium in the hope that it will better fit the plan."[54]

In the early days of the FIS, Sherwood could not create a government overseas radio broadcasting station. The president had strictly forbidden this in order to keep the good graces of the private radio industry. Sherwood was therefore forced to work with—and try to improve upon—existing shortwave outlets. This left the FIS in a peculiar position. Sherwood's organization was supposed to direct overseas propaganda, but it had to do so with the cooperation of a very recalcitrant radio industry. Throughout the first six months of its existence the FIS was little more than a think tank, a purveyor of ideas about propaganda without the means to effect those ideas.

Nevertheless, Sherwood set out to do what he could. The easier part of his task was technical. He upgraded the overall transmission power—which that very spring the BBC had declared too weak to enable British rebroadcast of American shows—by creating a system of leased land lines. The "bronze network," as it was called, allowed the FIS to coordinate existing stations and build up an overseas network.[55]

No matter how thorny the technical problems were, the corporate and political ones were worse. The private stations used the State Department as a buffer between themselves and the FIS. They hired a former foreign correspondent and foreign service officer, Stanley Richardson, to be their official intermediary with the State Department. Richardson was friendly with the State Department officer charged with working with the FIS, Michael J. McDermott, a conservative whose natural instincts ran counter to those of the propagandists.[56] All the Foreign Information Service could do was write daily news stories in English and send them on to Richardson, who read them, consulted with McDermott, and decided what parts of the FIS scripts to accept. It was a cumbersome system that generated continual conflict between private broadcasters and the propagandists. Richardson demanded cold, hard facts without "gratuitous editorial interpretation, innuendo or comment," whereas the propagandists argued that Richardson wanted news, not propaganda, and that their task was to serve American interests, not run a newspaper.[57] It was an impossible situation.

Pearl Harbor transformed broadcast propaganda. War gave Donovan and Sherwood the emergency they needed to effect a fundamental reorganization of American overseas broadcasting. The president at last agreed that the sentiments of private broadcasters could be violated, and on December 26 Sherwood cabled film, theater, and radio producer John Houseman to come to New York and take charge of a new government radio station – the Voice of America.[58] Through this single stroke the Foreign Information Service became a real propaganda organization.

Houseman came from the world of entertainment, and brought along his sense of show business. For him, he later wrote, news was "the raw material from which it was my job to fashion shows."[59] He was dramatic, intense, demanding, and full of energy; he worked ceaselessly and expected the same devotion from his staff. As one colleague recalled, Houseman seemed to consider sleep a luxury, and he denied it both to himself and those around him. Born in Romania to a British mother and an Alsatian Jewish father, he had been raised in France and England, spoke fluent French, Spanish, and German, and understood the sensibilities of both Europeans and Americans. His qualifications were superb, and he took on the Voice of America with gusto.[60]

Houseman's political instincts were liberal. He had spent several years during the Depression working for the Federal Theatre Project (FTP), a New Deal experiment in government-financed, locally controlled drama for the common man. During his years with the FTP Houseman headed the Negro Theatre Project at the Lafayette Theater in Harlem and, with Orson Welles, directed Project No. 891, the classical theater division of the FTP. A year later Houseman produced a radical and controversial musical, *The Cradle Will Rock*.[61] Like the other leaders of the Foreign Information Service, Houseman subscribed to the liberal Popular Front ideology of the thirties.

By late January 1942, he and Sherwood had arranged for three daily fifteen-minute broadcasts in German, French, and Italian to be relayed over the BBC. By early February the British had planned a permanent schedule for American rebroadcasts. American representatives in London reported that these trial broadcasts went "excellently, although the British registered reservations, worrying that the speed was 'too fast for clear audibility' and that the program overall was 'somewhat lacking . . . in vigor and interest.'"[62] By January, Houseman was ready to launch direct short-wave broadcasts as well. The Voice of America went on the air.

The Americans decided to use both direct short-wave broadcasts and British relays, which were medium- and long-wave transmissions, since each had their advantages and disadvantages. Relays could be heard in France far more clearly than direct shortwave, but the British tampered with the American shows in order to make the American product conform to British propaganda objectives. They edited what went on the air, and if they did not like the show at all they took it off, substituted a standby American record on an all-purpose subject, and told the Americans that reception had been bad.[63] The British were miserly at best in their allocation of broadcast hours, giving the Americans the least popular time slots and frequencies, and not even enough on-air time to satisfy the Voice of America.[64] But direct short-wave broadcasts, which could be neither edited nor altered, were subject to atmospheric interference and poor reception. It was hard for Europeans to hear American short-wave programs. So the Americans decided not to make a choice between them.

The leaders of the FIS and Donovan immediately began working to take over the short-wave channels that were still owned by the radio companies. The first station they acquired was the short-wave outlet of a powerful Cincinnati, Ohio, radio company called the Crosley station, or WLWO. Crosley was neither part of a broadcasting network nor an equipment manufacturer, and therefore had little investment in international operations. Of all the existing short-wave broadcasters, Crosley had the least to lose by cooperating with the government, and so on March 4, 1942, the station leased its daytime transmitting facilities to the Voice of America.[65]

With only a single station that spring the Voice of America was in a rather peculiar position as it became but one of several American overseas broadcasting services. European listeners heard only one British station broadcast over many channels, but they received an alphabet soup of American stations and programs. The Voice was thus put at a distinct disadvantage, especially in relation to the BBC. Overseas listeners could not, for example, rotate the dial to find better reception of the Voice on a different wavelength, or change channels to avoid jamming, as they could with the BBC. And most important, listeners were confused as to what the Voice of America exactly was, and who spoke for the American government. As Barnes complained to Sherwood that spring, "in these circumstances it is not reasonable to suppose that American radio can exercise a decisive influence upon the course of the war."[66]

The Voice of America supplemented its outlets only in June, when General Electric and Westinghouse agreed to lease their facilities. In September, under the growing pressure that came with planning for the invasion of North Africa, CBS and NBC leased their facilities. Shortly before the actual invasion the federal government ordered the last private station, World Wide Broadcasting Corporation (WRUL), to surrender use of its facilities to the Voice of America. In other words, it took until the end of 1942 for the government to gain control of all fourteen American transmitters.[67] The political success of broadcast propaganda depended on its facilities; the Voice of America could accomplish its goals only if it could be heard. Throughout 1942 the Voice of America was but one of several American short-wave radio stations.

Operations nevertheless expanded quickly. By March 1942 Houseman had established regional sections and set up news and script operations. The News Division supplied daily news roundups and gathered outside material, while the Special Events Section provided shows and speeches by Americans and foreigners who did not work for the FIS. By the end of the month, Houseman had fashioned the first daily broadcast pattern: a six-and-a-quarter-hour daily block of time divided between German, French, Italian, and English language broadcasting. Segments in each language went over the air at a specific time, the French every hour on the half hour, the German every hour on the quarter hour, and so forth. By April, the Voice was on the air twenty-four hours a day and was adding additional languages.[68]

The Voice of America soon became a universe of many worlds. News came from the wire services to the news and features desk. This desk edited and rewrote the news and then sent it on to censorship, or Control, which after inspecting the material turned it over to the language desks. Each language desk appraised and translated the material, using what was most relevant and suitable for the particular country for which it was intended. The atmosphere at the desks was always hurried and tense as the writers churned out story after story as the news came in, like waiters and cooks in a crowded New York coffee shop during a perpetual lunchtime rush.[69]

Shortly before airtime a producer came up to the language desk and asked for the scripts for the next show. He counted the lines in each script and figured out at what speed it could be read within the allotted time, after which he went to casting and asked for announcers for the show. The announcers went into the studio worried that they could not read their script with the speed, clarity, enunciation, and accent demanded of them without rehearsal, for which there was never enough time. The producer finally pulled the show together from behind a glass wall where he stood like a conductor, speeding up or slowing down the production with his hands and arms waving in the air. And then the Voice of America went on the air.

The heart of the Voice lay in the language desks. Each desk was distinct; each reflected a national personality. Sherwood and Houseman decided from the beginning to hire native language speakers so that their articulation and accent would be familiar and not jar the listener. Each desk was populated by exiles and émigrés who were often more interested in the fate of their country than in the diplomacy or welfare of the United States.[70]

The largest and most important language desk was France. The French language still held a unique place in Europe in the war years; it was spoken not only in France, Belgium, and Switzerland, but by the political and social elite of most of the continent. Furthermore, it was clear from the beginning of the war that when America attacked Germany it would be through France. In 1943, when Allied victory was no longer a question of if but when, the importance of France to the European balance of power became more clearly important. Propaganda to France assumed from the very start a standing of singular importance.[71]

To head the French desk, Sherwood and Houseman hired Pierre Lazareff, a French journalist with a towering reputation.[72] Lazareff had been born in Paris in 1907 to Russian Jewish parents. From his very earliest years he had gravitated to journalism and even as a young child had published little news bulletins. "I never once considered the possibility of any other profession," he reminisced in his autobiography.[73]

Lazareff was a dynamo, full of ideas and brimming with self-confidence. By the age of nineteen he had joined the staff of a midday paper, *Paris-Midi*.[74] He soon became the paper's editor and raised its circulation from five thousand to a respectable hundred thousand.[75] He shortly moved over to an evening paper, *Paris-Soir,* which he turned into a politically neutral, outstandingly successful commercial venture. By the last days of the Third Republic, the paper's readership numbered well over a million people, a tremendous figure for prewar France.[76] In May and June of 1940, as the Germans were sweeping through France, Lazareff courageously elected to stay with *Paris-Soir* until the Nazis actually took over Paris. Before June 14 he relocated his employees, arranged shelter for them in the south, and generally looked after their welfare. After France fell he fled to New York, where he tried unsuccessfully to publish an independent journal. Unable to find any other job he went to work for the Foreign Information Service in 1941, and in February 1942 he took charge of putting together a French desk for the Voice of America.[77]

The personal testimonies to his character remain a monument to his spirit. "He was wonderful to work for," recalled one Voice colleague who joined Lazareff's postwar French paper, *France-Soir*.[78] People would do anything for him, explained his wartime secretary, "because he was so extraordinarily warm and human. He treated everybody with great respect [from] the woman who cleaned his office to Eleanor Roosevelt."[79] He was lively and curious and never hostile, added another writer from the French desk. Before the war he enjoyed eating out with the messenger "boys" for *Paris-Soir*, but he knew everyone of importance in Paris. It was not unusual for Lazareff to invite to his home for an evening the American journalist Dorothy Thompson, the French minister of the navy, the playwright Henry Bernstein, the novelist Colette, and the French journalists George and Joseph Kessell.[80] Lazareff knew and collected "le tout Paris."

Lazareff worked hard to staff his desk at the OWI. He hired as his second in command the journalist-émigré Robert de Saint-Jean, with whom he had worked at *Paris-Soir*. He found other journalists, such as André Labarthe, the former Free French press attaché to North Africa, and writers and intellectuals of the caliber of Jacques Maritain, Denis de Rougemont, Philippe Barrès, and Julien Green. But many of his script writers were not professional writers when they joined the desk. Lazareff placed a French actress who had written some poetry in charge of the women's show and trained lawyers as journalists.[81] He hired refugees who needed the money and spoke little English as announcers, including such intellectuals as the anthropologist Claude Lévi-Strauss, the surrealist writer André Breton, and the budding actor Yul Brynner. Breton especially had a mellifluous voice and became a great favorite of Lazareff's. He chose his people, encouraged them, and molded them into the kind of writers and announcers he felt best suited his concept of the French language programs of the Voice of America. Moreover, he kept all these disparate, politically divergent, temperamental people in harmony. Members of the French desk occasionally fought with each other, but they all liked Lazareff and they wanted his respect. He created a spirit of fellowship and hard work, and people labored for him and because of him.

Throughout his career Lazareff avoided political positions. After the war was over he returned to France and established a successful news empire, but as one of his wartime friends recalled, "Pierre was more interested in political gossip than in politics." Lazareff adhered to a policy of political neutrality when possible and adaptability when necessary—what might be called, on the darker side, political trimming—throughout his career.[82]

Lazareff's talents and political adaptability had important consequences for the Voice of America. First of all, he built up a large and talented staff and sustained it with great esprit de corps. This was the staff that House-man later remembered as quick, elegant, and erudite, and whose shows he described as "models of precision and energy—examples of emotional, in-ventive, intelligent and well-aimed propaganda."[83] Lazareff's political neu-trality not only helped retain calm; it dominated the relationship of the French desk to the rest of the Voice and the OWI. Lazareff might scream and rant over issues that involved his French sensibilities, but he would never—even after the Americans collaborated with the former Vichy minis-ter of the navy Admiral Jean Darlan, or throughout the tortuous dispute between de Gaulle and the United States—argue with the American State Department. Sherwood argued. Warburg argued. Barnes and Johnson and Houseman argued. But Lazareff remained silent.

While Lazareff put together the French desk, Donovan developed admin-istrative machinery for propaganda policy. By March he had established the Planning Board, which operated through a series of regional coordinators responsible for the supervision of policies in specific areas.[84] The organiza-tion sounded better on paper, however, than it worked in reality. To begin with, the geographical distance between New York and Washington made New York feel criticized and Washington ignored. Sherwood disliked Dono-van's board so intensely that Sherwood boycotted the meetings. But most important of all, the Planning Board reflected Donovan's belief that propa-ganda should exert an immediate, palpable effect; it should mobilize people toward concrete goals.

Propaganda, Donovan believed, should directly counteract increasing Nazi hegemony over the continent. In late 1941, for example, the Planning Board cooked up a scheme to undermine Hitler's plans for a pan-European con-ference which Donovan reported on to the president. Donovan wrote the president that he, Donovan, "hoped that if it [Hitler's conference] could be given a bad name before it was called, it might never be convened."[85] He suggested giving the conference a nasty epithet, such as "Hocus-pocus Conclave" or "Punch and Judy Conference." These sorts of suggestions must have driven Sherwood and his colleagues in New York mad, and Sherwood went out of his way to avoid them. But by mid-spring, in any case, the Planning Board had sent so little guidance that Barnes charged that it had virtually ceased to exist.[86] Throughout the spring the Foreign Information Service therefore operated within a policy vacuum, which it filled with Brit-ish policy directives.

During the six months following the establishment of the Voice of Amer-ica Sherwood and Donovan made great strides in putting together both transmitters and a production staff so that when the station acquired more channels it would have the staff and programs to go on the air. The Voice slowly developed into a fully functioning government radio station able to generate programs for audiences throughout Europe, Asia, and Africa.[87] But its organizational problems remained acute. The conflict over propaganda between Sherwood and Donovan became so intense that it tore apart the fabric of the organization.

By the spring of 1942 the days of the Office of the Coordinator of Information were numbered. Donovan had come under attack on several flanks, and although he might have survived any single assault, he could not do so against so many opponents.

By that spring Donovan and Sherwood were at each other's throats. Sherwood had never viewed the FIS as a support for intelligence and subversion, but Donovan wanted propaganda to act as the initial arrow of penetration for covert actions. He did not care about standards of truth, and his policy men in Washington had constantly complained that the New York office paid too much attention to the requirements of radio production and good journalism and too little attention to the subversive potential of the medium. Sherwood wanted to build a Voice of America whose reputation could rival that of the BBC both for quality of production and reliability. The two men could no longer operate within the same organization.

Simultaneously, the Joint Chiefs of Staff fretted over the military implications of a free-wheeling, independent intelligence and covert operations organization. They worried that these activities should be put under military supervision lest the COI take action directly harmful to military plans. Therefore the Joint Chiefs campaigned to have the COI integrated into the military.[88]

The Bureau of the Budget—which acted as President Roosevelt's White House staff—disliked the untidiness of the bureaucratic arrangements.[89] The number of wartime information and propaganda organizations had exploded over the previous year and the result was overlapping assignments and administrative chaos. In the international arena the Office of the Coordinator of Information under Donovan broadcast propaganda to Europe, Africa, and Asia, while the Office of the Coordinator of Inter-American Affairs under Nelson Rockefeller distributed information to Latin America. On the domestic side there were several government agencies supporting civilian morale, of which the Office of Facts and Figures and the Division of Information for the Office of Emergency Management were the most prominent.[90] The Bureau of the Budget wanted to consolidate all these information services, domestic as well as international. Sherwood further increased the

Budget Bureau's anxiety over the current state of affairs with hair-raising stories of internal chaos and Donovan's propaganda philosophy. The FIS director's complaints fell on receptive ears since the bureau already disliked Donovan for his style of operation.

The pressure to dismember the COI grew increasingly intense. But bureaucratic reorganization needed presidential support, and Roosevelt, with his typical tendency to put off decisions, remained aloof from the fray. The president feared that any consolidation of government information services would generate public distrust of the administration and lead to accusations that the executive branch was trying to control news and dictate domestic propaganda. Nevertheless, the president's advisers pressed him to act and finally the Joint Chiefs of Staff decided that they wanted to integrate Donovan's covert and guerrilla warfare operations into the military as the Office of Strategic Services. Soon thereafter the way became clear for the establishment of an Office of War Information with both domestic and overseas branches. On June 13, 1942, Roosevelt signed Executive Order 9182, which consolidated the existing war information agencies in the Office of War Information—the OWI.[91] The Foreign Information Service accordingly became the Overseas Branch of the OWI, with the Voice of America as part of its operations.

Donovan's organization had existed solely as a foreign operation. The OWI, in contrast, controlled both foreign and domestic information. The Voice, along with other forms of overt foreign propaganda, no longer possessed the taint of covert operations, but the overseas propagandists henceforth had to work within an organization whose primary national visibility came from its domestic side, the Domestic Branch of the OWI. This allowed congressmen, journalists, and concerned citizens to accuse the OWI, and thereby Roosevelt and his administration, of manipulating news at home. It created fears that the president would use the OWI to help win yet another term in office. It provided constant ammunition against the OWI as a whole. And finally, the domestic side of the organization soaked up the time and sapped the energies of the OWI's leaders.

The Office of the Coordinator of Information had existed by military order, not executive order, and accordingly it had been funded through the president's special budget. The Bureau of the Budget oversaw the COI's expenditures, but Congress had no role. But once the president signed Executive Order 9182 the propaganda organization became an executive agency under the direct oversight of Congress.[92]

Although Congress suspended its judgment over large areas of the war effort, it was unwilling to do so over matters of direct domestic policy.

And domestic information was not only domestic policy; it was the government exercising authority in the sensitive domain of public opinion and political manipulation. By tying foreign propaganda to domestic information the Budget Bureau had opened a Pandora's box of hostility. Henceforth the Overseas Branch was subject to periodic legislative review, which Congress undertook with a vengeance. It did not destroy the Overseas Branch as it dismembered the Domestic Branch—by 1944 90 percent of the budget for the OWI went to the Overseas Branch and only 10 percent reached the shrunken Domestic Branch—but Congress did investigate and interrogate and make life thoroughly miserable for Sherwood, Barnes, Johnson, Warburg, and Houseman. Their time was devoted to the endless tasks of preparing reports, delivering testimony, and dealing with crusty congressmen whose overriding concern was to embarrass the Roosevelt administration. OWI leaders found themselves on the train between Washington and New York week after week after week, spending more time and energy fighting their domestic foes than waging war against the Axis.

The consequences of reorganization went beyond those of bureaucracy and administration, however, to the very nature of propaganda. When Roosevelt dissolved the COI he separated Donovan from overseas propaganda and the Voice of America. Donovan had linked propaganda to covert operations, and he had used the Voice of America as part of those operations. When Donovan left, American propagandists became free to broadcast a message in which resistance was a political and not a paramilitary act. It was the struggle of the common man for his own liberation. Moreover, once propaganda was severed from covert operations, propagandists had to redefine and defend their goals. They had to answer the question, Was the function of propaganda to arouse the listener to take direct action, or was there another, more inchoate but informational objective? What, put another way, was the relationship between Voice of America propaganda and American foreign policy? These were issues that would arise to haunt propagandists within little more than a year.

# 2

# *The Varied Context*

## *Creating a Propaganda Policy*

EXECUTIVE Order 9182 created the Office of War Information, but it did not include a procedure for formulating propaganda policy. The newly appointed director of the OWI, Elmer Davis, inherited that task since neither Donovan, nor anyone inside the former domestic information agencies, had left behind a workable system. But Roosevelt appointed Davis not for his organizational abilities but rather in order to reassure Americans that the new propaganda and information agency would be trustworthy and very American. A variety of suggestions for the job had floated around the White House, including Edward R. Murrow and William L. Shirer of CBS and Byron Price, then head of Associated Press, as well as writers such as Rex Stout. But the president selected Davis—whom Roosevelt called the radio commentator "with the funny voice"—because the Indiana-born and -raised journalist projected an image of integrity and an elusive quality of "Americanness."[1] The president, as always, acted with politics in mind rather than daily administration or a grasp of the art of propaganda.

Davis had begun his career in print journalism and later had become a free-lance writer, but he was best known as a radio announcer and commentator. As early as the mid-thirties he had made occasional broadcasts for CBS, but in 1939 the network news department recruited him as a nightly commentator, and he soon became a nationally famous radio personality. In a flat midwestern voice Davis broadcast five-minute programs in which he summed up as many as thirty news stories, blending them together with terse, sharp commentary. His ability to communicate masses of information in a minimum of time was outstanding; he would read a brief bulletin, follow it up with a single-sentence comment, and through it all give listeners a sense that they had acquired new insights. Davis was always at pains to identify his sources and explain his political positions, and he quickly earned a reputation for brilliant and honest reporting. By 1940 he attracted a nightly audience of twelve and a half million listeners.[2]

Over the spring of 1942 Davis began campaigning for a restructured wartime information agency, impressing liberal Americans with the need for reform. E. B. White wrote in the *New Yorker* that "of the twelve steps we would like to see taken in this war without delay, the first is the unification of the information bureaus and the appointment of Elmer Davis to head them up. . . . Our eleven other recommendations for winning the war will be presented as soon as the government acts on the first one."[3] The national press reacted to Davis's appointment with delight, describing him as "a liberal respected by conservatives" and "one of the best newsmen in town."[4] He had, moreover, a disarmingly American way about him, a quality Barnes later described as the essential "Americanism of his point of view." He seemed the perfect choice to head the OWI.[5]

Davis was an internationalist, but throughout the thirties he remained on the sidelines, in part because he supported the decline and fall of imperialism, which put him at odds with the British, and in part because he feared the consequences of interventionism for American safety.[6] Not until the Nazis swept through western Europe—and it became blindingly clear that the traditional European balance of power was shattered—did Davis fully drop his neutrality.[7]

By temperament as well as conviction Davis was neither a rebel nor a critic in the realm of foreign policy. He kept his broadcasts cautious and balanced. He never saw ethical issues as the determining political factor. He was convinced that foreign policy should rest on a global balance of power, although he simultaneously saw the war as a world revolution. To Davis the essential conservatism of American policy threatened to undermine the morale of the conquered peoples of Europe and set the United States on the wrong side of the war's moral issues.[8] As director of the OWI, however, he rarely dissented from the president's diplomatic policies. At least in foreign affairs, his politics were more conservative than those of Sherwood, Barnes, Johnson, Warburg, and Houseman.

Davis, moreover, concentrated on the Domestic Branch of the OWI. Perhaps he felt more comfortable directing propaganda at home rather than abroad. Davis argued, for example, that "the easiest way to inject a propaganda idea into most people's minds is to let it go in through the medium of an entertainment picture when they do not realize that they are being propagandized."[9] But he was not as aggressive toward the French as were his Overseas Branch colleagues. As one OWI official later recalled, "we thought that Elmer was a good man, a conservative, middle-western American, a good if not inspiring journalist." Although these philosophical splits did not surface in 1942, they ultimately widened fissures that tore apart the OWI in 1943 and 1944.[10]

Davis gave the new agency an immediate national respectability. He understood journalism and public relations, and he knew the members of the press corps and worked easily with them, but he was completely inexperienced as an administrator. Despite his efforts, his integrity, and his self-assurance, he lacked the know-how to take an issue and push it through a bureaucratic obstacle course. He was not aggressive enough to fight his way through the thickets of Washington politics. His ignorance of Washington politics in action was so enormous that when the president asked Davis if he, the President, should schedule Davis for a daily fifteen-minute meeting in the Oval Office, Davis said no. He had, moreover, no personal intimacy with the president, as did Sherwood. "I'm guessing that Roosevelt did not particularly enjoy Elmer Davis's company," one propagandist later mused. "I don't think that the president got much of a bang out of Elmer Davis; they didn't even drink the same things."[11]

Most important for the Overseas Branch, Davis concerned himself almost exclusively with domestic information. He believed that the American people were entitled to know the news and to understand the news. This commitment permeated his thinking about the role of the OWI and explains why he concentrated almost exclusively on domestic information. He defined his mission as the dissemination of war news to the American people: "You can't fight a war efficiently unless the people know how it is being fought," he declared.[12] The OWI's job was to give "the American people the fullest possible understanding of what this war is all about . . . where it is going [and] how our Government is conducting it. . . ."[13]

Davis wanted Overseas Branch propaganda to tell the truth, tell it intelligently, and tell it everywhere. He admitted the importance of selection and emphasis, but he believed first in the existence and then in the effectiveness of the bald fact. "Merely to know the truth is going to inspire" the citizens of enemy and enemy-occupied nations, he argued, "to a more stubborn endurance and resistance. . . ."[14] Davis envisioned the Overseas Branch as an international news agency and defined propaganda as information; propaganda accordingly was the broadcasting of the maximum quantity of news.[15]

The news, from headlines to stories to features, was to tell foreign audiences of American military, industrial, and economic superiority. For

Davis, however, news was effective because America was such a great nation. He believed that if the United States portrayed itself honestly, it would provide a beacon of light unto the world. He argued, moreover, that only straightforward news would create credibility. "We must establish at once," he wrote, "in the minds of our own people and the rest of the world that the United States government will tell the truth day in and day out about all developments. . . ."[16]

Davis chose Milton Eisenhower, youngest brother of General Dwight D. Eisenhower, as his chief administrative assistant, thereby reinforcing the domestic focus of the Washington OWI leadership. Eisenhower was a midwesterner from Kansas who had spent most of his career in the Department of Agriculture—the most domestic of all the federal executive departments—where he had been a protégé of Henry Wallace. In late 1941 Eisenhower assisted the director of the Bureau of the Budget in working with the Foreign Information Service, and then helped establish the Office of Facts and Figures. In the weeks following Pearl Harbor Roosevelt asked Milton Eisenhower to produce a study of all war-related information activities as part of a general review process. Six months later this resulted in the creation of the Office of War Information. In March 1942 Eisenhower set up the War Relocation Authority, charged with moving Japanese Americans off the West Coast. Three months later Davis brought Eisenhower into the OWI to oversee agency organization and coordination.[17] By 1942 Eisenhower had established a reputation as an organization man and public relations expert in the federal government with an affable manner and a mind of his own. But like Davis he possessed no experience in international affairs.[18]

Davis's career had not prepared him to direct the OWI. He had, in fact, accepted the position with the stipulation that the president would appoint an associate director, Milton Eisenhower, who was "skilled in governmental organization and information matters."[19] Davis confessed to Roosevelt that he knew nothing about administering an agency whose staff would soon number in the thousands.[20] Struggling amid tensions produced by a new and often cantankerous staff on the one hand, and dissatisfied executive departments and Congress on the other, Davis had neither the time nor the expertise to devote to his most urgent propaganda task: the creation of policy and a policy procedure. The State Department and the military gave him no help and much criticism; Congress constantly questioned his budget and attacked his agency; and his colleagues in New York doubted his judgment. His weakness as a leader left a vacuum that had to be filled. In the end, James Warburg assumed foreign propaganda policy leadership, working in concert with the British. But in order to understand how this came about

it is necessary to examine the attitudes and actions of the State Department
and the Departments of War and Navy.

The Overseas Branch propagandists fundamentally disagreed with the State
Department over American foreign policy. Sherwood and his colleagues had
a clear vision of their own mission. They wanted to use propaganda to fight
a war against Nazism and fascism and for democracy and freedom throughout the world. They supported resistance movements and Popular Front
coalitions and they decried American collaboration with the leaders of
Vichy in 1940, with Darlan in 1942, and with the Italian leader Marshal
Badoglio in 1943. They tried to use propaganda to make their vision come
true, and to push on the edges of foreign policy. The State Department
leaders, in contrast, were conservative men in every sense of the word. They
not only disliked left-leaning politics, but they distrusted new ideas.

This conflict threaded their approaches to the resistance in general, and
to the French Resistance in particular. Sherwood supported the Resistance
from his romantic and moral liberal view of foreign affairs; Barnes endorsed
it as a man of the left; Warburg believed in the revolutionary mission of
the Second World War. The Voice of America broadcasts used the Resistance to attack the Germans and undermine "the fundamentals of the German war machine. . . ."[21]

The State Department, for its part, did not condone the French Resistance. Roosevelt and the State Department had recognized the at best neutral Vichy government early in 1940 for a variety of reasons.[22] In its internal
memos the State Department did not even discuss the French Resistance
in 1940, 1941, or 1942. It was as if the department was saying by its very
silence that to support a resistance movement was too unorthodox to be
seriously considered by cultivated diplomats.

From the earliest days of the Voice of America, therefore, the propagandists were in conflict with the State Department. Although much of what
the Voice said supported State Department policy, disagreement was a
ground-base theme. At times it was muted, but it was always there.

The department's attitude toward propaganda reached back to the years
between the two world wars. The department first considered a government owned and operated short-wave station in 1929 when the head of
the Pan American Union, Leo S. Rowe, suggested that the State Department ask the Navy to build a station for the Union.[23] Rowe had been chief
of the Latin American division of the State Department before he took over
the Pan American Union in 1920. The department cheerfully listened to
the advice of this old and trusted friend. Accordingly, the department requested the Navy to construct a station. The Navy refused.[24]

Rowe dropped the issue until after Roosevelt's election in 1932, when he resurrected his campaign for American government short-wave broadcasting. The department again asked the Navy to set up a station, and the Navy again said no.[25] But although the department had, by 1933, twice supported Rowe's proposed station, in fact it had acted with ambivalence and hesitation.[26] Rowe continued to press his case for the next several years, until 1937, when he abandoned his crusade. After 1938 the department increasingly opposed an active government role in anything that put the department in the role of propagandist. When the Ickes committee issued a report urging the United States to counter vicious foreign propaganda, a department official responded that a government station would not be well received by the American people.[27] After Roosevelt's creation of the Foreign Information Service in 1941, the State Department gave little policy guidance. Instead, it demonstrated vacillation and bureaucratic paralysis.

During the years between the two world wars the State Department was staffed by native-born, Anglo-Saxon, Protestant, upper-middle-class Americans who came largely from the northeastern section of the country. They felt part of a self-conscious, cohesive world: "From the coding clerks to high department officials, all were regarded as 'fellow members of the departmental family.'"[28] These men had gone to the same colleges, and when they went to work they sought "gentlemen's" jobs.[29] They did not want to take responsibility for creating new activities that would mean more responsibility on their part, and they were afraid of initiating programs that would necessitate hiring experts who would supplant the more traditional foreign officers. The old State Department rarely accepted new ideas and even more rarely promoted them.[30]

State Department career men were uncomfortable with the idea of publicizing the department's positions in part because diplomacy, as traditionally defined, contained no place for public opinion. Based on the proposition that government officials would act in agreement with other government officials, international relations ignored popular opinion. The very idea of propaganda ran counter to the values of diplomatic relations and the ways in which career officers had understood their jobs.[31] This distrust of publicity techniques long predated the Foreign Information Service and the OWI. During the First World War the State Department had refused to cooperate with George Creel's Committee on Public Information.[32]

President Roosevelt disliked working with the State Department and felt that it would be the wrong department to take charge of an international information program. When the president wanted something done he typically created a new agency rather than reforming an existing one. The president's distaste for the State Department, moreover, meant that he had a complicated and distant relationship with the department's diplomats, whom he increasingly shut out of important foreign policy decisions. The more true this was, the more difficult it became for the department to guide OWI foreign policy decisions—and the greater the department's need to save face.

The fight over foreign policy, however, did not become intense until after the Allied invasion of North Africa in November 1942. Before then the New York leaders complained not so much about the substance of State Department policy as its flaccidity. Barnes fumed against the difficulties of doing "a consistent, honest, Henry A. Wallace job of psychological warfare in a country whose leaders do not know what they are fighting for . . . in a United Nations alliance whose leaders know all too well what they are fighting for."[33]

The tradition-bound, conservative State Department could not appreciate the enthusiasm and determination of a temporary wartime emergency agency staffed not by permanent bureaucrats but by journalists. The energetic OWI, on its side, failed to comprehend the reasons for, or appreciate any benefits from, the staid, slow, cautious attitude of the State Department. Their politics and ideologies were at odds. Both sides criticized each other, but once the smoke had cleared the propagandists realized that they did not have to consult with State Department staff or clear the Overseas Branch's daily and weekly guidances through State Department machinery since the department had no power to compel them to do so and, in 1942, little interest in taking up the fight.[34]

Relations with the military were no better. Although Davis initially reached out to the Departments of War and Navy and the Joint Chiefs of Staff, these gestures failed to result in any solid cooperation. In part, as with the State Department, Davis himself was to blame. Within weeks of assuming his new post, the director of the OWI abruptly approached Secretary of War Henry Stimson with the suggestion that the OWI, rather than the War Department's office of press relations, filter news to the domestic press corps. Stimson disliked the idea and worried that OWI successes at home might produce unintended but serious indiscretions abroad. He therefore discouraged any high level of cooperation.[35]

Like the State Department, both the army and the navy delegated the heads of the departmental information services to serve as liaisons, men with little say over the information policies of their own departments and less control over their departments' other policies.[36] Furthermore, the army and navy each had their own psychological warfare operations. Even if their liaisons had possessed the information and authority, military leaders were disinclined to pay attention to civilian operations, working as they did within a wholly military context and bounded by the parameters of the military world.[37]

Davis and Sherwood assumed that the Overseas Branch would coordinate its efforts with the Joint Chiefs of Staff through the Joint Psychological Warfare Committee, but Donovan made that impossible by taking over the committee and using it to emasculate the OWI. With Donovan in charge of the Joint Chiefs' propaganda organization, harmonious relations with the OWI became unlikely. The military, therefore, like the State Department, became peripheral to the policy-making procedures of the OWI.

By August it had become clear that no one in the Washington office of the OWI, nor anyone from any other government department, had taken charge of propaganda policy. No one had assumed the role vacated by Donovan. Policy leadership was open to anyone with the determination and ability to take charge.

It was James Warburg, deputy director for psychological warfare policy, who seized the initiative. Strong and driving, opinionated and sure of himself, Warburg possessed deep convictions about the nature and goals of the war and with that, the goals of U.S. international propaganda. By the fall of 1942 he began writing propaganda policy, and he ultimately became so central to policy-making operations that the OWI jokingly became known as the Office of Warburg Information.[38]

Each week Warburg took the train to Washington, attended the meeting of the Overseas Planning and Intelligence Board, and wrote the central directive—with a few suggestions from the board.[39] After his day in Washington he returned to New York, met with the Overseas Branch's regional heads, and explained the central directive. After working out weekly plans for their countries the regional directors resubmitted their proposals for approval to Warburg, who made sure that regional plans conformed with the central directive. Daily directives went through Warburg as well. The Washington office sent telegrams to New York on what material the Overseas Branch should and should not use. But it was Warburg who presided over the daily guidance meetings, and it was Warburg and the New York staff who formulated the specific instructions for the Voice of America as well as the other media of the Overseas Branch.[40]

Only an occasional script filtered back to Washington. The office there received no daily or weekly flow of either transcripts or recordings and therefore maintained no check on actual output. Davis, members of the Washington staff, or State Department and military officers might alter the central directive in Washington, but once Warburg took it back to New

York it disappeared from Washington's sight and moved out of its control.[41]

Warburg incurred resentment because of his independent procedures. He was admired, but often not trusted. Yet he represented the viewpoint of the leaders of the New York office, and this gave him his base of power. Sherwood, Barnes, Johnson, and Houseman all agreed with Warburg that the war was a fight against fascism and for democracy, and they all believed that this was not the viewpoint of the State Department or the military. They wanted to take the machinery of the Voice of America and use it to help the Allies fight the enemy and to portray America as a bastion of liberty. Separated from Washington by two hundred and fifty miles and susceptible to the heightened emotions within the New York office, the leaders of the New York office were suspicious of Davis, the State Department, and the military. They rejected the Washington viewpoint as unsuitable for propaganda. But it was Warburg who combined the determination and the self-confidence to push himself to the top and take charge of policy-making.[42] As a later director of intelligence reported, "He was agreeable with his equals and superiors, but with his inferiors he was very domineering. You could not discuss matters with him and he was intolerant of opposition."[43] As another intelligence officer phrased it, Warburg believed "that only he had the brilliance to formulate policy."[44]

For all his skill, however, Warburg did not, and could not, make policy single-handedly. He could not do so even in consultation with Sherwood, Barnes, Johnson, and Houseman, because the New York office lacked the necessary political intelligence. Warburg therefore turned to the British, specifically to his British counterpart, Ritchie Calder. Calder was a journalist who had become famous in England after writing a series of articles on the bombing of London. His reports earned him such a wide reputation that in early 1942 the Political Warfare Executive (PWE) recruited him and in August promoted him to the position of director of plans and operations.[45]

Over the fall of 1942 the two worked out a system whereby Warburg received, and then rewrote, PWE directives. The British thereby achieved great control over American international propaganda. Warburg described the process as one in which he and Calder jointly formulated policy. But Richard Crossman, a former Oxford don and journalist for the *New Statesman* who had recently been appointed German regional director of the Political Warfare Executive, belittled the effort as one in which Warburg only added "his own comments to our Directive."[46] Crossman may have exaggerated, but in large measure American propaganda policy toward Europe in 1942 was made not by the American State Department, the American military, or the Office of War Information headquarters in Washington, but by the British in London working with the Overseas Branch of the OWI in New York.

British interest in American overseas broadcasting dated back to 1940, when the State Department had suggested that the BBC rebroadcast NBC programs to counter Vichy collaboration with Germany. The British wanted to help the United States because they hoped the United States would replace British transmitters if and when the Germans destroyed them. The British also wanted American cooperation in expanding British monitoring services in the Far East, for which the United States was geographically well placed. But most of all the British, far more than their American allies, believed in the power of words—that is, in propaganda. They therefore viewed the State Department proposal as a means of "keeping alive and stimulating the democratic view of life, and of stating as powerfully as possible the achievements and purposes of the democratic nations."[47]

The BBC began monitoring American short-wave radio broadcasts in early January 1941.[48] They decided, moreover, not only to review NBC broadcasts, as the State Department had suggested, but to look as well at those of CBS and a private but noncommercial shortwave-only broadcaster called World Wide Broadcasting Company. After two weeks of review the British were not impressed with what they heard. "A cursory inspection of the monitored material," reported the BBC French program organizer, Russell Page, who a year and a half later would come to the United States to work with the Voice of America, "does not impress me as being of 'star' quality and that is what we need." It was not within Page's authority to decide whether the project should go through, but he wrote his superior that "though it is not my business I should strongly deprecate the rediffusion of straight news-bulletins."[49] Even the BBC representative in North America retreated from his initial enthusiasm, writing to the BBC office in March that "I am extremely critical of their [commercial] short-wave broadcasting Europeanwards. It seems only to be done as a gesture to the State Department . . . without enthusiasm and as cheaply as possible."[50]

The British therefore informed the Americans that the BBC would only retransmit World Wide programs, and not those of NBC or CBS. Unlike the commercial stations, World Wide broadcasts were not a string of wire service reports; far more than its competitors, World Wide editors shaped their stories to slant the news and support the British. But British efforts to rebroadcast World Wide ran into technical obstacles, and by April the British had to cancel their offer to relay World Wide shows.[51] But although this failure demonstrated deep problems in American short-wave broadcasting, it did not end British interest in using World Wide to extend British propaganda. The British began sending political propaganda directives directly to the British Security Coordination (BSC) offices in New York, which passed them on to World Wide, outlining British Foreign Office suggestions for the main propaganda themes to France for the week. The British rewrote their directives specifically for World Wide, and by the summer of 1941 they were sending their directives and monitoring World Wide broadcasts.[52]

A few months after the Foreign Information Service began operations, the British began shipping guidances to the New York office of the FIS, which then passed them on to World Wide. They were cabled weekly in cipher, but the Foreign Office did not hide the British authorship from the American propagandists, who understood and, although they did not like it, accepted the situation.[53] Moreover, Donovan's special relationship with William Stephenson, head of the BSC, facilitated British influence over World Wide. Throughout 1941 and into 1942 the British continued to feed policy directives to the American station through both the FIS and the BSC.[54]

By the spring of 1942, when the Foreign Information Service was a going concern and the Voice of America was on the air, the British expanded their efforts to influence American propaganda. To begin with, British relays of Voice of America programs allowed the British to exercise policy control over American broadcasts through editorial changes. The British wanted the American programs to reinforce the British viewpoint. As Ivone Kirkpatrick, controller of the BBC European service, recalled with classic British understatement, the Voice of America should provide "a demonstration of Anglo-American solidarity on the air." Years later he explained rather blandly that "in case reception [of American programs] were bad or the American broadcasts were rejected, we were supplied with stand-by American records on general subjects which could be substituted for the discarded broadcasts."[55]

The Foreign Information Service understood British intentions. During the spring of 1942, however, it was powerless to prevent British editorial interference. From London, Irving Pflaum, an FIS official who was there to help prepare news for the Voice of America, complained about British interference to Sherwood and Barnes: to no avail, he reported, he had reproached Kirkpatrick for repeated BBC editorial cuts. Barnes reassuringly responded that although the New York office found these cuts "disquieting," the Foreign Information Service had resolved to accept the situation, at least initially. British interference was the price Americans had to pay for British technical cooperation.[56]

British editing continued to generate bad feeling on both sides of the Atlantic. America policymakers disliked British censorship, and the British for their part objected to working with the Voice of America on the grounds that it constituted a direct threat to British credibility: "to being let down by those terrible mistakes that were being made all the time by the OWI."[57] The British did want a propaganda alliance, however, and so by midsummer they stopped editing American programs.

Although the British ceased tampering directly with American programs, they did not stop looking for ways to influence their ally's propaganda. In the late spring of 1942, concerned with the changes the establishment of a new propaganda organization might bring and how they might affect it, the British sent two men to see the president and to visit the Foreign Information Service. The senior man was David Bowes-Lyon, the youngest brother of the queen, a successful banker and a director of the Times Publishing Company. With the coming of war he had joined the Ministry of Economic Warfare and worked with the Secret Operations Executive (SOE), the British counterpart to the Office of Strategic Services. The other was Ritchie Calder.

Because Bowes-Lyon was the queen's brother, protocol dictated that he be invited to dine at the White House, and the story of his encounter there illustrates something of the British attitude toward their American allies. Dinner at the White House was a stag affair, with President Roosevelt, Secretary of State Hull, chief of staff General George C. Marshall, and Harry Hopkins, among others, in attendance. Conversation soon turned to German morale and—in June 1942—to how long the war was going to last. The Americans were convinced that German will was on the verge of collapse, an expectation that thoroughly amazed Bowes-Lyon. He asked them why they thought this. They responded that the White House had received monitoring reports of a subversive station of dissident German army officers called Gustav Siegfried Eins. The programs on this station, they said, revealed a major split within the German army over the future of the war. There was a faction of officers who believed that Germany had to lose, and that the Germans should surrender as soon as possible. What they heard on Gustav Siegfried Eins, the Americans asserted, showed that Germany was faring far worse than the British or Americans could have expected.

Bowes-Lyon said nothing. He knew that Gustav Siegfried Eins was not a German station, but a British secret operation located in Bedfordshire. His instructions, however, prohibited him from saying anything about covert operations such as this "black" radio station. So he sat through the dinner, saying little except that the British had been trying to find out about the station without any good guesses as to its significance. The moment he left the White House, however, Bowes-Lyon raced off to the British embassy and sent an urgent ciphered message to the director general of the Political Warfare Executive, Robert Bruce Lockhart, saying: by all means let us keep quiet about black (covert) propaganda to the OWI and be as cagey as possible with Donovan and the OSS, but should we not stop misleading the secretary of state, the chief of the army staff, and the president of the United States? Bowes-Lyon got permission to inform Roosevelt, but the British tendency to secrecy and manipulation had nearly worked against them. Their reluctance to tell the United States about covert radio all but convinced Roosevelt that the war was almost over–when in fact the Germans were still winning the war and America had not yet sent troops to the European theater.[58]

After spending a few weeks in the United States, Bowes-Lyon and Calder reported home that the American propaganda agency was about to be reorganized and the British should send a permanent mission to help the Americans improve their operations. The Foreign Office agreed and in July Bowes-Lyon returned to Washington, accompanied this time by Walter Adams, a British historian who had visited the United States before and who had made American friends while working to help German Jewish academics escape Germany.[59] Bowes-Lyon soon realized that his mission in Washington was insufficient to produce the kind of root and branch reforms he felt were necessary to bring the Voice of America in line with British broadcasting and propaganda standards. He therefore asked the BBC to send representatives to New York to work directly with the Voice. The BBC agreed and sent specialists for the German and French programs, Leonard Miall and Russell Page. They arrived in New York City in September.

Leonard Miall, former president of the Cambridge Speaking Union, had visited the United States twice before. He had been an original member of the BBC's German staff and intimately involved with the development of European broadcasting operations more generally. The BBC controller of European operations glowingly described Miall as "a thoroughly experienced operator who could write or deliver a script, coach a speaker, play a record and perform the other functions of a studio manager."[60] Russell Page was a well-established landscape architect who had joined the BBC in August 1940 as French program organizer in charge of features. Although his term within the BBC had not been as long as that of Miall, Page nevertheless combined a firm grasp of the organization of international broadcasting with a thorough knowledge of French society, politics, and propaganda.[61] Both men were young and attractive; both formed lasting friendships during their American tours of duty; both projected an affability that must have made their task–improving the output of the Voice of America and making it conform more closely with British foreign and propaganda policy—palatable to their American colleagues. Bowes-Lyon originally requested a BBC mission of a rather short duration, one or two months at most, but Houseman assigned Miall and Page a room next to his own, and they settled in, Page for nine months, Miall for two years.[62]

They were followed soon after by a visit from Crossman, a mercurial man with a pugilistic temper and a career that included radio broadcasting, local politics, and writing. Unlike Miall and Page, Crossman returned to Great Britain after three weeks in Washington and New York.[63]

British involvement in American propaganda operated through all three delegations: Bowes-Lyon and Adams in Washington; Miall and Page in New York; and at least briefly, Crossman, who shuttled between the two cities. Personal friendships and good working relations made it easier for the British to offer suggestions. Thus, for example, Sherwood regularly lunched with Adams when he was in Washington. In late September, while they were eating together, Sherwood took the opportunity to discuss with the British propagandist how the Voice of America might prepare the way for a possible diplomatic break between the United States and Vichy, and how the Voice could best exploit whatever happened. Adams cabled the question on to the PWE in London, and London sent Adams a series of suggestions for possible American propaganda lines, which Adams in turn passed to Sherwood.[64]

The British participated in American propaganda on the most intimate level. Miall and Page devoted their time and energy to the detailed work of production, format, style, and organization. They attended the editorial conferences, the daily political guidance meetings, and the central and regional directive sessions.[65] Miall cheerfully reported in October that the "new system of central directives [that he had suggested] has now started," but fretted that "still much has to be done, particularly in preparing material for regional directives."[66] When he was in New York Crossman discussed not only larger issues of organization but also specific propaganda campaigns.[67]

British influence extended down to such details as whom the Americans should appoint to head their language desks and how to organize those desks.[68] Miall and Page sent to London for recordings of jammed programs to demonstrate to Voice of America producers the actual distortions in listening caused by Axis interference, broadcast distortions that the American propagandists, isolated in New York, had not heard. Miall carefully explained the technical problems of maintaining listener interest "through heavy jamming with an audience tired, dispirited and cold."[69]

Overall, the British persistently argued for a general change in American programming. They worked to persuade the Voice's leaders to introduce personality speakers rather than rely on unidentified, impersonal announcers. They argued that Voice broadcasts should become more of a "Projection of America" rather than what one PWE report described as "a belated and frequently inaccurate version of the BBC."[70] American news stories, after all, were often "put to bed" five hours or more before they were broadcast in order to accommodate time for translation, policy oversight, censorship, rehearsal, and a two-hour lag in London for rebroadcast. As this necessarily stale American version of the news was sandwiched between other, BBC-originated news broadcasts, Miall suggested "a five minute news round-up somewhat in the style of American news commentaries rather than attempting to duplicate belatedly the B.B.C. bulletins." Furthermore, Miall added, "the second five minutes should be devoted to some aspect of American life . . . projecting in a human and lively way what is taking place over here. . . ."[71] Whereas Barnes and others worried at first that this might transform the Voice of America into a more parochial news operation, Miall reported that Houseman welcomed the suggestions and by mid-October had begun effecting them.[72]

The leaders of the OWI also needed British intelligence. They had to know as much as possible about living conditions, political beliefs, and the morale of the citizens of enemy and enemy-occupied nations. How could the Voice of America launch a campaign urging French peasants to withhold food from German occupation forces without knowing about crops, peasant attitudes, and local resistance? Donovan had intended to make intelligence work for propaganda, but after June he used his control over intelligence against the OWI.[73]

The British became concerned. Page and Miall, sitting in on the daily and weekly guidance meetings, received endless requests for information.[74] Thus, one of the many British assignments became making certain that British intelligence was available to the OWI leaders, who "relied quite a lot on British information because they had jolly little of their own."[75] Crossman initiated discussions on how to improve OWI intelligence, observing that this was the most important problem the British could solve.[76]

The British supplied the OWI with intelligence and in April 1943 sent Mark Abrams, director of the PWE Intelligence Unit, to work with the New York office of the Overseas Branch of the OWI. "Abrams," explained Miall, "came to show O.W.I. how to use intelligence for operational purposes . . . and he stayed to organize and direct the Operational Intelligence Division of O.W.I."[77] It was British intelligence, therefore, and not American intelligence that informed American propaganda. In this way the British maintained a constant degree of authority over Voice of America propaganda.[78]

The Americans worked closely with the British in London as well as in New York and Washington.[79] Sherwood had established, with Donovan, a London office in the winter of 1941–42.[80] In 1942 Sherwood sent Warburg to London to make preparations for a permanent OWI mission.[81] Personal relationships served the Americans in London, as they did the British in New York. Just as Miall and Page made friends and won respect in New York, so Warburg and the permanent head of the London office, Wallace Carroll, did the same in Great Britain. After fourteen years as a journalist in Europe for UP, several of which he had spent as London bureau chief, Carroll knew London well. He arrived there in September with instructions to harmonize the Allied propaganda agencies.[82]

Throughout the summer and fall of 1942 a procession of Americans and British crossed the Atlantic. The result was an integration of Anglo-American propaganda, and a large degree of British administrative and policy leadership. The situation was clear enough to be noted outside the OWI. John J. McCloy, assistant secretary of war, for example, found the situation disturbing and wrote in late November that "there are at present . . . dangers of too great an uncritical reliance upon the policies of the British as expressed in their Central Directives." He wanted American policy to be coordinated by the Departments of War, Navy, and State, and not "dominated by the British."[83] But in 1942 neither he nor others made a dent in the Anglo-American propaganda alliance. There was more harmony between the United States and Great Britain in psychological warfare than in almost any other arena of the war, and it became easy, almost natural, for the British to dominate the Overseas Branch, and for the Americans to accept the British propaganda lead.

The first Allied military campaign in the European theater of war, the Allied invasion of North Africa (Torch) launched on November 8, 1942, reinforced this intimate working relationship. After Roosevelt and Churchill agreed on an Allied invasion of North Africa, they selected General Dwight D. Eisenhower as supreme commander of the Allied Expeditionary Forces. By midsummer the two nations began planning for military action.[84]

That August, Warburg and Carroll suggested to Eisenhower that the Allied planners include propaganda—psychological warfare—in their overall strategy. Eisenhower agreed immediately. "I don't know much about psychological warfare," Carroll remembered the general saying, "but I want to give it every chance."[85] Eisenhower wished to avoid bloodshed between the Allies and the French and strove to achieve victory in North Africa at the lowest possible cost in human lives. Propaganda, the general reasoned, might further that goal. It could tell the French that the Allied troops were friends whose sole purpose was to drive out the Axis invaders.[86]

Eisenhower's decision reflected his philosophy of military administration. He wanted a fully integrated staff of American and British soldiers. He eventually incorporated within the Allied Force Headquarters (AFHQ) a combined operation known as the Psychological Warfare Branch, an amalgam of Americans and British, SOE and OSS, PWE and OWI. That August Eisenhower directed Carroll and Warburg to assign one man to work directly with the invasion planners.

Carroll and Warburg chose Percy Winner, a journalist with impressive credentials.[87] Like so many of the staff of the Overseas Branch, Winner had lived in Europe for many years. He had worked in North Africa as chief correspondent for the French wire service Havas, and in Rome for the American wire service International News Service. He had directed the International Division of NBC. He had joined the Foreign Information Service in its earliest days, and established close friendships with Warburg and Houseman and especially with Sherwood, who nicknamed Winner his "ferret" because Winner was such a short and wiry man. He was an eloquent and entertaining conversationalist, a copious memo writer, a self-promoter, and most important in 1942, an enthusiastic propagandist who believed in the importance of the job to be done and in his own ability to make the correct policy decisions all along the way.[88]

Winner, like Warburg, wrote propaganda directives in concert with British planners. "Propaganda policy should be made not by military commanders but civilian authorities," he wrote, and added, even more strongly, that "foreign propaganda policy does not necessarily stem from or agree with foreign policy . . . it must be drawn up with the *advice,* not on the *orders,* of the State Department" (emphasis is in original).[89] On one level, Winner's attitude reflected the intellectual independence of a good journalist, reinforced by personal ambition and arrogance. But beyond that, Winner believed that he and his colleagues understood the war better than did the State Department or the military. Like Warburg, Winner used propaganda to remake foreign policy.

From the beginning, the British and Americans portrayed the Allied invasion of North Africa as primarily American, which it was. Both sides hoped that America's neutral Vichy policy would make French North African officials accept the invasion. But the Allies did not in fact share a single policy toward France or French North Africa. The British supported de Gaulle and the Free French. The United States did not. Winner, like his colleagues in

New York, agreed with British policy and disagreed with American policy. Winner took the British line and wrote reams of guidances describing the Allied invasion as the beginning of a war of liberation. American propaganda reflected the independence of American policy planners from official American foreign policy and their close alliance with the British.[90]

Other threads wove together the Anglo-American propaganda alliance. The British worked gently to guide the American output. After the Voice of America went on the air the British trained American broadcasters in order to improve the output of the Voice, which the British, quite openly among themselves, considered terrible, despite Miall's and Page's very real and strong admiration for John Houseman and sincere friendship with the New York propaganda leaders. In part this disdain was based on cultural differences of style and taste between the restrained British and the more extravagant Americans. Mark Abrams, who came to America to transmit British intelligence, later remarked that the early Voice of America "was so hammy I remember shuddering." For Abrams, Houseman's tone sounded off, rather like "selling Colgate toothpaste, urgently."[91] In part it resulted from the remoteness of New York from the war itself and the effect geographic location had on the Voice of America. Miall explained of his own experiences, for example, that "when I was broadcasting from London to Germany, Germany seemed a terribly long way away, and it was very difficult to put yourself in the minds of people who were listening. . . . It was that much harder from New York." And so, "the fact that I had come from being bombed, and the blitz, and the war, and the black out . . . I could . . . myself identify the conditions in Europe . . . much more than people just reading newspapers in New York would."[92] For Miall the details of bringing over recordings of jamming to make the Americans hear the hardships of listening in Europe rather than merely letting them imagine these difficulties, or working over scheduling problems in order to make sure that the Voice of America did not go on the air when the French were asleep, were all extremely important parts of his job.

But the most important aspect of British interest in American propaganda was policy. The British, especially in 1942, wanted the Voice of America to reinforce the policy line of the PWE. That meant encouraging the Americans to talk about resistance, to oppose the regime of Vichy Vice Premier Pierre Laval, and to portray the U.S. role in the war as encouragingly and convincingly as possible. The goal of propaganda was to win the war. Toward France that meant restoring the self-respect of the French people and persuading them of the certainty of an Allied victory.[93]

American propagandists supported the French Resistance not as an un-

orthodox means of war, as did the British, but as an expression of political freedom and a way of securing a future democracy. In this area their
aims converged with British interests, which made it seem at the time that
they were in agreement with long-range as well as immediate British policy.
For the Americans, the British provided an attractive alternative to the State
Department. Sherwood, Barnes, Johnson, Warburg, and Houseman could
not work comfortably with the State Department. Nor could the State Department accept them. But the American propagandists could cooperate
with the British. And they did.

# 3

## An Agent of Resistance

### The Voice of America on the Air

JOHN HOUSEMAN established the Voice of America in February 1942 as an aggressive tool of warfare. An in-house report stated early in 1943: "Propaganda warfare is not merely a battle of words. It is a battle for people's minds and through their minds their physical actions."[1] The challenge was to create a special American radio propaganda style to accomplish these goals.

Houseman attacked his task with enthusiasm, vision, and talent. He was a commanding and charismatic man with an artistic vision and the force of personality to make his ideas come alive. As director of the Voice of America he could be found everywhere, talking with the announcers, directing the shows, editing the scripts, and providing a great fund of ideas for the propaganda broadcasts. As one British observer wrote home soon after Houseman left the Voice in June 1943, he was a natural propagandist, "an executive who combined dramatic ability with real driving power."[2]

He was an experienced radio producer. After abandoning a first career as an international grain broker in the wake of the stock market crash of 1929, Houseman made his way in the world of American theater. He spent the first few years of his new professional life staging works by Virgil Thomson, Maxwell Anderson, and Archibald MacLeish until in 1935 Houseman went to work for the newly created Federal Theatre Project of the Works Progress Administration, where he began his lengthy collaboration with Orson Welles.[3] Two years later Houseman and Welles started the Mercury Theatre, which in 1938 spun off the "Mercury Theatre of the Air."

For this series, Houseman and Welles adapted H. G. Wells's science fiction fantasy of an invasion from Mars, *The War of the Worlds*. In this terrifying radio drama Houseman and Welles used news reporting to create an atmosphere of authenticity, to persuade the listener that fiction was, in fact, reality. "New techniques of 'on-the-spot' reporting had been developed" for radio, Houseman later explained, and so "by copying every detail [we] found an already enervated audience ready to accept its wildest fantasies."[4] It was a sensational production that generated such fear among listeners that men and women living close to the supposed invasion site literally fled their homes in terror, heightening American consciousness of the power of radio to persuade men and women to act. "War of the Worlds" demonstrated how effective a propagandist Houseman could be and what influence radio could exert.[5]

As a radio producer, Houseman was very conscious of the importance of contemporary live drama to radio artistry. "My first decision," Houseman recounted, "was to get away from the single-voice news reporting of the private stations and BBC."[6] Systematic and continuous live international news coverage had begun in the United States when CBS first allowed Edward R. Murrow to broadcast direct reports from Vienna on the German occupation of Austria in March 1938; but by February 1942 the worlds news roundup had settled into a regular format, with an anchorman introducing news features and correspondents giving detailed accounts.[7] Network news was identifiable in three distinct ways. First, the networks took the audience around the world by pasting together a montage of reports, demonstrating thereby that radio could go anywhere and be present at any event. Second, these reports were of substantial length and were both personal and direct. Reporters were well-known men who created a direct link between event and listener.[8] Third, network stories tended to be based on eyewitness accounts. An NBC anchorman, for example, typically introduced a daily newscast by saying to his listeners:

Good morning. Time now for the regular round up of war news, with reports direct from the various capitals of the world. Our on-the-scene correspondents are standing by with direct coverage from the mid-Pacific, from London and from our nation's capital in Washington, D.C.[9]

In stark contrast, Houseman directed his announcers to introduce the Voice of America by saying:

VOICE: This is New York, the United States of America, calling the people of
       Europe.
VOICE: Every morning at this time you hear our voices from America,
VOICE: Telling you what this country is doing and thinking towards winning the
       war.[10]

Network news was a journalism of carefully chosen detail. It reflected a belief that "concrete terms produce more vivid impressions than abstract ones."[11] Through a "connoisseurship of facts" network journalism convinced Americans that it spoke the truth.[12] But Houseman thought it not only lacked energy and drive, but that it could not move listeners to take action. He wanted a broadcast style with freshness, vitality, and a distinct American sound.[13] He therefore chose his models from radio drama, radio documentary, and live political theater.

Radio has its own special artistic properties; its possibilities and its limits are unique to that medium. It is not only verbal, but aural; in its barest sense it is the art of what can be done with a microphone on one end and an amplifier at the other.[14] As the British poet cum BBC staff writer Louis MacNeice wrote, "Sound broadcasting gets its effects through sound and sound alone." In order to succeed, therefore, the radio writer must "forget about 'literature' and concentrate upon sounds."[15] Freed of a stage or screen, liberated from the visual element of production, during the 1930s radio producers and writers experimented with new broadcast styles. They discovered that radio dissolved barriers of space and time and enabled a rapid vaulting of audience from place to place.[16] They created dramas composed of many scenes stacked together: "a kind of overlay or rapid movement from scene to scene only possible in the flexible radio medium."[17]

Radio dramatists learned special techniques by which to transform their audiences from passive listeners to active participants. This feat, they discovered, could best be accomplished through dialogue rather than narration. The British writer and producer Martin Esslin described this process in his book about the variety of dramatic forms, *An Anatomy of Drama*. He recalled setting out to write a radio script in the late 1940s for the BBC World Service depicting an employment office as part of a positive image of Great Britain. "I could have written a purely literary, discursive description," he explained, one in which the narrator might say:

The official asks the applicant for a job to give him the relevant details. He is not unfriendly although he maintains a certain reserve and distance, yet at the same time it is quite apparent from the tone of voice he uses that he is genuinely trying to help the person in front of him. . . .

But, Esslin wrote, such a description would have sounded "like a very special pleading." Instead, Esslin broke up what he had to say into speech:

OFFICIAL: Do sit down.
APPLICANT: Thank you.
OFFICIAL: Now let's see. Your name is. . . ?

APPLICANT: John Smith.
  OFFICIAL: And your last job was . . . ?
APPLICANT: Machinist.
  OFFICIAL: I see.[18]

This dialogue invited the listener to come into the room and sit down on a third side of the desk. The listener became a participant.[19] It gave color to actions and brought to life what the producer wanted to tell the audience as drama brought home and vividness of the experience.

The most important American radio dramatist of the thirties was Norman Corwin. Among radio writers there were pro-Corwin and anti-Corwin factions, but no one else in the field was held in such esteem.[20] In 1939 Corwin produced a five-part series entitled "So This Is Radio," a group of plays dramatizing the art of broadcasting. He devoted the fifth installment to the role of music, but he did so not by playing music but by pasting together a montage of speeches.

  FIRST VOICE: This is a program about music, and a little about you.
 SECOND VOICE: It's going to be an unusual sort of program for a number of reasons, to wit:
  THIRD VOICE: Although it concerns serious music, you won't hear serious music.
 FOURTH VOICE: Although it concerns light music, you won't hear light music.
  FIFTH VOICE: Although it concerns a seemingly simple phase of radio, actually the subject is quite complex.
  SIXTH VOICE: Although this program is already one-thirtieth gone by, it has yet to make a formal opening announcement. . . .[21]

Corwin presented music through the abstraction of words. His dialogue was often very brief, but it moved the listener along at a fast pace. He used dialogue exclusively rather than a traditional narrative form, rejecting thereby the authorial voice. These were techniques Houseman used in producing programs for the Voice of America.

Radio documentaries also came into existence during the 1930s. They were part of a larger movement, which included films such as Pare Lorenz's *The Plow That Broke the Plain,* books such as James Agee's *Let Us Now Praise Famous Men,* and photographs such as those by Walker Evans taken to parallel Agee's text. Documentary expression was in turn part of the larger artistic movement of social realism which dominated the thirties.[22] The decade was an era of commitment in which liberals and radicals hoped to transform society through their plays, paintings, movies, books, photographs, and radio programs.[23]

Houseman was well acquainted with the most popular and important radio documentary program of the decade, "The March of Time." This was a fully scripted studio event. Originated in 1931 by *Time* magazine, each half-hour segment required a thousand hours of labor and an entire week of preparation. "The March of Time," both on radio and, after mid-decade, on film, provided its audience with a weekly dramatization of important events reenacted by a stable of actors adept at impersonation.[24] The series was exciting, and it became, as one radio historian has written, the "major example of how . . . the news story or essay on radio was most naturally cast as drama."[25]

The documentary provided a double influence. It showed that radio, along with film, live theater, posters, journalism, and photography, could become an artistic device of social commitment and propaganda. It also provided Houseman with a model for recreating news inside a sound recording studio, as had "War of the Worlds." Although "The March of Time" sounded less like the Voice of America than did Corwin's "So This Is Radio," the idea that news could be artistically reenacted proved crucial to the development of the Voice of America.[26]

Alongside radio drama and documentaries, live theater introduced the idea that nameless people could be used to express political ideas. This notion had its roots in the post–World War I German Expressionist theater.[27] Expressionists experimented with form in order to penetrate beneath surface reality and to illuminate man's inner world, for as the German Expressionist playwright Ernst Toller wrote, "by skinning the human being one hoped to find his soul."[28] Moreover, the Expressionists abandoned careful plotting and complete storytelling; instead they constructed their plays around a series of scenes that succeeded each other with rapid, almost cinematographic, speed.[29] Throughout the years between the world wars American writers such as Elmer Rice, Eugene O'Neill, and Tennessee Williams experimented with Expressionist dramatic techniques.[30] By the 1930s, the once-revolutionary forms had become literary conventions that Houseman in turn employed to create the broadcast style of the Voice of America.

Most important, live drama offered Houseman the model of agitprop theater and the more muted but artistically sophisticated Living Newspaper of the Federal Theatre Project in New York.[31] The Living Newspaper emerged from the postwar phenomenon of street theater. In Russia after 1917 the new Soviet government had organized theatrical troupes to support the revolution and inform the illiterate workers and peasants, but in Germany, where the postwar revolution had failed, political activists such as Bertolt Brecht and Kurt Weill used drama to attempt to overthrow the government.

There it became known as agitprop, or agitation and propaganda.[32] The director of the Federal Theatre Project, Hallie Flanagan, described the Living Newspaper as an effort to dramatize a new struggle: "to turn the great natural and economic social forces of our time toward a better life for more people."[33] It was, in short, a creative and inventive model for the Voice of America as a peculiarly American form of propaganda.

Agitprop adopted some of the techniques of Expressionism for political theater. The episodic form, for example, facilitated highly political plays without forcing unity of action.[34] Like Expressionism, agitprop portrayed archetypes rather than individuals. It altered and distorted dramatic dialogue to allow heavier use of political slogans, while it employed choral chants to represent the will of the people. Irwin Piscator, one of the leaders of the agitprop movement in Germany, wrote that "with a political revue I hoped to achieve propagandistic effects which would be more powerful than was possible with plays. . . . the revue offered a chance of 'direct action' in the theatre."[35] Agitprop, moreover, used "trivial [art] forms which have the merit of being clear and easily understood by all."[36] It was the sort of prose that news desk writers could grind out and that audiences huddled over their clandestinely owned sets could understand.

Houseman created an amalgam of these forms for the Voice of America. He decided that the Voice should "be represented by several voices of different quality and pitch carefully orchestrated to achieve a maximum of variety and energy."[37] He thus chose a rotating cast of four actors who never gave the listener a hint of individuality or personal recognition. The shows were produced with the fast pace and the episodic structure of a political revue. These were all hallmarks of thirties drama and experimental radio, but seen as a political act—as propaganda—it was agitprop.

Like network news, however, the Voice began every show with headlines, which set Voice of America propaganda in the traditional textual context of newspaper and radio news. Each headline was announced by a different voice:

FIRST VOICE: Laval is back in power in vichy [*sic*]. The American government will only make its position known when the composition of the Laval cabinet has been officially announced.
SECOND VOICE: On the Russian front Soviet troops have won several successes.
THIRD VOICE: Yesterday, throughout the day, the RAF [Royal Air Force] attacked German installations in Normandy.
FOURTH VOICE: President [Roosevelt] declared that the present war was a life and death struggle where the fate of our entire civilization was at stake.[38]

This technique extended from the headlines to expanded news accounts. "Yesterday," ran a report on the war in the Far East broadcast on August 5, 1942, there was good news on the fighting front in China:

FIRST VOICE: It came in communiqués from Lt. General Stilwell which announced that American warplanes are now fully cooperating with the Chinese offensive. Here is that important communiqué:
SECOND VOICE: American bombers and fighters attacked Japanese headquarters at Linchuan in the Kiangsi Province, dropping demolition and incendiary bombs while Chinese ground troops attacked.[39]

It defined features as well. One broadcast, for example, described the severity of Nazi rule and the consequences of the German plan to conscript French workers:

VOICE: Such is the law of Nazi Germany.
VOICE: All that is forbidden is required.
VOICE: Such is the voice Hitler wants to impose on the world.
VOICE: All that is forbidden is required.
VOICE: Such is the law the Vichy Kommandatur wants to impose on the French.
VOICE: Free Expression,
VOICE: FORBIDDEN.
VOICE: To be a patriot,
VOICE: FORBIDDEN.
VOICE: To eat enough,
VOICE: FORBIDDEN.[40]

The Voice projected an image of democratic masses and an industrious America committed to winning the war, since in thirties America the drama of the nameless person had come to represent "the people" in search of a transcendent national identity in a land of many regions and ethnic groups, and to assert the greatness of America. The very sound and form of the Voice of America, therefore, implicitly told the listener that the United States was innovative, strong, committed to democracy, and determined to fight for a better world for all. Houseman's broadcast forms told the oppressed of Nazi-occupied Europe to rise up and overthrow the Axis. The Voice of America was agitprop on the air, provoking the masses to resist.

The broadcast style of the Voice of America, moreover, implied the propagandists' definition of their audience. When Donovan conceived the initial goals of American propaganda, when Sherwood, Barnes, Johnson, and Warburg took over that task, and when Houseman created the station, they did not know who would tune in to the station—or, indeed, if anyone would do so. And although the OWI conducted audience surveys, these were inconclusive at best. Perhaps that was why the propagandists never articulated their concept of audience, for as one of the earliest Voice writers later recalled, "We didn't know whether we were talking to ourselves; we didn't know whether anyone was hearing us at all; . . . we were sailing, flying blind."[41] Nevertheless, Houseman and his colleagues did have an idea of audience, whether or not they consciously recognized or delineated it. Embedded in the text of their broadcasts was what literary critics call an "implied" reader – or an implied listener.[42]

There were no specialized programs in 1942 and even by early 1943 there was only a show for women and a show for labor. This deficiency was not for want of ideas, for a year later the airwaves were filled with such programs as a military show, a religious show, a European show, and a host of other specialized talks. The lack of specialized programming early in the history of the Voice of America rather reflected a concept of audience in which all of France – or any other nation – was considered as one. The listeners formed a "mass" who could be prodded into action through words alone, as a charismatic leader could ignite a crowd through his speech and personality. Just as the shows stripped away the individuality of the announcers, they denied individuality, or uniqueness of interest, to members of their audience. Throughout 1942 the leaders of the COI and then the Overseas Branch of the OWI told the French that America was democratic, energetic, and egalitarian, and they encouraged their listeners to overthrow their German and collaborationist rulers. With great flair and élan, Houseman created a broadcasting style to accomplish this twin mission.[43]

Important as were the forms of the radio shows in expressing the propagandists' goals, Houseman, Sherwood, and the leaders of the Overseas Branch concentrated their efforts on the content of the programs and the specifics of foreign policy. Voice of America broadcasts to France covered three categories, each of which included both news and features. First, the station discussed domestic French politics. Second, it relayed battlefront news and reviewed overall developments in the war. Finally, it told the French about America – its spirit, its strengths, and its hopes for the world after Allied victory. Propaganda to France is the story of these three themes.

Throughout the period of the COI and Donovan's direction, the Voice concentrated on discussions about internal French politics and the political leadership of the premier of the Vichy regime, Marshal Philippe Pétain, and the vice premier, Pierre Laval. It encouraged the French to resist any further collaboration with the Nazis and obliquely encouraged rebellion against Vichy.

Official American policy toward Vichy France had three basic aims: to ensure that the French fleet would not be used against the United States, to make certain that the Axis powers would not secure French African and Caribbean military bases, and to dissuade the Vichy government from further collaboration with Germany.[44] To effect these ends the American government had established diplomatic relations with Vichy, and on January 4, 1941, President Roosevelt appointed Admiral William D. Leahy as American ambassador in the hope that the president could thereby disengage France from outright Axis collaboration.[45] The United States also accepted Marshal Pétain as the best of Vichy. The president and the State Department believed Pétain would not hand over the country's remaining military assets to the Germans; he was, they believed, America's best French hope.

Initially, Pétain's vice premier was Pierre Laval, the son of a village entrepreneur who had climbed the political ladder of success in the Third Republic.[46] Laval was America's villain—"an ideal scapegoat," as one historian has written, "a symbol of evil incarnate."[47] Laval believed that the Germans would win the war and that France's interests therefore lay in full and wholehearted cooperation with the Nazis.[48] Laval fell from power in December 1940. But in February 1942 the Germans demanded that Pétain reinstate Laval.[49] The Americans threatened to break off diplomatic relations. Hitler retorted that if Pétain did not reappoint Laval, Germany would take aggressive measures.[50] Pétain capitulated. On April 14 the Vichy leader announced that he would reinstate Pierre Laval. Roosevelt recalled Leahy to Washington, and relations between the two nations deteriorated.[51]

The Voice defined French politics as a choice between collaboration and resistance, and within this context repeatedly discussed Vichy leadership. Throughout February, March, and early April 1942, the station avoided attacks on the marshal himself. Once Pétain accepted Laval's return, however, policy directives began instructing the French desk to criticize the marshal, albeit with care not to use personal insults or invective.[52] But enemy number one was Laval, and that was where the propagandists aimed their fire. Bear down on Laval, directed on April guidance, "as a traitor and as a German agent."[53] The directives spoke with urgency, and by late April stories about Laval showed a definite distaste; Laval was a quisling who would never succeed in his traitorous goal of appeasing the Germans.[54] By mid-May the Voice's call was clarion. "Today it is Laval and not Pétain who governs Vichy. And he does so as a puppet of Hitler."[55] *Laval* became a propaganda code word, warning the French that collaboration would lead first to oppression and ultimately to invasion.

Voice of America propaganda concerning Laval was not, at least immedi-

ately, out of line with State Department policy. The State Department intensely disliked Laval and saw him as the opening wedge for increasing
German control.[56] Where the propagandists differed from official foreign
policy was in their assessment of the implications of Laval's return. The State
Department thought it highly unlikely that French political events would
increase resistance or generate violent action against Laval and the Vichy
government. The French, they argued, would deplore Laval's return, but
in the end they would acquiesce, with a shrug and a comment that at least
he was a clever man who might obtain concessions from the Germans; they
would remain apathetic to events around them.[57] The State Department
advocated a wait-and-see tactic: do nothing for the time being.

The propagandists disagreed. For them exhortations against Laval were
part of a far more general and important support of the French Resistance.
Whereas the State Department believed that there was virtually no resistance within France and that events would not change that fact, arguing
that French domestic resistance had no role to play in American foreign
policy, the propagandists advocated direct support of resistance on all levels.
"Put in material which suggests, but does not call specifically for, the assassination of Laval . . . and other key traitors," exhorted one directive.[58]

The propagandists understood the frailty of the fledgling French movement for resistance, which in early 1942 was embryonic at best. So they set
about selecting relevant news items from around Europe, working with
them as imaginatively as possible, to create an image of a Europe alight in
the flames of resistance. They talked about Dutch confrontation, for example, and Czech sabotage of Nazi trains.[59] A feature on a Canadian para-
chutist who single-handedly killed scores of German soldiers before he took
his own life exemplified the will "to second the resistance of the French
patriots."[60]

The summer of 1942 witnessed a crucial turning point for wartime France
as Germany began subjecting the French to the increasing rigors of the wartime economy, rationing food, deporting massive numbers of Jews, and finally, in September, instituting the hated *relève,* or relief system. Soon after
Germany attacked the Soviet Union, the Wehrmacht began drafting German factory workers into the army. The Nazi government, short of manpower and unwilling to turn to German women, began staffing factories
with foreign workers. During the winter of 1941–42 the French voluntar-
ily contributed nearly 150,000 such workers, who at the time were seeking
better wages and working conditions than they could find at home. But
French enthusiasm did not last, and by the spring of 1942 there were very

few French workers willing to go to Germany. The German need for foreign labor continued to increase, however, and in May the Nazis demanded that the Vichy government press more Frenchmen into service.

The dirty work fell to Pierre Laval. He first tried a scheme of voluntary compliance, but the plan did not work, nor did it placate the worried French, despite a massive campaign to woo the French out of their homes and into German factories. In September, therefore, Laval agreed to pursue a more stringent system of labor recruitment. According to the relève system, the Germans could draft French workers in return for the repatriation of French prisoners of war.

The relève gave American propagandists an issue for their first major direct propaganda campaign.[61] Guidances advised the Voice to portray French workers as hostages, to predict Germany's failure to keep any of its promises, to explain the German need for French manpower, and to describe the poor living conditions of French workers in Germany. By October, the Americans accelerated the campaign against the relève, describing Laval's measures as an agreement to convert France into an agricultural province of the Reich. "The main general theme may be that Germany is systematically depopulating" occupied countries.[62]

Houseman created two shows in response to the relève: a show for labor and a show for women, although of the two campaigns, labor predominated. "The time has come to start a new and very powerful line in our manpower campaigns," dictated the central directive for the week of October 10.[63] The question of labor presented "the strongest argument of all to the conquered peoples," and the directive therefore suggested broadcasting the message that "any man who leaves France is not only helping the Nazis — is not only becoming a hostage — is not only exposing himself to air raids — but through his very absence from his own country is assisting in its murder."[64] The labor show regularly began with the statement that this was the Voice of America calling the workers of France. It enumerated again and again what the relève meant for the working classes and for France: the destruction of French industry deprived of its best workers; the separation of men from their families; and a program to sterilize France. "It is the France of tomorrow," a feature of October 12 told its audience, that Hitler "is assassinating today."[65]

The women's program developed around the same themes. The Germans were not conscripting women, but the Voice leaders assumed that they could address women by appealing to the French commitment to family and stability. Wives influenced their husbands. "We should stress the role of

French women in developing national morale," suggested a French directive early in October, "taking privations upon themselves and their children and helping their men in the fight for the liberation of France."[66]

By mid-September, French features began praising resistance rather than urging it, marking thereby a slight shift in propaganda tactics and goals. They cited the failure of the relève campaign as proof of successful resistance. "From now on . . . your resistance is a proven fact. . . . By refusing to volunteer, you have made Hitler lose decisive hours . . . by your resistance you are directly contributing to our common victory." The Voice hammered home again and again a message of success and hope for the common Allied war goals.[67]

It was a small change, but an important one, for what it reflected was a different view of resistance. The previous spring there had been no American troops in the European theater of war, and the Russians were still losing on the eastern front. Six months later the Americans were planning their attack through North Africa, and although such plans could not be announced, they did give hope and a new attitude to the propagandists. Everyone knew that the Russians were beginning to win in the east and that the British had turned a corner in North Africa. Resistance no longer had to sustain the hope for the defeat of the Axis; now it could be seen as part of a wider Allied effort. In October this was still a muted and secret thought, but its effect can nevertheless be discerned. It reflected, moreover, a shift in propaganda theory with the change in control from Donovan to Sherwood, from COI to OWI. For Donovan resistance was an arm of covert operations, whereas for Sherwood and his colleagues resistance was not a military act but a political statement.

Despite these important differences between Sherwood and Donovan, both propagandists supported the idea of resistance. The State Department never even considered the French Resistance as a potential political ally, unlike the British, who nurtured the French Resistance with men, money, and material support. American support of the Resistance was impossible once the United States had decided to recognize the Vichy government. Moreover, unlike the British, the Americans did not consider France an essential element in the postwar balance of power.[68] Finally, both President Roosevelt and State Department policymakers actively disliked General Charles de Gaulle.

For the propagandists, however, resistance was part of the framework in which they saw the war itself. It began with how they defined the war and its goals. For American liberals in general—for readers of the *Nation* or the *New Republic,* for followers of Reinhold Niebuhr, Henry Wallace, or David

Dubinsky—the fight was, from the very beginning, a two-front struggle. It was a war to defeat fascism abroad, and it was a struggle to define the future at home. Liberals consciously and repeatedly linked American democracy with the end of fascism and oppression in Europe and Asia. Thus Niebuhr wrote Dubinsky two months before the Japanese attacked Pearl Harbor that as far as he was concerned, the goal of the American government should be to connect "the fight for democracy on the foreign front with the domestic issues" of the New Deal. And Herbert Agar said in the *Nation* that if the United States were to survive it would have to "carry on two struggles at once; a struggle at home to show that we mean democracy and a struggle abroad against the murderers of freedom."[69]

Popular Front liberals argued that the world needed a democratic revolution, and that the United States should be at the forefront of that revolution, laying down the foundations for a new international world order.[70] For this reason liberals were willing and often anxious to make an alliance with antifascist coalitions, which were a continuation of the Popular Front movements of the thirties. They identified American opposition to their own political goals with the State Department's international free-trade conservative policies under Cordell Hull. The liberals argued that conservatives in international policy refused to examine the roots of fascism, or the role that had been played by the business and professional elites in its development. Liberals believed that if the United States followed the lead of the conservatives the nation might win the war, but it would lose the peace.[71]

When Joseph Barnes talked about doing an honest, Henry A. Wallace job, he was referring not only to the vice president but to a symbol of the liberal viewpoint. "This is a fight between a slave world and a free world," Wallace said. "Just as the United States in 1862 could not remain half slave and half free, so in 1942 the world must make its decision for a complete victory one way or the other." He went on: "The people's revolution is on the march, and . . . when the freedom-loving people march, when farmers have an opportunity to buy land at reasonable prices and to sell the produce of their land through their own organizations, when workers have the opportunity to form unions and bargain collectively, and when the children of all the people have an opportunity to attend schools . . . then the world moves straight ahead."[72] This was the New Deal at war, the fight for which Sherwood, Barnes, Johnson, Warburg, and Houseman had enlisted. When Wallace spoke of the world as half slave and half free he might have been quoting from Sherwood's play *Abe Lincoln in Illinois*. And Warburg articulated this ideology in *The Isolationist Illusion* when he wrote that "an order permeated with justice demands that all those who are affected by the exercise of any power—political, social, or economic—must have a voice in deciding to whom that power is delegated and how it is exercised."[73]

Throughout 1942 the issue of resistance remained the single most important focus of Voice of America propaganda. This emphasis was possible in large measure because the State Department—and Congress and the military—did not interfere with what the propagandists said during the first year of the American war effort; indeed, they gave the propagandists virtually no guidelines at all, leaving the propagandists free to follow both their own political instincts and those of the British, who saw their opportunity and flooded the Overseas Branch and the Voice with political directives. This situation was to change in 1943, after which news about the war and the Projection of America became increasingly important, while propaganda for resistance steadily decreased. But that is the story of 1943.

In 1942 the Voice of America was suffused with the sound of agitprop—the whole of any broadcast often sounded like an episodic political revue—but Houseman especially emphasized this radical style in propaganda about resistance. It was here that he wanted to address all of France, to tell the French people to rise up and overthrow the fascist oppressor, both in Vichy in the south and Occupied France in the north. It was here that he wanted to provoke direct action, as Piscator had tried to do in Germany after the First World War and street theater players had attempted in the United States in the twenties and thirties. It was here, most of all, that Houseman wanted to convince the audience that it was part of the action, not a group of disengaged individuals listening to a well-constructed political argument. Thus the Voice broadcast in September an agitprop play entitled "The Front of Resistance," using news bulletins as dialogue, blasting out the news and wringing every emotional nuance from it.

VOICE: The third front, the front of RESISTANCE to the Axis in the occupied countries, becomes so active that Germany is seized with anguish. Her press and her radio mirror her confusion. And as the reprisals increase, the movement gains momentum.

VOICE: The Germans don't publish the number of hostages killed in Paris, but it has been learned that among those who recently were shot, were a professor of mathematics, Jacques SALOMON, a philosopher, Georges POLITZER and one of the leaders of the Metal Workers Syndicate of the Parisian region, JOURDIN.

VOICE: No! Repression doesn't put a stop to resistance. Far from it. The NYE DAG, a Stockholm paper, announced, from authorized sources, a number of acts of sabotage that took place recently in occupied France. The list is impressive. Listen:

VOICE: At *Issy-les-Moulineaux*, six radio transmitters used by Goering's Luftwaffe were destroyed in an old Ford plant.

VOICE: At *Argenteuil*, in a merchandise shed, fire destroyed several railroad cars. In a cable factory, work was interrupted for six hours.

. . . . . . . . . . . . . . . . . . . . . . . . . . . . .

VOICE: Far from being impressed by the terror the Germans attempt to impose, the French spend their time inventing new ways of showing their hatred for the invader.

. . . . . . . . . . . . . . . . . . . . . . . . . . . . .

VOICE: Here, in the United States, we all know that conquered France will never be subjugated and that she is awaiting her liberation through the victory of the United Nations.[74]

Stories about resistance, Laval, and Vichy politics dominated the Voice of America throughout the year, but by late April the Voice also informed its French listeners about Allied military successes in the Pacific and in Russia.[75] The propagandists knew that the Soviet Union now sustained the brunt of the fighting in Europe and that the British were no longer the lonely heroes they had been in 1940, and they carefully broadcast news about American assistance to Russia and built up both the British and the American war efforts.[76]

After the June 1942 reorganization of the COI into the OWI the Voice continued to inform the French about the war, hoping that short, briskly presented war reports would attract an audience. The leaders of the Overseas Branch assumed that the French wanted information about the war itself. The Vichy Ministry of Information censored foreign news, as did the Germans in Occupied France. This was one reason why Sherwood and his colleagues had argued with Donovan over the strategy of truth: the French wanted reliable news accounts, and so the Voice of America should establish its credibility. War news played an important role in accomplishing this goal, for although the propagandists carefully chose what stories to include and what pieces to exclude, they did not explicitly distort the truth.

Telling the story of the war was not always easy in 1942. Although in retrospect the Axis lost the war in Europe over the course of that year as the British gained ground in El Alamein, the Russians withstood the Germans at Stalingrad, and the Americans invaded North Africa, throughout the summer of 1942 news was grim.[77] Nevertheless, the propagandists talked at length about the Russian front, the North African front, and the still-to-come second front.

Good news from the Russian front was sparse. Directives suggested only that the Voice emphasize its admiration for the Russian people and army, and show American solidarity with its ally.[78] News writers painted a portrait of a successful Soviet national defense. "The Soviet troops are counterattacking vigorously in Voronezh on the Don front," the 11:30 A.M. news of July 16 told French listeners. "Despite the German superiority, the Russians [have] succeeded in driving them back in certain areas."[79] Small news items could convey optimism; for example, a French language show said that "the Soviet navy's air force in the Baltic [has] destroyed . . . three of the Axis gunboats, one patrol boat, and one armed transporter."[80] American propagandists understood the desperation that stalked the Russian front, but by a careful selection of news stories, all of them true as far as Overseas Branch leaders could ascertain, they implied that small victories augured larger Russian successes and devastating German defeats.

Features allowed the French desk writers a chance to make explicit arguments. This was both an advantage and a disadvantage. Small news items, modestly mounted, were likely to be believed by overseas listeners. The unstated argument for Allied victory would be unconsciously completed by the listener, who would integrate news into a total war picture without questioning the American version of events. Features, on the other hand, challenged the listener to question and rebut.

In August, the leaders of the Overseas Branch began a campaign to counteract German claims to victory in southern Russia. The Americans directed a series of arguments that embraced an overall picture of the eastern front, including predictions that the Germans had stretched their communications and supply lines too thin. "We might indulge in speculation which might compel them to fight on two fronts," suggested a directive on August 10.[81] But although the strength of the Russians was played up, the OWI warned its writers and producers to do so with care and not to overplay their story.[82]

The war in North Africa presented some of the same propaganda problems as did the Russian front. Throughout the summer of 1942, Rommel's forces camped at El Alamein. The Germans had not yet taken the eastern Mediterranean or the Suez Canal, but they were poised on the brink of doing so, and from July to October the war news from eastern North Africa was grim. As in reports about Stalingrad, OWI guidances instructed the Voice to concentrate on what the Germans had failed to accomplish, not on what they had actually done. Thus, in August the Voice pointed out that Rommel was as far from his goal as he had been in June.[83] But unlike reports on the Russian front, the Voice played the British battle in the desert very cautiously. "Stick closely to the United Nations' communiqués in our handling of the news," advised an October guidance note, reflecting British policy.[84]

American propaganda about Stalingrad and the British desert war took two approaches to what was, in both cases, distinctly bad news. In Russian news the Voice of America had a free hand since the American propagandists had no links to their Soviet counterparts; but in British news their English colleagues and allies directly influenced the Voice's coverage. In the first case the Voice of America broadcast flowing, dramatic, overstated narrative prose features. In the second case, warned by the British that enthusiasm might harm the war effort rather than help it, the Voice broadcast a portrait of British soldiers calmly biding their time in the desert. The British wanted to keep expectations for military success to a minimum, and the Voice followed that line; the Russians could not communicate their desires to the American propagandists, and the Voice made up its own line.

The biggest propaganda problem in the summer and fall of 1942 was the promised Allied "second front." "Do not report recent press stories casting doubts on U.S. intentions," warned a June directive.[85] Voice writers used ancillary military actions to demonstrate Allied good intentions, describing, for example, Royal Air Force bombing raids as an "augury of future offensives by land and air."[86] Directives in August carefully instructed the Voice to be as strong as possible–in the vaguest terms.[87] The Political Warfare Executive again set the goal: "Stick to the line that immense and systematic offensive preparations are being made–and that we can say nothing about time or place. . . ."[88] American broadcasts told stories about mounting Allied strength, troop buildup, and British and American air power.[89] The Voice told the French that when the American troops came it would be more than just a raid, but that lengthy preparations were necessary for success.

The American propagandists, however, were pressured at home by their own political commitment to saying more than merely denying the negative. They wanted the United States to launch a second-front attack; they wanted the United States to prove itself a firm ally of the Soviet Union and to free the peoples of Europe from Nazi oppression. The propagandists therefore used bombing raids and disruptions of the French transportation system to give life to the promise of a second front. Here they used techniques of drama and agitprop. One play, for example, had anonymous characters talk with "Uncle Sam," who repeatedly stressed American victories, with choral punctuation in the agitprop manner.[90] "On the Near Eastern front as on all other fronts of the total war, America is attacking," Uncle Sam told the French. For "America is waging a total war, until total victory, for a total peace." The propagandists used experimental radio and agitprop drama to bring alive American intentions and to generate a sense of excitement and expectation, and they used anonymous voices to pro-

ject the will of the whole of the American people, bent toward doing all
they could to win the war.

The third component of American propaganda to France was news and
features about the United States, what the propagandists called the "Projection of America." Three issues initially governed this campaign: U.S. military strength, American national character, and the nation's postwar aims.
Policy directives on American production and military strength, however,
were few in number and expansive in scope, repeatedly directing broadcasters to reiterate the critical importance of the battles still to be fought in
the coming year and to detail America's herculean war production efforts.
Such instructions implied that, although temporarily hidden from view, the
American military stood on the brink of supplying the essential materiel
and military force for Allied victory. The Voice of America should therefore broadcast positive news concerning American military operations.[91]

The Planning Board of the COI warned the Voice to stay clear of overly
hopeful statements. Broadcasts were to forbear from intimations of immi-
nent military effort. "We avoided any promise of immediate offensive action," Donovan reported to Roosevelt, referring to the southwest Pacific,
"but we used [the] line, 'if this is not victory, it is at any rate the assur-
ance of victory.'"[92] American propaganda had to work between the limits
of excessive glorification, which might provoke military expectations the
nation could not fulfill, and drab modesty, which could discourage resistance within France.

The Voice broadcast news accounts of American arms production, and
the numbers of ships and planes, tanks and guns, while not enumerated,
were exaggerated. To implement this line of argument, the Voice used book
reviews, newspaper stories, presidential press conferences, and military and
executive department statements. The French desk, for example, released
the president's figures on increased Lend Lease aid, pointing out that "daily,
America is getting more and more involved in the conflict and is always going to farther fighting fronts."[93]

Accounts of the enthusiastic spirit of Americans complemented descriptions of U.S. military strength. They portrayed idealized beliefs and characterized American international political goals. Voice of America programs
revealed a national mood in which citizens from all walks of life were "determined to make huge sacrifices to beat the Axis."[94] There were dramas that
detailed the courage and heroism of the American combat forces. One such
tale was that of a Captain Wheless, a navy airplane pilot who shot down
seven Japanese planes in May and whom President Roosevelt had honored

in a nationally broadcast speech. Voice writers created a drama in which they interspersed the president's real words with the fictional thoughts of Wheless. "Just as I was charging upon the objective, my gunner shouts at me: two chasing squads, one on the left and one on the right. I could have plunged into the clouds or made a detour, but my position was too good." In terms worthy of the Red Baron, Wheless went on: "I plunged down."[95]

The propagandists described an idealized United States, a land of mobility and freedom, where unity of will existed alongside diversity of background. America's postwar goals were European liberation from Axis tyranny and achievement of the Four Freedoms enumerated by Roosevelt early in 1941: freedom of speech and worship, and freedom from want and fear. Unlike propaganda about European domestic politics and specific areas of foreign policy, there were few immediate objectives to be achieved and little room for political argument. Sherwood and Donovan disagreed over the extent to which propaganda should be used as an instrument of insurgency and over whether or not the United States should publicly and explicitly support the government of Marshal Pétain, but they agreed on the importance of portraying America in a positive light.

After the formation of the OWI in June, Houseman expanded the Projection of America. Leonard Miall and Russell Page persuaded the Americans to talk more about the United States. This, the Englishmen argued, was the most important task before the U.S. propaganda station both because the BBC could broadcast war news at least six hours before the Voice could, and because it was extremely important for Europeans to learn about the United States. America was isolated politically and geographically, and most foreigners knew only what they had learned from American movies and magazines; America was a land of gangsters and cowboys and Indians, a country led by political leaders uninterested in European affairs.[96] The propagandists therefore expanded their programs, portraying the United States as a nation of overwhelming industrial and military potential. They told the world that America was strong, that already its strength was helping the Allied war effort, and that in the future it would do more. In June, directives suggested stories about industrial production, war machinery, and the American traditions of practicality and industrial know-how as well as engineering achievements.[97] By September, guidances warned programmers to make American productive power as palpable as possible: "not [an] ivory tower matter."[98] Stories were to be hard and driving, and production talk was to be confined to that which had been done, was being done, or was about to be done; most important, it was to avoid vague promises that might leave the French listener feeling abandoned in the wash of present realities.[99]

The second part of the Projection of America remained that of national character: citizen morale, fighting strength, and commitment to democracy. The labor and women's features provided excellent vehicles for these themes. Women's features, for example, allowed the Voice to paint American women as hard-working, frugal, industrious, generous, and above all else, determined to help the war effort. French desk writers showed American women as committed to France, eager to know the French, and resolved to fight for French liberation.[100] The United States had geared up its production lines and witnessed a psychological transformation from a people satisfied with their own isolation to a nation of committed internationalists eager to beat the Axis.[101] The Voice of America portrayed Americans as eager to go to war in dramas, straight narratives, and through quotations from American leaders—whenever possible, from presidential addresses.[102]

"American war aims today are not merely to secure and maintain the Four Freedoms for Americans, but to help establish them throughout the world."[103] The Projection of America campaign, finally, was to explain America's goals for peace and its vision for the postwar world. This was the most difficult assignment of all, as President Roosevelt gave little guidance. The president was keenly aware that Woodrow Wilson's rhetoric and George Creel's propaganda had helped defeat Wilson's goals after World War I. Roosevelt therefore eschewed bold talk and easy promises and limited his speeches to avoid building up public emotions and expectations.[104] The State Department, moreover, acted with deliberate caution and provided the Overseas Branch with little foreign policy direction.

Before November 1942, therefore, the president's major postwar guidelines were these enunciated in the Four Freedoms and elaborated in the Atlantic Charter, the same goals to which the leaders of the Overseas Branch were themselves committed. "The United States . . . must once again fight on all the world's battle fields for these essential liberties: liberty of expression, of religion, and the right to live protected from need and from fear," they broadcast.[105] They talked as well about a new league of nations, an international organization that would prevent future wars.[106]

The Projection of America did not specifically use agitprop methods, but it did employ the experimental techniques of thirties drama. These forms reflected a search for a "real" America and the variety of efforts made throughout the period to define American civilization as a unique New World culture, one that was equal, if not superior, to that of the Old World. America had shut its gates to the flood of immigration in the twenties; it had grown increasingly urban; its citizens had moved around the country in unprecedented numbers. It thus became the task of the thirties to define what was truly American. Artists and writers self-consciously searched for a "usable past." It was an era of a new nationalism. This search for culture merged with the ideal of social commitment. Amid the cracks and strains produced by the Great Depression, writers and artists searched for new ways to understand the reality of economic crisis, and then the means to transmit their ideas to the world at large.[107] The new art was a social realism that idealized the group, the community, and the movement; Americans became a "folk" whose Americanness transcended their ethnic and regional differences. This concept of folk in turn became a means of defining the collective identity of the American people.[108]

These ideas were taken up and translated by artists and writers of all kinds. Carl Sandburg reflected this movement in his poetry as did Thornton Wilder in his plays, to name but two examples outside the realm of radio. In broadcasting it produced a kind of drama which worked through the literary device of typical and nameless people. Paul Green, for example, the progressive southern playwright, composed a radio drama, "Citizen for Tomorrow," in which average Americans across the nation speak up to defend freedom. Green wrote the play for a host of voices—from the past and the present, from the North, the West, the East, and the South, from all walks of life—who one by one presented their ideas. It was this kind of thirties experimental drama, this sort of choral chant to America, that Houseman echoed in the Projection of America.[109]

"Listen to the story of American arms," an announcer called out. "Listen to an American manufacturer":

VOICE: We are concentrating our production on the "bombardier en pique" bomber.
VOICE: We organize the resources of our different factories, large and small, so that the best equipped for any given work gets the contract.
VOICE: We use mass production. Our workshops, all very large, have conveyer belts on which the planes advance slowly and regularly from the assembly to the end.

. . . . . . . . . . . . . . . . . . . . . . . . . . . . . . . . .

VOICE: We attack the enemy wherever he is. We attack him ceaselessly, everywhere and every time we meet him.
VOICE: On the five continents.
VOICE: All over the world.
VOICE: On all seven seas.[110]

It was a very American sound. British radio propaganda, by contrast—even in its earliest years when it, too, had employed drama to convey its propaganda points—had a more subdued effect.[111] It was also a radical sound, too radical for American leaders in Congress, the State Department, and the military. Houseman's singular style of radio propaganda could not, and did not, last through the war.

After the creation of the OWI, the Voice of America broadcast with increasing zest and policy independence. Not yet restricted by the course of American foreign policy, and no longer under the ruling hand of William Donovan, Sherwood and his colleagues projected America as the last bastion of liberty and freedom, the world's democratic hope. This goal was accomplished through a three-pronged approach that provided information about French politics, news about the war itself, and descriptions of the United States of America. The leaders of the Overseas Branch broadcast news about nearly every aspect of the war, from the British and American bombings of German industrial plants to American soldiers fighting in Guadalcanal, from life in Vichy France to reports about American congressional elections, and more. But they concentrated on a few important issues, such as the relève and the coming second front, and through these they told listeners that, despite events currently to the contrary, America and her allies— including the French Resistance—would win the war and liberate France.

In November the Allied invasion of North Africa brought a shift in direction, albeit slowly executed, as the United States committed itself to active warfare in the Atlantic theater of war and became enmeshed in increasingly complex and difficult diplomatic and military alliances. Before the invasion, the propagandists worked to improve the output of the Voice according to their own ideas and political goals, with the advice and help of the British. Afterward the Voice slowly came to rely on straight news, and by 1944 it consciously avoided conflict with American foreign policy. It was in these early months of the war, therefore, that the leaders of the Overseas Branch most clearly imposed their political vision on American propaganda and the Voice of America.

# 4

## After Torch

### Propaganda and
### American Foreign Relations

WHEN William J. Donovan and Robert E. Sherwood created the Foreign Information Service in 1941, they set in place the administrative machinery for overseas broadcast propaganda. Their inauguration of the Voice of America in February 1942 was the next critical step in the history of American propaganda. Throughout the following months they and others effected additional changes in the structure of the administration of overseas propaganda. But these shifts did not alter the essential nature of American international radio propaganda.

The next important transition in overseas propaganda followed the Allied invasion of North Africa, the military operation known as Torch. Until the Torch campaign was launched the American war effort in the European theater of operations existed more in theory than as a military reality. The months between Pearl Harbor and the North African invasion were, in a sense, the American equivalent of the "phony war," the period of expectation but inaction which had hung over Europe during the fall and winter of 1939–40. With Torch the Allies went on the offensive in western Europe.

The months between the invasion of North Africa in November 1942 and February 1944, when the leaders of the Overseas Branch were forced out of their positions because their politics were too radical, form a middle period of American wartime external radio propaganda. Thereafter the war in Europe revealed changes in American foreign policy, domestic politics, cultural expression, and propaganda. The transition itself, however, took place during these axial months of war.

The war dictated shifts in American foreign and military policy. In mid-July 1942, President Roosevelt sent his chief White House adviser, Harry Hopkins, the chief of staff of the U.S. army, George C. Marshall, and the chief of naval operations, Ernest J. King, to Great Britain to hammer out an agreement on a second-front attack. Invasion planning began with the selection of General Dwight David Eisenhower as field commander for the Torch invasion, and planning hastily moved into action. On November 8, 1942, the Allies landed in Casablanca, Oran, and Algiers.[1]

The initial reaction to Torch was jubilant. The Allies were now launched on a course that would defeat the Axis. Then, within days of the Allied landing, General Eisenhower announced that he had appointed the Vichy minister of the navy, Admiral Jean Darlan, to head the new post-liberation government of French North Africa. Darlan was anathema to antifascists. He had reorganized the Vichy police force along the lines of the German gestapo; he had handed French hostages over to the Germans to be shot; he had authored anti-Semitic decrees; and he was passionately anti-British. He was, wrote one OWI leader, "a Judas who delivered his own country-men to the torturers, a symbol throughout Europe of the evil fascism of collaboration—this was the man now recognized by the Americans as the supreme French authority in North Africa."[2] Eisenhower, with President Roosevelt's agreement, had exploded a political bomb.[3] If the Allied war was being waged to defeat Germany and the Axis, how could the Americans forge an alliance with a prominent Nazi collaborator?[4]

Eisenhower had sound military reasons for his appointment of Darlan as civilian head of French North Africa. The American general commanded only about 110,000 men, whereas the French troops in North Africa numbered 120,000, plus two hundred fifty tanks, more than a hundred fifty combat planes, and the French fleet.[5] The French army officers in Morocco and Algeria were right-wing anticommunists who were loyal to Marshal Pétain.[6] And the Allies aimed to conquer North Africa, from Casablanca through Tunis, which meant subduing and administering lands along a coast that stretched more than twelve hundred miles. Eisenhower reasoned that the Allies could not govern such vast territories without the support of the already existing colonial—now Vichy—administrative structures. But no matter how logical his plan was, Eisenhower's decision marked a political as well as a military divide.

This American action, Warburg wrote of the Darlan agreement, "indicate[s] to the world that when we 'liberate' a country we shall make a practice of putting our friends in jail and turning the liberated country over to the enemies of democracy." Sherwood worried that it "confirm[s] the impression that while Americans talk a lot about the Four Freedoms they can be hoodwinked by any treacherous gangster who offers them collaboration."⁷ And Wallace Carroll, working in London, observed that "from the outset of its intervention in the European theater of war, the United States had allowed itself to become identified in men's minds with the forces of reaction which were anathema to the great majority of the European peoples."⁸

The propagandists were Popular Front liberals who believed they were fighting a war against oppression and for democracy. President Roosevelt's speeches on the Four Freedoms and the Atlantic Charter had spelled a broad devotion to a future freed from the plagues not only of hunger and fear, but oppression and political tyranny. The president, however, moved away from these liberal war aims. The State Department increasingly viewed the OWI leaders as radicals attempting to subvert American policy. The military wanted propaganda to act as an adjunct to war, and not to politics. The war changed. The goals of all these groups became more visible and pronounced. Their mutual animosity became harder to contain.

The commitment of American troops to active combat in the European theater of operations, and the increasingly certain prospect of victory, drove the U.S. government to a series of diplomatic and military decisions. The process by which these decisions were made became crucial to American propaganda because it governed the relationships between the propagandists and the president, the State Department, and the military. Overseas propaganda was, at least in theory, an expression of American foreign policy. But the means by which that policy was made during the Second World War, and how it translated into propaganda, was complex and often confused. The growing split between propagandists and the State Department and the military—and less visibly with the president—was reinforced by daily bureaucratic conflicts.

In November 1942, Roosevelt approved General Eisenhower's decision to work with Admiral Darlan. Six weeks later Darlan was assassinated. By January 1943 the president had to choose between Generals Honoré Giraud and Charles de Gaulle, both of whom claimed the moral authority to lead a "free" France. Roosevelt supported Giraud. The sixty-three-year-old general, who had been captured by the Germans in 1940 and escaped in April 1942, fitted well with the overall American view of foreign policy. He was a military man with military rather than political objectives. Unlike de Gaulle, Giraud never claimed to speak for France in the councils of the United Nations, or sought to exchange ambassadors with the Allied governments. He articulated one clear ambition: to fight the Germans to victory and French liberation.[9] He was politically neutral and a war hero, and he provided the perfect foil for Roosevelt, who preferred many small local provincial French governments to a centralized authority. Giraud would preserve America's peace table "trading position" on the future of France and of Europe.[10] But Giraud did not have the force of personality, the political vision, or the moral authority of de Gaulle.[11]

De Gaulle had personal strength. By the spring of 1943 it was clear that he would dominate French politics. The president nevertheless vigorously opposed recognition of Charles de Gaulle and his French Committee of National Liberation (FCNL). "I am fed up with de Gaulle," Roosevelt wrote Winston Churchill that June. "I am absolutely convinced that he has been and is now injuring our war efforts and that he is a very dangerous threat to us. . . ."[12] As early as May 1943 he wrote Churchill that when the Allies liberated France "we will have to regard it as a military occupation run by British and American generals" rather than as the civilian government advocated by de Gaulle and the FCNL.[13] And again, in November, the president wrote Cordell Hull that he was convinced "that no final decisions or plans concerning civil affairs for France should be made at this time. . . . The thought that the occupation when it occurs should be wholly military is one to which I am increasingly inclined."[14]

There was more to Roosevelt's attitude than personal animosity. Once the United States collaborated with Darlan, it had wedded itself to a policy of expediency which could only be justified on the grounds that American foreign policy would consist of temporary measures until the war was won. Only then could a French government be established, and only then could American diplomatic policy toward France become a matter of serious engagement. The president thus rejected any role for de Gaulle in overall policy, according to which Roosevelt sidestepped any commitment to postwar France. He hid his determination to postpone a decision under an avowed respect for the wishes of the citizens of France and a pledge to allow them to express those wishes through immediate postwar elections.[15] He compartmentalized the war into two tightly sealed sections: military victory and long-range diplomatic goals. Roosevelt argued that first the Allies had to win the war, battle by battle, and then, at the peace conference table, conjure the postwar world into existence. In the context of this vision de Gaulle, with his strong commitment to his own future as leader of France, and the FCNL had no place. Roosevelt rejected them as long as he could.[16]

The president shied away from interpreting the war as a fight over ideology or transcendent political philosophies. He feared creating a crusade that might arouse expectations he could not satisfy, or that might rip open the unity of purpose on which he had built the American war effort. He had seen President Wilson do this in the First World War, and Roosevelt was determined not to repeat what he interpreted as Wilson's fundamental mistake. Thus, from the very beginning Roosevelt subordinated the defeat of fascism and the victory of democracy to the goal of a speedy military victory.[17]

Finally, Roosevelt opposed treating France as a major power. He had little faith in France's ability to establish stable domestic politics, having witnessed, albeit at a distance, the shifting leadership of the Third Republic. The rapid collapse of France in May and June 1940 had, moreover, suggested that the majority of the French favored—or at least did not oppose—the Nazis, and the president accordingly decided he could not rely on the French. De Gaulle wanted the complete restoration not only of France but of its empire, envisioning the nation's return to the pantheon of world leaders; Roosevelt favored restoring only an independent France with a rather modest place in the world.[18] For Roosevelt, the future of the postwar world lay not in Europe, nor in the traditional balance of power, but in the cooperation of a few nations, among which were to be the United States, Russia, China, and Great Britain—but not France.

Roosevelt's determination to push aside issues of foreign policy and concentrate on military victory continually frustrated the leaders of the Overseas Branch. Most particularly it angered Sherwood, Barnes, Warburg, and Johnson. In 1943 the propagandists employed the Voice of America and the other media of the Overseas Branch to express their own firm belief that the objective of the war was not simply military victory but the defeat and destruction of National Socialism as a political system. They supported de Gaulle as part of that new world order, in part because de Gaulle was the symbol of the French Resistance, the one man who in 1940 had stood up against the Germans; in part because in 1943 de Gaulle worked with the Resistance forces within France; and in part because the British backed de Gaulle and the FCNL.

The propagandists did not direct their discontent with foreign policy toward the president, however, but toward the State Department. The route that lay between foreign and propaganda policy wound its course through the State Department, and the propagandists were part of the uncomfortable relationship between the president and the department. Roosevelt did not just ignore the department; he chose many alternate advisers, among whom numbered such New Deal liberals as Harry Hopkins, Samuel Rosenman, and Robert Sherwood. Roosevelt wanted to keep his political options as open as possible, and in 1942 it seemed reasonable to give support to resistance groups in Europe, who were still the only allies of the United Nations on the continent. The Overseas Branch of the OWI and its mouthpiece, the Voice of America, were therefore useful to the president in preserving these liberal options. But the State Department did not support resistance movements, especially in France, where American policy had publicly accepted Pétain and the Vichy government.

Over the course of 1943, as the Allies began to win the war, European resistance generally and the French Resistance in particular became increasingly less useful. The option that the propagandists had been providing thus decreased in importance, and eventually it became a liability. But the direct conflict over U.S. policy toward resistance did not surface as a confrontation with the president, who was far too wily to allow such a collision, but with the State Department.

The State Department had never supported resistance in France—indeed, it had rarely even discussed it, and never as a serious political option. State Department policymakers supported Giraud, disliked de Gaulle, and accepted the primacy of military victory. As Hull cabled Murphy in May 1943, "Our one primary consideration and concern in the African campaign is the waging of battle until the continent is conquered, and we see no reason, therefore, why political or other considerations should be allowed to interfere with the military effort now proceeding."[19]

The diplomats believed the propagandists were radicals. In the years before the war, for example, the American embassy in Moscow had thought Barnes (who was then the *New York Herald Tribune* correspondent in the Soviet Union) was a Stalinist and his wife an out-and-out communist. "This was one of the things that troubled relations with the State Department," Wallace Carroll later argued. Despite the fact that there was no truth behind the allegation, it fitted in with the department's view of the world.[20] Symptomatically, the department used its passport office to keep those whom they suspected of being left wing, such as John Houseman, from traveling abroad.[21]

The State Department merged its distrust of and anger at the OWI with its frustration over its own hobbled role. Throughout 1943 the department's participation in foreign policy-making decreased, but the criticism leveled against it for precisely the policy it had not authored—but for which it remained publicly responsible—grew. Liberal critics waged their own war on such actions as American recognition of Darlan in North Africa and of Marshal Badoglio in Italy. Elmer Davis noted in January 1943 that conversations with Hull had became needlessly prolonged because Hull "continually drifts off into defense of his record."[22]

Over the course of the year, profound disagreements over basic issues of ideology were reinforced by petty and abrasive matters of daily administration, bureaucracy, and public image. The State Department became convinced that it was important to control the OWI. But instead of coordinating department area desks with propaganda language desks, the department authorized Robert Pell, head of the Office of Public Information, as the department's official liaison.[23] From the perspective of the propagandists, this meant that the desk chiefs could not meet with French regional specialists in the State Department to discuss issues of immediate concern.[24] From the French desk, Lewis Galantiere, the area chief of policy, repeatedly sought advice from the department. When Giraud visited the United States, for example, Galantiere asked the department how the general's trip was to be treated in the news. He received no answer.[25]

The leaders of the Voice of America asked for quick answers. They had news shows to produce, and they could not wait days or weeks for their replies. The very ethos of newsmen, whether on the air or in print, was to get the news out as fast as possible. But the State Department was not staffed by men trained to this way of thinking. The diplomats wanted time to consider policy questions, take matters up with their advisers, consult their records, and generally pursue all angles of a question. These approaches were mutually exclusive.[26]

Finally, when it came to the really tough matters of policy decisions, the State Department could not give the propagandists the answers they sought because the department did not have the power to make important propaganda decisions. This left department policymakers often frustrated, a frustration that they vented on the leaders of the Overseas Branch of the OWI and especially on Sherwood, Barnes, Warburg, and Johnson. In one sense that anger was justified: the propagandists were using propaganda to try to steer the direction of foreign policy. Yet in another sense this anger was reinforced by the particular view of the diplomats, who not only saw the propagandists as would-be policymakers, but as part of a national movement of political liberals and radicals who were out to destroy the State Department.

In 1942 the leaders of the OWI had found the State Department silent on too many issues. The department had not provided the propagandists with clear policy guidance, and so they had turned to the British for political leadership. Then in 1943 Sherwood and his colleagues found themselves locked into conflict with the department over the liberal propaganda policy that the department had refused to help formulate. OWI liberals could find no common ground on which to talk to the diplomats, and their mutual anger crackled.

The rift left the Overseas Branch vulnerable to accusations that it was not the mouthpiece of U.S. foreign policy. It severed the OWI from what should have been a crucial bureaucratic alliance. It meant that the propagandists continued to rely on British policy directives rather than on American instructions. It bred in the leaders of the OWI a commitment to their own opinions and a determination to do all they could to stop the United States from repeating what they saw as the terrible foreign policy failure of the Darlan deal. Only after Sherwood, Barnes, Warburg, and Johnson had left and the new, more politically accommodating leaders of the Overseas Branch withdrew propaganda from controversial liberal political positions and moved the Voice toward "straight" news and information could the OWI and the State Department begin to work together smoothly.[27]

If the State Department was locked into battle with the Overseas Branch of the OWI, the military took a distinctly different position. Unlike the State Department, the army, particularly under the leadership of General Eisenhower, created its own propaganda branch. Early in the planning stages for Torch, Eisenhower recognized the potential importance of propaganda. Propagandists accompanied the Allied troops as they landed in North Africa. But the real military organization for propaganda did not crystallize until May 1943 with the creation of the Psychological Warfare Branch (PWB) of the Allied Forces Headquarters, which in a somewhat reorganized form generated in 1944 the Psychological Warfare Division (PWD) of the Supreme Headquarters, Allied Expeditionary Forces.[28]

From the perspective of the military, the evolution of the PWB proved very important. Originally, military leaders found the OWI propagandists who had gone out to North Africa a constant irritant since the liberal propagandists hated Darlan, generally supported de Gaulle, and argued against the military's occupation policy in French North Africa. Throughout the winter and spring of 1943 this situation produced near warfare between the two groups. With the creation of the PWB in May 1943, however, the OWI sent out a new propaganda leader, C. D. Jackson, a Time-Life executive who knew how to play bureaucratic politics and was determined to win the support of the army. Jackson was not a Popular Front liberal but a conservative internationalist. He gained the cooperation of the military. Thereafter the friction between the military and the propagandists gradually waned.[29]

The fact that the PWB (and later PWD) was composed of both Americans and British had important repercussions. The PWB created an unexpected context in which the Anglo-American alliance for propaganda continued. Combined operations dictated dual leadership and a partnership of purpose; each operation had an American director and a British co-director and was staffed by men from both sides of the Atlantic. The Americans had always found their British colleagues congenial, and they continued to do so.

With the active engagement of American troops the war front lured the propagandists. The war front meant action, a fact of considerable importance to journalists, who largely staffed the Overseas Branch and the Voice of America. The war transformed the New York station into a backwater; the Voice of America broadcasting from New York City became increasingly removed from events. This change was accelerated by the establishment of a relay network in North Africa in February 1943 (and in 1944 by the creation of a radio station entirely devoted to propaganda in London). News from New York was handicapped by the time difference across the Atlantic, and by the fact that news reports first reached Algiers, or later Sicily and London, and from there had to be communicated back to New York, where the language desks wrote the stories and aired them. The stations in North Africa and London could broadcast, at least to the French, over medium- and long-wave transmitters, which made these programs far more accessible than the short-wave transmissions from New York. These circumstances underscored the feeling in New York that the Voice of America was very distant from the war.

This remoteness forced the New York broadcasters to consider increasing the airtime the Voice devoted to the Projection of America. As early as August 1943, Leonard Miall, writing to the BBC, told his superiors that "it is now openly recognized by the London office of O.W.I., and by a substantial section of New York . . . that the Voice of America from New York can never hope to compete with European and Mediterranean transmissions . . . as a primary source of world news. . . ."[30] Allied victory moreover made it essential that Europeans understand a United States that remained distant and isolated. That, argued Miall, was New York's unique mission.

All this reinforced not only the importance of the war, but of the military. In this sense the military was distinct from the State Department, for although it was unclear who really made foreign policy, there was no doubt that the military was fighting the war. By mid-1943 the Overseas Branch had developed a strong ambivalence toward the military. On the one hand it applauded successful battles, if not always the grand strategy of peripheral warfare, but on the other hand the OWI fought with military leaders over propaganda policy.[31]

American propaganda leaders, however, were not as divorced from American attitudes toward the supremacy of military as diplomatic policy as they believed themselves to be. They fought with the military and held the State

Department in disdain; they raged against the president's policy toward de Gaulle; they felt closer to the British propagandists than the policymakers of their own country. Yet they understood that military victory was the most crucial part of the war effort, and that to the oppressed peoples of Europe nothing was more important than an end to hunger and misery. Victory would come first, and then, riding the back of conquest, would come a democratic and just world order. It was over this second, political vision that Sherwood, Barnes, Warburg, and Johnson fought with the State Department and, indirectly, the president, while accepting the American emphasis on military victory. As Sherwood wrote, "All our propaganda is in support of and intended to facilitate military operations with a view to gaining total victory in the shortest possible time."[32] It was this vision that later allowed the Overseas Branch to bow to the president's insistence on victory first, politics later.

Finally, the relationship of the propagandists to the president, the State Department, and the military altered over the course of 1943 because the meaning of resistance—at least for France—changed, both within the American corridors of power and among the leaders of the FCNL. In 1942 the French Resistance had been minuscule in reality, but extraordinarily powerful as a symbol. Very few Frenchmen had actually joined the underground struggle during the first few years after June 1940, but the idea of an organized resistance created the hope that the French people would liberate themselves and, in the process, purify the French body politic of the reactionary and proto-fascist elements within it. For American liberals the French Resistance gave truth to the idea that the war was being fought for domestic rejuvenation and liberalization in all countries. As Freda Kirchway wrote in the *Nation*, "We [American liberals] intend to underline the revolutionary character of the war and help develop a political strategy through which the democratic elements in all countries may overcome the forces of reaction and capitulation. . . ."[33] In 1943 the newly formed FCNL underscored this hope by declaring that it was "the pivotal force from which radiates the French movement en masse." And its leaders proclaimed that their political goals were "subject to the will of the French people" albeit "as soon as that will can be expressed."[34]

De Gaulle and the leaders of the FCNL, however, also knew that success meant the military liberation of France, and that military liberation necessitated Allied—British and American—troops invading France. Therefore, no matter how uncomfortable political discord made the military effort, both the French and the Americans recognized by mid-1943 that the Resistance forces had to aid the Allied invasion forces.

This recognition transformed the meaning of French resistance. By the fall of 1943 resistance no longer meant the revolutionary will of the French people, or the guerrilla warfare of men and ideas against fascist oppression. It meant political negotiations over the role of the Free French Army. It decreed an increasing alliance with the United Nations military forces. And it necessitated the creation of a civil administration within France. When the Allied troops arrived, there existed local governments loyal to de Gaulle, ready to take over civil administration.[35]

This change cut the ground from beneath the ideology of the liberal propagandists. In 1942 the Voice of America had broadcast a message of active resistance, of agitprop. But in 1943 the Voice advocated the coordination of French underground support of concrete Allied military measures. The propaganda solution was an increasing reliance on military news, which muted the ideological message of resistance while it reinforced that of the coming liberation.

It is interesting to note that no matter how enraged the leaders of the Overseas Branch became at American foreign policy, the writers of the French desk never allowed themselves the luxury of such sentiments. Neither Pierre Lazareff nor his colleagues ever publicly protested the American alliance with Darlan and Giraud, not did they openly criticize Roosevelt's steadfast refusal to work with de Gaulle. The French writers observed, years after the war was over, that they felt at the mercy of the Americans, from whom they earned a precarious living in a country where many of them could barely speak the language.[36] The French desk was made up of exiles and émigrés, and no matter how angry they might get at propaganda, they defined their role as a conduit for American policy. When they objected so strenuously that they could no longer abide by official policy, they quit; they did not fight. "Warburg could object, so could Cowan," recalled one staff writer. "But the French! You just bide your peace." In any case, they worked under the curb of the Office of Control, which censored all broadcasts.[37] In the broadest of terms, the French desk went with the policy set by Roosevelt and the military and agreed on by the State Department, a policy that put military aims first and French political goals a distant second.

Although the Allies quickly conquered Algeria and Morocco, they soon met stiff opposition from German troops in Tunisia. In an atmosphere of hard slogging, the Allies agreed to defer for the time being a cross-channel attack and contain their land-troop efforts in the Atlantic theater to the Mediterranean. When the Allies defeated the Germans in North Africa in May, they moved on to Sicily. By August they were in mainland Italy.

Whatever the ultimate tactical and strategic merit of these decisions, from the viewpoint of well-informed civilians the Allied military campaigns of 1943 thwarted German victory, but they did not bring Allied success. The Mediterranean campaigns had achieved limited objectives – the elimination of Vichy and Italy as Axis assets – but they had not crushed the German army. In fact, the most important victories had not been won by the British or Americans at all, but by the Russians, who had defeated the Germans, at overwhelming human cost, at Stalingrad. Stalin increasingly came to regard the Americans and British as ineffectual at best, double-dealing at worst. He saw the Anglo-American decision not to open a second front in France as a decision to achieve Allied victory at the price of Russian lives. The issue of the second front therefore weighed heavily on the Americans by late 1943, as the Allies remained bogged down in Italy and the British continued to press for further Mediterranean operations. It was in this context that Roosevelt, at the Tehran conference in November–December 1943, announced that a second-front attack would be mounted in late spring 1944 in order to placate the Russians.

The year 1943 was thus one of military success mixed with stalemate. It brought real war news – often good news, but not news of victory. By the fall of 1943 it meant, for the propagandists in the Overseas Branch, hope laced with frustration as the Germans demanded more labor, food, and industrial production from their conquered subjects, and as living conditions across Europe deteriorated. Victory remained elusive and the expectations of what peace would bring continued to be undefined.

If the war was measured in battles, foreign policy was expressed through conferences. Casablanca, Trident, Quebec, Moscow, Cairo, Tehran: Roosevelt and Churchill, and finally Stalin, and their leaders of missions traveled around the globe from the United States to Canada to North Africa to the Middle East. In the January following the launching of the Torch campaign Roosevelt met Churchill in Casablanca, Morocco. The president wanted to silence domestic and international criticism of his "collaborationist" policy in North Africa, and thus it became important to him to demonstrate that he could bring together de Gaulle and Giraud.[38] Moreover, in the midst of what was becoming a stiff battle in Tunisia, and knowing that Anglo-American military action was not a second front and could not satisfy Stalin, Roosevelt tried publicly to maneuver his way out of a complicated diplomatic problem. On the last day of the conference he bought time with a grand gesture: the doctrine of unconditional surrender.[39] In the middle of a war that the Americans were still only half fighting, at least in comparison with the beleaguered Russians, the president said he would not give up the fight until total victory had been won.[40]

The Americans and British defeated the Germans in Tunisia in May, and that month Churchill and Roosevelt met in Washington to set future goals for the war. Churchill still argued for peripheral action rather than a direct attack through France, and he pushed for the invasion of Italy. The prime minister won this time, and in late May he traveled to Algiers to meet with Generals Marshall and Eisenhower. On July 10 the Allies invaded Sicily and a week later moved on to the mainland.[41]

The political repercussions of the invasion of Italy became as disheartening to American liberals as the aftermath of Torch had been. Just as Eisenhower collaborated with Darlan in North Africa, in Italy he decided to work with Marshal Pietro Badoglio, the Fascist whom the king of Italy appointed to take Mussolini's place after a coup removed Il Duce, but not the Fascist party, from power.[42] Roosevelt went along, and at the Quebec conference in mid-August recognized the Badoglio government as a co-belligerent. Roosevelt's move was disheartening. It meant, in midsummer of 1943, that the Americans had neither launched a second front nor used what victories they had won to define a peace, to end fascism or to establish democracy. It was hard for the propagandists to tell France, or Europe, that the United States was fighting to spread democracy while it was cooperating with Italian Fascists. July marked a low point from which neither the end nor the meaning of the war could be seen.

Nevertheless, beginning at Quebec Roosevelt began affirming the importance of a second front, thus opening the way for Russian participation in the conference procedure Roosevelt and Churchill had created.[43] Stalin cabled the president that he was ready to talk, and in early November the foreign ministers of the United States, Britain, and the Soviet Union met in Moscow and agreed to closer collaboration in all spheres. Here the Americans issued, and the Russians agreed to, a Four-Power Declaration proposing the nucleus for a general postwar security system, thus beginning to shed light on how victory could bring lasting peace.[44] As Isaiah Berlin reported back to London from the British embassy in Washington, the news from the Moscow agreement "was greeted with excited jubilation on all sides."[45]

Tehran was the last of the year's conferences. Many issues were discussed by Roosevelt and Churchill, who finally met with Stalin, but again the western leaders promised a second-front attack, now concretely planned for late spring, and again the leaders talked about a postwar world organization. Moscow and Tehran had begun to give political definition to the postwar world and ammunition for the propagandists.[46]

From the perspective of the propagandists, the events of 1943 divided the year into four sections. First came the months of military action in North Africa, from November 1942 to May 1943. Second was an interlude of hope for the ideologically defined liberal war effort, the moment between the end of the Tunisian campaign and the beginning of collaboration with Badoglio. Then followed the depressing months of August, September, and early October, when the propagandists despaired of Roosevelt's giving them the kind of direction for which they greatly hoped. And finally came the Moscow and Tehran conferences, the Four-Power Declaration, and the planning for a postwar peace-keeping organization as the basis for the doctrine by which to set the sails of their propaganda. These were the marking posts of the year, and the evolution of the propaganda directives followed them.

In the months between November 1942 and early May 1943 the propagandists argued, in their most general themes, that America was now involved in hard, daily fighting and that the war effort had to be seen in its whole, global perspective. These two themes were tied together for several mutually reinforcing reasons.

Faced with the necessity of talking about the war in North Africa, and explaining to the peoples of Europe that the United States was still fighting for liberation from the Nazis, the propagandists turned to strictly military news. "We should avoid the political developments in North Africa," said a directive in December 1942.[47] "Stick to hard news and avoid all comment on political personalities" articulated another guidance in January.[48] By April the directives included such instructions as "since there is no effective way of alleviating French disappointment over the postponement of de Gaulle's trip to Algiers, it is better to maintain the emphasis on military developments in North Africa. . . ."[49] The propagandists rationalized the importance of keeping to the military side of events, because "news about Allied action will have a more massive effect. . . ."[50] This emphasis on military news was a marked shift away from the more dramatic and ideological propaganda broadcasting style of 1942.

Straight-sounding military news became a device to distinguish American information from German propaganda, a means to project an image of realistic and truthful news rather than fantastic and deceitful psychological warfare. "If our approach . . . is tough, factual, military and confident, based heavily on the facts of our new offensives," urged a directive in December, "it will sharpen the growing contrast between the tone of the United Nations statements and the . . . ideological line of the Axis."[51] The propagandists understood that Europeans were saturated with Nazi propaganda and increasingly distrusted anything that sounded or looked propagandistic. This was one extremely important reason why the Voice of America became increasingly journalistic in tone and style, and this shift was paralleled in developments in poster propaganda, for example, where the Americans increasingly used low-key photo montages and other journalistic and realistic visual formats to present their message.

But radio propaganda as journalism was also a way of preserving the ideological goals of the Voice of America: the fight for democracy and against fascism; the commitment to a new world order along with a belief in the importance of domestic reform. The new political framework demanded new artistic and propagandistic strategies. News allowed the propagandists to emphasize the liberal thrust of the war. The American fighting forces were presented as part of a global war in which all of the United Nations took part and in which the Soviet Union fought as America's ally. The emphasis on military news as global warfare meant that the Voice of America could take a stand against U.S. isolationism. It enabled American propagandists to argue against the re-creation of traditional spheres of influence. Most of all, it helped them define the future peace and create a meaning for the war as an effort to bring about not only the end of fascism but a peace based on worldwide cooperation, about which not more could be said in the months following the Torch invasion than that "when victory was won, [the] United States would take part in organizing the world for peace and security in all countries."[52]

Victory in Tunisia lessened the immediate importance of war news.[53] But there was more of a shift in May than a temporary abatement of fighting necessitated. Propaganda leaders knew that they had been swept along by the events in North Africa, reporting increasing amounts of war news. In May they stopped short, as it were, and examined this policy. They paused and questioned whether the framework of news, especially military news, was drowning their political message. They wondered if they had chosen the wrong strategy. "There is one lesson which we should learn from our experience in the immediate past," a central directive instructed in mid-June.[54] The military events of any day or week must not be allowed to crowd out political news, and the news must always be put into a broad political context. The critical themes became to defeat Germany, split the Axis, achieve unconditional surrender, and persuade the French (and all of Europe) that the United Nations would win in a victory that would benefit the subject peoples of Europe.[55] The propaganda directives generated a sense that the Voice of America broadcasts could do more than ward off defeat; they could help bring victory.[56]

In May, June, and July there was an enthusiasm for the task. The expectations generated by this enthusiasm made the propagandists feel, in the brief period between Mussolini's resignation and the appointment of Marshal Badoglio, that propaganda could commit the United States to a goal of political warfare which promised the defeat not just of Germany and Italy, but of Nazism and fascism. But the propagandists were wrong in their expectations. Eisenhower again chose collaboration, and Roosevelt again supported the general's decision. The American government's decision to work once more with a Fascist leader demanded a reevaluation of propaganda.

The propaganda directives changed in their expectations over the fall of 1943. Military news took on a new purpose and propaganda function. In August, September, and early October the propagandists increasingly came to accept the necessity of concentrating on military events, and to make a virtue of that necessity. Again and again central directives called for military news rather than warning not to let military events overshadow political policy. "Our main theme is to drive home the military strength and unity of the United Nations," recommended an exemplary directive in August.[57] The propagandists still warned that political developments were crucial, but the fervor behind the message was gone.

Following the heels of this discouragement came the Moscow conference, and with it the American commitment to both a second front and a post-war peace-keeping organization. Once again, the propagandists searched to find a transcendent meaning to the war within which they could embed their propaganda. They found their solution in the outcome of the Moscow conference, which marked, the central directive of November 5–12 said, "the political turning point of the war." The conference, the directive asserted, manifested "the political and military unity of the United Nations." It provided all the material the propagandists needed to drive home Axis defeat, and not just Allied victory but also "the political machinery with which we intend to win the war and organize the peace" as well as "the objective for which we are fighting."[58] Between the lines one can almost hear Sherwood, Barnes, Warburg, and Johnson shouting with joy that finally they had proper ammunition with which to fight the war as they wanted to fight it. Military news became a declaration of self-confidence and coming victory. The Projection of America followed suit. It, too, was intended to proclaim self-confidence and demonstrate that a democratic America would direct postwar settlements toward a lasting, just, and democratic peace.

Behind this developing reliance on news, on factual information reported in as concrete and matter-of-fact a style as possible, lay a changing assumption about propaganda. Gone was the dramatic, agitprop style of Houseman's efforts of 1942. As the directives show, the propagandists grew to believe that their task was to persuade their audience that victory would come, that the Axis would crumble, and that it was in the best interests of the French people to align themselves with the United States. To achieve these aims, propagandists merely had to report events. Persuasion, in other words, was best accomplished not by a head-on attack, but by indirectly presenting information. If the audience thought it was being propagandized, if it felt an onslaught of words, it would recoil. But information, artfully presented, was an entirely different matter. In addition, the propagandists implied that as long as they restricted themselves to covering the news they could either comply with Allied policy or bypass it.

But 1943 was a turning point. It was the middle year between belief in the effectiveness of agitation and dramatic forms of persuasion broadcast within the vacuum of foreign policy and fear of Allied defeat on one side, and commitment to a strictly informational reporting style created to support American foreign policy and boost Allied victory on the other. Sherwood, Barnes, Warburg, and Johnson, and their like-minded colleagues in the Overseas Branch, believed that propaganda could mold and influence foreign policy. Propaganda, in other words, was not merely an expression of policy made by others. The propagandists believed they could make their own version of American foreign policy come true. They believed they were right; they argued that they understood the foreign influence of American policy in ways that the State Department, and even the president, did not; and they used the Voice of America to enter the foreign policy debate between members of Roosevelt's administration.

Most of all, they believed in the power of words. Once spoken, once made public, words could change the course of events. Again and again central directives warned the writers and editors of the language desks not to use terms that would "commit" the Russians to any particular action or "commit" the Germans to take military action.[59] *Commit* is an interesting word to apply to propaganda, and the directives used it over and over again.

The leaders of the Overseas Branch became increasingly disturbed at producing propaganda in support of policies with which they disagreed. They found themselves in a position in which they had either to mute their beliefs, or to try to use propaganda to alter American foreign policy. Barnes, Warburg, and Johnson, and to a lesser degree Sherwood, chose the latter course. In the debate over what relationship propaganda should bear to foreign policy, they believed that propaganda could play an important role in foreign policy-making, and that it could do so by stating the objectives of that policy before the peoples of the world. As one propagandist argued, propaganda need not stem from, nor agree with, foreign policy; it should be drawn up from the advice, but not at the orders, of the State Department.[60] He might have added the president as well.

The leaders of the Overseas Branch believed they could make a difference in more ways than through shaping the political beliefs, or even actions, of their audience. Through the power of their words they wanted to influence the foreign policy of the State Department in what was, from their perspective, the best way they could work to help the United States win not only the war but also the peace. They hoped to redirect foreign policy through the power of their propaganda. But they met, head on, the resistance of the president, the State Department, the military, and Congress. The ensuing political blaze consumed Sherwood, Barnes, Warburg, and Johnson in its flames.

# 5

# The Propagandists and the Federal Government

## The Political Struggles of the Overseas Branch

THE YEAR 1943 proved the watershed in the relationship of the Office of War Information to the federal bureaucracy. Here again, the months between the Allied invasion of North Africa and Roosevelt's decision to fire the leaders of the OWI in February 1944 formed a period of transition. By 1944 the early liberal leaders had left the OWI. Thereafter, propaganda concentrated on military victory, and the Overseas Branch grindingly spun out its remaining days until the end of the war.

The story of the struggle between the Overseas Branch and American domestic political leaders began with William Donovan, who renewed his attack on the Overseas Branch in the early fall of 1942 when he opened the question of who should operate propaganda in the pre-invasion planning for Torch. Donovan had resented the Overseas Branch of the OWI since the reorganization of June 1942. Preparations for Torch presented him with an opportunity to attack the propagandists. Active warfare was sure to make propaganda more important, especially as it became a handmaiden to military operations, and military planning for propaganda gave Donovan, now a member of the Joint Chiefs of Staff and head of the Office of Strategic Services, a new lever to pry overseas propaganda loose from the OWI. In August 1942, therefore, Donovan reasserted his agency's right to take charge of propaganda activities abroad, and in September he presented his case before the joint military planners.[1] Three months later the Joint Chiefs of Staff asked Donovan to assume responsibility for overseas propaganda.

The leaders of the OWI were furious. Sherwood, Barnes, Warburg, and Johnson all offered Davis their resignations in protest. Davis calmed them down and set out to repair the situation. Accompanied by Sherwood and the British head of mission of the Political Warfare Executive, David Bowes-Lyon, Davis went to the White House to present the propagandists' case before the president. But Roosevelt was indisposed, irritable, and inattentive, unable to concentrate on the dispute between the OSS and the OWI — which was a very minor issue compared to the major problems of foreign policy. Although the president slowly began to express his support of the OWI, midway through the conference news of Admiral Darlan's assassination shattered the meeting. Roosevelt dismissed the propagandists and, turning his full attention to international affairs, did nothing to resolve the OWI-OSS struggle.[2]

In early January 1943, Roosevelt left Washington for North Africa and the Casablanca conference, where for ten days he conferred with Churchill about future Allied plans. The struggle between Davis and Donovan, the OWI and OSS, became increasingly remote to the president, who quite typically ignored it, as if to solve it through procrastination.[3] When Roosevelt returned from abroad, however, Harold Smith, director of the Bureau of the Budget, again raised the issue of propaganda administration. Smith urged the president to issue an executive order reaffirming OWI control over all overseas propaganda.[4] Roosevelt did so.

The battle won, Smith and the Bureau of the Budget joined hands with Davis and Milton Eisenhower in demanding that Overseas Branch propagandists put their house in order and move propaganda policy planning from New York to Washington. Davis and Eisenhower felt divorced from the workings of the Overseas Branch, and were upset that they had no control over what went out over the Voice of America. As Eisenhower wrote the head of the Domestic Branch in January 1943, "I . . . am suffering from a sinking feeling deep inside. Elmer Davis doesn't know what OVERSEAS is DOING. Neither do I." Eisenhower went on: "I seriously question that anyone in Washington does. . . . If we [the Overseas Branch] are supporting Federal policy, it is almost accidental."[5]

Sherwood and his New York colleagues wanted policy to stay in New York in order to thread it into the hourly broadcasting operations and make it express their own political beliefs rather than those of the State Department, the military, or the Washington organization.[6] Edd Johnson rationalized to Bureau of the Budget investigators in late March why he objected to putting policy in Washington while keeping operations in New York. Take a story to be broadcast to European workers, he said; if it was an important story it must go on the air with the shortest possible time lag: the Voice of America "cannot wait for Washington to digest this material." Policy plans may look good on paper, he went on, but any delay in getting news out was a decision, and a policy decision. "If propaganda warfare is planned in Washington it is possible to state objectives, but the job of translating the directives into scripts requires adjustments. In radio propaganda the microphone is boss."[7] Action, in other words, dictated policy. Not surprisingly, neither Johnson nor his colleagues could persuade the Budget Bureau men to let policy planning stay in New York.

The Bureau of the Budget thus temporarily settled the conflict between the OWI and the OSS, but in so doing reopened the still unresolved question of the relationship between the New York and Washington offices. The OWI in New York needed leaders in Washington to defend the agency to politicians and bureaucrats, and the propagandists in Washington needed producers, writers, and announcers in New York to use the city's radio studios and news services. But it was a terrible arrangement. "It is impossible to work a combined operation from New York for political considerations," Leonard Miall wrote to London, reporting on the current reorganization plan, "and it is impossible to move everything to Washington for technical and financial reasons. Therefore the divorce between policy direction and actual output is getting worse, and in my opinion can never be solved."[8]

By June 1943 Sherwood and Davis had fallen out. Sherwood, angry at Davis for exerting so much authority over the New York office, wrote him that "you were appointed to your job by the President, and I was appointed to my job by the President. But that does not give you dictatorial powers over all of OWI. . . ." The chasm between New York and Washington steadily grew.[9]

The Bureau of the Budget, moreover, had exacerbated the rift between Davis and Sherwood without resolving the dispute between Donovan and the OWI. The new executive order gave the OWI charge of overseas propaganda. In retaliation Donovan refused to give the propagandists intelligence reports.[10] Still not content, Donovan began attacking the OWI through his friends in Congress.

It was easy for Donovan to work with members of Congress, many of whom disliked the president and distrusted the OWI. Although Donovan himself was neither an isolationist nor a Roosevelt hater, he chose his allies from conservatives who were determined to prevent the president from winning a fourth term in office.

The spring of 1943 brought with it one of Congress's semiannual investigations. Twice a year Davis, Sherwood, Barnes, Johnson, and others devoted endless hours to preparing and then presenting their testimony. Congressional attitudes split along party and regional lines because Republicans and southern Democrats saw the OWI as an outpost for the New Deal. Congress reserved the greatest part of its hostility for the Domestic Branch of the OWI, which conservative congressmen denounced as a means to use taxpayers' money to keep the Democrats in power.[11] But although the Domestic Branch and the Overseas Branch were separate—divided, as Barnes recalled, "by very, very heavy walls"—they did go by the same name and were both headed by the same director.[12] The Overseas Branch suffered from guilt by association.

Suspicion of the Overseas Branch became clear throughout the endless hours of congressional hearings. Sitting at long tables gleaming with high-gloss polish, behind piles of reports, books, photographs, and press clippings, legislators chipped away at the executive agency. The hearings held over the spring of 1943 were not the worst the OWI were to endure, but they took their toll. "The only real bombshell," Miall reported, exploded when Senator "Johnson of Oklahoma got hold of a book of memoirs written by Lania of the German section." It was not a political book, and no objection was taken to its political content. But there was "a passage . . . describing Lania burying his head in some good lady's bosom." This snapped Johnson into action. "Throughout the proceedings he kept saying 'but this is sheer filth—but this is disgusting.' . . ." Finally he posed a question. "Do you believe, Mr. Sherwood—and you, Mr. Barnes—that a man of such low moral fiber is fit to work on the international broadcasts of the United States of America?" Finally, Johnson marched out of the room "with the book firmly under his arm."[13]

This sort of question—and there were others—devalued the work of the OWI and the Voice of America and left the agency leaders feeling abused. The sessions were nerve-racking and debilitating; they sapped and diverted energies and lowered morale. Houseman recalled with special loathing that, "[although I have] spent many hundreds of hours in my time cringing before persons who were in a position to grant or deny me money for causes I considered valuable and important, these congressional hearings were different; they were less concerned with the quality or the value of our operation than with the deep-rooted political conflicts in which we played only a subsidiary part and of which we were never fully aware."[14] The hearings of that spring may not have been the worst investigations into OWI operations but Congress did lop off $3 million from the Overseas Branch's budget for 1944, reducing it from $27 million to $24 million.[15]

Donovan played on these congressional suspicions and partisan positions. He was a Republican, which put him in good standing with members of the opposition party such as John Taber. Like Donovan, Taber was from upstate New York. The New York congressman hated Roosevelt and opposed all matters that were even tinged with New Deal liberalism, and he was the ranking Republican member of the House Appropriations Committee. In a "deep rasping voice that penetrated to every part of the House Chamber," this man who was known alternatively as "the watchdog of the Treasury, John (Cash and Carry) Taber, and the fiscal vigilante," tried to destroy the OWI. "We're not going to use a knife to cut down Federal appropriations," Taber was fond of saying, "we're going to use a sledge hammer."[16]

Early in 1943 Taber became convinced that the Overseas Branch had promoted President Roosevelt abroad in ways that would prove destructive to American democracy. "The deification of one man as the leader of a country . . . is Fascism in its simplist form," he argued.[17] Although by the summer of 1943 Taber had let up on the Overseas Branch and begun to concentrate his attacks on the Domestic Branch, his relationship with Donovan made the congressman's anti-OWI actions look like a conspiracy. "It would appear from the facts," Sherwood wrote Hopkins, "that [Taber and Donovan] are engaged in another attempt to change, by irregular means including drastic reduction of OWI's budget for overseas work, the assignment to OWI of responsibility for propaganda warfare. . . ."[18]

The leaders of the OWI believed that Donovan also turned to his friends in the press, most notably to Arthur Krock, Washington bureau chief for the *New York Times*.[19] Krock was one of the nation's most powerful journalists with extraordinary contacts throughout the capital. When Krock had taken charge of the *Times*'s Washington bureau in 1932 he had been a Roosevelt supporter, but he turned against the president in 1936 after Roosevelt tried to pack the Supreme Court with supporters of New Deal agencies and policies. By the outbreak of World War II Krock was a thoroughgoing conservative. He still had his friends in the administration—he was close to Secretary of State Cordell Hull, for example, as well as to Donovan—but his enemies included Undersecretary of State Sumner Welles and Harry Hopkins, both of whom Krock viciously attacked in cruel, stiletto prose. As Isaiah Berlin, head of the Special Survey Section of the British embassy in Washington, wrote to the Foreign Office, Krock was a man "who veers between the extremes of vindictive spite and sycophantic flattery."[20] Krock did not need Donovan to arrive at the conclusion that the OWI was excessively liberal if not downright communist-leaning and in need of trimming; but if Barnes and Warburg were right that the two were in alliance, the men made a good team.[21]

Barnes may also have been a lightning rod for Krock's dislike. Barnes had worked as a reporter for the *New York Herald Tribune* in Moscow for many years, during which time American embassy officials had suspected him of communist sympathies. Despite his strong support of Wendell Willkie, Barnes retained his reputation as being a supporter of the left. Krock could easily have come to distrust Barnes and, by extension, the New York office of the Overseas Branch and the Voice of America. In any case, Barnes told Leonard Miall that Krock had warned the OWI in June 1943 that it needed only one major slip for the OWI to be out—and the OSS to take over.[22]

Soon after the congressional investigations ended, Krock wrote a column that amounted to a threat against the OWI. "The comparative immunity of the foreign department of the OWI from the axe of Congress," Krock claimed, "has furnished one of the most curious incidents of this session." The Overseas Branch, he asserted, was spared only because congressmen did not know the Voice of America; they did not listen to overseas broadcasts; they were forced to rely on what the propagandists told them about their operations. But this was sure to change, he warned. "It won't require more than one glaring slip to gain the support of a number of anti-fourth-term Democrats." He went on: "There is a strong disposition to turn over all foreign propaganda to the military authorities, functioning through the Office of Strategic Services," a propaganda outfit that "Congressional critics . . . have good cause to believe [has] been brilliant and effective."[23]

Krock and Donovan's opportunity came later that month. On July 17, 1943, General Eisenhower decided it was time to follow up Allied successes in Sicily with the invasion of mainland Italy; two days later the Allies made their first aerial raid on Rome. Allied bombs shattered Italian political resolve. The Fascist Grand Council met and voted to change the existing government; soon Mussolini was arrested. King Victor Emmanuel III, who had known and approved of the coup, appointed Marshal Pietro Badoglio, a member of the Fascist party since 1927, to take Mussolini's place. What followed was chaos. Badoglio announced over the radio that the Italians would stay in the war, but neither the Germans nor the Allies believed him. Everyone expected Badoglio and the king to take Italy out of the war; the issue became how to make the most of these developments while avoiding the debacle of another Darlan deal. These events set the stage for the single biggest domestic battle in which the OWI was ever embroiled.[24]

The leaders of the Overseas Branch, as we have seen, believed that their most important task was to use the Voice of America in such a way as to prevent the recurrence of another Darlan deal—to use propaganda to shape American foreign policy.[25] Sherwood, Barnes, Warburg, and Johnson wanted to tell the world that the United States was bent on establishing and preserving democracy, not on maintaining order and political stability at all costs, or upholding a conservative and oppressive status quo, as the Badoglio "deal" implied. They tried to project an image of American politics which conformed to their ideals of what they wanted America to be: reform-minded, idealistic, and committed to worldwide political and economic justice. They not only wanted the Voice of America to tell Europeans all these things about the United States, but they wanted these things to be true; they wanted propaganda to move Europeans to action, but they also hoped to influence the State Department, the military, and Congress.

On learning of the events in Italy, Warburg therefore issued a guidance to treat Mussolini's resignation calmly, without the celebration that would imply an overthrow of fascism. He told the language desks to "emphasize that Badoglio's first words upon assuming command under the Fascist King had been a promise to keep Italy fighting for the Nazi-Fascist cause, and to make it clear that the war against the Fascist Italian regime would continue irrespective of the palace revolution."[26] Warburg phoned Sherwood in Washington and cleared the guidance. One of Sherwood's aides contacted a lower-level man at the Joint Chiefs of Staff and two regional specialists at the State Department. But it was a Sunday evening, people were hard to reach, and no real approval was received. Nevertheless Barnes, Warburg, Johnson, and their colleagues felt that they were right, and they followed their instincts.[27]

The immediate question was how to treat the story, how to make it clear to overseas listeners that this change in leadership did not spell an overthrow of the Fascists or a move toward constitutional monarchy in Italy. How could the Voice explain that the Fascist party was still in power?

First, the English language desk wrote a very neutral ten-line story headlining the news. It said only that Mussolini had resigned and that the king had appointed Marshal Badoglio to succeed him as premier. This statement was followed by a longer bulletin containing Badoglio's announcement that the war would continue, the comment that Badoglio had assumed Mussolini's pledge to Hitler, and a concluding remark that Mussolini had met with Hitler only the week before. The Voice of America's second news report implied that the king's appointment of Badoglio was a continuation of the same Fascist regime.[28]

Warburg then went on the air with his own commentary, not as James Warburg, but as John Durfee, a political commentator on the Voice of America English language program. There were several reasons why Warburg used a pseudonym. The most personal and obvious was that Warburg came from a wealthy, prominent family of European Jewish bankers. Warburg was a name to be avoided in Allied propaganda. But Warburg had not invented the practice of using a pseudonym; it was done by the British and by the Axis as well.[29] Warburg had begun using special names for personal, "signed" commentaries over the winter of 1942–43. As he explained in defense of his nom de plume, "The same words spoken by an individual carry more weight than if they are merely spoken by a nameless announcer."[30] He thus became Wallace Herrick in analyzing military developments and John Durfee in covering political events.

As Durfee, Warburg broadcast what he believed to be the basic political tenet of the Allied cause: "The American people are fighting a war against Fascism and this war will go on irrespective of whether it is Mussolini, or Badoglio, or the Fascist King himself who forces Italy to continue to fight for Hitler. . . ." They were fighting words. Warburg told the world that America would not cut another infamous Darlan deal.[31]

Warburg, Johnson, and Barnes also searched for an independent commentator who would underline the position of the Voice of America and the Office of War Information. The first well-known journalist to criticize the king's move was the *New York Post* columnist Samuel Grafton. Warburg decided Grafton's comments were worth using. The Voice of America recorded them, and they went out exclusively on the English language transmission. Grafton's remarks were hard-hitting. "Fascism is still in power in Italy," he told his audience. "It has put on a new face; that's all." He went on to utter the words by which the episode became known. "The moronic little King, who has stood behind Mussolini's shoulder for twenty-one years, has moved forward one pace." There was more: "I do not feel in any sense that history has been made today. . . . This is a political minuet and not the revolution we have been waiting for."[32] It was strong material. Grafton's anti-Fascist views expressed what Barnes, Warburg, and Johnson wanted to say. But the broadcast was not meant to provoke domestic controversy, and no one in the New York office expected Grafton's commentary to be picked up by an outside listener, let alone an eager American journalist.

That Sunday night the *New York Times* radio critic, Jack Gould, was sitting in his small study, a room barely large enough to accommodate his desk, chair, and collection of radios. On the top floor of his rented Greenwich Village house he listened regularly and professionally. Gould had long made it a practice not only to tune in domestic radio, but to include the short-wave broadcasts of both the Voice of America and the BBC. At 8:00 P.M. on July 25, he picked up the English language broadcasts of the Voice of America. He decided he had a newsworthy story and phoned the *Times* office.[33] The night editors met and decided to play the story on page 3 in measured, quiet tones.[34]

The story may have been understated and somewhat buried on Monday, but on Tuesday the paper carried it on the front page of the paper. Gould wrote Tuesday's story in a vivid style that implicitly criticized the OWI. The Voice of America broadcasts, he said, characterized King Victor Emmanuel as the "moronic little King," pulling out the one phrase of Grafton's commentary most likely to jangle the nerves of American conservatives.[35]

Gould phoned Barnes, an old friend, that morning and told him that "he had been writing the story and playing it up heavily under orders from Krock."[36] Krock himself took the news and wrote a piece in which he accused the agency of violating State Department policy. He charged the OWI with undermining military action and condemned its staff as procommunist subversives. The Office of War Information, Krock wrote, spoke with an "'ideology' that conforms much more closely to the Moscow than to the Washington-London line." His venom increased: "The New York shortwave department of the OWI deliberately and constantly borrows from these sources to discredit the authorized foreign policy of the United States Government, or to reshape it according to the personal and ideological preferences of Communists and their fellow-travelers in this country."[37]

Krock's blasting story was picked up across the nation. Barnes spent the day answering phone calls from newspapermen. Patiently he explained that the phrases referred to were but a minuscule part of the Voice of America's output for the day, but clearly, no matter how often or with what good grace he reiterated his line, the story was making waves.[38]

On Tuesday, Barnes began getting calls from Washington. Milton Eisenhower phoned. The Voice of America should refrain from smearing the new Italian regime. It was an early sign of what the Washington reaction would be. Sherwood rang. He had been closeted with the president for days working on a presidential address, and had sustained the brunt of the official backlash. He upbraided his deputy in no uncertain terms.[39]

Roosevelt initially rebuked the New York office, but by Wednesday he had softened his line. There are several possible reasons for his doing so, although the president never explained why he changed his attitude from anger to neutral acceptance. Roosevelt and Krock were long-standing enemies, which would have made the president all the more willing to react stubbornly and rebelliously against Krock's furious prose. Roosevelt would thus have to forgive, at least temporarily, the OWI's political transgression.[40] Moreover, the president had been burned once by the fiery liberal reaction to his acceptance of Admiral Darlan. With a presidential election a little more than a year away, he wanted to avoid a repetition of that episode. He needed the support of liberal-minded voters and the liberal wing of his party, and he softened his stand on the incident of the moronic little king accordingly.

Roosevelt's instinct was reinforced by word from the State Department, in which Hull made it known that he was not gunning for the OWI.[41] The department was, in mid-1943, torn by internal dissent, especially by differences between Hull and Sumner Welles. Reports of administrative chaos, and rumors of a Budget Bureau report chastising the internal workings of the department, filtered through the capital. Moreover, Krock had attacked the State Department as part of his campaign against the president, a tactic that made him heartily disliked by the diplomats. In all, the State Department and the president had little to gain by withdrawing support from the OWI in early August.[42] The whole sequence of events had a storybook quality. First came an attack, unprecedented in its intensity and viciousness, and then, two days later, peace—and with it, political advantage.

There was no serious threat from any other quarter. Congress continued to bombard the OWI, but it made no further budget cuts in overseas operations that fall. The State Department was itself in a serious state of disarray as Sumner Welles was attacked and deposed in a battle over leadership which only quieted down in October when Roosevelt appointed Edward Stettinius as Welles's successor.[43] The State Department continued to criticize the OWI, but it made no real effort to exert control. For the moment, relations remained quiet.[44]

Notwithstanding the appearance of victory, the affair of the moronic little king felt to the New York leaders like a drubbing. It drained the office of energy. "After its last bouleversement over 'John Durfee' and the 'moronic little King' broadcast," Isaiah Berlin reported to the Foreign Office, the OWI "is leading a somewhat troglodyte existence."[45] By late summer Houseman had left the New York office for Hollywood. Barnes was spending much of his time in Washington, either filling in for Sherwood or fending off hostile congressmen. Edd Johnson, who as chief of the Office of Control was the main news editor, retreated to a quiet position as an administrator, leaving the tape machines for a more remote sanctuary "behind an outer office, behind a swinging door." Edward Barrett, the editor of the basic news and cable wireless services, immersed himself in his daily routine, while Lou Cowan, Barnes's deputy director, focused his energies on "making records of domestic transmission in neutral countries." Only Warburg remained enthusiastic and full of drive, eager to make the most of the OWI's victory over the OSS.[46]

As director of policy, Warburg was a Washington-based man, not a denizen of the New York office. But he became the champion of the New Yorkers. Warburg decided that it was important to keep all the regional editors closely informed on the developments in Italy following the moronic little king debacle. Liberally, at times indiscreetly, he showed the regional editors his memos to the Overseas Planning Board in which he appealed for a clear policy line while justifying the Voice of America against outside attack. In the process Warburg took on a new shine; he "became the protagonist of the forgotten men." The staff of the New York office saw Warburg as their leader who had defended the Overseas Branch and the Voice of America on the night Mussolini fell. He brought the New York staff news of Washington and kept them informed of large events within the government. He took the time and the trouble to find out how the New York staff felt about the course of events, and he seemed to be able to do something about it.[47]

Warburg did more than open up communications. He wrote and engineered a new staff order that supplanted the past spring's plan of posting seven regional chiefs in Washington. In its place Warburg created a system of three main divisions in charge of propaganda to America's allies, propaganda to the Pacific, and propaganda to Europe and the Middle East. With this bureaucratic shuffle, Warburg transferred policy control from Washington to New York. The engine of policy creation became the New York Editorial Board with Edd Johnson as its chief. The purpose of the Editorial Board was to integrate policy and operations. To this end the principal editors for each language section sat on the board and became part of the guidance process. Although the regional directors in Washington still met and kept their nominal position, New York functionally superceded them.[48]

Warburg's system reflected and enlarged the old "we" versus "they" split between New York and Washington. From Warburg's standpoint the new committee was brilliantly composed of men who had become intensely loyal to the Overseas Branch's policy director. "It is not without significance," Miall observed of these changes, "that the men who will form this Editorial Committee are those who now feel a particular bond of loyalty to Warburg."[49]

Moreover, the leadership in Washington was, temporarily, losing its energy and will. Milton Eisenhower, Davis's right-hand man and associate director of the whole of the OWI, left. As early as May 1943 Eisenhower had begun considering whether, how, and when to leave the OWI. Kansas State College offered him the position of president, Ike encouraged his brother to take it, and that settled the issue; in late August Milton Eisenhower departed for Kansas.[50] Milton had been the force behind bringing policy control into the Washington office. Without him that control again slipped away.

Davis, too, hit a low point in his career as head of the OWI. Not only had he to defend the Overseas Branch; his job was to break the waves of criticism that relentlessly crashed on the Domestic Branch. It was a thankless and impossible task. By the fall of 1943 Congress had whittled down the Domestic Branch to a pittance: only 10 percent of the whole of the OWI budget went to the Domestic Branch.

Warburg took advantage of these events. He was an enormously talented, personable, and warm man who easily reached out to other people. One of his colleagues observed of him that he was a "good communicator. If you asked him a question you got an answer very quickly. . . . he realized that you were out on the end of a wire, that you needed guidance, and it would come back."[51] If Warburg saw a need, and he thought he had an answer that seemed to fit the pieces of the puzzle as he knew them, he acted. He did not wait to write all the memos and check with everyone around him; he did not bring the leadership along in the process; he acted. His vision, intelligence, and absolute sense of independence at times served him well, and at times undercut his accomplishments. In September 1943 it got things going.

Once Warburg initiated the New York Editorial Board, he and Sherwood began discussing what move the Overseas Branch should take next. They weighed jumping still farther away from Washington, to London. Sherwood therefore asked Warburg to go to England, take a look at the London OWI office, and consider whether or not to move the main Overseas Branch abroad, closer to the war front and to the British.

Warburg went. He suggested to Sherwood that it would be a good idea to move the operational headquarters for short-range propaganda forward. But he argued that it could not be done under the aegis of the presiding head of the London office, Wallace Carroll.

Carroll had joined the Overseas Branch when it was still the Foreign Information Service. In 1941 he had just returned from Europe, where he had lived for over ten years. Carroll was thirty-eight years old in 1943, a midwesterner from Milwaukee who had become a journalist straight out of college when he went to work for United Press. He stayed on with UP, rising up the ranks. In 1928 he had gone to London, then moved on to Paris, and then to Geneva to cover the League of Nations. In 1939 he returned to London to head the office there, and remained through the early months and years of war until the spring of 1941, when he joined the first convoy of British and U.S. war materials sent to the Soviet Union, witnessing Russia's front lines in the very first phase of the Soviet war against the Axis.

When Carroll returned from Europe John Winant, American ambassador to Great Britain, suggested to Davis and Sherwood that they use Carroll's skills by sending him to head the office in London. Davis and Sherwood readily agreed. Carroll went.

At first Carroll's attitude toward American foreign policy, and especially toward the relationship of propaganda to foreign policy, seemed much the same as Sherwood's or Warburg's. His background was in so many ways so similar to theirs. For years he had worked for and with Edd Johnson's brother, Earl Johnson, one of the heads of United Press. He was a member of the international journalists' club. And he seemed to see issues in the same way they did. Those on the right in British politics, for example, categorized Carroll as a member of the left. When the *New York Times* journalist Harrison Salisbury interviewed the British newspaper magnate Lord Beaverbrook, Beaverbrook expounded to Salisbury how Wallace Carroll, the former UP London chief, then with the OWI in London, was a leftist.[52]

Carroll had written a series of award-winning articles on Russia in which he extolled the communist government, including its leader, Joseph Stalin. He used his stories to persuade the American people that Russia would make a good and reliable ally. And so he wrote articles confronting issues such as religion and godlessness in Russia. He went to church in Russia, he wrote not atypically, and saw there "a thousand worshippers [who] bowed their heads in the mellow shadows of the Yelokhovo Cathedral . . . to receive the blessings of Metropolitan Sergei, acting patriarch and primate of the All-Russian Orthodox Church." Carroll attacked the question of communist control and the destructiveness of Stalin's purges. Yes, he said, every officer of the Soviet Red Army has a political commissar at his side. But the system works, he argued. Commissars are there "to tell the stokers, mechanics and other men who do the dirty work that they're heroes." From the Russian front he wrote that the Red Army was pushing the German army steadily back. "I have seen the Red Army working, calmly and efficiently," he told American readers. "Everywhere the troops appeared well fed, well equipped, well clothed and in excellent spirits."[53]

Carroll's was the voice of a Popular Front liberal who believed that an alliance with Russia was necessary to win the war and bring freedom and democracy to the peace. Or perhaps Carroll was merely willing to work with the devil in order to defeat the Nazis. In any case, by 1943 differences between Carroll and the New York leaders had become apparent.

On one level these differences were personal and professional. Carroll complained he could not get instructions from Sherwood. All he got, he remembered, was "a great silence." When Sherwood did finally cable him it was to accuse him of "failure to communicate." After a while Carroll could stand the tensions and difficulties no longer. "I thought," he explained, "if he won't talk to me maybe he'll talk to somebody else. And I quit."[54]

But it was Warburg's trip that triggered Carroll's decision to resign. Anger and frustration piled on top of sixteen-hour days, two attacks of jaundice, and sheer exhaustion. It felt terrible, Carroll explained, to be so undermined, "to have somebody snooping around saying what do you think about Carroll. . . . this was a hell of a way to undercut your chief of mission."[55]

A month later Carroll left London, "as bitter a man as ever I have encountered," commented Sherwood's assistant.[56] Carroll told Davis that he could no longer work with the OWI as it was constituted; he charged the New York office with denying him sufficient cooperation. The failures of the OWI, he asserted, turned on the operational inadequacies of New York, and especially on Barnes, Warburg, and Johnson. Warburg, Carroll added, was unacceptable to the British, to the American embassy, and to military leaders on both sides of the Atlantic. Although Carroll's claim was certainly not true of Warburg's relationship with the Political Warfare Executive, it was true of his relationship with John Winant, the American ambassador to Britain and Carroll's old friend.[57] Warburg could not fight back with his usual vigor that fall. Throughout late October, November, and much of December he was ill, too sick to travel from New York to Washington.

But there was more to Carroll's fights with Sherwood and Warburg and his resignation in 1943 than personality and the inevitable tensions of running a satellite office at a three-thousand-mile reach under wartime conditions. Carroll believed that the role of propaganda was to explain and support American foreign policy, not to make it. He did not always approve or like American policy. He disliked Darlan, for example, and thought Eisenhower and Roosevelt had made a dreadful mistake in recognizing the former Vichy minister as head of North Africa. But he did not believe it was his role to change that policy. Rather, the propagandist's job was to ameliorate relations and to sell American policy, regardless of the difficulties any policy created. He concerned himself more with immediate military victory than with long-range consequences of peace. And his disagreements with American policy, unlike those of Warburg or Barnes, were never so deep as to bring him into harsh conflict with the State Department. Carroll in fact got along well with the State Department, which even offered him a job in March of 1944, a job he unhesitatingly turned down.

For Davis, who also was not at war with American foreign policy, Carroll's discontent and resignation proved the last straw. First Warburg and Sherwood had moved policy from Washington to New York, next they had threatened to transfer it to London, and finally Warburg had so enraged the London office of the OWI that its leader, plus his deputies, had resigned. Davis could not tolerate the situation. As Carroll himself recalled, this latest tempest "increased the frustration on Davis's part and his awareness that the Overseas Branch was not running very effectively."[58] But Davis was too soft and kind a man to behead others. He needed someone who could help him put the OWI back together, regardless of the pain it might cost; he had to replace Milton Eisenhower.

He turned to Edward Klauber, an old friend from the days during the First World War when he had worked for the *New York Times*. Davis had become so close to Klauber that he had asked Klauber to be his best man. Klauber had moved over to CBS in the 1930s, but the two men remained in touch. Klauber had lobbied for the network to hire Davis as a news commentator. It was not an easy battle to win, for Davis had an arid voice and a dry style that deadened radio's eyewitness style of reporting. The news department hung back from hiring him, but Klauber pushed, and won, and by the early forties Davis had became one of CBS's most successful commentators.

By 1943 Klauber had built a strong reputation as a radio journalist. In the early 1930s the president of CBS, William Paley, had put Klauber in charge of the news and public affairs section of the network. Radio journalism in those days was more an adjunct of advertising than the serious journalistic enterprise it was to become; it sounded more like Walter Winchell than Edward R. Murrow. But schooled by years in print journalism, and especially by his association with the *New York Times,* Klauber insisted that CBS's news coverage be objective and straightforward and that it inform its listeners as accurately as possible of the events of the day. News, he dictated, was one of the most important underpinnings of a democracy, and it was the job of good radio news "to help the listener to understand, to weigh and to judge, but not to do the judging for him."[59]

Klauber's news philosophy was to play an important role in shaping the Voice of America in 1944, after he had assumed a great deal of influence within the Office of War Information. But in the late fall and winter of 1943–44 it was a second attribute that he had cultivated as Paley's assistant which became crucial to the development of the propaganda agency. Under Paley's tutelage Klauber had become a totally committed, single-minded organization man. As an administrator he learned to subordinate himself to his chief, and to make an institution function. He excelled at taking charge, and he enjoyed exercising power. Despite his personal force, however, he determinedly remained a shadowy figure in the background, an *éminence grise,* anxious not to seem to be taking over. "America's number one number two man," he liked to call himself.[60]

Klauber brought to the OWI his passionate commitment to an objective, informative news style, his long-standing friendship with Elmer Davis, his administrative talents, and his ability to devote himself completely to what he saw as the best interests of the institution and its leader. For Klauber there was no administrative distinction between a government agency and a private corporation, and he assumed that the OWI should function as smoothly as CBS. This assumption entailed that policy should be set at the top and adhered to all along the line; that the nerve center of the OWI should remain in Washington, and Washington alone; and that Elmer Davis should be the single head of the organization, and not Sherwood, Barnes, or Warburg. Klauber did not create the power struggle between Washington and New York or between Davis and the leaders of the Overseas Branch, but he had the political skills and strength of character to win it.

Klauber went to bat for Davis. He formally accepted his new post on December 1, 1943, and rapidly came to the conclusion that the Overseas Branch of the OWI was the only part of the organization that mattered. He traveled to New York to take a look at operations there, attended a meeting of the Editorial Board, and immediately realized that New York had become the effective center of all overseas propaganda policy. He recommended that the Editorial Board be dissolved, pushed Davis to take a more active role, and moved to pull the organization back to Washington.[61]

Early in January, therefore, Davis began reorganizing the Overseas Branch. He wrote to Roosevelt, explaining that the New York office had been reduced to chaos and confusion. Davis informed the president that as head of the OWI he had "relieved" Sherwood of all operating duties and fired Barnes, Warburg, and Johnson.[62] A few days later Sherwood took his own case to the president.[63]

Roosevelt disliked making clear-cut decisions between friends, and this struggle presented him with definite problems. Sherwood, on one side, was a White House regular and a close friend of the presidential adviser Samuel Rosenman. Davis, on the other side, was still popular with the public—always an important factor in Roosevelt's calculations—whereas

Sherwood was not. Moreover, Davis had the backing of the Bureau of the Budget.[64]

On February 2, 1944, the president called the two leaders in to see him. He said he did not want to lose either of them and instructed them to go into the Cabinet room and work out their differences.[65] When they emerged they had agreed on a solution. Davis would remain head of the OWI, and gain control of the organization. Sherwood would move on to London to take up where Carroll had left off, thereby saving his face and the president's but removing himself from effective power. Barnes, Warburg, and Johnson were to go. Weeks later, in London, Sherwood sobbed on Ritchie Calder's shoulder that he had bartered Barnes, Warburg, and Johnson for the "Dixie-crat" vote because Roosevelt needed the congressional support of the southern Democrats.[66] But the three propagandists felt they had been sold down the river. "Elmer . . . insisted upon his original demands," Warburg angrily wrote Sherwood, "and you have apparently acquiesced in them. . . . Had you not surrendered, I should have refused. . . ."[67]

The day after he demanded their resignations, Davis took a train from Washington to New York, where he called a press conference. There Davis portrayed an amicable situation. Barnes, Warburg, and Johnson, Davis told the gathered journalists, had decided on their own to leave the OWI, despite a current manpower shortage in the organization.

The three men were enraged. They gathered at Johnson's apartment, gloomily downing vodka and preparing public statements for the journalists, who had agreed to come hear the other side of the story. When the reporters finally arrived, one of them began by reading out Davis's statement and then asked the now ex-leaders if they had anything to add for the record. "No," said Barnes, short in his response. Warburg aired his anger in public. "I would like to clear up one misapprehension," he said. "One does not resign from a war. I resigned because I was asked to resign." Johnson bitterly added: "I have just carried out the first instruction Elmer Davis ever gave me."[68]

The New York staff felt shattered. They gathered for a farewell party following Barnes, Warburg, and Johnson's final press conference, drinking heavily while they waited an hour or more before the three men could join them. "As a party," Miall commented, "it was more like a wake." Then Barnes, Warburg, and Johnson entered the room. "The effect was electric," Miall recorded. "Cheers rang through the hotel for many minutes on end. Someone started 'For they are jolly good fellows' and chorus after chorus was repeated until Warburg said aside 'if this goes on any longer I shall blub like a baby.'"[69] After much discussion and pleading the New York staff agreed to stay on. Lou Cowan, despite his own depression about the turn of affairs and serious misgivings of conscience, took Barnes's job.

Cowan was well liked and a born mediator. Unlike most of his colleagues, he had not come to propaganda through journalism, politics, or writing. He was a public relations expert and radio producer who had first acquired an interest in propaganda in college, when he had taken a course at the University of Chicago with Harold Lasswell, the sociologist who was the leading American expert in the field of propaganda during the twenties and thirties.

Cowan did not try to become an academic, however. He was an ambitious son of a Lithuanian Jew, and he wanted to earn both fame and fortune. Radio, still a brand-new business in the thirties, was wide open to the newer immigrant groups. A young talented Jew could rise to the top, and for Cowan it provided the right mix of intellectual challenge, professional advancement, and financial reward. He started out in publicity, but soon began packaging his own shows, which by the opening of the war included "Kay Kyser's College of Musical Knowledge" and "The Quiz Kids."

As war approached Cowan became restless and worried. On his honeymoon in August 1939 he could not tear himself from his old Zenith portable radio, and spent the first weeks of his marriage anxiously waiting for news that Germany had invaded Poland. When war came he searched Germany for relatives, and then other Jews whom he could save by bringing them to America. By 1941 he knew he had to pour his energies into the war effort. Classified as 4-F with a bad back and weak ankle, he joined the Radio Division of the Army Bureau of Public Relations. There he created shows such as "Command Performance" and "Hymns from Home." His job, he recalled, "was to supply ideas for subject matter that might interest an audience. It was not to operate any part of the Bureau." In early April 1942, Cowan moved over to the Foreign Information Service. At first he was on loan to Sherwood as liaison with the army, but a month later he became assistant to John Houseman. In July 1943 Cowan took over the Radio Program Bureau, where he stayed until 1944.[70]

Cowan had long acted as a mediator within the Overseas Branch. He had never been political. When he turned twenty-one he had registered as a Republican because his uncle was a Republican, despite the fact that he generally supported Roosevelt and the New Deal. He saw the war as a crusade against fascism. He was politically naive, but he was abundantly charming. "He had presence," recalled the head of the Low Countries desk. "If he entered the room, you knew it: the voice, the manner of speech, the hands . . . he was very sympathetic."[71] Cowan got on with everyone and commanded respect for the job he did. He handled personnel problems and smoothed tempers. He daily replaced those who resigned with new recruits. He boosted egos of men and women who were underpaid and frustrated, angry at government policies or at each other or at the unfairness of a room without a window. And he did so calmly and sympathetically. He made people feel that he cared about them.

The very arrangement of his office reflected his sensitivity to others and ability to mediate between people. He had a large corner room with high windows, which he furnished with a glass-topped conference table. "People use their desks as a psychological moat," he believed. "In England I once had an appointment with Lord Ormsby-Gore and found him waiting for me at a desk actually raised on a platform, making him not only separate, but higher than anyone who came to talk to him. I found it all very uncomfortable."[72] Cowan tried to put people at ease. It was typical of his style that he sent out for coffee and sweet rolls from a nearby Schrafft's as soon as he smelled trouble brewing.

"Many people were waiting for a lead from him," wrote Miall, "and he probably saved the impending disintegration."[73] Edward Barrett stepped into Sherwood's slot and Carroll assumed Warburg's role. Barnes, Warburg, and Johnson, like Houseman before them, all left government service permanently. The work went on, but it was the end of an era.

The crisis of 1943 not only produced changes in propagandists and propaganda; the incident of the moronic little king and the consequent shifts within the OWI reflected the progress of the war. By mid-1943 the Allies had effectively won the war, and ultimate victory was only a matter of time. This is not to underestimate the hardships and cost of the last years of the war, for they were very brutal years indeed, to be paid for in soldiers' and civilians' lives across Europe and Asia. But the outcome of the war was no longer in doubt. America thus had to face a very different set of questions from those the threat of defeat had presented in 1942. The pressures and demands placed on the Overseas Branch of the OWI and the Voice of America sprang out of a need, inchoate though it was, that propaganda also had to recognize these questions and come up with solutions. But although the propagandists may well have understood the importance of the implications of victory, they were unwilling to shelve their beliefs or accept a conservative ideology in which global stability meant something other than achieving worldwide justice, democracy, or the end of fascism. The incident of the moronic little king was, in that light, a symptom and a result of the political changes generated by the course of the war.

Practical consequences slowly emerged. The Overseas Branch became integrated into Washington policy-making, and relations with the State Department grew smoother. The State Department accepted the new regime in the Overseas Branch as it had never accepted the old, and Barrett, Cowan, and Carroll professionally accepted American foreign policy even when they personally disagreed with it. They were, in other words, willing to act as conduits of official policy. The Bureau of the Budget approved of the new order, and stopped pulling at the Washington leaders of the OWI to clamp down on the New York office. The OSS and Donovan never again threatened the working establishment of the OWI. Even Congress became a bit happier with the state of affairs.

If external politics were easier, however, the New York propagandists never fully recovered their enthusiasm for the job. A few moved on to London, others quit over the following weeks and months, but most stayed on, at least through D-Day. The episode of the moronic little king produced a sense of alienation from American foreign policy, however, and in turn a narrowing of focus. The propagandists tended to concentrate on the daily issues of their jobs, to think of their work in terms of craft and daily news. No longer was there a Warburg to press for a propaganda formulation that would lead American policy where he wanted it to go: a fight against National Socialism and oppression of all kinds and a commitment to a more democratically run world. Accordingly, the importance both of the Projection of America and of military victories increasingly defined the style of the Voice of America.

Relations with the British also fundamentally changed. Much of the cooperation between London and New York had been forged through the political vision of Warburg and his friendship with Ritchie Calder. Warburg wanted to work as closely as possible with the British Allies, and he established procedures to achieve this aim. Davis, Barrett, and Carroll, on the other hand, prevented the institution of a joint directive in London, a project that had been dear to Warburg's heart. By mid-1944 the Overseas Branch ignored the Political Warfare Executive's mission as much as it could without being openly hostile and stopped initiating discussions of propaganda problems with the British. They "adopted an attitude of studious evasiveness to every approach," Lord Ritchie-Calder later bemoaned. "After the departure of Sherwood [as head of the Overseas Branch], and the appearance of his successors, the intention of OWI became that of steering clear of PWE."[74] It was, indeed, a new order.

The men who directed the Overseas Branch in 1943 gave the propaganda organization, and its struggles within the American government, a distinctive character. But the fall of Sherwood, Barnes, Warburg, and Johnson was not just a personal tale; it was one that came as a consequence of tensions brought to the surface by the Allied invasion of North Africa and the incident of the moronic little king. Henceforth, the Voice of America would have to defend a policy that the liberal leaders of the Overseas Branch could not tolerate. It was the basic dilemma on which Sherwood, Barnes, Warburg, and Johnson had foundered. The Voice of America was just that—the voice of America—and those leaders in Washington who demanded that the Overseas Branch conform to official policy ultimately had to win the struggle of who would control the organization. It was only a matter of time.

# 6

# Who's Listening?

## The Role of Changing Mass
## Communications Theories

A FUNDAMENTAL shift in the radio propaganda of the Voice of America mirrored the administrative upheaval that transformed the Overseas Branch of the OWI. By the time Sherwood moved to London and Barnes, Warburg, and Johnson left the OWI, Voice propaganda had changed in its tone and style, in its conception of its audience, and in its goals for American propaganda. The Voice of America had moved from agitprop, directed to the masses in Europe, to news, spoken to the many and diverse citizens of France who, it was hoped, would greet the American liberators.

On one level this alteration began with the departure of John Houseman. In March 1943 the State Department refused to grant Houseman a visa to travel to North Africa. Three months later he quit and returned to show business.[1] Perhaps no one could have replaced Houseman. Certainly no one did. But toward the end of the summer, Sherwood and Barnes appointed Lawrence Blochman as the new chief of the Radio Program Bureau and Werner Michel enlarged his role as chief of the broadcasting division of the Radio Program Bureau.

Blochman was a journalist who, in the 1930s, had left the newspaper world to become a detective story writer, novelist, and translator of French literature. He was a solid man with a wry sense of humor and a large fund of jokes. Friendly, agreeable, and generally easygoing, he was also meticulous and involved in all levels of radio propaganda. He worked hard, for example, to find extra spots for the time-short Low Countries desk, and he regularly attended the morning meetings of the various language desks. It was typical of his approach that at the French desk morning meetings he would stand at the back of the room smoking a chain of cigarettes and quietly observe what went on. He was a political liberal who stood up for his principles, but he was neither a radio man nor a natural propagandist.[2] Nor was he charismatic. He ruled his roost with a light hand, and finding that the language desks functioned well on their own, he let them go to it in their own ways. He was not an innovator, but rather he "ran the propaganda machine" thoroughly, cheerfully, and competently.[3]

Werner Michel oversaw production. He allotted airtime to the language desks and determined which producer would work on what program, decisions that carried with them policy implications. What time of day the French labor show reached its audience, for example, made a difference in who could be expected to listen to it, and how it would be written.[4]

Michel, like Houseman, was an Alsatian equally fluent in German, English, and French. He had come out of the world of theater, where he had been a stage producer as well as a conductor, composer, and lyricist. After he immigrated to the United States in 1938 he worked on two Broadway musicals, but in 1939 CBS, looking for multilingual announcers for its shortwave service, asked Michel to announce and write shows, and he took the job. Two years later a friend called and asked Michel if he wanted to leave CBS, and if so to go down to Madison Avenue and meet John Houseman, who had just started the Voice of America. "So I went down there," Michel recalled, and Houseman came "storming out of the door, bigger than life as he always was. . . ." After a perfunctory interview Houseman hired Michel and told him to begin work.[5] But Michel never rivaled Houseman in influence and never imposed his own sense of radio or propaganda on the Voice of America.[6]

The only other radio man who might have assumed Houseman's role was Cowan. But Cowan spoke no foreign languages. He could thus not speak directly with Pierre Lazareff, for example, or with most members of the French desk—or any other language desk. Nor did he see his role as that of editor or producer. Unlike Houseman, who was European and sophisticated, Cowan was a midwesterner, born and raised in Chicago, with a background in publicity and quiz shows and variety programs. His strength lay in his ability to mediate between people and factions. Despite his years spent working in American radio and the interest in propaganda he had absorbed from Harold Lasswell, Cowan did not interfere with the contents of the language desk programs. Like Blochman, he gave the desks great creative latitude.[7]

Houseman was replaced by men who allowed the Voice of America to become less dramatic and creative, and who converted the Voice into a station that broadcast straight journalism. Blochman, Michel, and Cowan were conduits for a new propaganda approach intended to inform the many citizens of France, rather than provoke them to action. The shift in leadership was not the basic reason why Voice of America propaganda changed, but it released the Voice from its early and radical broadcasting patterns.

The changes in Voice of America propaganda in 1943 reflected a rethinking of mass communications theory which took place during the war. Voice propagandists reported on listening patterns in Europe, and then evaluated these reports within the framework of already existing studies of public opinion. Alterations in the assumptions behind these studies indirectly affected the propagandists. The leaders of the Overseas Branch worked, in other words, within an intellectual climate that was changing, helping to transform Voice of America propaganda.

Under the leadership of Leonard Carleton, the Bureau of Research and Analysis of the OWI collected and analyzed as much data as it could on listening patterns throughout Europe. These studies were augmented with intelligence from the BBC monitoring service. The Analysis Bureau staunchly defended the American propaganda effort. To support this position it poured out a steady stream of bulletins showing that Europeans listened to the Voice of America.

The leaders of the Overseas Branch used these reports to justify the OWI budget and to answer repeated congressional demands that the propagandists demonstrate the effectiveness of the Voice of America. The Voice of America thus had two distinct audiences—the peoples of Europe, whose actions and thoughts the propagandists were trying to influence, and Congress, whose approval the propagandists had to win in order to secure financial and political support. Congress was the Voice of America's most skeptical client, to whom it had to sell its product.

The Bureau of Research and Analysis provided OWI leaders with important political ammunition. Sherwood, Barnes, and Warburg could say, for example, that the OWI representative in London had reported closely questioning at least a hundred French refugees, and claimed that "Frenchmen all over France of all social, political and economic groups, listen eagerly . . . to the Voice of America from London. . . . Radio propaganda has played a tremendous role in keeping alive faith and hope in liberation . . . and in stimulating resistance."[8] Or the propagandists could pull out another report stating that "a French submarine captain listened to the Voice of America very frequently and found it superior to broadcasts coming from Algiers or from London."[9] This was the sort of material the Overseas Branch needed in order to hold up its efforts before congressmen whose main concern was that the government get the greatest value for the taxpayers' dollars. In this important respect the Analysis Bureau proved useful and successful.

But the Analysis Bureau encountered serious problems in its attempts to collect and analyze data about overseas listening patterns. The heart of the problem lay not in the OWI's ability to persuade congressmen, but in grappling with the complex and difficult issues of whether or not people listened to the Voice of America, who those listeners were, why they listened, what they wanted to know, how they could be further encouraged to listen, and most difficult of all, how these listeners interpreted what they did hear—when they did hear it.[10]

Although some of the problems faced by the Analysis Bureau were peculiar to war, many were inherent in the nature of audience research as the field had developed in the late thirties and early forties. The wartime efforts were part of larger trends within the field of mass communications.

The field of public opinion studies took on new life after World War I, when political leaders, intellectuals, and educators became concerned with understanding the profound influence propaganda—through speeches, newspapers, magazines, posters, and leaflets—had exerted on both enemy and home populations during the Great War. After the war there had issued a great flood of autobiographies, magazine articles, and serious academic studies aimed first at understanding the art of propaganda and then combating it. The most outstanding of these books was Harold Lasswell's *Propaganda Technique in the World War,* published in 1927, but it was only one among many. Americans wanted to safeguard democracy from the seemingly insidious effect of propaganda—a term invariably used in its most pejorative sense. Propaganda was, according to Lasswell's classic definition, "the control of opinion by significant symbols," from which public officials felt they could not guard American citizens.[11] Moreover, the seemingly rapid and devastating effects of German propaganda after 1933 reinforced the fears of propaganda first generated in World War I.

These examinations merged in the thirties with a newer set of social science advances American market research was working out. In the 1930s the growth of commercial radio broadcasting increased the importance and profitability of this research. Radio, which unlike newspapers or magazines could not count its audience by tabulating the number of issues sold, had to discover ways to prove the dollar value of broadcasting time to potential advertisers. Radio researchers therefore began directly sampling the au-

dience. Networks, individual stations, talent firms, and advertisers all wanted
the information and subsidized this field of research.[12]

In the late thirties these two academic specialties—propaganda studies and
radio market research—merged to form a new research field called mass communications. The questions of political behavior addressed by propaganda
theorists, and of listening habits addressed by market researchers, combined
in a broad investigation of audience behavior and the influence radio listening had on American citizens.

The two most important figures in this new field were Paul F. Lazarsfeld
and Harold Lasswell. Lazarsfeld, a Viennese sociologist who had fled the
Nazis in the mid-thirties, became director of the Office of Radio Research,
first at Princeton and later at Columbia University. Lazarsfeld's goal was
to examine how radio broadcasters got their message on the air and how
it came to be accepted by listeners. He wanted to know what effect radio
was having on society, an interest that had long-range implications for
American public policymakers. He and his institute took a very broad view
of the subject, ranging in their investigations from interviews with soap opera
fans to the relationship of radio to nationwide trends in popular music to
the psychology of radio commercials.[13]

Simultaneously, Harold Lasswell, a professor at the University of Chicago, continued his studies of the influence of mass communications on
the American people. Unlike Lazarsfeld, Lasswell did not confine his pur-
view to radio but included political speeches, newspapers, and the entire
range of political communications. It was Lasswell who formulated the standard paradigm for researchers in the field: who, said what, to whom, and
to what effect. Like Lazarsfeld, Lasswell was convinced that he could measure the effect of mass communications on society and politics.[14] He went
so far as to criticize his own early work for its lack of clear social science
method, by which he meant "the sampling, recording and summarizing
of sources."[15]

Out of this work, particularly that of the Office of Radio Research, five
major research techniques became the standard operating procedures for
the field, especially for the measurement of radio audiences. First, the investigator could use the poll, or the short interview. Second, he or she
could set up a panel of respondents, which allowed repeated interviewing
of the same listeners over a period of time. Third, the researcher could conduct an intensive interview. Fourth were community studies. And finally,
radio broadcasts themselves (or propaganda) could be examined through
content analysis.[16]

Despite an interest in following such lines of scholarship, the Overseas

Branch propagandists obviously could not use these methods of radio audience measurement in the same way as could the domestic practitioners. Audience research in the thirties and early forties depended on personal interviews, written responses, and telephone surveys that were predicated on a wide and scientifically determined sample of the total audience. The investigator could, for example, poll a carefully chosen group of American households by telephone, calling up to ask if the respondent was listening, and if so, to what program.

Researchers of domestic listening habits encountered many pitfalls, not the least of which was the honesty of respondents, who might well claim to be listening to whatever program they felt the interviewer thought was the most educational or popular show on the air at that time. But if these ratings were flawed, domestic research had better tools than anything available to the analysts of overseas propaganda, who could not interview people living in Lyons, Rheims, or Nancy, let alone those in Berlin, Frankfurt, or Rome. There was simply no means by which American propagandists could directly question listeners in Europe.[17]

Because polls could not be taken in Europe, the OWI substituted interviews of refugees. This method, however, raised the fundamental question of the accuracy of the sample. Whom to interview had become, by the beginning of World War II, a major component of the emerging science of audience measurement. Any survey, researchers soon learned, was only as good as the accuracy with which it was planned and taken. To be valid, a sample had to be crafted in such a way as to create a miniature scale of the larger world of the radio audience. Thus, the technique by which investigators selected samples was fundamental to the very process of the audience survey.[18] But those who left Europe in 1942, 1943, and 1944 were those whose lives were threatened or those who hated fascism. Given the politics of these refugees, how much could they know about the listening habits of the supporters of Marshal Pétain, or the fence-sitting *attentistes* of Vichy France? The problem was compounded by the fact that it was illegal to tune in to Allied radio. People who did violate the law kept the fact that they listened to the Voice of America a guarded secret; it was a clandestine act of resistance in and of itself, and not an activity of which one spoke lightly or openly.

If interviews with refugees provided a problematic source of information, other methods were worse. Analysts read letters written directly to Allied stations, but the question of who wrote these letters applied here too. As one British investigator wrote, "Granted that letters are a sample – in the sense that they are a fragment of a larger whole – the difficulty is that there can be nothing in the letters themselves to throw light on the size or nature of this larger whole."[19]

Researchers combed newspapers and read intercepted mail, but these sources were subject to intense Axis censorship and therefore presented another set of thorny problems. The only remaining research tool was content analysis of enemy programs. Researchers listened to enemy radio for any attempt on the part of the Axis to respond to American propaganda. An answer, they assumed, indicated that the enemy had heard the broadcast and decided to reply because they worried about the effectiveness of that particular American broadcast or propaganda line. But the Axis program might merely mean that the Voice of America broadcast had been picked up by a German, French, or Italian monitor, not that ordinary citizens had listened to the show. Furthermore, propagandists on both sides of the Atlantic increasingly avoided responding to what the other side had said. They felt that to do so would tempt their own listeners to reset their dials to enemy radio, and they feared that any response would be interpreted as political or military weakness. Moreover, French authorities monitored a broad band of stations, including German Occupied Radio Paris, Vichy radio, the BBC, and the Swiss Radio Sottens, so that the Americans could never be sure to whom the Axis was responding.[20]

Content analysis proved useful in understanding much about the Axis, from morale to policy, but it was not as successful in illuminating the extent and or nature of overseas listening. This problem was, in fact, anticipated by propaganda analysts. As Lazarsfeld and Robert K. Merton wrote in 1943, "The major task of content-analysis is to provide clues to probable responses to the propaganda. But this is not enough." What was needed, they argued, was "interviews with members of audiences; interviews of a special type, which we shall call the 'focused interview.'" But this technique was not available to the researcher of international propaganda in wartime.[21]

The BBC, which conducted extensive research on listening habits in enemy and enemy-occupied nations, occasionally opened its bimonthly surveys with a caveat to the reader. Interviews, the BBC explained, constituted the single most useful body of evidence. But even they "cannot . . . be held to represent a reliable cross-section of the French audience, and still less of the total potential audience." In the report of June 18, 1943, for example, over 14 percent of the total respondents were Jews—out of a national percentage in France of 0.5 percent. The vast majority of interviewees came from the upper professional or middle classes, whereas fewer than 5 percent were women. "The industrial population of the large cities," warned the report, "is represented only by employers, by politicians . . . and by a Christian Trade Union leader, himself a black-coated worker." This, bemoaned the BBC, left only a few Bretons, whose coastal residence made escape relatively easy if the need should arise, to "speak direct for 'le petit peuple.'" Their evidence, the BBC researchers admitted, "could not possibly stand peacetime scientific tests."[22]

The American propagandists understood these limitations, and few of them believed the Analysis Bureau reports.[23] Many were not inclined to take seriously the findings of a group of academics and often did so only after they had gotten to know personally the social scientists doing the work.[24] When asked how carefully he paid attention to the audience surveys issued by the Bureau of Research and Analysis, the head of the Low Countries desk responded, not at all. The bureau's sampling, he explained, was "like a lottery ticket. . . . There was an effort, but I believe it was a wasted effort."[25]

Edward Barrett's criticisms were even stronger. In September 1943 Barrett, then head of the Office of News and Features, wrote to Sherwood and Barnes from London that radio listeners naturally and always tuned in to the station they heard best, the one that had the strongest and clearest signal. For this single reason, Barrett told his colleagues—without taking up the issue of the competitive quality of the two nations' broadcasts—Europeans almost always chose the BBC and not the Voice of America. "American stations are simply not in the running," Barrett reported. "I know you have heard this before, and I know it is an unpopular conclusion in New York, but please, for God's sake, let's take it seriously this time and not brush it aside because Lennie Carleton has been able to find a few fragmentary reports and use them as the basis for a story of thousands around the world listening regularly to American stations." Others have told you just what I am saying, Barrett pleaded. They even argue that "the number of persons listening regularly to the Voice of America *direct from America* is less than the number of people in New York working on the shows. I am inclined to agree."[26]

Skeptical as the propagandists were of audience reports, they did listen to some suggestions for change and used them to promote a transformation of the Voice which they felt was necessary for other reasons. This raises the obvious question of why, when they did not believe the evidence presented by the researchers, the propagandists seemed to listen and obey. The answer is that they listened because they wanted to do so, and they obeyed their own instincts rather than the suggestions of social scientists, whose reports reinforced the direction in which their thinking was already moving. This is a crucial distinction. The propagandists were not operating according to rules established by social science theory; they were flying, as it were, by the seat of their pants. This absence of any systematic sociological or psychological foundation to their work allowed them to adjust American propaganda quite freely to the changes they felt, or sensed, were taking place in Europe. Social scientists therefore became useful when they provided the propagandists with justifications for what they wanted to do in any case. Leonard Doob, the Yale sociologist and prominent American expert on propaganda and public opinion who became head of the Overseas Branch's Bureau of Overseas Intelligence, wrote that "policy-makers were more than eager to be guided by research findings when a report seemed . . . to justify one of their own propaganda ideas."[27] The chief of the Low Countries desk put forth the same explanation more bluntly. He listened to these critiques, he explained, because he could "not believe that somebody would listen, at the risk of his or her life, to the radio, to hear some literary masterpiece. It's that simple."[28]

What the propagandists heard reinforced their ill-defined, unarticulated but growing sense that the era of agitprop had ended. In mid-1943, the Voice of America had to create a new broadcasting style in response to the demands of the war and the reality of American foreign policy. The liberal propagandists found political news freighted with such unpalatable decisions as Roosevelt's determination to accept Marshal Badoglio as the new prime minister of Italy and his continued unwillingness to recognize de Gaulle or the French Committee of National Liberation. At the same time, the propagandists knew that European audiences were saturated by propaganda of all sorts, especially Axis propaganda, and that in order to penetrate the increasingly thick wall of indifference to rhetoric and the whole variety of techniques of persuasion, the Americans had to sound neutral and newsworthy. Audience reports lent a special legitimacy to a shift in propaganda strategy which was already taking place.

Complaints from abroad may have only underscored these trends, but the propagandists listened. Tales of discontent began coming into the Overseas Branch during the spring of 1943. As early as March, the American chargé d'affaires ad interim in Tangier cabled that his French informants found the Voice of America filled with too much talk—*bavardage*—and too little news. What they did like, he went on, was the BBC program "Les Français Parlent aux Français," thirteen minutes of detailed news followed by crisp commentary.[29] The flow of complaints had increased by the following summer. The BBC monitoring report spoke in no uncertain terms when it said that "the thirst for news . . . is a universal phenomenon. . . . While the strain and stress of everyday life in France today causes people to turn to the radio for news of their coming liberation, it also makes them turn away from every broadcast other than news." Listening in France was illegal, while the Germans continued to demand French labor and materiel; in this environment what was said had to be serious. Anything that seemed either chatty or, worse, too overt an attempt to persuade or manipulate – what the listeners thought of as "propaganda" – had, the BBC report warned, to be shed. The French were in no mood to put up with drama or publicity campaigns. "All words are at a discount in a country haunted by hunger and deportations."[30]

American surveys began repeating the same line. "Every listener wants 'direct, straight and unvarnished' news," Percy Winner, Sherwood's close friend and colleague, cabled the leaders of the Overseas Branch in September.[31] And by November the Bureau of Information was instructing the Voice that straight news was best.[32] The message had been sent, and by mid-1943 the Voice of America heard it and began acting accordingly.

"More news" was as much a plea for a change in content as it was a request for an alteration in form. But audience reports also criticized both the use of four voices and the impersonality of agitprop characters. The multiple voices, the American listening post in Bern reported, sounded disembodied to the French. They tended to confuse listeners rather than grab their attention.[33] "People have to keep re-tuning their ears to various voice levels," the OWI representative in Spain argued, and they had to do so against a background of static and jamming.[34]

By September Werner Michel's weekly guidance reported that "semi-dramatic styles of presentation are often harsh and dull. . . . No one wants to be shouted at. . . . They want the news unbiased, and trustworthy . . . presented sincerely and, perhaps, pleasantly." The guidance jettisoned the very idea of multiple voices and agitprop drama. "This does not by any means imply that readings need be monotonous or colorless," the guidance concluded. "To speak intelligently requires interpretation. To interpret requires absolute comprehension of text and context."[35]

The BBC used named commentators and speakers and employed single announcers, the OWI representative in Spain pointed out, and thus the British broadcasts felt recognizable, familiar, and comfortable to their audience. The Voice of America, on the other hand, "is the voice of a ghost. [Listeners] are unable, as yet, to imagine what the body looks like (or should we say what the soul is like)."[36]

The Voice of America staff began to wonder if U.S. propaganda was believable. The pattern of multiple voices and agitprop forms, a listener report made in the late summer argued, sounded flat and uninspired. "We listen to your broadcasts but we don't feel that you are talking to us. . . . Every hour we hear the same . . . voices talking impersonally to an audience that needs, above everything, presence." The American reporter admitted to a certain skepticism about these complaints. After all, the relationship between broadcaster and listener was too complex to be so easily defined or measured. "But when a high percentage of the audience agrees that a broadcast is colorless, we should take notice."[37] Thus, listener reports justified a shift in American propaganda necessitated by diplomacy and war.

The propagandists read the audience reports and listened to British arguments against a background of changing social science theories on the achievable goals and potential effects of propaganda. American social scientists slowly reworked theories about the mass media and their ability to influence readers or listeners. Although little of this thinking was directly concerned with the Voice of America, the propagandists nevertheless heard the arguments. Like rumors whispered in a crowd, inspiring anxiety, these ideas influenced the propagandists' thinking because they were part of a changing intellectual climate that challenged the effectiveness of agitprop propaganda.[38]

Rethinking mass communications theory began with research into the nature of an audience: who, heard what, and why, to paraphrase Lasswell's earlier formulation. Before the war social scientists commonly held the view that the thoughts and opinions of the radio listening audience could be altered through the conscious manipulation of a whole range of symbols and arguments. This assumption emerged in large measure from the thinking of late-nineteenth-century European academics who addressed the question of the nature and behavior of the crowd, and in particular, that of revolutionary mobs. In the twentieth century sociologists on both sides of the Atlantic delineated theories of what they labeled mass society. These theories presumed that industrialization, and with it urbanization, mass transportation, and communications, had transformed social relationships. People's lives were no longer lived within the context of small, cohesive primary groups such as family, guild, and church. Instead, men and women now led lives governed by a new anarchic individualism. The old universal values were gone; an educated elite no longer existed to shape opinion and taste; mobility created increasing anxiety over individual status and place; each individual took many roles and played them in a succession of situations. Because of this, theorists of mass society argued, the individual had lost a coherent sense of self, and the stage had thus been "set for the charismatic leader."[39]

These ideas influenced the fields of public opinion and mass communications as they emerged and changed during the twentieth century. In *Social Psychology*, published in 1924, Floyd Allport argued that people did not have to be congregated in one physical spot in order to behave like a crowd. Ten years later Allport's brother Gordon, working with Hadley Cantril, directly applied this notion to radio. Radio broadcasting, Allport and Cantril wrote, could make the individual listener believe "that others are thinking as he thinks and are sharing his emotions." Thus radio, "more than any other medium of communication, is capable of forming a crowd mind among individuals who are physically separated from one another." The radio audience could become more than a crowd: "The fostering of the mob spirit must be counted as one of the by-products of radio."[40]

*[handwritten marginal note: Psychology of Radio (1935)]*

In the mid-thirties the American sociologist Herbert Blumer reopened the discussion of the nature of the mass society, and by extension the mass audience.[41] A mass, he argued, was "an elementary and spontaneous collective grouping . . . an anonymous group." The behavior of such a collection of individuals transcended what any particular person within it might or might not do. It was not a crowd. Crowds needed to be physically collected in one geographic place so that the individuals within that crowd could influence each other through their heightened moods and tensions. A mass, on the other hand, was the aggregate of many individuals whose lives were not governed by collective traditions, rules, or organizations that in the past had guided people's political actions. Blumer examined the radio audience through his lens of *mass,* or collection of random individuals. He argued that it was because people were uprooted from their moorings by geographic migrations, changes in occupation, and a new, intense exposure to newspapers, films, and public education that they responded so intensely to the propaganda campaigns of World War I and Nazi Germany.[42] In an era in which "impersonality has supplanted personal loyalty to leaders," Lasswell wrote in a concurring spirit, persuasion "must now be done by argument."[43]

The concept of a mass audiences led theorists during the twenties and thirties to assume that opinion could be grandly molded by propaganda. As Daniel Katz wrote in 1940, modern public opinion was less subject to the influence of an objective event than it was to the "agencies of symbol manipulation."[44] Writing about the success of Houseman and Welles's production of "War of the Worlds," Hadley Cantril argued that radio was by its very nature the best possible medium not only for disseminating information, but "for arousing in [the American people] a common sense of fear or joy, and for exciting them to similar reactions directed toward a single objective."[45] The majority of social scientists in the years between the two world wars believed that radio, and with it radio propaganda, was an overwhelmingly powerful weapon that could be aimed at the masses of people who, in turn, could be thereby persuaded to take action. It was a lesson relearned and reinforced by Hitler's propaganda campaign presaging his blitz-krieg across western Europe, which seemed to prove that wars were now to be fought not just by guns and bullets, but by words.

Pervasive as this faith in propaganda was, by the late thirties there were signs that it was already breaking down.[46] In 1939 Hans J. Speier observed that the more distant an audience was from the reality of an event, the more easily persuadable it was. But if citizens knew simple facts about the course of, for example, a war, more abstract manipulations of symbols, such as references to patriotism, would not change their opinions.[47]

An attack on the concept of the mass audience began wholeheartedly with research done by Lazarsfeld and his colleagues. In 1943 Lazarsfeld and Robert K. Merton published the results of some of the work they had been doing on domestic radio and film propaganda. They defined propaganda as "any and all sets of symbols which influence opinion, belief or action," and they argued that propaganda had to date been far too generally discussed with little real empirical research. This deficiency, they declared, they had set out to correct.[48]

Lazarsfeld and Merton included a discussion of audience. Any audience had to be understood as first and foremost a general collection of individuals, all of whom have different "states of mind on the given issue."[49] They could not be assumed to be malleable, their minds a kind of tabula rasa, as was implicit in the theory of the mass audience favored by Katz, Cantril, and Blumer. People held long-established opinions and possessed their own volumes of information, and anything a propagandist told them would be judged against that background. Thus, Lazarsfeld and Merton reasoned, if propaganda flew in the face of what the audience already believed, these discrepancies would damage the credibility of the propaganda and not change the audience's point of view. No amount of conscious manipulation of symbols could shift the weight of preexisting knowledge and belief. Propagandists therefore had to be careful to appraise the state of mind of their intended audience. Lazarsfeld and Merton presented a concept of audience which was fragmented and diverse. Accordingly propaganda, to be effective, had to address selected audiences rather than general ones.[50]

Lazarsfeld and Merton drew quite specific conclusions about what all this meant for the propagandist. To be effective, propaganda had to be governed by facts. It had to pander to a desire for "specific, almost technological information." It had to rely on concrete incidents and circumstantial details, which would lead listeners to where the propagandist wanted to take them but not arouse their suspicions. Propaganda, Lazarsfeld and Merton argued, had to be something akin to education; U.S. wartime propaganda had to teach listeners slowly about America and American war goals in order to dispel distrust and plant a new faith. "If propaganda is restricted wholly to exhortation, it runs the risk of intensifying distrust," they concluded. "The propaganda of facts can be utilized to supplant cynicism with common understandings."[51]

Lazarsfeld again transformed mass media studies with *The People's Choice*. In this book Lazarsfeld and two colleagues, Bernard Berelson and Hazel Gaudet, conducted a series of interviews with six hundred men and women on what they thought and for whom they would vote in the 1944 presidential election. The voters repeated a startling theme: personal discussions consciously and directly influenced their thinking; newspapers, magazines, and the radio barely figured in their conscious decisions.[52] Lazarsfeld and others subsequently reformulated the theory of the flow of information. Whereas before Lazarsfeld's studies social scientists had believed that information followed a "one-step" flow, henceforth they defined a "two-step" flow, according to which the media spoke to a national elite, who in turn addressed the common people.[53] Thus Hans Speier came to believe that propaganda campaigns should focus on selected groups in a foreign population "whose self-interest, predisposition and organization are conducive to deviation." To Speier, writing in the mid-fifties, trying to reach the enemy population at large had become obsolete.[54]

Over the course of the Second World War social scientists began to reject the notion that the audience was some magical equation of mass and crowd. They no longer believed that propaganda could transform thought or action. In between the propagandist and the audience lay a whole series of intervening factors, ready, as it were, to ambush the unprepared propagandist.[55]

The changes in social science theories indirectly undermined the assumptions that lay behind agitprop propaganda, which had assumed the immediate effect of radio broadcasting. The new theories challenged the very notion of a mass audience. They supported the growing interest in news as propaganda, in what Lazarsfeld and Merton had so aptly described as the propaganda of facts.[56]

These changes demanded a reworking of the propagandists' style of programming and their definition of the goals of propaganda. "The purpose of propaganda warfare is to divide, confuse, and subvert the enemy; stimulate and command the allegiance of friends and potential friends," an in-house report had stated in the winter of 1943. It went on to define propaganda. "Propaganda warfare is not merely a battle of words. It is a battle for people's minds and through their minds their physical actions." Propaganda, the essay argued, "is not the short-wave radio program but the act committed because of the message carried by that program." As the conductors of the orchestra of radio voices, the "OWI's main task is . . . active resistance . . . encouraged through great emphasis upon acts of sabotage in other occupied countries."[57]

Werner Michel proclaimed an end to the era of agitprop in a broadcasting division guidance of September 26, 1943, just three months after Houseman had left New York for Hollywood. Henceforth the style of broadcasting was to be closer to that of domestic American news and the world news round-up. Voices were to change only with a shift in subject matter, and not as a means of bringing drama or characterization to the news.[58]

What he, and the Radio Program Bureau, intended was that propaganda was not to be conceived of as directed at "the masses," but at "politically allied individuals [who] listen" to the Voice of America. This view reflected a new philosophy of propaganda and a different conception of audience. The theory that the mass media could influence their audience directly through what academics called a one-step flow of information justified the liberals' proposal that they could tell the French to rise up and expect that French listeners would do so. It was part of the intellectual context of the liberal propaganda of Sherwood and his colleagues. The adoption of the theory of a two-step flow of information removed that context and justified the new conservative order of news. Propaganda after 1943 was meant to inform a wide variety of Europeans. It aimed to educate them about America in order to convince them that the American, and Allied, occupation of post-liberation Europe would be benign. It told them about the course of the war in order to bring them along with events, and it prepared them to help the Allied invaders. It emphatically did not seek to incite popular resistance. Voice of America broadcasters were to talk about the United States "in a simple, direct fashion . . . if they can sound convincing about their own beliefs without being pompous, they can make friends."[59] No longer was Voice of America a radio theater of agitprop. It was a carefully designed newspaper delivering a message of liberation.

During the 1930s, art was an agent of change. John Houseman's Voice of America was based on what had become, by 1941, an instinctive assumption about the role of the artist in society, within which the applied arts of the mass media were weapons in the battle for a better world.

Reality, according to this view, was not a stack of facts, waiting to be recorded and put in order, there to inform or instruct. Reality imposed on the artist the obligation to take information and rework it in a special vision of life and society and man's relationship to that society. Art was to be used to make the world a better place by presenting images of what had to be changed and the benefits that social, political, or economic reforms could bring. Art could transform society.

The relationship of the artist to society altered in the forties. "The present problems of documentary film-making," a British filmmaker reflected in the years following the Second World War, "are not the sole products of its own shortcomings, they inevitably reflect the social, cultural and economic thinking of the time." He continued: "In the 'thirties there were issues to be fought over. . . . today, the urge for reform has dimmed, and with it the incentive to make films to inspire action. Instead there is a parrot cry for information. . . ."[60]

The shift in the role of art emerged from larger political alterations. Henry Luce, for example, the publisher of *Time* and *Life* magazines and founder of one of the largest American media empires, observed the coming change with remarkable prescience in *The American Century,* which he wrote in 1941. Britain could not win the war alone, he stated. "America and only America can effectively state the war aims of this war." He continued: "The big, important point to be made here is simply that the complete opportunity of leadership is *ours*" (emphasis in original). America was on the brink of becoming a world power that would dominate international relations and world trade in the immediate future.[61]

The United States entered this future, however, with more fears than proposals for how to handle its new opportunities. "As we look toward the future, Luce began his book, "we are filled with foreboding." America did not know how to become a world power. Luce tried to give the country a blueprint for the future. "To lead the world would never have been an easy task. To revive the hope of that lost opportunity makes the task now infinitely harder than it would have been before."[62]

Luce was a prophet of a new U.S. imperialism. He wanted Americans to shape world trade, to train the future leaders of the world, and to make sure that at least enough of the world remained democratic and supportive of the United States to enable it to thrive. It was, as he said, "our time to be the powerhouse from which the ideals spread throughout the world . . . lifting the life of mankind from the level of the beasts to what the Psalmists called a little lower than the angels."[63]

Luce may have been the Rudyard Kipling of mid-twentieth-century America, but his faith in the United States and his ideas for the future help explain why the role of the artist in America altered during and right after the war. Before the war Americans knew that the nation had to change in order to meet the challenge of the Depression and a fraying social order. Everyone had a potential role to play in the process of winning that struggle. But once the war came, once it had become clear that America and her allies would win the war, and in the process of fighting the war, once the American economy had returned to prosperity, the United States was no longer under siege from poverty and despair.

Beginning in 1943, as Allied victory became only a question of time and the future role of the United States in the world order could be glimpsed, the new enemy became success. The gift of world power generated a confusion that thrust Americans back into themselves: to basics, to facts, to letting things speak for themselves. As C. Wright Mills wrote in 1959:

> The very shaping of history now outpaces the ability of men to orient themselves with cherished values. And which values? Even when they do not panic, men often sense that older ways of feeling and thinking have collapsed and that newer beginnings are ambiguous to the point of moral stasis.[64]

This change in sentiment had many repercussions. The shift from a belief in a one-step to a two-step flow of communications–from the direct influence of propaganda on an audience to the indirect influence of information on leaders, and through them on followers–emerged from a growing disbelief in the power of words, or art, to change society. This retraction was grounded less on observation and a "scientific" approach to the study of society than in long-term social goals.

The propagandists saw these changes in terms of the world around them. They believed that the incident of the moronic little king had provided a demarcation line between what Warburg, Barnes, and others saw as a liberal stage and a State Department–directed, conservative stage in American overseas propaganda. It made them understand that the war was no longer about resistance and political democracy, but sheer, hard, military victory and Allied occupation. American propaganda could no longer revolve around themes of self-liberation, as the Voice had originally done.

The propagandists knew that victory meant the Allied occupation of Europe. This single fact determined the new direction American propaganda had to take in 1943 and, to an even greater extent, in 1944. In 1942, while the question of who would win the war hung fire, the possibility of Allied occupation remained irrelevant. But after 1943 it became the crucial point of American foreign policy and American propaganda. Henceforth, the main goal of the Voice would be to educate Europeans to accept the coming of the American liberators. As the leader of the Low Countries desk later observed, "The only features I felt were of interest were to show friendship on the part of America and the might of America, because the mightier America, the sooner liberation." Features after 1943, he explained, were to reveal a "cultured America, and not an uncivilized wild America, to permit American military government. That I felt was useful; but the rest. . . ."[65]

From the summer of 1943 on, it became increasingly clear that the job of propaganda was to educate the French to accept the Allies. The French could help in this process, but acts of resistance, no matter how fulsomely praised, were part of the larger Allied war of liberation, which the French could neither initiate nor control. Although all talk of resistance was not abandoned, propaganda had to change from mass incitement to individual education.

When social scientists argued that the mass media could not mold opinion but only provide facts, they had retreated from the forefront of the battle to build a better society. When propagandists came to believe that the best job they could do, for America and for the world, was to provide information, they too had withdrawn from the task of remolding society.

# 7

# *Broadcasting the News*

## *From Guidances to Programs*

THE CHANGES that took place over 1943 reflected the certainty that the Allies had won the war and that victory was only a question of time. Consequently, the Voice increasingly portrayed the Resistance in France as a sign that the French people, unlike their Nazi collaborationist government, had never abandoned the Allied war effort. The existence of the Resistance, the Voice now implied, demonstrated that France was at war on the side of the Allies. No longer was France neutral, or what the French themselves had termed *attentiste*. As a guidance noted the following February 1943, "The world recognizes that France now is resuming its natural position, as the spearhead of European resistance to the domination of the Germans."[1]

After victory in Tunisia this message expanded. Allied victory had become more certain, and American propaganda predicted the crumbling of the Axis. "Without inciting to revolt, the tone and tempo of our output should pick up in intensity," argued a guidance that May. "We should make people . . . feel that something is happening—something over and above our military successes—and that they have a part in it. The Axis [is] falling apart from within."[2] It was a theme that remained, in its largest outlines, constant throughout 1943. "Our overall task . . . remains the same, and will probably continue unchanged for some time to come," explained a central directive in December 1943: "to maintain France as an important factor in the defeat of the common enemy . . . by recognizing and encouraging resistance appropriate to the strategic situation."[3]

By the summer of 1943, the Voice was reporting acts of sabotage within France which, by their very size and success, constituted propaganda for resistance. "Of 120,000 French workers designated for forced labor in Germany," the radio said that August, "only 20,000 could be sent across the Rhine." It concluded with words meant to encourage those who were afraid to defy the Germans: "In many places those workers who evade don't hide any more. The whole population is with them. The local authority, even if they wanted to, would be powerless to execute their orders."[4]

The German labor campaign had become furious and destructive. Manhunts were increasing within France. By March, over two million French workers were prisoners in Germany.[5] Support for Pétain and his government slowly waned after the Germans invaded Vichy, the Allies liberated the French empire, and the Germans intensified the relève.[6] Propaganda against the relève became a way of reaching an already sympathetic audience, and it pervaded Voice broadcasts throughout 1943 as it had during 1942.

The campaign against the relève did not eliminate propaganda encouraging the French to resist the Germans in other ways as well. The Voice suggested sabotaging German transportation systems in order to maim industrial production.[7] It encouraged soldiers and sailors to join the Resistance.[8] And it tried to persuade French peasants to withhold their crops from the Germans.[9] "Our men, our wheat, our wine, our machines and our raw material must not be handed to the Germans," urged a broadcast in August. "Sabotage everywhere. Sabotage absolutely everything which can be in any way useful to the Germans."[10] But labor remained the most important and best issue with which to hammer home resistance to German demands on the French.

But if resistance provided a constant theme, its uses and meanings changed in critical ways over the course of 1943. American propagandists quickly realized that resistance would provoke Gestapo reprisals. It was therefore bad tactics for American propagandists to encourage the French to take action when the Americans themselves were not on French soil, armed and prepared to back up their exhortations with protective military action. Accordingly, they began distinguishing between covert acts of sabotage whose authorship the Germans would not be able to uncover and overt acts that could bring swift vengeance. As early as February, a regional directive advised the French desk to tell its listeners to take care "while committing acts of resistance [so as] not to provoke mass arrests, deportations or more drastic reprisals by hasty or ill-considered action."[11]

The British influenced the Americans. By March, the PWE and the BBC were complaining that Voice broadcasts overstressed French resistance and that their programs employed too rousing a tone. The Americans would incite the French to general sabotage or revolt, the British argued, at a time when the French were beginning to feel that a cross-channel invasion, in reality still more than a year away, was just around the corner.[12] American propagandists accordingly muted their tone. They continued to advise the French to make subtle forms of resistance, although even so they increasingly suggested that this be done within the framework of a resistance organization rather than as lonely and single acts of defiance.[13] But caution was increasingly urged. "Repeat . . . our admonition to remain calm and take no unorganized premature action of a kind that endangers their lives," a directive in July instructed.[14] And, with the encouragement of the British, the Voice began repeating specific warnings and instructions issued by the French clandestine radio station, "Honneur et Patrie."[15]

Caution led to a distancing of Voice of America propaganda. By the summer of 1943 the propagandists no longer directed the French to take action, as they had in 1942 and early 1943, but instead reported on events in France, citing as their source French or European papers or enemy broadcasts. The factual tone removed the Voice from the role of exhorter to that of reporter. In January the Voice program on the "Resistance Front" quite typically began:

VOICE: In every country oppressed by Germany, resistance is growing.
VOICE: The German recruiting agents double their efforts to hire workers from the occupied countries.
VOICE: But the workers know that when they go to work in Germany, they are neither more nor less than civilian prisoners.[16]

But seven months later an equally typical news piece urging resistance went like this:

The workers of Lyons have addressed a new appeal to the French people, to exhort them to resist the Nazis and to sabotage the German war machine by every means at their disposition;
Frenchmen, declares the appeal. . . .[17]

By August, the Voice made the French speak to each other, or took stories from European papers and American correspondents. The Voice had become the channel through which information was passed on to the French people.

Important as were changing conditions within France, as well as mounting British dissatisfaction with Voice output, the fundamental reason why the Voice of America toned down its propaganda on resistance lay with the American war effort and American foreign policy. After the Torch invasion, American military commitment in Europe grew. No longer did resistance have to substitute for an Allied military force, nor did the Americans want it to. The function of resistance, at least for the Americans, changed. Increasingly, the Allies hoped that the Resistance would provide local support for Allied troops of liberation.[18]

The Voice began to define the Resistance as French preparation for the coming Allied invasion. In June, the propagandists dropped the very term "resistance" and substituted in its place "the movement of liberation."[19] By July the facts of the case had become even clearer. "France can be liberated only by the total military defeat of the Axis power and the driving of the Axis invaders out of French territory," a regional directive pronounced.[20] By August, instructions had become explicit. Frenchmen were to make sure that they worked within an organizational structure that was prepared to help the liberation forces. Every individual "should determine exactly what service he could render to facilitate the task of the Allied forces. . . ."[21] In November, Warburg met with Ritchie Calder in London to create joint OWI-PWE plans for propaganda to France over the coming winter. The resulting document expressed their views on what were to be the major propaganda goals of both countries. Propaganda was to persuade the French to pour their energies, once devoted to passive or active resistance, into support for the Allied forces to liberation: "to complete the process of sustaining, preparing and mobilizing the French people, in the period prior to military operations, for active cooperation now, during military operations and after liberation, within the framework of United Nations plans."[22] Even for Warburg, the meaning attached to mobilizing the French for war had changed. In 1941 and 1942 it had symbolized resistance as an uprising for democracy and freedom. But by 1943, and especially into the last years of war, it meant Allied victory, French cooperation, and American power.

The year following the Allied invasion of North Africa also witnessed significant changes in what the Voice told its French audience about military events and the progress of the war. As with the topic of resistance, war coverage was not merely a matter of reporting the news. The propagandists selected specific themes that the language desks then translated into news and features. The question we must ask, therefore, is what messages the propagandists attempted to convey through their coverage of military news.

There were two distinct periods in propaganda about the military progress of the war during 1943: the half year between the Torch invasion and victory in Tunisia on May 13, and the half year that followed. Before June the propagandists were still afraid of military defeat, or at least of a war prolonged to the point of unendurable exhaustion. Nevertheless, for the first time military events pointed to a turning of the war: the Allied invasion of North Africa, the Russian victory over the Germans at Stalingrad, and the Allied victory in North Africa. The propagandists experienced an enormous sense of relief and reported the events with undiminished enthusiasm until the lull in the war in the European theater in late May and June gave them time to reflect on and rethink the role of political objectives within the daily propaganda output.

On a concrete level there were great advantages to this emphasis on war news. The propagandists believed that stories of victory were overwhelmingly more effective than had been any of the propaganda ammunition they had possessed throughout 1942. As a guidance written soon after the North African invasion stated, "news about Allied action will have a more massive effect on French workers and people than editorials about what the French have, are [or] will do."[23] War news had other advantages. It was a means of avoiding discussions of topics the propagandists felt would hurt their cause, such as the Allied collaboration with Admiral Darlan. One directive advised the French desk: "Avoid the political implications of developments in North Africa."[24] There were other reasons to stick close to hard, military reporting. Trying to second-guess troop action in the midst of battle was tempting, especially as American newspapers occasionally did so. But doing so ran the risk of reporting what had not in fact happened and making misstatements that might run counter to military objectives or harm long-term goals. The guidances warned the propagandists to adhere to communiqués and not race on ahead.[25]

The military message in the first half of 1943 was one of mounting success that would bring with it political liberation. In the second half of the year the theme shifted to Axis defeat and coming Allied victory but no longer addressed political rewards. In part this change was due to the victorious Tunisian campaign, and a new tone can be dated to the directives of June. But it was also a result of the episode of the moronic little king. Because the State Department, the military, and Congress all watched over Voice of America propaganda to see that it did not run outside the grooves of official foreign policy, the propagandists retreated to, or perhaps more aptly were forced into, the safe harbor of hard news. This was the lesson of the summer of 1943. It came slowly, and Warburg repeatedly tried to inject political content into the war reports, but the overall picture presented by the Voice had henceforth to remain solidly military and strictly reportorial.

In war-starved and German-oppressed Europe, where living conditions had deteriorated badly and the issues of hunger, disease, and cold dominated the lives of most ordinary people, the principal question was when relief would come. The propagandists understood the importance of Allied military initiative, and a new tone of confidence emerged after the victory in Tunisia. "Create the conviction in the minds of our audiences that the Axis powers have failed," a central directive of late June stated, "a United Nations victory is inevitable."[26] The Voice could now put war news within what they called "purposeful solidarity" against "purposeless desperation . . . and disintegrating solidarity."[27]

As with news of the Resistance, particular themes remained constant throughout the year, threading together the output and giving consistency to the broadcasts. What changed over the year was not so much the major issues as how these issues were used and what images were thereby sketched.

Throughout the year the propagandists carefully and repeatedly described the war as global. Fighting took place not only along the southern periphery of the Axis—North Africa and Italy—but on the eastern front of the Soviet Union, in the Atlantic Ocean, in the air, and in the Pacific and Far East. This multiple-front war—in which the Resistance was significantly called the Resistance front—was a coalition effort in which the major Allied partners, Britain, the United States, Russia, and China, were joined by many other nations, from France to Australia. Thus if the war was not going well in one place, the Allies might be winning battles somewhere else. Propaganda pictured the Soviet Union as a firm ally of the United States and Britain and defined the all-important Russian victories such as that at Stalingrad as part of a united effort. The very size of the war effort and the number of countries that made up the United Nations lent substance to the notion that the Allies would eventually have to win because they were more numerous, prosperous, and strong. The Voice of America presented to its French audience all parts of the war effort, from domestic American production to the bombing of Germany and France to the battles in the Pacific, as united.

The most pressing political and military issue behind the theme of global warfare was the question of a second front. The Soviet Union was bearing the brunt of the war, a fact that all three leaders, Stalin, Churchill, and Roosevelt, knew but from which they reached different conclusions. Churchill, who was the most adamant in insisting that the British and Americans stick to the strategy of peripheral warfare, wired Hopkins in the spring of 1943: "I think it is an awful thing that in April, May and June, not a single American or British soldier will be killing a single German or Italian soldier while the Russians are chasing 185 divisions around."[28] But chasing divisions around avoided confronting the reality that the Russians were losing millions of soldiers and citizens. Stalin repeatedly demanded that the British and Americans launch a second front, a request that the propagandists had to meet by explaining the rationale behind the American and British delay. One means was to link the Russian front to the rest of the war and to insist on the war's global nature. But that was not enough.

Throughout the winter and spring the propagandists talked not about a second front, but about the encirclement of the Axis, a euphemism of sorts, an attempted answer to Stalin's demands.[29] After June, however, the propagandists began to confront the issue of a second front by saying that the Americans and British had gone beyond North Africa into Italy and direct confrontation in Europe. In July, a central directive argued that "stress should always be placed upon the fact that we are bringing the enemy to battle and forcing him to accept losses in men and resources."[30] By August the propagandists were more direct. "To overcome impatience over a second front: show that we are moving towards the liberation of Europe . . . as rapidly as possible."[31] But the leaders of the Overseas Branch knew that they were using words to paste over what was an unequal military burden. "It is not important to get into the arena of second-front argument," a directive instructed in October. There was no way, in fact, to argue the case head on, the directive continued, "in view of the great present disparity between the land effort of the United States and Great Britain and that of Russia."[32] Therefore the propagandists continued to present the American war effort in Europe in other ways, the most important of which was, as it had been in 1942, the Allied bombing of Germany, Austria, and France: the "air front."

The air war was important throughout 1943, but after June it assumed an even greater importance. As a guidance explained in August, the propagandists were to juxtapose Soviet ground action with Allied air action over Germany.[33] The "air war on Germany means that war is going on within Germany just as much as if Allied ground troops were fighting there."[34] The Voice repeatedly argued that the Americans and British were fighting the Germans directly by bombing their production centers and transportation systems, impairing their ability to fight by draining materiel and energy and demoralizing the German nation. Warburg articulated this view under one of his pseudonyms, Wallace Herrick, the Voice's military analyst who broadcast in English but whose opinions were quoted by the other language desks. "It is more and more evident," Warburg-alias-Herrick wrote, "that the effect of the Anglo-American air bombardments upon the German production centers and upon the German transport networks is beginning to have an effect on the war front itself." He went further, explicitly maintaining that the air war was impairing the ability of the Germans to fight the Russians. "The German armies on the field," by which he implied those on the Eastern front, "are thus more and more isolated."[35] By the end of the year the Voice was still broadcasting much the same sort of news. "Thursday in broad daylight, powerful formations of flying fortresses and American liberators," the Voice announced in mid-December, "have bombarded the military and industrial installations in the Northwest of Germany."[36]

The war had progressed, the Resistance in France had escalated, but the Americans were no closer to a second front in September than they had been in February. Only after Tehran could the Voice talk about opening a second front, and it was still a matter of expectations. Such promises were important, but they were balanced by the fear that excessive hopes would debilitate the people of France.

The broadcasts about military events projected a set of images about the war, international relations, and the United States. Propaganda about the war became increasingly self-confident, sure that the Axis was crumbling and the Allies would win. This self-confidence was reflected in the very nature of the shows. In May the Voice spoke in assertions that stretched beyond the truth. They exhorted listeners to accept claims that were on the edge of credibility, through the pounding of voices demanding that the listener hear and believe:

VOICE: In Tunisia, the Germans are dying or surrendering. But, as in Stalingrad, they surrender more than they die.
VOICE: The Germans are surrendering, and they are surrendering without conditions.
VOICE: As Roosevelt and Churchill declared at Casablanca, there is no other possible outcome for the Axis powers.
VOICE: Beaten on the battlefield, they surrender unconditionally or they die.[37]

By December the broadcasts had assumed a journalistic tone of impartial facts. This did not make them any less "propaganda." The broadcasts continued to be conscious attempts to use all available symbols to persuade the audience to the propagandist's point of view. What the change in tone reflected instead, as we shall examine at fuller length later, was a belief that a more remote and journalistic style, one in which the viewpoint of the propagandist hid behind the references and impartial style of the broadcasts, would prove more effective. Thus, in December a typical broadcast on military events ran like this:

VOICE: America at war speaking.
VOICE: Wednesday in broad daylight, heavy bombers from the American 15th air

force army struck very powerful blows against the enemy communications lines between Germany and Italy. The central point of these communications lines is the Brenner Press. Wednesday, American pilots bombarded Innsbruck, a great railroad center in Austria, on the way to the Brenner. It is in Innsbruck that the railroad going from the southwest and the north of Germany cross on their way to Vienna and Italy.[38]

War news about the Russian front and the second front implied that the wartime alliance between the Soviet Union and the United States was holding fast. By casting an image of a global war in which events in Russia were matched by battles in the Pacific, in North Africa, in Italy, in the Atlantic Ocean, and in the skies over Germany, the Voice told the French that the Americans were fighting in much the same ways as were their Russian allies. Military news told French listeners that the United States was fighting hard for victory against the Axis, working toward the ultimate goal of the liberation of France and Europe.

Throughout 1943 the Voice of America steadily built up an image of the United States through the Projection of America. In a sense this was what all Voice propaganda was about: interpreting the meaning of the Resistance through American eyes; explaining the progress of the war in American terms; and telling the French how the Americans felt about French politics, the Axis, the Anglo-American-Russian alliance, and all the other issues that bobbed up and down, like so many markers, on the vast sea of the war. But there was besides a specific category of propaganda whose goal was to draw a flattering portrait of America. This campaign, like that of military news, fell into two halves—that which came before victory in Tunisia, and that which followed. Unlike propaganda about the military progress of the war, however, the shift in the Projection of America began over the spring of 1943, after the Allies had taken Algeria and Morocco and the Russians had won at Stalingrad.

Before March, the major themes of the Projection of America had been American war production, growing American military readiness, and American determination. The Voice, in other words, issued a steady stream of stories on the potential power of the United States. This propaganda was a song of praise about what the United States was getting ready to do, could accomplish, would bring about—in the future. But by mid-March the propagandists felt it was time to shift gears as Europeans now knew that the Axis would lose and the Allies would win the war. "They want to know two things," a directive suggested; "how soon will it end?; and what are we going to do with the peace?"[39]

Accordingly, the central directives called on the propagandists to revise the Projection of America. The Voice was still to drive home the day-to-day contributions the United States was making toward Allied victory. It was still to emphasize materiel production, especially in shipbuilding and airplane construction. But henceforth "production figures are no longer valuable unless directly related to military events."[40] Programs on industrial production were to become a less prominent feature of Voice propaganda.

"In projecting what sort of country and what sort of people we are," a directive told the desk writers, "the emphasis should gradually drift away from mere size and power." This, the propagandists felt, was no longer important. America had already proved herself to be a strong nation, and the world knew that the United States would assume a major role in the postwar world. The Voice therefore did not have to emphasize this. Rather, it was to tell the French, and the rest of Europe, "what sort of people Americans are, [and] how they are going to use their power." Especially in the halcyon days before the debacle of the moronic little king, the Voice's message was that the United States aimed to help bring peace and democracy to the war-torn countries of Europe, purposes in which the peoples of Europe would unite "because they are for the common good of all men everywhere."[41]

The propagandists began linking American industrial production to military action. "Otherwise," a directive pointed out, "we shall give the impression that we think we can win the war in our factories."[42] The United States had passed from a preparatory stage to "a new state where all power and effort may be devoted solely to the active prosecution of the war in the field."[43] The propagandists achieved this emphasis by writing stories on war materiel in the field. There was a show about portable pipelines, for example, replete with discussions of joints, elbows, and hydraulic pumps, a new and complex American industrial development that eliminated the need for fuel depots on the front.[44] Weapon production was linked to battles. In early November 1943 a regional directive told script writers to churn out stories on airplanes. The Voice followed instructions, using such material as an announcement from Donald Nelson, director of the War Production Board: "Considering airplanes in particular, production in November reached 8,789 planes, 427 more than were made in October."[45]

The Voice continually praised American democracy. It was, as a directive said in January 1943, a "form of government [which is] practical, workable . . . even in time of crisis."[46] The phrases most often used were "dynamic democracy" and the "great laboratory of democracy." The Voice took pains to tell its listeners about strikes and social dislocation in order to explain that imperfections were the beauty of the system. The tone of these stories grew in self-confidence throughout the year as victory came closer. A sense of American power lay behind the actual words of the directives, a belief that the United States was a great nation and a world power. Accordingly, bad news was to be told along with the good, as "the story of our successful accomplishments will be much more convincing if we occasionally tell about our mistakes and failures." The words rang with pride and self-assurance.[47]

But if there were continuities, there were also critical changes. Most important, the Voice increasingly had to talk about America's postwar goals. Although this task was always the most difficult of the Voice's various duties, it was one that had been easier in 1942 than it became in 1943, after American collaboration began first with Admiral Darlan and then with Marshal Badoglio. Before the Torch invasion the president's goals were most clearly stated in the Atlantic Charter and the enunciation of the Four Freedoms, political objectives to which Sherwood, Barnes, Warburg, Johnson, and their colleagues enthusiastically adhered. These vague commitments left the propagandists free to say whatever they wanted, and the Voice spoke of the war as a battle for liberty and an end to future wars.

By June, Warburg and his colleagues believed that the time had come to orient the Projection of America toward postwar goals. This new orientation required discussing Allied unity, describing Allied intentions toward the reconstruction of France and of Europe, and talking about a future world organization that would ensure peace and security. These topics, then, became the major themes for the Projection of America in the second half of 1943. Certainty of eventual victory made postwar planning essential to give meaning to the war and to the hardships Europeans had endured.[48] But there was little the propagandists could do to manufacture a policy that did not exist. The directives often remained vague, emphasizing the importance of planning for a postwar organization to ensure an international order based on justice and liberty.[49] It was only in November, with the Moscow conference and the passage in the Senate of the Connally resolution, that the Voice felt it had real political ammunition in a clear mandate for a postwar peace-keeping organization.[50]

The most immediate and therefore the most important issue for the French desk was that of the postwar reconstruction of France itself.[51] It was, however, a particularly difficult issue to confront as the president had said that the United States would not take a political stand or support any candidate as the future leader of France. Roosevelt, and therefore the Voice, justified the American position by arguing that the United States would guarantee free elections after the war was over, but what this stance actually reflected within the American government was a firm commitment to Giraud.[52] It was not very good material with which to work.

The Voice played up the doctrine of nonintervention. "We should pay particular attention at this time to the projection of the United Nations' policy of non-interference and disinterestedness in the internal political situations of other countries," stated a regional directive in June. But the propagandists believed that this was not enough, that the doctrine of noninterference was a mask for policies with which the propagandists disagreed, such as collaboration with Darlan and support of Giraud to the exclusion of de Gaulle. Therefore they retreated from the issue: "Emphasis should be restricted to military unity and cooperation among the Allies," the guidance instructed the French desk.[53] The furthest the Voice could push the issue was to tell the French that the Americans would not try to rule France once the nation had been liberated. "Civil government is in the hands of French civil authority wherever Allied troops have appeared."[54]

The French desk substituted friendship for politics. Again and again they wrote stories describing the good will and cooperative nature of the Americans, who not only trained for battle and fought with enthusiasm, but who admired and liked the French. The French desk inaugurated an entire show devoted to this subject, "Franco-American Friendship," written by Albert Guerard, a French-born professor at Stanford University and a regular contributor to the *Nation*. Guerard stated his objective when he told his audience, in October, that "during this series of talks I have repeatedly told you . . . the words of President Roosevelt: 'there are no two other nations more united by the links of history and mutual friendship than the peoples of France and the United States of America.'" Because the Americans so admired the French, Guerard implied, the United States would work toward positive French domestic goals, ill defined as these were.[55]

The images cast up by the Projection of America were those of a powerful nation committed to war and to the postwar goals of peace and democracy. The United States possessed vast human strength, portrayed through such stories as a news piece on the six million American factory workers. It possessed technical strength, revealed through items on innovations and developments like portable pipelines. It possessed military strength, depicted through news about airplane production.

The picture of America at home was more complex than that of a strong and innovative nation committed to victory. The portrait included the cracks and fissures of coal strikes, election fights, and congressional disputes, all of which were at least mentioned in the belief that such stories told the

French that the United States had the self-confidence of a successful democracy. The Voice could reveal these strains because they were essentially unimportant when contrasted with the vast strengths of the American system of government.

Finally, the Voice told the French that America would keep French national interests uppermost in its policy decisions. Through stories of friendship and cooperation, the Voice penciled a sketch of mutual interests and postwar political agreement that went beyond the immediacy of foreign relations and presidential policy to the hopes of the propagandists themselves. More than in any other area of propaganda, the Projection of America, although bound by the realities of foreign policy, remained rooted in the propaganda of 1942. Above all, it was a propaganda of ideology, a hope sung out for a liberal, antifascist, aggressively democratic conclusion to the war.

In the spring of 1943, Edd Johnson and the Office of Control established a central writing desk, Basic News, which produced sample news stories and headlines and passed them on to the language desks to be rewritten in the various languages. After the introduction of this new system the desks did not originate their own news bulletins except when news items had to be specially written for a specific audience.[56] The news programs were therefore quite distinct from features, which the desk writers continued to create independently. For this reason, headlines and news bulletins most accurately reflected the overall propaganda philosophy of the Overseas Branch.[57] They formed the core, if not the bulk, of the propaganda of the Voice of America.

The form of the headlines, which introduced and concluded each fifteen-minute language segment, changed during this period. In November 1942, four announcers read the day's headlines:

FIRST VOICE: General Eisenhower stated that he was very satisfied with the progress of the American forces in French North Africa.
SECOND VOICE: Meantime, in Libya, the British Eighth Army is continuing to pursue the enemy, which has been routed.
THIRD VOICE: Our Russian Allies have repelled German attacks everywhere along the eastern front.
FOURTH VOICE: In the South Pacific, our forces have made new advances on the island of Guadalcanal in the Solomon archipelago.[58]

By the fall of 1943 the style in which the announcers spoke the headlines implied a new philosophy of radio propaganda: "We are reminding you of the principal events which happened during the last twenty-four hours," the now single voice of the news broadcaster told his listening audience. He continued on, alone:

> *In Russia* the red army has enlarged its bases for offensive operations on the right side of the Dnieper river, north and south of Kiev, as well as close to Kremenchug. Farther north the Russians have advanced in the direction of Vitebsk, liberating 150 towns and villages in twenty-four hours. In the South, Soviet forces are liquidating the last German troops in the Taman peninsula.
> *In Germany* the American flying fortresses violently bombed the port of Bremen on Friday. Close to Bremen the navy shipyards of Vegesak were successfully attacked. One hundred and forty-two German fighters were gunned down. Thirty bombers and three allied fighters have not come back to their bases. In the night of Thursday the RAF bombed Stuttgart, Munich, Friedrichs Haven. During friday [*sic*] night, the RAF again bombed Germany.
> . . . . . . . . . . . . . . . . . . . . . . . . . . . . . . . . . . . . . . . .
> *USA* Seven new merchant ships have been launched.[59]

The propagandists calmed down the headline style. In September, Werner Michel, chief of the broadcasting division of the Radio Program Bureau, instructed his staff to restrain the style of the programs, both in the scripts and the acting. Emphasize instead, he suggested, a sober reporting of the news.[60] The pace at which the announcers read the news was, accordingly, considerably slower in October than it had been the previous winter. The style of the voices had taken on a steady and serious quality.[61] News headlines were no longer lines in a drama; "too frequent changes confuse the listener," Michel advised his producers.[62] Instead, they became a stream of information that sounded reliable and authoritative.

Drama is fiction; it mimics reality. But journalism is nonfiction; it recounts reality. The message the propagandists implied, therefore, was that the American station gave its audience plain, unadorned facts.[63]

This shift in style and format was even more pronounced in the longer news stories that followed the headlines. In late December 1942 the Voice told its listeners about Allied successes in North Africa through four announcers:

> FIRST VOICE: Since the beginning of the operations in French North Africa, the Allies have shot down or destroyed 277 enemy planes, and lost only 114 of their own.
> SECOND VOICE: Nothing could be better proof of the U.S. secretary of war's recent words:
> THIRD VOICE: "On the Tunisian front Allied aviation showed a constant superiority over the enemy."

FOURTH VOICE: You have just heard the main excerpts from the U.S. secretary of
    war's last communiqué, in which he paid a tribute to the Allied
    pilots' successes on the Tunisian front.[64]

By January many news bulletins were already announced by a single voice.
Shifts of place and time were made by pacing and emphasis, rather than
by different voices. The announcer's voice, and his authority, were outside
the action. "In Tunisia," a bulletin of mid-January stated:

the French troops, helped for the first time by the flyer *Lafayette,* have occupied
German positions in the northwest of Kairouan and in the area of Bour Davouss,
a little bit farther to the south. Northwest of Kairouan, the forces of General
Giraud proceed equally in the reduction of Italian troops who are surrounded in
the mountains.[65]

The first story was related by four different announcers, three of whom articulated discrete voices of authority. The first was the omniscient narrator,
who told the listener what had happened during the day's fighting. The
second shifted perspective and played the role of the drama's storyteller, explaining to the listener the identity of the next speaker. The third played
a character, the U.S. secretary of war Henry Stimson, and the fourth returned to the role of the second voice, the master of ceremonies addressing
members of the audience. This shuttling of perspective made sense within
the context of drama, where different actors play different roles and audiences expect to follow rapid shifts of character and attitude.

In the case of the bulletin of the following month on the Mediterranean
front, however, the now single voice was that of an omniscient narrator.
Whereas in the previous piece the Voice writer not only told what was happening but showed it through voices and characters, here the writer adhered
to the narrative device of telling without explicitly acknowledging the existence of an audience, thereby implying objectivity.

In both examples there was what literary critics call an "implied author"
who spoke in special ways to the audience. The very act of communication,
the way in which the news was told, set up a relationship between listener
and speaker in which each took on a special role. By ignoring the audience
and creating the fiction of impartiality, Voice writers created an "implied
listener" who believed what he or she was told by the authoritative, distant,
all-knowing Voice of America.[66]

By May, news bulletins were all single-voiced productions that were, on
the whole, both longer and slower. They had become journalistic war stories,
full of small authenticating details, written by staff members who now signed
their stories. In reporting on the Mediterranean front in mid-May, for example, a Voice announcer told his audience:

The first British army has just sealed the entrance to Cap Bon peninsula, advancing from Tunis up to Hammammet. According to agency dispatches, the armored units of the first army have occupied Hammammet Tuesday at dawn and taken 5,000 prisoners.[67]

The changes in style are striking. Before, the Voice writer would have told the listener in general terms where the action had taken place. But here he quite specifically described the army as having "sealed" up the enemy and told the listener not merely that this had taken place at Cap Bon, but at the entrance to the peninsula. Through the terse conventions of journalistic prose the writer said to the listener, We, the Voice of America, have it on expert witness that the British are winning the battle against the Axis in Tunisia; the British have isolated Axis troops in an area from which there is no likely escape, and will now take these soldiers prisoner. Once having established the most important news first—Allied military success—the Voice writer selected a few details through which he both authenticated the news and gave it emotion. Only an eyewitness could have known that the victory was won by armored units, that they had taken a specific number of prisoners, and that the victory had taken place at a certain time of day. These facts thus underlined the appearance of veracity in the report.[68]

The authoritative sources cited in these bulletins also changed. No longer were the news bulletins of the Voice either without a direct quotation or reference or, as had frequently been the case, based on Allied military communiqués. Increasingly they used and acknowledged journalists and press agencies, both American and foreign. American war correspondents were often mentioned by name. Voice writers lifted newspaper stories and put them nearly intact on the air. They recounted news stories from foreign papers with ever greater frequency. They cited stories from neutral Switzerland and Sweden in an attempt to display the Voice's own objectivity.

Voice writers increasingly filled their bulletins with references to an original text. They often avoided making an independent assertion; all ideas and thoughts were anchored to the weight of some independent, external authority. In one short, fifty-word bulletin, a Voice writer quoted from both a Swiss and a Swedish paper. It was a three-paragraph story, in which all three paragraphs began with the now magic words: "According to . . ."[69]

This shift from multiple-voice plays to single-voice news stories that were based on outside sources emphasized the reliability and objectivity of the American radio station. The Voice of America spoke in terms that were increasingly concrete and factual. In an atmosphere in which "propaganda"— the attempt to persuade people to adopt one political belief over another through symbols embedded in language—was discredited both abroad and at home, precise information sounded neutral. It made American propaganda credible abroad and acceptable at home.

News reporting created a distance between audience and events. The dramatic style of Houseman's Voice had brought the audience to the event as the audience became part of the story. But news stories replete with official quotations and a remote authorial voice established distance and command. Increasingly Voice writers used the passive voice or impersonal form to indicate a weighty authority. "In Italy, the Allied advance is going successfully," a news story said on October 9. Or again: "In the Yugoslavian sector an important local activity continued to be seen."[70] The use of the passive voice and impersonal form conveyed a reliance on some higher, and therefore trustworthy, authority.

By the end of 1943, the broadcast style of the Voice indicated a definite notion of audience. It was for this reason that the Voice began creating special shows such as those about labor, women, the military, and youth. Underneath the decision to produce these special-focus shows lay the assumption that different techniques drew different listeners, and that the Voice of America could not speak to the nation of France through any single style.

The overall changes in propaganda techniques transformed the features of the Voice of America in 1943 in ways that paralleled the alteration of headlines and news. These changes emerged from discussions among the leaders of the Voice of America and the French desk about what kind of broadcasting created effective propaganda. Was it artistic, dramatic radio, or was it clear, informational journalism? Could radio propaganda persuade people from one position to another? Should the Voice attempt to provoke acts of sabotage and resistance, or should it suggest to its European listeners that they wait for the Allies?

The chief of the French desk, Pierre Lazareff, believed it was essential to make the French language propaganda as personal as possible, for otherwise, he told his superiors, the French would never listen. The French, he advised, were, above all, a highly individualistic people. For them, anonymity meant nothing; they would suspect anything that seemed official. Moreover, he warned, the French saw in America a nation that lacked soul. Broadcasts from the United States had to avoid anything that lent the impression of being mechanical, or spiritually empty.

Lazareff blamed what he defined as a dismal state of broadcasting affairs on the conception of propaganda which he believed reigned within the Overseas Branch. "So long as all material in the scripts which is slightly colorful or personal is hunted down in the name of sacrosanct principles . . . we have to cut, clip and prune so carefully . . . that either one of two things happens," Lazareff wrote: "the authors end up by being afraid to write anything at all, or else their work consists of little jobs made to order, an assembly-line type of work which entails no unpleasantness, and which brings as its reward the smiles and pats-on-the-back on the part of all persons in the office."[71] For Lazareff, the key to good propaganda was the same as the key to a good newspaper: hire good people, trust their judgment, and allow them to do the job as they see fit. He felt that the Overseas Branch, with its directives, Basic News, Control, and the niggling fights that affected all daily work, undermined the kind of confidence any good propaganda operation needed.

Lazareff's view of how to run a propaganda organization mirrored his concept of audience. He assumed that listeners were intelligent, made up their own minds, and cared about what they heard: he never talked down to his audience. If the OWI, he argued, would consider the Frenchman who tuned in to the Voice of America at the risk of his life, "the obstacles might be surmounted and the shackles removed that prevent us from speaking to him from America . . . and it might be possible to speak heart to heart, man to man."[72]

Lazareff introduced signed commentaries in earnest over the summer of 1943. By September, he and his colleagues had introduced to French listeners daily commentaries by Philippe Barrès, Julien Green, Pierre Martel, Pierre Dulac, Georges Bernier, Raymond Mesnil, and Pierre Lansac, periodic addresses by Lewis Galantiere, Albert Guerard, and Harold Jeffries, and weekly speeches by Jacques Maritain. "All are meant to endow our broadcasts with the note and personality which they lack," Lazareff explained.[73]

Lazareff argued against broadcasting translations of Basic News items; instead he wanted the French desk to write and deliver its own material. He urged the Overseas Branch to accept individual initiative and responsibility. "I am attacking a rigid system which *paralyzes all our efforts, and emasculates all our energy,*" he wrote (emphasis in original). He asked writers to read the directives and interpret them as intelligently as they could, according to their temperament. "And that is all."[74]

There was, in other words, a shift that took place in the French features which paralleled the changes that occurred in Basic News. The feature writers cut down their use of voices. They wrote stories that were more concrete, filled with details of fact and supported by newspaper and other sources. They gravitated to a journalistic style of radio broadcasting.

Over the course of 1943—or from the watershed of the North African invasion on one side to the expulsion of Sherwood, Barnes, Warburg, and Johnson on the other—Voice of America propaganda changed in both content and form. This transformation did not take place at any single moment; the shifts came about slowly. Like body weight, lost or gained, their cumulative effect was unrecognizable until the old clothes no longer fit the new shape. Propaganda about the Resistance altered most dramatically over the summer, the emphasis on and nature of military news began to shift in the spring, and programs devoted to the Projection of America changed gradually in reaction to American collaboration with Darlan and Badoglio and again in response to the Moscow and Tehran conferences. At the same time the broadcasting style of the Voice underwent a gradual revision from the beginning of the year.

Participants dated the transformation of Voice of America propaganda to the episode of the moronic little king. In a sense they were right. The Overseas Branch had been attacked and its liberal leaders defeated. As early as the first part of August 1943 Warburg wrote to Davis and Sherwood that there were two major ways in which American propaganda could help shorten the war: by driving home the inevitability of Axis defeat, and by persuading the peoples of Europe that their only hope for a lasting, secure, and democratic peace lay in Allied victory. "It is in the carrying out of this second part of our assignment that we are hampered by the limitations of present policy," Warburg complained. It was true, he went on, that American propaganda possessed a great array of verbal weapons, from the Atlantic Charter to Roosevelt's Four Freedoms speech, and that the United States could point to its accomplishments in the world, from the Good Neighbor policy to the Lend-Lease program. But there was a grave danger that "in our anxiety to prevent disorder, we may make ourselves the agents of preserving in Europe the very political and economic status quo which gave birth to the Communist revolution and to the Fascist and the Nazi counter-revolutions." He went on:

Our present attitude suggests that we do not want an anti-Fascist or anti-Nazi revolution at all, that we are afraid of it, and that we will not "take the lead and give it the backbone of our military power." Once this conception of our war aims takes root in the minds of the people of Europe, they will regard us not as liberators, but as agents of reactionary suppression.[75]

This fear was bred by the incident of the moronic little king; it was the reason why the propagandists thereafter wondered what message, beyond that of sheer military victory, they were to convey to the oppressed peoples of Europe. As Miall wrote in his diary on July 28, the events around the broadcast of the moronic little king "may well have been climacteric in the history of the O.W.I."[76]

It is only when seen from the perspective of time that the importance of the single event of the moronic little king story, although critical, diminishes in proportion to a variety of other causes: the influence of the British, the departure of John Houseman in June, the declining belief in the power of propaganda to generate action, the increasing certainty of Allied victory, and finally, the larger view of Roosevelt's continued reluctance to establish clearly defined postwar goals.

By the beginning of 1944, the propagandists had changed their definition of persuasion. Propaganda could not move people to action. Instead, it could inform and it could present an attractive picture of the United States. An in-house description of Overseas Operations written in late 1943 stated that the "OWI never urges specific sabotage . . . [because] a listener huddling over a radio doesn't want to be told by someone in New York that he should risk his life."[77]

The Voice had stepped back from its audience. It had retreated from exhortation to information, just as its language shifted from the active voice of drama to the passive voice of journalism. In April 1943, Warburg wrote to Davis that the mission of propaganda was "to keep alive hope of liberation and stimulate resistance to the enemy forces of occupation."[78] A year and a half later Edd Johnson described the reigning philosophy within the Overseas Branch as "news, news and news."[79]

# 8

## Sailing Between Wind and Water

### Propaganda and American Foreign Relations, 1944

THROUGHOUT the first two years of operation of the Voice of America the leaders of the Overseas Branch of the OWI tried to mold opinion abroad and influence policy at home. The events of 1943, however, forced the propagandists to reevaluate those goals. By 1944 there were new leaders of the Overseas Branch of the OWI who implemented a revised philosophy of propaganda and made different assumptions about the proper relationship of propaganda to foreign policy. These men saw their role as expressing, rather than creating, foreign policy. Propaganda became the handmaiden of foreign policy.[1]

Throughout 1944 the relationship of the Overseas Branch to the State Department and the military steadily improved. Edward Barrett, Louis G. Cowan, and Wallace Carroll worked hard to smooth relations. Their success was especially noteworthy because they did so within the framework of the president's refusal to recognize Charles de Gaulle and the French Committee of National Liberation. The propagandists believed that Roosevelt's policies eviscerated their efforts; as Carroll later recalled, "because of the rigidity of Roosevelt, our propaganda to France was never terribly effective."[2] One intra-office cable explained that the OWI had to represent a government that was anti-Gaullist while assuming a friendly public attitude toward de Gaulle. It is the belief of the OWI leaders, the cable explained, that "the only persons [inside France] who are entirely informed of the clash between

[de] Gaulle and Washington are the political leaders of organized resistance, and if we disclosed the conflicts as they are . . . the population at large would be bewildered and angered." Thus, continued the cable, "it is our feeling that . . . OWI has successfully sailed between wind and water. . . ."³

American foreign policy in 1944 and 1945 lacked clarity. The United States was going to become a world power, but the nation had yet to define what that power was to mean. No political philosophy immediately replaced the liberalism of the early war years.

The men who took over from Sherwood and his colleagues were not conservatives who opposed the approach of the early founders of the Voice of America. They were committed internationalists, they accepted the Soviet Union as America's ally, and they wanted to create a democratic and prosperous postwar world without oppression or political tyranny. But they were willing to work with the State Department and the military and they were comfortable within a bureaucracy in which they lost as many fights as they won. The most important issue, in other words, was the relationship of propaganda to foreign policy.

Roosevelt's attitude toward de Gaulle and the French Committee of National Liberation became increasingly rigid over the spring and summer of 1944. By January the Allies were deeply enmeshed in planning for Overlord, the projected invasion of France through Normandy. These plans raised important military questions about how the Allies would govern newly liberated France and the extent to which they would rely on French civilian authority rather than rule France as a conquered territory.

The roots of the problem lay in the aftermath of the Torch invasion. The events of 1943, from the storm of protest after Eisenhower's appointment of Darlan to the disillusion following the general's accord with Badoglio, made it imperative that the Allied forces find better ways to govern newly liberated territory. The War Department therefore created a Civil Affairs Division to handle issues of civil administration in formerly occupied regions.⁴ Eisenhower had bypassed de Gaulle for Darlan in 1942, but by the summer of 1943 the American general knew de Gaulle's political strength. The French leader meanwhile pressed for American recognition of the FCNL, which was headquartered in Algiers. Eisenhower agreed, requesting recognition in June 1943. But the president told the general that he was to grant recognition "under no conditions."⁵

Eisenhower feared getting bogged down in civilian affairs. He wanted the cooperation of the French Resistance movement to conduct sabotage operations on D-Day and collect information on German troop disposition and movements. He knew that the French Resistance would follow de Gaulle. It would obey Eisenhower in return for Free French participation in the liberation of Paris and control of civil affairs in the liberated areas of France.[6]

Throughout the spring of 1944, pressure mounted for Roosevelt to recognize de Gaulle and the French Committee of National Liberation. Within the War Department both Henry Stimson and John J. McCloy supported recognition of de Gaulle and the FCNL, and within the State Department Cordell Hull joined the chorus of support.[7] In the weeks before the Normandy invasion General Eisenhower repeatedly petitioned the president to relent on his position toward de Gaulle. But no movement was discernible until July, when de Gaulle came to the United States for a six-day visit. On July 7 McCloy, together with Secretary of the Treasury Henry Morgenthau, presented Roosevelt with a proposal for a new approach to the FCNL, which would be given the status of a "de facto" authority.[8] On July 11, the day de Gaulle left for Canada, Roosevelt finally pronounced that he was willing to accept the FCNL—by this time the self-appointed Provisional Government of France—as "the de facto authority for the civil administration of France."[9]

Progress again stalled. The president moved no closer to recognizing the FCNL, the Provisional Government, or the authority of de Gaulle for the remainder of the summer, despite the fact that as French territory became liberated the need to establish civil authority increased. In August the Allies liberated Paris, with the French Gaullist General LeClerc leading French troops into the city, a clear symbol of Allied recognition of de Gaulle's authority. De Gaulle soon arrived in Paris himself, appointed Major General Pierre Joseph Koenig as military governor of the city, and took control of government buildings.[10] Roosevelt still did not relent. In September the president met with Churchill in Quebec, still unwilling to alter his position. On September 19 Roosevelt sent Hull a memo, restating that "the Provisional Government has no direct authority from the people. It is best to let things go along as they are for the present."[11]

General Eisenhower finally forced the president's hand. Determined that the Allied forces, now moving on toward Germany, should not get bogged down in the job of controlling France, Eisenhower reported on October 20 that he was turning over the zone of the interior to de Gaulle. On October 23, the United States recognized the new French government of Charles de Gaulle.[12]

Roosevelt left no clear answer, in letters, memos, or recorded conversations, as to why he so relentlessly refused to recognize de Gaulle and the French Committee of National Liberation. His obstinate stand remains something of a mystery. In general, historians have been divided in their approach. Some view Roosevelt's implacable hatred of de Gaulle as personal, reinforced by his larger view of French and European politics. Others assign the basis of Roosevelt's policy to a more comprehensive worldview sustained by the president's personal animosity.[13]

Secretary of War Stimson inspired the first view when he wrote that "to the President, de Gaulle was a narrow-minded French zealot with too much ambition for his own good and some rather dubious views on democracy."[14] Roosevelt had at best a dim view of France itself: it was, he believed, a defeatist nation that did not deserve a leader who insisted on its grandeur and invincibility.[15] As one historian has written, Roosevelt's policy toward France was a product of the president's determination to postpone political decisions for the postwar world and concentrate on military strategy while the fighting was still going on. This was a view supported by General Eisenhower himself, who wrote in his memoirs that Roosevelt consistently talked about North African problems in terms of military occupation of enemy territory, of "orders, instructions, and compulsion." Despite Eisenhower's attempts to remind the president that the Americans were not trying to govern a conquered country, but win over allies to whom they could turn over internal affairs and gain military and political support, Roosevelt "nevertheless continued, perhaps subconsciously, to discuss local problems from the viewpoint of a conqueror."[16] This was an arrogant and willful Roosevelt, riding roughshod over North Africa. France and de Gaulle could be scrapped and disregarded and humiliated, not out of any clear policy on the role postwar France would play, but out of a "contempt for a nation proven incompetent at social and economic reform, unable to defend itself against its neighbor even while claiming a preemptive right to rule underprivileged peoples."[17]

The other side of the historical debate focuses on longer-range, less personal issues. Roosevelt's policy toward France emerged from his initial decision, made in 1940, the recognize and work with Vichy, a decision based on a set of pragmatic assumptions about the course of the war. By 1944, Roosevelt feared civil war in France and the consequences such an internal cataclysm could have, first on the conduct of the European war, since it would threaten American lines of communication, and later on the future of western Europe.[18] Most important, Roosevelt not only wanted to postpone decisions on the shape of the world to come until after military victory had been achieved, but his political vision, inchoate though it still was in many regards, rejected the traditional balance of power in Europe, in which France had played a pivotal role. The postwar world was to be

governed by an alliance composed of Great Britain, the United States, and
the Soviet Union, all of whom would cooperate to maintain world peace.
There was no room in this holy alliance for France, much as de Gaulle
might hammer at the door. The quarrel between Roosevelt and de Gaulle
was therefore not just a matter of personality or historical coincidence. It
emerged from Roosevelt's belief that the old balance of power must end,
and that the era of European dominance in world affairs had concluded.[19]

It was a recognition of the supreme importance of the eagle and the
bear, of America and Russia, which rendered all other powers secondary
at best, admitted only under the protective wing of one of the two great
powers, as the United States, through its "special friendship," admitted Great
Britain. De Gaulle, on his side, struggled hard to defeat Roosevelt's vision,
not only during the war but as president of France more than a decade
later. The hostility between these two great leaders reflected not animosity
between the two men themselves, but the incompatibility of their political
philosophies.[20]

The second interpretation is more historically satisfying, but the first,
Roosevelt's personal distaste for the Free French leader, was more apparent
to the propagandists in 1944. They had to live within the confines of a policy they did not fully understand, but which they had to obey. Roosevelt
imposed the tone of and established the limits on what the propagandists
could say as the Allied forces of liberation moved through France. The
propagandists could scream with rage–and so they did–but they could not
move the president.

The propagandists might have reacted differently to a well-defined policy,
which they could have analyzed and then supported or opposed. Instead,
the president's obstinacy generated confusion and frustration. But in a strange
twist, it made peace with the State Department and the military easier. By
the summer of 1944 both had a seemingly more liberal policy toward France
than did the president.

After Sherwood and his colleagues left, the State Department made over-
tures toward the new propaganda leaders. It was indicative of this new attitude that in March 1944 Secretary of State Edward R. Stettinius wrote
Ed Klauber encouraging the OWI to expand its activities in North Africa,
which, Stettinius and the department hoped, "constituted a useful testing
ground for new methods which might be used later in Metropolitan France
with a view to promoting better Franco-American understanding."[21] Relations with the military also improved, although they remained more complex than those between the Overseas Branch and the State Department.
The military, like the State Department, had not acknowledged the impor-

tance of psychological warfare before or during the first years of the war. But in 1944 the Allies were winning the war, which put a premium on war news and gave the military a great deal of influence.

By the spring of 1944 the leaders of the OWI in New York and Washington, the Psychological Warfare Division (PWD) in London, and the Psychological Warfare Branch (PWB) in Algiers were chanting in near-unison that the United States should not only recognize but also work with the FCNL. On the daily level of details and local committees, the propagandists abroad effected a fair degree of cooperation with the French. In North Africa, for example, the French worked with the Americans in planning and writing leaflets designed for distribution in France, while the Americans helped the French make films to sustain the morale of the French army. But it was hard slogging in the face of official American policy, and American propagandists complained that this policy was making their job difficult.[22]

In North Africa the spokesman of dissent was William R. Tyler, chief of the French division of the PWB as of March 1944 and, after midsummer, chief for the whole of the western Mediterranean. Tyler was an exceptionally well-connected American with many years of radio propaganda work under his belt. He was born in Paris in 1910 to American parents with a diplomatic background and had been educated in England, first at Harrow and then at Oxford. In 1935, Tyler returned to America to work as a banker until the late thirties, when he abandoned his first career to study fine arts at Harvard University. In 1940, WRUL recruited him to broadcast to France, along with another Harvard student who would end up in PWB, Douglas Schneider. In 1942 Tyler moved from WRUL to the OWI. In March 1943, after the State Department denied Houseman his visa, Sherwood asked Tyler to go to Algiers and sort out radio operations there.[23]

Tyler was an exceptional propagandist. He knew and got along with the broad range of British and American representatives in North Africa, from diplomats to propagandists, from Houseman to Eisenhower and from Murphy to Sherwood.[24] He was bilingual and tricultural. Moreover, he was working in Algiers, close to the Mediterranean war front and next door to the headquarters of the FCNL, with which he cooperated on a daily basis, planning and negotiating schedules and programs for what became, after the summer of 1943, United Nations Radio. If any single American propagandist was suited—by temperament, education, background, and geographic location—to mediate between American policy and French reality, it was Bill Tyler.

As early as December 1943, Tyler found himself warning against the results of American policy toward France. "We are not neutral in this war," he wrote. The United States was fighting for certain principles, principles that were embodied in certain men and expressed by certain political trends. America could not stand on a policy whose fulcrum was the avoidance of "imposing upon the French a regime they have not chosen."[25]

Tyler had to meet daily with the French, with whom he found negotiations increasingly difficult. He blamed American policy for creating insuperable problems for the Free French, who then passed these problems on to the PWB. The Americans in Algiers, for example, found themselves in the ridiculous position of not being able to air a message from the French Committee of National Liberation or the Provisional Government—because they were not permitted to broadcast the words "French Committee" or "Provisional Government" in any American program. Roosevelt's policy hamstrung the PWB. A typical case ran something like this: in early June, the Gaullist commissioner of the interior, Emmanuel d'Astier, spoke over Radio France, the Free French radio station in Algiers. The French cut a recording of the speech and sent it around to the Americans to use on United Nations Radio. The Americans, much to their chagrin, could not use it because the commissioner's speech had referred to de Gaulle as "president of the Provisional Government of the French Republic." Nor did the Americans feel they could ask the commissioner to bow to American policy and make a whole new speech. All they could say was that, should the commissioner want to make another recording, "without the references in question, we should be only too pleased to broadcast his message."[26]

These sorts of encounters weighed heavily on Tyler and his colleagues, who repeatedly wrote to the leaders of the OWI in Washington and New York, complaining that "it is impossible for you quite to visualize how very great the problems are that face us," and warning that such breakdowns would have far-reaching repercussions.[27] The OWI directives did not suit the needs of propaganda as seen from Algiers. Tyler and his colleagues therefore kept trying to influence the directives of OWI policymakers in Washington—"to respond to them," as a colleague of Tyler's in the PWB recalled, "instead of simply apply[ing] them." At best, however, the "responsive" directives choked up into inarticulate groans. "Stress but do not emphasize," read one guidance on how to report a presidential speech. Stress but do not emphasize? "In the musical comedy that we never completed," said the colleague, "the conga number was 'stress but do not emphasize.'"[28]

What is important here is not what Tyler and his colleagues felt and cabled to their opposite numbers in New York and Washington, but what they did not say or do. Despite Tyler's diplomatic connections, he and his colleagues kept their arguments inside the OWI. Working on the firing line, in daily contact with the FCNL, PWB propagandists became upset with policy, felt frustrated and angry, and aimed their complaints at their colleagues in America. But they never disobeyed official policy. PWB North Africa, despite the pressures of the spring and summer of 1944, did not imitate Warburg's independent line over the moronic little king.

From London C. D. Jackson, by then head of PWD Supreme Headquarters, Allied Expeditionary Forces (SHAEF) under Eisenhower as supreme commander, articulated the same objections to American policy as did Tyler from North Africa.[29] By June the PWD was pushing hard on Eisenhower to modify his invasion message to include references to de Gaulle and the FCNL, but without success.[30] As in North Africa, no matter how heated the argument became, no one suggested going against the guidelines established back home. When Percy Winner wrote to Barrett in March suggesting that effective propaganda meant speaking directly, "without being shackled" by the American "cautious do-nothing while waiting-to-see political policy of avoiding anything which may be interpreted as a commitment," his attitude was an anachronism.[31] By 1944 Winner, of whom Sherwood had been "extravagantly fond," and who had been with the Overseas Branch since its earliest days, had gained a reputation as a brilliant man "with a considerable capacity for getting into and causing trouble."[32]

Even Sherwood had modified his views of the appropriate relationship of propagandist to policy by June of 1944, perhaps because he felt exiled in London, cut off from domestic American politics. He no longer enjoyed his former easy access to the White House or his closeness to the corridors of power. His relationship to Davis and Klauber remained painfully sore. He had never gotten along easily with Carroll, nor had he established any close ties with Barrett, who told Sherwood in one breath how important his continued leadership was and in the next that he would have to quit the OWI were he to support actively Roosevelt's bid for a fourth presidential term.[33] Working under these pressures, Sherwood had lost his belief, and perhaps his confidence, in a propaganda line independently arrived at, a belief that had vanished with his privileges and connections.

In any case, Sherwood did not know how, from London, to forge a policy on the FCNL or de Gaulle in June 1944. On his way to Algiers he cabled Davis and Barrett that the PWB needed something better by way of a policy line than it had. Where, however, could anyone get such a policy? From his end Barrett suggested that Sherwood take the dilemma to the London Policy Coordinating Committee (LPCC), a kind of would-be court of last resort. Sherwood agreed to meet with the LPCC, and attempted to persuade it to cut through the thickets of Roosevelt's policy. But much as Barrett and Sherwood wanted to pass the buck, the American members of the LPCC would not take it.

Less than a week later Barrett, along with Davis and Carroll, urged Sherwood to try again. Probably against his better judgment, Sherwood again agreed to meet with the LPCC, again to no avail. The members of the committee would have none of it. "On this touchy material," Sherwood responded to his colleagues in Washington, a policy "recommendation from [the LPCC] would only serve to give annoyance. . . ."[34] Sherwood wanted Davis, Carroll, and Barrett to deal with the problem, clear it up, and give him, and the propagandists in London and Algiers, a better line to use. Davis, Carroll, and Barrett wanted Sherwood to use his London base to cut the gordian knot of American policy toward France. But Roosevelt was unwilling to have his policy severed, and by early July Barrett had to admit that he had been unable to get any satisfactory ruling from the White House.[35]

As with the PWB and PWD, what is important here is not just the frustration bursting from the cables sent between Sherwood and OWI leaders in the United States. It is the fact that the propagandists saw no way around the dilemma. They wanted to influence policy, but they could not do so. On the far side of the Atlantic, Sherwood was forced to accept Roosevelt's foreign policy as it was. Like Barrett, Cowan, and Carroll, he had come perforce to see propaganda as a mere handmaiden to foreign policy.

It was not that the propagandists, whether in the United States, London, or Algiers, necessarily liked or even supported de Gaulle and the FCNL. Douglas Schneider, writing Barrett from Algiers, began with the caveat that he was definitely not a "blind supporter" of either de Gaulle or the FCNL. Of de Gaulle, Schneider reserved his opinion; of the members of the French Committee of National Liberation, Schneider considered them "men of not quite top-flight, first class caliber."[36] Galantiere, known for his conservative views, was by no means the only man in the OWI in 1944 who was unsympathetic toward de Gaulle. Pierre Lazareff, for example, did not support de Gaulle.[37] But support for de Gaulle and the FCNL was not the issue for the propagandists; political reality was. Roosevelt's policy undercut good propaganda. The propagandists complained that American policy toward France was repeatedly and grindingly negative. "We cannot recognize"; "We do not know"–these were the policy lines handed down to the propagandists. Somehow, they argued, policy had to be presented in a positive way so that the United States was not just a foot jammed in the door of liberation but a nation prepared to help France in a concrete, meat-and-potatoes, this-is-what-we-will-do-for-you sort of way. Lofty statements about friendship, Lafayette, and the brotherhood of arms established in World War I only washed over the issues without dissolving any of the problems.[38]

Related to this issue were questions of image and timing. Propaganda along the lines of American policy seemed only to reinforce the idea that the United States had rebuffed France. Even remarks that might have been perceived as useful failed to project any positive view of America. The president, the propagandists pointed out, reacted negatively to issues rather than boldly stepping forward.[39]

What the problem boiled down to was not a question of the content of the president's policies, but their form or packaging. This became the paramount issue for the pragmatic new leaders of the Overseas Branch. As Schneider said, after ticking off his laundry list of complaints, "all that goes above may sound like a plea for the recognition of the FCNL as Provisional Government. It is not." He went on: "Apart from the fact that such a plea would scarcely be realistic, I fully realize . . . that PWB, like OWI, applies and does not formulate policy."[40] He could not have stated the case more clearly. The propagandists now saw their job as merchandising American policy, not transforming it.

The evolving relationship of propaganda to foreign policy can be viewed from another direction by briefly examining the propaganda guidances sent over to the Voice of America on a regular basis. Carroll was in charge. Each Saturday he would meet with his regional specialists, with whom he would examine the news, look at intelligence reports, and then draw up a central directive for Europe. Within that framework each area specialist—the historian Leo Gershoy for France, the Austrian social psychologist Hans Speier for Germany—would draft individual plans. Next Carroll would sit down with Speier—whom he later described as "an ace . . . he had a great scholarly background, but he was the decisive man"—and edit and polish the material. This draft plan would go to the Overseas Planning Board, attended by Elmer Davis, David Bowes-Lyon, and representatives from the OSS, Rockefeller's Office of the Coordinator of Inter-American Affairs, the Joint Chiefs of Staff, and the State Department. If Barrett came to Washington for the meeting, which he occasionally did, he would preside; otherwise Carroll would take the chair. At this time the various departments had their chance to state their objectives, which, recalled Carroll, they seldom did. Carroll then sent the central directive to New York, London, and Algiers. He would travel to New York at least twice a month, if not every week, to meet with the various language desks, Control, and representatives from the other media. "The idea was," explained Carroll, that "we tried to bring the people who were going to have to use the directives into our thinking: bring them along" and make adjustments accordingly. Carroll then returned to Washington and sent out the final version of that week's central directive.[41]

By mid-1944, a reading of these directives indicates, the function of propaganda was no longer to define the war or provide it with a transcendent meaning for either American policymakers or European listeners. It aimed instead to support and extend American military victory; to provide information to listeners who were eager for hard news, either on the eve of liberation or in the midst of battle; and once liberation had been achieved, to give the French access to news about the United States. As a directive of early June said: "We must concentrate our time and wordage on the essential news which our audience will demand. . . . We shall have no time for home-made appeals, exhortations and denunciations."[42]

It is easy to understand the concern manifested in this directive for essential news; it was, after all, the last central directive to be issued before the invasion of Normandy. But implicitly to label earlier Voice propaganda as "home-made appeals, exhortations and denunciations" was discordant. It was as if Carroll and his colleagues had taken the opportunity to criticize the propaganda that had gone before. The guidance seemed to announce that the old-style propaganda was no longer relevant, implying that the agit-prop style of 1942, and its milder descendant of 1943, was mere rhetoric and denunciation. What made good propaganda was whatever supported and extended military victory. "As the world military and political situation ripens," ran a central directive in early May, "certain changes in the larger role of propaganda and information become appropriate and necessary." From that time on "our output must . . . reflect the fact that the United States, more than ever before, is involved in the direct military steps necessary to rescue and reestablish European civilization."[43]

By July this idea had become even more concrete. "Psychological warfare is of little value when it lags behind military events," stated another directive. "It is of maximum value when it runs boldly ahead of military events and shatters the enemy's will to resist before he has been beaten into submission." In the simplest terms, American propaganda was henceforth to proceed as if victory were around the corner, when it was in reality still a year away—a year of very heavy, destructive fighting. Propaganda was to persuade Europe, and especially the Germans, that the Allies had won, and with this conviction, to "make the Germans, the occupied countries, and the neutrals act on it." The only content that mattered was that which pounded in the reality of Germany's defeat.[44]

After France had been liberated, the goal of propaganda remained informational in its tone and form. It was to set forth news about America in ways that the French could use. Only through information, the propagandists argued, could such an indirect program work. The political goal was "to consolidate, intensify and perpetuate Franco-American friendship and cooperation." It was not that a democratic Europe was an insignificant objective; the restoration of democratic institutions was an important propaganda theme. But propaganda was to act as an underpinning for American foreign policy, in the broadest of definitions. It was to lay the groundwork for the policies determined by the president and the State Department.[45]

Underlying this shift was the reality of coming Allied victory. What both could and should be said in 1942, and even in 1943, differed from what could and should be said as the Americans landed on the beaches of Normandy and fought their way toward the German border, and as Russian troops inexorably moved toward the eastern boundary of Germany. Listeners in Europe increasingly wanted to know what was happening, and only that. Nothing else mattered. Everything else was an encumbrance, an obstacle to knowledge of where the troops were, who had won the latest battle, how close the fighting was to home, and how cruelly the war, and the Germans, were treating those in their path. If American propagandists wished to hold their audience, they realized they had "to discard ruthlessly all trivia . . . and to put aside minor themes and campaigns which may have served a purpose in an earlier state of the war" but did so no longer.[46]

The coming of victory necessitated a change in propaganda and in the attitude of propagandists toward policymakers. In order to support victory, the leaders of the OWI had to line up behind the president, the military, and the State Department. This change in turn forced a transformation in the philosophy of propaganda and attitudes toward policymakers.

Davis transferred Sherwood to London and fired Barnes, Warburg, and Johnson as part of the process by which the goals of the war were slowly, if inchoately, being defined by the president. The propaganda arm of the U.S. government could no longer be run by such outspoken liberals. In this sense, the original leaders of the OWI were symbols of important trends, not causes in themselves.

The original leaders of the Overseas Branch were men with firm political convictions. They were entrepreneurs, with a vision of the product they wished to create. Sherwood, Barnes, Warburg, and Johnson worked within a political vacuum in 1942 which gave them license to act according to their own political instincts; they worked with blinders on, looking forward, not sideways. They were thus protected from having to make the compromises that become necessary with peripheral vision. They wanted Roosevelt's foreign policy to conform to their own ideals, and propaganda was their tool to make it so.

The new leaders were symbols of a new order and products of a new situation. By 1944 the OWI itself had grown into a large bureaucratic organization, while the State Department and the military had become increasingly interested and involved in OWI activities, further expanding the organizational complexities and tensions within the OWI. The era of entrepreneurship had ended, and the time for executive administration had arrived. Barrett, Cowan, and Carroll were administrators willing to subjugate their personal beliefs to overall government policy. They were compromisers, men who could work with a diversity of people and smooth over consequent difficulties and tensions. A member of the French desk later described Carroll as "intelligent, moderate and conciliatory in his opinions."[47] And a writer from the English desk painted Cowan as "the Eisenhower [of the Overseas Branch] . . . he was the man who could keep these things in balance. . . . he was able to make this thing work."[48] Because of the shift in the nature of the OWI, it henceforth needed men who were willing to cooperate with the Departments of State, War, and Navy, men whose role was to be conduits of official policy.

The reports of the Bureau of the Budget witnessed this change. "When Mr. Warburg was with the Overseas Branch," read a report of June 1944, "there was much more of a tendency for the OWI to try to influence foreign policy. . . . Since Mr. Warburg has left, OWI has worked much more closely with the State Department."[49] Half a year later, the bureau reported that not only had Warburg and Barnes left: "Davis, Barrett and [Leonard] Doob are trying to find out what the policies of the Department of State are. They want to conform to these policies. They are interested in getting out the news."[50] In early November Phil Hamblett, Carroll's successor as chief of the London office of the OWI, told the assistant executive director of the Overseas Branch, Thurman L. Barnard, that General McClure of PWD SHAEF had asked what OWI's organizational responsibility was for the creation of policy. "I have explained," Hamblett said, "that it is our job to implement national policy rather than to create it. . . ."[51]

Wallace Carroll was crucial in implementing the change. In London, Carroll had worked closely with H. Freeman Matthews of the State Department. By 1944 Matthews had gone home to become head of the Office of

European Affairs. When Davis asked Carroll to take over Warburg's job as head of OWI policy and operations, Carroll first contacted Matthews in order to cover his bases and to explore what the relationship of the Overseas Branch to the State Department would be. According to Carroll, Matthews responded, "I know relations have been bad, but if you will come back, I will see to it that there will be very close cooperation between the State Department and OWI." Matthews went on: "You'll get our intelligence, and you'll get such policy guidelines as we can give you, and if you meet with any obstruction from the desk and so on, let me know and we'll straighten that out." Matthews's enthusiasm marked a breakthrough, Carroll argued: "This was the first time there was this prospect."[52]

Just as Warburg's style had been to act according to his own political instincts, so Carroll's was to work within a given political structure as carefully and competently as possible. As director of the London office of the OWI, Carroll had watched the leaders of the Overseas Branch wage war with the State Department and concluded that the independent decisions made in New York City had led to chaos and immobilization. The role of propaganda, he later wrote in *Persuade or Perish,* was to explain U.S. foreign policy sympathetically, even to explain mistaken policy sympathetically. There were reasons for U.S. foreign policy—policy decisions were not made in a vacuum—and propaganda should broadcast these reasons to the rest of the world. The place to alter foreign policy, Carroll concluded, was within the State Department and the White House, not outside; propaganda should work within the existing structure and function as part of an overall process.[53] For Carroll, Warburg had a shiny brilliance that reflected the shape of the immediate dilemma, but not of the long-range problem. In contrast to Warburg's individualistic style of decision making and implementation, Carroll typically used the meetings of the Overseas Planning Board not to plan policy—with more than twenty people usually in attendance this would not have been possible—but to bring representatives of the Departments of State, War, and Navy along in the process, make them feel included in the decisions, and work through possible disagreements before they became disputes. "Meshing them in a bit," Carroll later described it.[54]

Carroll's thinking was typical of the later leaders of the Overseas Branch. Hans Speier wrote that foreign policy was not the province of the propagandist. When foreign policy became public knowledge, it would then become ammunition for propaganda.[55] Paul Linebarger, an army lieutenant assigned to the OWI who later published a book entitled *Psychological Warfare,* argued that when propaganda diverged from foreign policy it would boomerang back against the propagandists, because actual policy would in-

evitably catch up with and contradict the spoken word.[56] And Daniel Lerner,
working for both the PWB and PWD, stated that the role of propaganda
was to argue policy, not make it, and thus "help win the war on terms acceptable to the victors."[57]

This chapter began by asking how the relationship between propagandists
and official foreign policymakers evolved over the course of 1944. Good relations between the OWI and the military and State Department came largely
as a result of an acceptance of the role of propaganda on the part of the
military and the State Department, and the realization by the OWI that
propaganda had to be the aid, not the initiator, of foreign policy. Hans Speier
later described the role of the propagandist in a way that sharply reflected
the shift in perspective which had occurred since the beginning of the war.
Describing what he saw as the tendency of propagandists to focus on short-
range issues, and of diplomats to concentrate on long-range issues, Speier
wrote that "the cooperation between the statesman and the propagandist
can in some regards be compared with the relations between a husband who
wants to save and a wife who likes to spend."[58]

This attitude in turn reflected an emerging philosophy about the nature
and goals of propaganda. Sherwood, Barnes, Warburg, Johnson, and Houseman had believed that propaganda was a weapon in the war for men's minds,
and hence their actions. It was as important as military battles. This belief
was the legacy of the thirties, with its faith in the power of the word, and
of the myth of Nazi propaganda as an invincible force.

It was not by accident that Undersecretary of War John J. McCloy had
called propaganda a "military necessity" in 1940, without which the United
States would be "unprepared to defend [itself] against a weapon which has
played a most important part in Hitler's success both in peace and actual
war." He argued that "we might better be short of other modern weapons
than this one, for anti-tank guns cannot stop ideas."[59] This striking phrase
is well worth stopping to consider: anti-tank guns cannot stop ideas; ideas,
in and of themselves, are powerful weapons, equal in strength to the latest
military technology. Ideas, according to McCloy in 1940, mattered, and
propaganda could influence events and win battles.

It was not an accident that by 1944 McCloy had long stopped concerning himself with propaganda. Not only were the Allies winning the war—
although the overwhelming importance of that single fact cannot be under-
estimated—but also McCloy, like others of that time, no longer believed
in the power of words to win, or to lose, wars. Thus, wrote Speier, propaganda campaigns, no matter what their strength or cleverness, could never

be as important, or as final, as military campaigns. Propaganda could not substitute for sheer military strength. Ideas did not matter as they once had. Propagandists accordingly stopped believing in their power to influence foreign policy and in the ability of the Voice of America to win the war.

Looking at this shift from the perspective of time, the transformation seems to have traveled a smooth and easy path, at least for those not hurt in the crossfire of institutional warfare. But even for those who stayed and whose own attitude toward propaganda changed, and for those whose careers were created by their wartime successes, these alterations did not take place without inner struggle or a sense of loss. Recording the events of D-Day in his daily appointment diary, Cowan wrote that all the preparations the Overseas Branch had made had borne fruit. "One had the feeling," he proudly set down, "of organization and of steadiness of experienced hands. People knew what they were doing. All the general plans had been so well spelled out that little doubt remained in the minds of the key operators." But as Cowan concluded his entry, his feelings of nostalgia, of regret for the beliefs once held and for the commitment and energy once experienced, emerged. "It was nothing like the night of North Africa," he lamented, "but I suppose nothing shall ever be like the early days of OWI."[60]

# 9

# D-Day, Liberation, and the End of the OWI

## The Administrative Struggles of the Overseas Branch and the Voice of America, 1944–45

THE LIBERATION of Europe provided a new military and diplomatic context for the propagandists. Victory was the goal for which they had long been striving. But victory condemned the OWI and brought confusion and retrenchment to the Voice of America. Accomplishment led to collapse.

Voice of America propaganda was conceived as ammunition in a war of words that paralleled military battle. It was what William Donovan had called the initial arrow of penetration, and Ritchie Calder the fourth fighting arm of war. These views of the Voice's function implied a critical question in 1944. If propaganda was an arm of war, what role could it have in peace? And if propaganda was but one weapon in a growing arsenal, was it powerful enough to be worth preserving as the Allied tanks, fighter planes, ships, and guns proved their might?

Military preparations for the invasion of France began in earnest in 1943. By January 1944 the British and Americans had created a joint propaganda plan for France, and by mid-April Washington began sending out guidances dictating a balance between confidence in military operations and recognition of the hazards that were inevitable in such a difficult amphibious operation. The French language shows accordingly used news of the air war offensives to create a feeling of intensity about the war effort. They advised listeners that the United Nations had chosen a time and place for its attack, and that they would be the first to announce the invasion. They underscored the ability of the United States to launch an amphibious operation in Europe while pursuing large-scale warfare in the Pacific. They increased the frequency of campaigns of caution–the "Avis"; they played up the role of the French Resistance; and they stressed Franco-American friendship.[1]

By May specific plans had been made for what the propagandists called the H-hour broadcast, which was to begin with a communiqué from the Supreme Headquarters of the Allied Expeditionary Forces. A battery of transmitters from the United States, North Africa, southern Italy, and Great Britain were to be ready to announce the landings and broadcast instructions. Civilians in Normandy were to be told to leave their homes and stay off the roads. Instructions were to go out to those whose jobs put them in a position to aid the forces of liberation. Feature shows were to be canceled, except those dealing directly with military operations. Special events recordings were prepared weeks before the landing, giving the military background of the landing operations themselves.[2]

Steadily the Overseas Branch, and with it the Voice of America, put its full weight behind the coming invasion. It was a period of intense labor in which the stresses of the winter were muted by the excitement of the job ahead. But the issues that had torn the OWI apart were not resolved. There remained questions of what kind of organization the Overseas Branch should become, what its political goals were, how it should relate to the White House, State Department, and military, and how it could get along with Congress. There was, as well, the dilemma of who listened to American short-wave broadcasts and what the value of radio propaganda was. These questions grew after D-Day and liberation as the French, and then all of Europe, regained its independence.

One symptom of the continuing political stresses within the Overseas Branch was Sherwood's extended stay in London. In the spring of 1944, Davis and Klauber had sent Sherwood abroad for a short visit, after which he was to return home and gracefully relinquish active control of the Overseas Branch.[3] Instead he stayed on, ostensibly waiting out the congressional budget hearings. His anger at the new regime oozed through the lines of the letters he sent back home. "Let Elmer and Klauber handle this by themselves," he wrote, referring to the congressional investigation into the recent OWI shake-up, "and schmooze their own way out of the embarrassment, with me far away."[4]

Beneath what appeared as administrative wranglings Davis, Klauber, and Sherwood were fighting about the nature of propaganda. Sherwood believed in crafting a weapon of war in which the message should undermine the enemy's morale, further the Allies' military and diplomatic goals, and project a vision of postwar democracy. Klauber, Barrett and Davis did not disagree with this overall goal, but they chiefly aimed to propose a propaganda of information. The job of the Voice of America was to tell the truth, as closely and objectively as possible, and to project military victory. Barrett, as head of the office of news and features, produced unedited information, leaving it to the desks to adapt the material—if they felt it was required. Shaping the news, Barrett implied, was not the job of the propagandist.[5] Carroll stated in a special long-range guidance that "our only choice is to do a *straight-forward informational* job in our long range media" (emphasis in original).[6] Klauber brought to his job a passionate commitment to objective news. News, he believed, supported democracy and, in turn, the American war effort. It was the journalist's job, and in 1944 and 1945 the propagandist's function, "to help the listener understand [the news], to weigh and to judge, but not to do the judging for him."[7]

This reliance on facts—toward which the Voice had been steadily moving since 1943—reflected a growing discomfort in the United States with propaganda and doubts about its legitimacy. Once the United States had fully engaged its resources in the war effort, what the propagandists said, what postwar goals they projected, mattered. In 1942 Sherwood, Barnes, Warburg, Johnson, and Houseman had been able to create an ideological, democratic, agitprop type of propaganda because the Allies were losing the war, and news alone could not produce effective propaganda. Before the Allied invasion of North Africa, American war aims were, moreover, inchoate. The liberal propagandists therefore filled this void with their own hopes and beliefs. Precisely because they linked domestic politics and foreign policy, however, their ideas angered members of the State Department, the military, and Congress. Their propaganda could not survive the war itself, especially once the president had narrowed the political options of the war to military victory and unconditional surrender.

Historians have argued that as time passed the OWI increasingly came under the control of the State Department and the military.[8] There is no doubt that after February 1944 the Overseas Branch worked with the State Department, the Bureau of the Budget, and the military more and more comfortably. Many of the old tensions disappeared and a new cooperative spirit flourished, although as late as September 1944 Cowan would still observe in his diary that it had been a "very stormy 9 o'clock meeting. . . .

The State dept. rulings have not always served our propaganda purposes and the consensus of opinion was that we should retain [our] position."[9] But to observe this amelioration is not to demonstrate that the State Department dictated propaganda policy. First, the State Department under Roosevelt often did not control critical areas of foreign policy, such as the decision whether or not to recognize the French Committee of National Liberation and de Gaulle. Thus, although State Department agreement was essential for bureaucratic harmony, it had little to do with the most important aspects of propaganda policy. Second, the State Department never actively controlled the OWI, and so both propaganda policy and propaganda operations remained essentially matters of cooperation. Third, the State Department, as we shall explore later, remained uncommitted to broadcast propaganda as an instrument of foreign policy. What the State Department wanted was to ensure that propaganda did not contradict State Department policy; it did not pursue propaganda as an extension of foreign policy. It exerted negative control without setting clear positive goals.

Finally, the State Department could not effectively control propaganda because it did not have a coherent long-range policy plan of its own for France or for Europe—or for the postwar world. Owen Lattimore, director of policy for propaganda to Asia, summed up the problem of State Department policy control—or lack thereof—in a talk he gave in New York City in mid-September 1944. What is the United States stand on postwar European colonialism in Asia going to be, he was asked, and what will be the corresponding position of the OWI? His answer was illuminating. "That is one of the biggest difficulties we have in actual operations in the Pacific," he said. "Simply that we do not have a clear declaration of national policy one way or the other." He went on to argue that "if it were just a matter of operations you could handle it if you had a clear policy saying you were going to back them, also, if you were not going to back them." But the State Department had provided no such guidance. "We don't have it one way or the other," Lattimore reported regretfully.[10]

In October 1944, faced with the lack of any coherent long-range foreign policy guidance, the Overseas Branch and the Voice of America backed away from the problem of how to create policy—in direct contrast to the days under Sherwood, Barnes, Warburg, Johnson, and Houseman, when the leaders of the Overseas Branch had relied on their own goals in the absence of State Department clarity. But in late 1944 the operational plan for France stated that "in preference to stories on European policy, use articles on the history of U.S. foreign policy in the Pacific, such as the Philippines."[11]

Continued British attempts to guide and manipulate Voice of America propaganda further demonstrated the State Department's lack of firm control over propaganda output. As late as April 1944 Walter Adams of the Political Warfare Executive mission in Washington wrote home that the British representative to the French desk heavily influenced the OWI's French regional directives. "So . . . if there are points you particularly want to see in OWI output," he confidently penned, "it would be helpful if you would let the mission know by cable. . . ."[12] The British, in other words, were still exploiting the lack of State Department authority much as they had done in 1942, albeit on a diminished scale.

The larger political and ideological issues were also influenced by operational concerns. The propagandists became increasingly convinced that overseas audiences only wanted to hear hard news. To saturated European ears everything else sounded too much like Nazi propaganda. OWI intelligence warned that the French desired "to listen only to news and to avoid assiduously anything that was, or was believed to be, propaganda."[13] As one Psychological Warfare Division officer reported, the preoccupation of the French after D-Day was the military situation, or as Lazareff himself pointed out, war news would be all the French would want to hear as the war itself became an increasingly intimate French concern.[14] These sorts of reports, filed again and again, made the Voice's move toward an emphasis on relaying information seem practical and necessary rather than ideological. It was as if the French themselves were arguing on Klauber's behalf, asking for news by which to make their own decisions.

The BBC reinforced this view through its monthly audience reports. In April the BBC pointed out that because European listeners were becoming weary of propaganda, they were increasingly turning to broadcasts not intended for them, such as the BBC Home Service and the Voice's English language programs. Allied propaganda therefore must avoid ill-planned discrepancies that the Axis could then exploit. One solution to this potential problem was a measured retreat from political programs to the safer terrain of military news.[15]

The shift to hard news as liberation propaganda was also reinforced by a series of administrative trends that were political in their implications. There was growth, and consequent fragmentation, of the overall organization. There was continuous demoralization within the staff of the French desk of the Voice. And there was negative evaluation of audience.

Ever since the Allied landings in North Africa, American propaganda operations had expanded. In North Africa the Americans established not only a radio broadcasting station, United Nations Radio, but cooperated with the British in the Psychological Warfare Branch. Over the summer of 1943

General Eisenhower extended combined psychological warfare to Italy, and radio broadcasting began in southern Italy. When Eisenhower moved from the Mediterranean to London for the launching of Overlord he again decided to continue psychological warfare, reconstituting efforts in the Psychological Warfare Division. By the spring of 1944 the OWI staffed not only the London office of the OWI but also the expanding PWB and PWD operations.[16]

The OWI also moved abroad through a growing number of outposts. The first was established in Iceland early in 1942, and the number of such posts steadily grew in 1943 and 1944. It was in France that combined military psychological warfare operations met and merged with OWI outposts. Here the Americans were not conquerors but allies of a liberated, self-governing France. The PWB and PWD thus had to fold and become civilian extensions of the OWI. Soon after the invasion the PWB in France became the Allied Information Service. When France ceased to be a theater of military operations the already established Allied Information Service office in Paris became the United States Information Service, a model the OWI followed for the rest of the continent.[17]

From the perspective of radio broadcasting, the largest growth came during the spring before the Overlord invasion, when the Americans set up a special radio station in London. The OWI created what was known as the American Broadcasting Station in Europe, or ABSIE, in order to reach western Europeans over their medium- and long-wave receivers. Most Europeans owned, or had access to, medium- and long-range sets, but far fewer possessed short-wave or all-wave receivers. Moreover, medium- and long-wave transmissions were always easier to find on the dial and, once tuned in, easier to hear than their short-wave equivalents. The Americans hoped, therefore, that ABSIE would expand the Voice of America's radio audience.

ABSIE held a unique place among wartime propaganda broadcasting stations.[18] It both was and was not an outpost of the Voice of America, and it both was and was not the Voice of the Supreme Headquarters of the Allied Expeditionary Forces (SHAEF).[19] New York, for example, sent ABSIE American comments on the important events of each day, descriptions of the American war effort, news of the United States and the war in the Pacific, and discussions of postwar problems from the American standpoint.[20] New York cabled guidances known as Nycasts three times a day.[21] But ABSIE also originated its own shows, broadcast BBC programs, and transmitted broadcasts from UNR in North Africa.[22] Furthermore, ABSIE obeyed PWD directives, and over the course of the months following Overlord, broadcast eighty-six military-originated instructions written explicitly as the Voice of SHAEF.[23]

ABSIE solved technical problems, but despite its potential importance, the Overseas Branch and the Voice of America never fully supported the London station. It was not planned as anything more than a stopgap measure intended to go off the air ninety days after victory in Europe. And the Voice of America and the Overseas Branch did not have enough men and women to run two complete organizations, one in New York, the other in London. Yet the very existence of ABSIE necessitated creating and staffing a second Voice of America.

This spread was experienced not only in space, but in time, for when it was midnight in New York it was early morning in London or Paris. The complexities of placing a telephone call, or reaching a decision by cable, became daily difficulties. Phone calls had to be booked ahead of time, and conversations had to be conducted in guarded language. Letters took weeks to cross the Atlantic Ocean, whereas even to cable a message could take as long as forty-eight hours, including the time needed to code, decode, paraphrase, mimeograph, and distribute it. Nycasts could take two or three hours to transmit, too long to be effective should a story need immediate action.[24] The Overseas Branch expanded, and as it did, central control fragmented.[25] As a consequence, straight news became the most workable sort of propaganda.

As the Overseas Branch grew, the need for more trained propagandists accelerated correspondingly. The draw of Europe was intense. Europe was where the action was and New York, always remote, felt increasingly like a backwater, out of touch, irrelevant to the progress of the war. The needs of ABSIE, the PWD, and the USIS pushed men out of New York, and the excitement of the war front pulled them to Great Britain and France. As Leonard Miall observed in July 1944, one of the major forces behind what he called "a progressive change-over [to] straight-forward informational activity" was "the removal to London of the personnel most interested in political warfare."[26]

When Barrett became director of the Overseas Branch he tried to solve these problem by placing first-class people in key jobs and then relying on their good sense. He assumed that they understood general policy and therefore neither needed nor used directives. But Barrett could work this way because he believed that propaganda was information. As the news reporting of the Voice of America became less subject to shaping and crafting, policy direction became increasingly unimportant, and arguments with the State Department over postwar policy goals diminished in proportion.[27]

Over the spring and summer of 1944, morale within the New York French desk plummeted, reflecting the struggles of the Voice to maintain a quality station in the face of steep obstacles. First and foremost, continuing American rejection of de Gaulle demoralized the French desk. Furthermore, French staff members were eager to return home and take part in the process of liberation in order to establish their own postwar careers. They left in droves, and there was a severe drain of talent from New York. In April Lazareff himself moved to London to set up ABSIE's French language desk. Later that month a member of the PWD French language staff who was on leave in New York reported, dazed and upset, that he had come back "to see that we were really scraping the bottom of the barrel for personnel."[28] ABSIE operations lowered French desk morale since despite his considerable talents, Lazareff was unable to create a first-rate operation in London. For the French writers and announcers this deficiency certified the shortcomings of their own wartime careers at the moment when they were finally able to worry about their future professional prospects. They had hoped that ABSIE would promote their prestige in France, paving the way for their repatriation, but instead they felt it did the opposite.[29]

D-Day returned enthusiasm and confidence to the French desk, but it was a temporary palliative to the increasing malaise that had taken root. Over that summer the tensions created by the president's policy toward de Gaulle eroded whatever good feelings remained. Lazareff's successor quit, and then his after that, so that by August Michel Rapaport was the fourth man to take charge of the desk within five months. By mid-July, a BBC representative wrote home that "the state of affairs in the French Section of O.W.I. is simply hopeless." Things had gotten so bad, he reported, that even "the amelioration of Franco-American relations cannot settle the crisis."[30]

Internal rot affected the kind of propaganda the desk could turn out after D-Day. By late June, the obstacles to writing scripts had become serious. Rapaport worked hard to get writers to carry on, but he often found himself composing three or more programs a day to fill the gaps. The news desk ceased to produce a news bulletin for every show; instead, it brought in news items as they came off the wire service tapes. This new practice reflected the injunction to concentrate on news and information, especially during the cross-channel invasion, but the French desk writers in general, and the news desk in particular, had collapsed to the point where merely getting through the day was their primary goal.[31]

Victory, liberation, and American policy toward de Gaulle thus decimated the French desk, which by late summer had lost almost all of its original staff. Those who remained tended to be Americans who possessed few of the skills that had once made the French desk the most exciting and vibrant of all the language desks. There was no longer a group of men and women who could create, or announce, the propaganda; they were, rather, "third rate writers who became writers 'par la force des choses' [by the luck of circumstances]," accompanied by "various secretaries who stay there because they can't get a job anywhere else."[32] Increasingly, New York broadcasts became duplications of ABSIE programs or shows of no interest to the French. By the end of the summer, Lazareff bitterly complained that it had become difficult to accept New York shows for retransmission, but that there was no time in London to rework the New York product.[33]

As if this was not enough, by the spring of 1944 the leaders of the Overseas Branch concluded that very few French listened to the Voice of America. Reports from interviews with French exiles repeatedly told the same story: the French did not tune in the Voice of America; the BBC was the station of choice. "Listening to London seems to have settled into a regular habit for most people," came one report. But "listening to U.S.A. stations is non existent in spite of the fact that . . . America is more popular than Britain in many quarters in France."[34] Audience "ratings" remained poor. The OWI concluded that only about 10 percent of the French listened regularly to American broadcasts, whereas more than 90 percent—virtually all those who had radio sets—listened to the BBC. "As more than one listener has said," an intelligence survey reported, "there was no reason to listen to 'La Voix de l'Amèrique' since it 'added nothing to what people automatically took from London.'"[35]

These intelligence reports proved a crushing blow for the Voice of America. What, the propagandists asked themselves, could they accomplish if no one in France or Europe listened to them? And if no one in France tuned in the Voice during the spring of 1944 and the period before and after D-Day, how much smaller an audience would the Voice command after the invasion succeeded and France had been liberated? The reports told the propaganda leaders that the Voice of America had failed to attract a loyal audience in war; what then, should the Voice do in peace? Over the course of 1943 the Overseas Branch and the Voice had lost their clarity of mission. During the months before the Overlord invasion and the weeks surrounding D-Day, the organization began to fragment and deteriorate. The war had changed American propaganda. Military victory began the process, but liberation completed it.

On August 25, 1944, Allied troops entered and liberated Paris. Three months later the war was over in France. It took another winter and spring of stiff fighting to defeat the Nazis, and another three months beyond that to beat the Japanese, but while the war was still being fought in central and eastern Europe and in the Pacific, the French slowly began rebuilding their country.

Liberation presented the propagandists with a new context in which to work. Even before the Allies drove the Germans out of Paris, members of the French Resistance began broadcasting over the facilities of Radio Paris. Soon the French inaugurated their own post-liberation radio station, Radio Diffusion de la Nation Française (RDF), controlled by the Ministry of Information. RDF news quickly became known as thorough and objective.[36] And not only did newly liberated France have its own radio station, it also had independent newspapers and magazines. The French thus no longer had to rely on foreign broadcasting for news since they had their own news services once more. Moreover, with liberation the French became openly hostile to anything that resembled propaganda, whether from the United States or from any other outside source.[37] Thus whatever the Voice of America said, it had to say unobtrusively, in tones that were as calm, factual, and nonpropagandistic as possible. Broadcasts had to stay neutral on domestic French politics and the French had to be reassured that the United States would act toward them in a friendly and cooperative manner.[38]

The Voice of America had also learned that it could not successfully compete with the BBC.[39] The American relays through the BBC and even ABSIE had more often than not been taken by the French as just so many more British broadcasts. American relay programs were often identified as "London." When refugees were interviewed about their listening habits, they reported that they frequently assumed they were listening to the BBC when they had heard ABSIE. Even if listeners heard that ABSIE was American, they usually believed it was nevertheless British; the skeptical European assumed that the adjective *American* was merely a camouflage and not a real identification.[40]

The first set of questions American propagandists had to face, therefore, was how they could persuade the French to listen to the Voice of America, when the French were satisfied with their own news and broadcasting system and preoccupied with their own domestic problems of postwar rehabilitation. What kind of radio station should the Voice of America become in order to woo the French?

From Cowan's diary, which he kept between D-Day and the V-E Day, a picture emerges of the leaders of the Voice of America first recognizing the need to change the nature of the Voice, and then working out plans for how to do so. As early as June 22, a little more than two weeks after the invasion of Normandy, Cowan met with Blochman to discuss the future of the Radio Program Bureau. They agreed that Blochman should spend a week analyzing the existing short-wave shows, after which they would review program schedules "with an eye to cutting down as much as possible." Already the two men knew that whatever the Voice had been during the war, it could not stay the same, and that direct short-wave transmissions to France would attract fewer and fewer listeners.[41]

By early August, Cowan had become convinced that short-wave broadcasting had to be cut even more drastically than he had originally planned. The director of the Voice, Werner Michel, had been reducing shows, but when Cowan met with Michel on August 3, the chief of Atlantic operations gently chided Michel for not paring programs back more vigorously. Get rid of "a thousand more transmissions a month," Cowan suggested.[42]

Within another month, short-wave programs were disappearing. Cowan and Blochman met again in early September to review the scheduling, after which Cowan happily recorded that "the program pattern is changing rapidly; should be settled within a few days." Later in the same day Cowan had lunch with Barrett and again discussed short-wave programming. Barrett agreed that short-wave radio had served out its term, and that the Voice ought to slash at least thirty-five hundred to seven thousand programs a week. "This is in line with my own feelings," Cowan noted.[43]

Simultaneously, Cowan and his colleagues began considering what American international radio could do after the end of hostilities and what they wanted it to be like. Once they had agreed that the Voice of America could not compete for a French audience they either had to create a new radio plan or virtually go off the air. For his part Cowan was quite clear in his general thinking. Radio, he believed, remained an important tool of international relations; an American voice in France, and Europe, was worth pursuing. The new American radio, however, would have to represent American policies and American society abroad "through unusual and special programming," which was, he felt, the only way "to get an audience."[44]

American radio to Europe would have to be broadcast over relay stations, which as long as the war lasted would be ABSIE and UNR. Some of these medium- and long-wave programs would be news, especially news of the United States and the war in the Pacific, but on the whole, Cowan believed, a French audience could not be built simply on news coverage. The information function of American radio would have to diminish in liberated areas, and other ways would have to be found to get listeners. American radio should be entertainment, features, round-table discussions, and special talks. As early as mid-July, Cowan enthusiastically recorded in his diary that he had decided to do a half-hour program from Hollywood each day. He wanted variety shows, musicals, and dramatic condensations of movies. He would relay these shows through ABSIE, but he would also record them and send the platters to France, where they could be played over local stations. "If this plan should go through," he confided to his typewriter, "we ought to be able to steal the entire French audience."[45]

To do this, Cowan decided that the whole format of the Voice of America had to change. Houseman had created a schedule of fifteen-minute language programs in quarter-hour rotation. According to this schedule a French program, for example, might go on the air at 8:00 P.M., an Italian one at 8:15, a German at 8:30 and an English at 8:45. All languages were rotated and were heard abroad more or less frequently depending on how often they were played. This schedule made sense in the midst of war, allowing a maximum number of broadcasts in the key languages and enabling the European listener to tune in throughout the day for the latest news updates. It was, in other words, a schedule created for clandestine listeners who wanted to hear news.[46]

Once the clandestine listener had moved out of his hiding place, begun reading French newspapers, and started tuning in local French radio stations, however, this schedule became obsolete. Such was the problem Cowan addressed when he decided that the Voice of America, by relay and shortwave, had to change to block programming. "We will have to take a block of time," he wrote, "perhaps an hour or two hours, and program that in a manner similar in form to domestic programming."[47] Perhaps two hours of prime-time radio would be all the United States would relay abroad. What was wanted, after all, was the kind of quality radio that would attract an audience, not around-the-clock listeners. If the French knew that every night America was on the air with something good to hear, maybe they would tune in. Embedded in this two-hour block would be American news, the Projection of America, discussions intended to promote American policy abroad, and programs that would build bridges of Franco-American friendship.

Cowan implemented some of his ideas, but he could not successfully put the most important of them into effect. The Voice began broadcasting Hollywood shows, music, and other entertainment. By September 1945 the French station RDF rebroadcast one and a half hours of American programs a day, including music, a series of Hollywood programs, and features such as "L'Amèrique depuis 1939" and "Echos d'Amèrique."[48] But Cowan could not retain the writers and announcers he needed to create first-rate shows. By September 1945 much of the programming was turned over to a master radio desk, which wrote shows in English to be translated into other languages as needed. This allowed the Voice to eliminate personnel and bypass the problem of an inadequate French language staff, but it could not reproduce the Gallic flavor that the BBC still had, and which would have been necessary to attract a sizable French audience.[49] Cowan could not create quality French broadcasts.

With liberation, therefore, the leaders of the OWI reconstructed the nature of the Voice of America. There was, however, a second and perhaps more difficult set of questions about what kind of goals the American government hoped to achieve through postwar propaganda. The British and Russians were convinced by 1944 that propaganda should play a part in their postwar foreign policy. They believed that during the period immediately following liberation they should broadcast their ideas, their aspirations, and their peace plans. They wanted to forge links between the French government and the governments of Britain and the Soviet Union, and they considered radio the ideal medium through which to conduct a propaganda of peace.[50]

The Americans had no unified or clear vision of what goals propaganda should achieve, or even what sort of agency should survive the war. Organizational decisions implicitly defined longer-range objectives. There emerged three possible ways of organizing information activities after the war ended. First, a government information service might operate within the State Department. Second, an independent agency, similar to the OWI, might be formed. Third, the private sector could shoulder the burden, with each company supporting its own efforts and working in loose coordination with the government.[51]

The early founders of the OWI and the Voice of America, such as Sherwood, Lazareff, and Cowan, at least initially put their weight behind the last of these three options: the United States should turn international information work over to the private sector and the government should gracefully bow out. Sherwood spelled out his ideas in a memo he wrote to Davis just before Sherwood quit the OWI for Roosevelt's campaign. He recommended that the Overseas Branch drastically reduce its operations. The very fact of such a move, he argued, would appeal to a Europe saturated with propaganda and exhausted by war. Besides, he pointed out, American propaganda, in its leaflets and magazines, its posters and publicity, was too wealthy in tone and texture; it flaunted American money and created bad feelings. Most startling of all, he suggested that the government dismantle the Voice of America and that overseas broadcasting be left to private radio companies.[52]

During the war, he wrote with eloquence, there had been a "moral (but tangible) . . . legitimacy of the term 'Voice of America.'" But, he went on, "with the war ended in Europe I feel that it would be patently dishonest to describe as the 'Voice of America' broadcasts which are subject to rigid control by the directives approved by the State Department and the Joint Chiefs of Staff." They could not do so; they would not, in peacetime, be qualified to interpret the real voice of America, "which is, eternally, many voices." Here was the last word from the man who had originated the Foreign Information Service in July of 1941 and was the founder of American overseas radio propaganda. These were the thoughts of a man who believed that America was composed of many people entwined as one, a nation of nations, woven together in a complex fabric known as the United States. It was the very diversity of the peoples of America that Sherwood spoke of here, and which he felt so strongly could not be translated through a government bureaucracy. It was not that Sherwood loved the private broadcasting companies, but rather that he believed a permanent government station would become just another flat, unimaginative, stolid organization, wedded to an equally unimaginative and stolid foreign policy. It would not represent the American people. "It would become increasingly apparent to the discerning listener that U.S. Government controlled broadcasts were telling no more than a carefully selected part of the truth," he argued. Better to be rid of it.[53]

Lazareff refined Sherwood's ideas. With liberation, the head of the French desk pointed out, France would have its own radio station. The British and the Russians planned to continue broadcasting information and propaganda programs, but unlike the BBC, the Voice of America had never had a sizable audience. Nevertheless, America should not be the only great power left without a voice in France, and, Lazareff argued, "radio is the best, most direct and most rapid means" of communicating ideas and opinions between nations. Therefore, like Sherwood, he suggested that the United States rely on private broadcasting stations, who had the best resources to create high-quality programs and who could expect not only to gain great national prestige, but to be allowed, in time, to have their programs fully sponsored.[54]

Cowan also believed that private broadcasters had to fill the hole created by the shrinking Voice of America, although he also believed that a small government-owned and -operated Voice of America should continue to exist. NBC and CBS, he suggested, should create programs to fill the two-hour blocks of time he advocated for post-liberation programming. Moreover, he saw no reason why these programs could not be supported by advertising, within certain limitations. These broadcasts, Cowan argued, could be fitted into an overall American propaganda and information program through directives created by a board composed of government officials and representatives of private interests.[55]

These men pointed out an essential dilemma. The Voice of America had failed to attract an audience, and as Lazareff especially knew, the French desk had disintegrated with liberation. There was good reason to despair of any future for the Voice. But equally there was no reason to believe that private broadcasters would do after the war what they had not done before – provide good international radio services. Sherwood, Lazareff, and Cowan thus pinpointed the dilemma without providing a workable alternative. Since the Voice of America had failed to attract an audience during the war, there was no reason to suppose that the station could possibly improve afterward, especially since it was sure to be attacked by Congress, shorn of its budget, and left bereft of a talented staff. And yet America could not retire from international radio and leave the field to the British and the Russians.

This dilemma prompted Barrett to outline his own ideas to Davis.[56] It was important to continue international information in the postwar world, Barrett wrote, and therefore he advised establishing a small U.S. information agency that would report to the secretary of state. Short-wave radio, however, had failed expectations; it could not compete with British broadcasting, and ABSIE would have to fold soon after the war ended. Barrett could advise neither continuing the Voice of America nor destroying it, and therefore suggested creating a foundation to operate American short-wave broadcasting facilities. It was an unrealistic proposal that had no future, but it accurately reflected the confusion with which propagandists viewed the Voice. In a larger sense, Barrett's suggestion emerged from the growth in the size and scope of the federal government which the war itself had forced. Americans lived in a new environment of big government burdened with large responsibilities, but still thought as they had in the days of small government with minimal responsibilities. Foundations were one way to fill the space between new functions and traditional viewpoints.

For the OWI, all these suggestions were inconclusive. The Voice did in fact allow for a mixed system of broadcasting between public and private sectors. Since September 1942 NBC and CBS had contributed programs, albeit under strict supervision and subject to Control. By early 1945 the number of shows the networks broadcast abroad had increased. The results were not good. NBC and CBS contributed time, but not the kind of energy for which Sherwood, Lazareff, and Cowan had hoped. The Voice of America, for example, now concentrated on entertainment and the Projection of

America, but the private companies had made no such switch; instead they continued to broadcast news and information in much the same way as they had done in 1944. NBC and CBS shows were boring, badly presented, and poorly timed. Some French programs ran short and ended with musical fills; others were too long and concluded with a race against the clock; musical themes drowned out the voices of announcers; and programs obliterated station identification.[57] Nevertheless, without a good alternative, this mixed system limped along through the end of the war and into the early postwar period.

If the propagandists had no workable suggestions, the U.S. government, especially the State Department, had even less vision. The State Department had never understood how propaganda – or information – might prove an integral part of its operations, how it could be used as an instrument of foreign policy, or even why an equal voice in Europe was important. Perhaps C. D. Jackson hit the mark when he wrote in mid-1945 that "the State Department never got over its jealousy at the creation of this war emergency organization, whose charter would have been within the State Department charter had the State Department been competent to take on the assignment."[58] The department's ambivalence toward propaganda – its desire to control it combined with a continuing suspicion of it as an instrument of diplomacy – paralyzed postwar propaganda planning by the State Department. This hesitation was, moreover, deepened by a general tendency on the part of the State Department to move slowly and plan gradually.

The result was that by 1945 the State Department had not created a postwar plan for propaganda. In a general but vague sort of way the department did support the OWI by 1945. In the face of congressional opposition in mid-1945, as the House of Representatives attempted to cut propaganda appropriations by more than half, the State Department came to the defense of the OWI. Joseph C. Grew, acting secretary of state in June 1945, wrote to President Truman and Secretary of War Stimson, urging them to help the OWI. The department, Grew wrote, regarded the work of the OWI "as important and, indeed, at present indispensable to the most effective conduct of American foreign affairs." But he added a caveat that conveyed the department's position even more forcefully than all the words of support. "We in the Department of State," Grew wrote, "have neither the funds, the specialized personnel, nor the legislative authority to undertake such activities at the present time."[59] The State Department, in other words, would support the OWI, but saw no way to continue that agency's work.

The State Department turned to a special external committee for guidance on postwar propaganda plans, which reported in mid-July 1945 that there should be a continuing government program, that it should be located directly within the State Department, and that its main job should be to supplement and help the work of private communications companies, from broadcasters to news agencies. The government's role, this committee hoped, would be "positive but limited."[60]

On August 31, 1945, Truman signed an executive order abolishing the OWI and transferring its propaganda functions to the State Department, renaming it the Interim International Information Service (IIIS). The department was not happy with this solution, however, and did not give the IIIS its full support. The IIIS limped along, deserted by almost all the OWI leaders, who by the fall of 1945 had returned to private life.

Although the State Department's position was mixed, that of Congress was clear: it wanted to end any program of international information and propaganda. Congress, like the State Department, was acting in long-standing character. It believed that propaganda was at times harmful because the OWI harbored subversive, communist elements who were, or might be, using the resources of the American government to promote global communism. At best, Congress thought propaganda without value and not worth the money. The House especially had never liked the OWI. It had all but destroyed the Domestic Branch in 1943 and allowed the Overseas Branch to continue only because it played an ancillary military role in the war. Fighting Congress had always been one of the most important, and difficult, roles of the leaders of the OWI.

By the summer of 1945, as the life span of the OWI was drawing to a close, the propagandists anticipated a severe budget cut in the operations of the Overseas Branch in general, and the Voice of America in particular. Congressional budget slashing was expected and dreaded, but it also fulfilled the ambivalence the propagandists themselves felt about the Voice. Not that they would have recommended large cuts; they would not have done so. But after the liberation of France the propagandists had compromised with failure, and combined that compromise with their deep commitment to propaganda and information. In an odd sense, by 1945 congressional hostility confirmed what had already become a reality: a muted Voice of America.

The Office of War Information folded with the end of the war. Its demise was not a singular act against the propaganda machinery of the Second World War, however; it was part of a fever of reconversion which coursed through the American body politic at the end of the war. The fact that the OWI was unpopular in Congress and with the press did not help, of course, and the White House instructed the OWI to deliver its own liquidation plans within two days of victory over Japan. The propaganda leaders handed their deliberations to the White House at three o'clock in the morning of August 18, after a meeting that had begun the previous afternoon and lasted twelve straight hours. On August 31 President Truman abolished the OWI.[61]

The Voice of America did not end in 1945 but rather was transferred, along with other information activities of the Overseas Branch, to the State Department. There it remained for the next few years, badly staffed and demoralized, a shell of its former self, going through the motions without well-defined political goals to inform its spirit. It was an institution on the defensive, for with the end of hostilities what could be the future of "a weapon of war wielded . . . on behalf of one's country"?[62] Could there be a role for propaganda in peacetime?

In May 1946 the new director of the IIIS, William Benton, wrote a letter to the publisher of the *New York Times,* Arthur Sulzburger. In it Benton defined his postwar position on propaganda. He complained that Sulzburger had narrowly and unfairly dismissed both propaganda and the efforts of the Voice of America as the process of distorting the news "in order to create specific impressions abroad about a specific situation in which we have specific interests." It was as if, Benton went on, Sulzberger had charged the U.S. government with engaging in sinister activity: "that what the State Department is doing is what the German, the Italian and the Japanese governments did" during the war. No, Benton retorted, that is not the case. His answer tells much about how he defined propaganda and its political goals:

> The fact is that we try to present as objective a news report as is humanly possible. . . . It means we present the "unfavorable," the good about America with the bad. We do not want to do more than that. We do not need to. Even if we wanted to do otherwise, we couldn't get away with it. . . . Our objectivity must be antiseptic to the point of dullness.[63]

What is singular about the conclusion of the American experience in wartime propaganda during World War II was the continued national reluctance to engage in propaganda, or to use international broadcasting, to further American diplomatic goals. Not only did private companies refuse to take on the job; so did the federal government. The United States remained unwilling to support a serious international broadcasting station until 1947, when the cold war defined the enemy and revived the uses of propaganda. But in 1945 the cold war was still in its formative stages and American foreign policy was largely predicated on Roosevelt's international and cooperative vision.

The Allies destroyed the propaganda organizations of Germany, Italy, and Japan. But in 1945 both Great Britain and the Soviet Union saw propaganda and information as part of their postwar foreign policy and worked hard to continue as well as improve their international broadcasting operations. The United States, alone of the Allies, did not do so. It is testament to the strong American aversion to propaganda, and it gives witness to the powerful American sentiment against government involvement in broadcasting. It also reflects a basic American reliance on military strength rather than complex foreign policy maneuvers to achieve national ends, and indeed, the lesson of two world wars had been that American military strength and national resources prevailed when needed.

Once the war had been won the United States had to face the question of its political and economic goals. By 1944 the liberal ideology of the thirties did not provide adequate answers. To the extent that liberals continued to attach themselves to the president's policies, they did so through the United Nations in alliance with the Soviet Union and the United Nations Relief and Rehabilitation Administration. But administration policies were fully accepted and supported by the old enemies of the OWI leaders: the State Department and the military. If one's beliefs are defined by one's enemies, State Department support confused the issue of who was a propaganda liberal and who was a conservative.

No political philosophy, moreover, replaced the liberalism of the early war years. What was needed in the last years of the war was a long-range postwar plan that Roosevelt would not provide, and no one else could give. In the face of this dilemma the Voice of America retreated to a broadcast style of hard facts and verifiable quotations.

Why did the United States engage in overseas propaganda when there was such a small audience and so little domestic support? In 1945 Americans were ambivalent over whether—and if so how—to relinquish their traditional isolation. They sought the benefits, both economic and political, of world domination. They relished the idea of an American Century. But they could not bring themselves publicly to accept the burdens required, including an open and official campaign to influence world opinion in time of peace. They could not bear to give up their self-image as an independent republic and replace it with that of an empire. The continued operation of the Voice of America thus proved especially problematic after the war, for the Voice in peace symbolized global domination.

The Voice remained on the air nevertheless. Despite its small wartime audiences and its consequent sense of failure, there was no choice but to keep the Voice of America operating. Roosevelt had initiated the propaganda broadcasting station in part out of deference to Sherwood and Donovan and their conviction that they could help win the war, but also because he realized that the United States had henceforth to engage in external radio propaganda quite simply because the rest of the world was doing so. America could not be left out. Radio demanded use, abroad as well as at home. Before the war, private radio stations had used the international radio frequencies and acted as unofficial American propagandists, but after the war the radio industry refused to shoulder that burden. The federal government therefore had to do the job. Britain broadcast around the world. The Soviet Union broadcast around the world. So too did France, Italy, Chile, and Egypt; Ethiopia had done so as early as 1935. Having no choice, the United States limped along in the radio brigade until 1947, when the cold war infused the Voice with new meaning and energy.

# Epilogue

AMERICAN overseas propaganda did not stop after the end of World War II, but it did change. Although President Truman abolished the OWI in late August 1945, the Voice of America remained on the air. And although the OWI folded, some propaganda administration continued within the State Department, albeit on a smaller scale. The operations that had been established in 1941 remained a permanent feature of American international policy. But in many important ways, propaganda after the Second World War became significantly different from what it had been between 1941 and 1945. Propaganda in peace could not be what it had been in war.

When Truman dismantled the OWI, he directed the secretary of state to formulate a program "to be conducted on a continuing basis."[1] From September to December 1945 the State Department took over operations under the Interim International Information Service under Archibald MacLeish, assistant secretary of state for public and cultural affairs. Truman's explicit goal was to establish some mechanism "to see to it that other peoples receive a full and fair picture of American life and the aims and policies of the United States Government."[2]

MacLeish soon left and William B. Benton, an advertising man, educator, and publisher, took over. Benton's job was to sell his program to Congress and to the State Department. Neither was enthusiastic about a permanent propaganda agency. Benton therefore took a circumspect approach, promising that his organization would create information, not propaganda. It would not be a full-blown information agency competing with private interests such as CBS and NBC, but it would be an effort "to fill the gaps." He cut expenditures to the bone, slashed Voice programming, and let go, or did not replace, nearly three-quarters of the staff. Congress further decreased appropriations until funding for the Voice, and propaganda under the State Department, hit rock bottom in 1946–47.[3] Congress eliminated all funds for propaganda in 1946, and Benton's organization was saved only by the efforts of Truman and Secretary of State George C. Marshall.[4]

That year, 1946, witnessed another bureaucratic reorganization, and the fall of 1947 yet another. But throughout propaganda remained a function of the Department of State.[5] Over the summer of 1947 a group of congressmen traveling abroad became aware of the cold war in Europe. America needed to be defended against a new enemy: the Soviet Union. When Congress convened in January 1948 it passed the Smith-Mundt Act, the first formal postwar act authorizing the American government to engage in overseas propaganda. The act provided for "an information service to disseminate abroad information about the United States, its people and policies promulgated by the Congress, the President, the Secretary of State and other responsible officials of government having to do with matters affecting foreign affairs."[6]

By the late 1940s propaganda became increasingly caught up in the cold war. In February 1947 the Voice inaugurated its Russian service. The tone of the Voice hardened, and it concentrated its efforts on Russia and eastern Europe.[7] The budget of the Voice rose from $8.9 million in 1947 to $16.1 million in 1948. By 1952 the Voice was broadcasting in forty-six languages, twenty of which were spoken in iron or bamboo curtain countries.

In 1953 the propaganda administration remained a division of the State Department, but it was reeling under attacks by Senator Joseph McCarthy. If an American agency for international propaganda was to survive, something had to be done. President Eisenhower therefore began a quiet but concerted effort to clarify the functions of a propaganda program. The administration undertook one examination, the Senate Foreign Relations Committee another, and the House yet a third. All recommended removing propaganda from the State Department. In June Eisenhower submitted a plan to Congress, consolidating all foreign information programs and operations into a new, independent organization known as the United States Information Agency, or USIA. The State Department was to provide policy guidance, the military to cooperate in policy planning. The plan went into effect that August.[8]

The administration structure of propaganda remained relatively constant after the creation of the USIA. Gone were the days of yearly reorganization under the State Department. Only President Carter overhauled the agency. In 1975 he reshaped the USIA into the International Communications Agency. Carter's decision reflected his desire to make propaganda more responsive to international audiences. He wanted to integrate cross-cultural concepts into American propaganda and to demonstrate U.S. appreciation and respect for other nations and other cultures. The new agency was to "tell the world about our society and policies—in particular, our commitment to cultural diversity and individual liberty."[9] Cultural communication and mutual understanding became the new propaganda goals, and the International Communications Agency was Carter's instrument to realize those aims. President Reagan dismantled Carter's work, however, and as part of his renewal of cold war ideology he revitalized the old USIA in his propaganda campaign against Russia and for global stability.[10]

The overall administrative story was thus quite simple. The OWI folded and in its stead Truman placed a shrunken propaganda program within the State Department. The cold war then revitalized the need for and role of propaganda, and in 1953 Eisenhower created a successor agency to the OWI, the USIA. With a few changes that agency has survived to the present.

The sense of continuity was reinforced by the governmental realities of running an independent executive agency for external propaganda. Congress continually questioned the Voice of America and the USIA about their operations, and right-wing inheritors of the Taber tradition took pleasure in browbeating the propagandists, just as Taber and others had throughout the war. Congress underfunded propaganda administration. As early as 1948, during the hot years of the cold war, House representatives accused the Voice of excessive liberalism and indecency for broadcasting selections from John Gunther's *Inside USA* (a passage stating that Texas had been born in sin and New England conceived in hypocrisy) and from Works Progress Administration guidebooks (a section on Wyoming, portraying Indian maidens as running foot races "undressed and unfeathered"). Congress investigated.[11]

In February 1953, Senator Joseph McCarthy opened hearings on the Voice. Neither Truman nor the State Department, which was itself greatly demoralized by attacks from the junior Senator from Wisconsin, defended the station. In April Congress reduced the station's budget and cut broadcasts to noncommunist nations.[12]

Relations with Congress improved after the McCarthy era, but they did not fundamentally alter. In the mid-sixties J. William Fulbright, chairman of the Senate Foreign Relations Committee, supported the Voice, but without enthusiasm. "I have great difficulty in finding any favorable reaction to the Voice of America," he complained, "but that is a matter of opinion." But he voted yes: "I supported [it] but I do not have any great faith in it."[13] By the early seventies Fulbright had abandoned even this tepid support and accused the Voice of being a cold war relic. Propaganda cost too much money, he argued. Why should Congress fund the Voice to broadcast cold war rhetoric while Nixon jetted to Peking and Moscow in search of détente?

Fulbright evidenced a mainstream distrust of propaganda. Congressman John J. Rooney, a Brooklyn conservative and chairman of the House Appropriations Subcommittee on the State Department and USIA, renewed the spirit of John Taber. Congressional sessions in the sixties "were wearing, abrasive . . . nickel and diming, haggling over budget cuts, arguing for restorations, justifying salaries, programs and general expenses in the face of vocalized dislike."[14] President Kennedy's USIA director called these meetings his "exercise in self-restraint."[15] That in itself was a restrained epithet with which Barnes, Cowan, Sherwood, and Carroll would have agreed.

At best, the propagandists found themselves in the unenviable position of trying to get money from a congress whose political divisions inhibited them from making any clear presentation of their case. They feared that anything they said, whether seemingly left- or right-wing, would be used against them. At worst, the propagandists found themselves enmeshed in a battle over executive power between Congress and the president.[16]

Nor did relations with the White House and the State Department improve. Presidents came and went, but except for Ronald Reagan, none gave wholehearted support to propaganda, nor did they take an active interest in the Voice of America and the successor agencies to the OWI. President Kennedy did not give the director of the United States Information Agency, former CBS newsman Edward R. Murrow, advance warning that the United States was about to invade Cuba at the Bay of Pigs. Nor did Kennedy consult Murrow on how to handle the Cuban missile crisis until after the fact.

Lyndon B. Johnson never liked the USIA and as a senator had favored cutting its budget. When he became president, as early as 1964 he reduced funding of the USIA by $5 million. "With little support from the White House," one observer wrote, "U.S.I.A. officials year after year troop over to the Capitol at budget time to ask for their money. There, Congressmen ask them some searching questions about the effectiveness of the USIA. Apparently the answers are not compelling enough to elicit a vote of confidence, or a larger budget for the Agency."[17]

The State Department also continued to lack any great interest in propaganda, despite the fact that propaganda administration remained housed within the department from 1945 until 1953. Even Congress found the department's negligence appalling. In 1953 the U.S. Advisory Commission on Information reported "a singular lack of enthusiasm and imagination in the [State] Department's development of the information program. . . . Instead of initiating and carrying on a fresh, dynamic program, the Department converted it into a low-level and secondary operation. It soon became apparent that the Department was . . . interested in conforming the information program to its own long-established conventions. . . ."[18]

Within propaganda operations other trends that had surfaced during the war and plagued the wartime agency continued. The Voice of America remained separate in its operations and identity from the rest of overseas propaganda, and even when its offices moved to Washington, in 1953, the old strain of "we" versus "they" held sway. The broadcasters found the propaganda bureaucrats too stuffy and stifling. "We at the Voice," wrote Henry Loomis, Voice director from 1958 until 1965, "are more conscious of our immediate contact with our audience, and therefore more acutely aware of the problems of cross-cultural communications. . . . We believe our audience judges us as radio," he continued, pinpointing the wellspring of conflict, "while some of our colleagues assume that the audience considers a commentary by the Voice as authoritative a statement of U.S. policy as a statement by the Secretary of State or the President."[19] And Loomis's successor, John Chancellor, concurred when he wrote that "the USIA suffers . . . from too many career employees suspended in a sort of civil service aspic. . . ."[20]

There remained inherent problems in linking the broadcasts of the Voice with the foreign policy of the State Department and White House. The Voice continued to structure its programs around the news, adding features as trimmings. But to be interesting and competitive with other short-wave world services, news had to contain the latest up-to-the-minute information. News ordinarily came into the Voice over the wire services, and there was therefore little time to consult the State Department or White House. Sometimes the Voice restricted what it said about a story, such as conflict between Pakistan and India, or fighting in the Middle East. But foreign leaders regarded a one-line Voice story as an indication of official U.S. interest in, or reaction to, that event. News reporting, of any sort, was not neutral.

The OWI leaders had long struggled with this problem. The fight over the broadcasts after the abdication of Mussolini – the moronic little king episode – had demonstrated both the difficulty propaganda leaders had in reaching the State Department and the price they paid for not strictly following administration policy. Roosevelt's decision to fire Barnes, Warburg, and Johnson and to remove Sherwood to London may have been extreme, but the difficulty of meshing fast-breaking news into State Department policy decisions continued to be problematic and unsolvable.[21]

The Voice of America moreover remained remote from events in the rest of the world and struggled to evaluate, or even measure, its audience. For example, it altered its broadcasts to Greece during the late sixties at the insistence of the Greek military junta. U.S. relay facilities in Greece, through which the Voice beamed its programs to eastern Europe and the Soviet Union, gave Greek military leaders political leverage, even though American foreign policy already supported the junta. Spyridon Granitsas, a Greek journalist in exile who free-lanced for the Voice of America, spoke before a congressional investigating committee in 1970 and pleaded for change. The Voice, he insisted, was a voice with no ears; "it never heard the wishes, the desires, the voices of other people." But if this imperviousness was so in general, after the junta the Voice gave the impression that it sent its "message with the approval and embrace of the military junta." Add to this, he railed, a more general insensitivity. The Voice would broadcast to Greece stories on U.S. agricultural surpluses, terming them "provisions." "Thus we believe," Granitsas complained, "that other people will think that we are provident and that agricultural surpluses do not exist in the United States. This kind of terminological manipulation is pretty thin, and at least in Europe, is not believed." By 1970, he despaired, no one in Greece tuned in the Voice.[22]

The American propagandists continued to have difficulty evaluating and measuring their audience, despite constant pressure from Congress to do so as proof of the Voice's appropriations value. It was, to be sure, far easier to interview listeners, and to that extent to measure listening. But more subtle questions remained. For example, should Americans broadcasting to China speak in flawless Mandarin, thus exhibiting their educational credentials, or should they speak the corrupt dialects of the greater proportion of the Chinese themselves? And if such minor problems proved vexing, how much more complex were questions of policy, strategy, content, audience, and effects of the Voice of America broadcasts to the People's Republic of China—or anywhere else? Evaluation of effect and audience, or what those who tuned in really heard, remained elusive.[23]

American propaganda continued to be, as it had been during the war, a two-fronted endeavor. It was enmeshed in complex issues of domestic politics, wherein the Voice was caught up in battles without either presidential support or a local constituency. As before, the battle for survival at home often proved more draining and difficult than the battle abroad.[24]

Yet if the domestic context remained the same, the propaganda itself—from its staff to its political goals and its relationship to foreign policy—did not. Wartime propaganda proved a special case. What came after the war was new and different.

When the war ended, the exiles and outcasts who had populated the desks of the Voice of America went home. They had not come as permanent émigrés, but as temporary refugees. They had always intended to return to their native lands as fast as possible, and through their broadcasts they tried to shorten the war and quicken their departure. The very work they did—the broadcasts they wrote, edited, or announced—became for them both testimonies of their wartime loyalties and portfolios of wartime achievement for postwar employers.

The men and women who graced the French desk were a stunning assemblage of French talent. Pierre Lazareff, chief of the desk until he left for London and ABSIE in 1944, was France's most brilliant newspaper editor. He created cohesion among the members of the desk, and he worked tirelessly to create an authentically French sound. He stamped his style on the French desk, creating a special unit that was not merely a collection of experienced writers and journalists, but Lazareff's own creation.

He had working for him men and women of great intellectual and artistic talent. Writers included the philosophers Jacques Maritain, Helene Iswolsky, and Denis de Rougemont. There were novelists and poets such as Julien Green and Yvon Gaul. There were critics and intellectuals such as Leon Kochnitzky, who had once been private secretary to Gabriele d'Annunzio and who later published seven volumes of poetry, translated Shakespeare's sonnets into French, edited *La revue musicale* as well as newspaper criticism of art and music, and spoke Russian, Polish, Italian, English, and German as well as French. Rachel Bespaloff had written about Greek mythology, and was a regular contributor to *Nouvelle revue française* and the *Revue philosophique*. Dolores Vanneti had been an actress in Paris, Georges Pitoeff an actor. Philippe Barrès was a prolific journalist whose father, Maurice Barrès, had been one of France's most eminent journalists. The announcers numbered many famous and talented Frenchmen such as André Breton. They all lived in an intense, hothouse environment in which they did not work five days a week for eight hours a day and then go home, but toiled seven long days a week and lived, ate, and breathed the French desk. If single, they roomed together. Married or not, they slept with each other. They talked to each other and about each other. They were a world unto themselves.

It was a world that moved to the cadences of the French language. André Breton refused to learn English lest he pollute his French. Lazareff himself spoke little English, and was forced to communicate to the outside world through a series of interpreters. The French desk—indeed all the language desks—wrote, spoke, and thought behind the nearly impermeable membrane of the language barrier, connected to the rest of the Voice and OWI only by a few bilingual translators.

Together they formed an amazing collection of talent. But with the end of the war they fled New York for France. Even those few who remained in New York left the Voice as quickly as they could. For them, propaganda was an exclusively wartime activity, and with the end of war they wanted no more of it. But as long as they were there they gave the Voice unequaled talent and, above all, immediacy. They were emotionally still in France.

What distinguishes their experience from that of political refugees who came to the Voice of America after the war is that the French desk staff were on the winning side. They possessed a sense of connectedness without the bitterness of permanent exile. They had passion and enthusiasm for their cause, but they never became mired in their status as refugees, railing against the fate they could not change. And they were not in New York very many years; indeed, some of the most important French desk writers, such as Jacques Maritain, stayed with the Voice for only a year. They were thus enabled to express the enthusiasm and freedom of the Gallic spirit which could not be duplicated in the Voice after the war. Their cause was just, it was going to win, and then they would go home. As one desk writer later observed of postwar Voice of America broadcasts to the Soviet Union, "When I listen, sometimes I think it has been written in 1918 and not in 1986. But we on the French desk, don't you think that we were aware of how to speak to the people we left two years ago?"[25]

The postwar Voice never again had such a brilliant assemblage of writers, editors, and announcers. Nor were the top positions filled with men of such conviction and passion, talent and experience as Robert Sherwood, James Warburg, Joseph Barnes, or John Houseman. The administration of postwar propaganda machinery became a civil service bureaucracy that attracted not only journalists but civil servants, foreign service career officers, and political appointees. The civil servants especially were steady and sound and often excellent, but the excitement of the war years could never be recaptured or duplicated.

What differentiates peacetime propaganda most significantly from wartime propaganda, however, is its relationship to foreign policy and policy goals—and leaders' conceptions of how to achieve those goals. During the war the chief propagandists, Warburg, Barnes, Johnson, and Houseman, thought that they should play a direct role in creating American foreign policy. They believed in the righteousness of their liberal definition of war aims, and they intended to project these aims over the Voice of America. Warburg, for example, argued that it was "part of our function to see that the National Policy is not hopelessly compromised by a flock of apparently disconnected, but actually closely interwoven, acquiescences. There is a great danger that in our anxiety to avoid disorder, we make ourselves the agents of preserving that very political and economic status which gave birth . . . to the Fascist and Nazi anti-revolutions."[26] And Sherwood's friend and confidant, Percy Winner, argued more extremely that "propaganda policy does not necessarily stem from or agree with foreign policy. It must be drawn up with the advice, not the orders, of the State Department."[27] Warburg later argued, after he had been forced out of the OWI, that American wartime propaganda had failed not because of the propagandists, but because American ideology, and therefore foreign policy, was too conservative. Thus in the future, he suggested, propaganda should help liberalize foreign policy.[28]

By 1943, however, there were propagandists who clearly disagreed with these OWI liberals. Daniel Lerner wrote that the makers of foreign policy should define the goals of propaganda, and Hans Speier argued that the foreign policy goals of propaganda should remain the province of State Department diplomats. Wallace Carroll stated that the independent decisions initiated in New York led to chaos and then immobilization. For him, the main role of propaganda was to explain American policy sympathetically—even mistaken policy—as there were always reasons for policies, and these reasons were not all bad. As Richard Crossman aptly phrased the problem, propaganda should be the handmaiden of foreign and military policy.[29]

This shift in the relationship of propaganda to policy was not confined to the United States; it occurred in Britain as well. BBC propaganda, like Voice of America broadcasts, was originally highly dramatic and creative. The most famous early BBC tactic was the *V* campaign, which urged listeners throughout western Europe to signal their resistance to the Axis by splashing their walls and streets with the letter *V* — *V* for victory and *V* for freedom.

In Britain, as in America, official foreign policy came ultimately to control propaganda output. The propagandist Richard Crossman, speaking years after the end of the war, explained that the *V* campaign "made us understand that psychological warfare may do more harm than good unless it is strictly coordinated with diplomatic and military activity."[30] Propaganda, Crossman came to believe, could not be an independent arm of government; it could not work miracles on its own; it could succeed only as an advance guard of clearly defined policy, whether that of the Foreign Office or of the British Chiefs of Staff.

BBC propaganda therefore also took on an increasingly objective-sounding, journalistic tone. As Crossman explained, "What sounded objective to the home audience sounded like propaganda to the Germans. If we had put out the B.B.C. home bulletins in German, it would have been written off as flagrant propaganda." Propaganda, he continued, "has to be as concentrated and as apparently objective, informative, and concise as possible." For, said Crossman, speaking in the instance of the Germans, but in terms applicable to the broad reach of British overseas broadcasting by 1944, "what they wanted was news."[31]

The first OWI leaders created a propaganda supporting and promoting resistance under a united front, left-liberal European leadership; the second set of leaders turned propaganda toward news and information, and relied on military victory instead of political promises or ideologically defined goals. As Daniel Lerner observed in explaining how difficult political ideology, goals, and promises became even for the propagandists to find in State Department and White House directives, "The less clearly Allied statesmen committed themselves, the less risk they ran of alienating one or another member of their coalition."[32]

After the war ended, the debate over the relationship between propaganda and foreign policy continued. But the lines of argument changed. During the Second World War the more liberal and independent-minded propagandists used their product to push at the edges of foreign policy and thereby change it. But with the beginning of the cold war in 1947, liberal and independent propagandists advocated a propaganda of information, of objective news. During the war the more conservative leaders had avoided the stickier debates over foreign policy and relied on journalistic information. But after 1947 the conservatives were far to the political right of any of the major leaders of the OWI. These new men used propaganda as a weapon of the cold war, a position the new liberals argued against under the objective-sounding rubric of journalistic standards.

Edward R. Murrow in many ways personified the liberal propagandist during his tenure as director of the USIA under President Kennedy.[33] Murrow came to the job from a career of more than twenty-five years in radio and television journalism and a deep commitment to independent, reliable, and objective reporting. He agreed to join Kennedy's administration because he believed Kennedy would not only stand up to the Russians—for 1960 was still very much a cold war year—but bring standards of excellence and liberalism to the administration of the U.S. government. He thought that to be effective the Voice of America had first of all to achieve credibility. "We are not operating in a closed society," he had told the Committee on International Information Activities as early as 1953, when Eisenhower was exploring how to restructure propaganda administration. "There are too many alternative sources of information to permit successful slanting. We should," he therefore argued, "above all else attempt to achieve credibility, for the measure of our success will be the degree to which we are believed."[34] Or as John Chancellor argued during his period as head of the Voice of America from 1965 until 1967, "selling America was a matter of being truthful. The persuasiveness of the commentaries stemmed from the credibility of the news."[35]

To this end Murrow tried to establish a Voice of America that would be a "radio mirror" for the enormous diversity of American culture and opinion. Murrow's policy met its test over the Cuban missile crisis in the fall of 1962. Although Murrow wanted to further American interests through journalism reflecting the range of American opinion, including opposition to Kennedy's policy over Russian missiles in Cuba, as director of the USIA he could not do so. Murrow found himself in the miserable position of compelling the Voice to adopt a monolithic tone that in essence merely repeated what Kennedy or his secretary of state said. Government policy won over any propagandist's opposition, just as it had during the days of the OWI. But what is crucial is not that the debate existed, but that liberal opposition to presidential cold war policy expressed itself through an adherence to the standards of American journalism and the relating of objective information, rather than an insistence on the inherent righteousness of the foreign policy in question.

With the beginning of the cold war, conservatives undertook to substitute propaganda for the guns, tanks, planes, and men of active warfare. As the Voice director Foy Kohler said in December 1950, "Propaganda must be made a potent weapon in an effort to avoid another great conflict."[36] When the cold war became hot, as during the war in Vietnam, propaganda became one-sided in favor of official American policy. And under the direction of President Richard Nixon's USIA director, Frank Shakespeare, the Voice of America was to "portray and advocate the ideas we believe in."[37] Central to these ideas were the direct goals of American interests and the power of democracy and capitalism.

During the cold war the United States was engaged in a war of ideology, but not of active fighting. Words again served in the place of military might, as they had in 1942. The struggle for the minds of men was again termed as important as military engagement. After the cold war began to command the direction of propaganda and the Voice of America, liberals who opposed what was happening took refuge in the only ideology that could counter the pressures of the cold war: a free press and objective journalism.[38]

Yet the goals of propaganda in peace, however fragile that peace, could not possibly be the same as they had been in war. During the Second World War, military ends were always paramount. The Allies had to win, and this single fact could substitute, at least temporarily, for any more complex political aims. The target of victory gave propaganda special functions. It aimed to disarm the enemy psychologically, in preparation for the coming invasion. The approaches to how this end could be accomplished were various, and OWI leaders and the Voice of America experimented with a fair number of them. But even so, war gave propaganda a reasonably clear role to play. Thus a liberal, left-leaning politician such as Richard Crossman, working out of the Psychological Warfare Branch of Allied Forces Headquarters in North Africa, or the Psychological Warfare Division of Supreme Headquarters in London, could argue for the necessity of propaganda acting as a handmaiden of policy.

No such clarity could exist in peace. There was no military goal with which propaganda could intertwine. And political goals, even such strong and often repeated aims as besting the Soviet Union in a cold war, disentangled into numerous and complex strands of ideas on close examination. The cold war could be argued to have played a more important domestic than foreign policy role in the 1950s. But if this was the case, how was propaganda to further which end? As long, however, as the propagandists saw themselves as doing a job akin to what had been done in war—indeed, which was on a continuum with what had been done in war—they could not analyze the reasons propaganda became increasingly difficult to effect.

The American government continues to support a United States Information Agency, but debates over the USIA and the Voice of America still periodically flare up. Does the United States do a good job of presenting itself to the world—and of winning the minds and hearts of men and women around the world? Should propaganda be based on the standards of objective news as developed in the American press, both electronic and print, or should different principles govern the broadcasts of the Voice of America? Should there be a propaganda agency at all in time of peace, or should our communications be left in the hands of the private media?

The answers to these questions are a matter of individual political philosophy. But perhaps when debating the merits of an official instrument of propaganda, it is important to bear in mind that the present-day Voice of America, and the USIA, are distinct from the wartime Voice and the OWI. War presented special needs and opportunities that are not or cannot be duplicated in peace. And just as the war itself transformed propaganda, so the peace that followed again changed America, and the propaganda that new society produced.

The history of the wartime Voice of America and the OWI cannot, therefore, justify the present-day propaganda. Nor can the history of the Voice and the USIA be seen as a straight-line continuum. But that statement does not in itself answer the question of whether, or how, the United States should conduct propaganda—or information dissemination, or publicity.

We live in an era in which every major power, and most minor ones, have their own propaganda services. International short-wave radio (and increasingly television) is used by nearly every nation to speak to the governments and citizens of other nations. Accordingly, not to take part in this effort is, in the latter half of the twentieth century, unthinkable. To engage in propaganda—to broadcast to the world over the Voice of America, and use the other instruments of the USIA—has become a necessity of contemporary global politics.

*NOTES*

*BIBLIOGRAPHY*

*INDEX*

# Notes

Collections of archival sources which are frequently cited in the notes are referred to in the following shortened forms:

BBC Archives  BBC Written Archives Centre, Caversham Park, Reading, England.

BOB Records  Records of the Bureau of the Budget, Record Group 51, National Archives, Washington, D.C.

Barnes Papers  Papers of Joseph Barnes, in the possession of Mrs. Elizabeth Barnes, New York, N.Y.

Cowan Papers  Papers of Louis G. Cowan, Columbia University, New York, N.Y.

Davis Papers  Papers of Elmer Davis, Library of Congress, Washington, D.C.

FSP Records  Records of the Foreign Service Posts of the Department of State, Record Group 84, National Records Center, Suitland, Md.

Ickes Papers  Papers of Harold L. Ickes, Library of Congress, Washington, D.C.

Jackson Papers  Papers of C. D. Jackson, Dwight David Eisenhower Library, Abilene, Kans.

Lilly Papers  Papers of Edward P. Lilly, Records of the Joint Chiefs of Staff, Record Group 218, National Archives, Washington, D.C.

McCloy Papers  Correspondence of John J. McCloy, 1941–1945, Records of the Office of the Secretary of War, Record Group 107, National Archives, Washington, D.C.

Miall Papers  Papers of Leonard Miall, Taplow Village, Berks, England.

ONI Records  Records of the Office of Naval Intelligence, USDIA 373-001725, National Records Center, Suitland, Md.

OWI Collection  Sound recordings in the Office of War Information Collection, Division of Motion Pictures, Broadcasting and Recorded Sound, Library of Congress, Washington, D.C.

OWI Records  Records of the Office of War Information, Record Group 208, National Records Center, Suitland, Md.

PRO, FO 371  Records of the Foreign Office, Public Record Office, London.

PRO, PWE Records, FO 898  Records of the Political Warfare Executive, Public Record Office, London.

PS Files    President's Secretary's Files, Franklin D. Roosevelt Library, Hyde Park, N.Y.

Rosenman Papers    Papers of Samuel Rosenman, Franklin D. Roosevelt Library, Hyde Park, N.Y.

SD Records    Records of the Department of State, Record Group 59, National Archives, Washington, D.C.

Sherwood Papers    Papers of Robert E. Sherwood, Houghton Library, Harvard University, Cambridge, Mass.

Warburg Papers    Papers of James P. Warburg, John F. Kennedy Library, Boston, Mass.

WD Records    Records of the War Department General and Special Staff, Record Group 165, National Archives.

## Introduction

1    Sound recording, August 5, 1942, LWO 12487, reel 21A3, OWI Collection; Werner Michel, interview with author, April 24, 1983; Robert Newman, interview with author, February 20, 1986; Michel Rapaport Gordey, interview with author, November 6, 1985.

2    Harold D. Lasswell, *Propaganda Technique in the World War* (New York: Knopf, 1927).

3    For the development of early American broadcasting see Susan Douglass, *Inventing American Broadcasting, 1899–1922* (Baltimore: Johns Hopkins University Press, 1987); Susan R. Smulyan, "And Now a Word from Our Sponsors . . . : The Commercialization of American Broadcast Radio, 1920–1934" (Ph.D. diss., Yale University, 1985); Erik Barnouw, *A Tower in Babel: A History of Broadcasting in the United States to 1933* (New York: Oxford University Press, 1966). For an authoritative discussion of the origins of British broadcasting see Asa Briggs, *The History of Broadcasting in the United Kingdom*, vol. 2: *The Golden Age of Wireless* (London: Oxford University Press, 1965).

4    Erik Barnouw, *The Golden Web: A History of Broadcasting in the United States, 1933–1953* (New York: Oxford University Press, 1968), 7–9.

5    Stanley Leinwoll, *From Spark to Satellite: A History of Radio Communication* (New York: Scribner's, 1979), 114; Llewellyn White, *The American Radio* (Chicago: University of Chicago Press, 1947), 17. For a discussion of the development of shortwave see also Michael Kent Sidel, "A Historical Analysis of American Shortwave Broadcasting, 1916–1942" (Ph.D. diss., Northwestern University, 1976); George Sterling, *The Radio Manual* (New York: Van Nostrand, 1928); J. B. Morecroft, "The March of Radio," *Radio Broadcast*, August 1924, 296–97; Joseph Baudino, "A History of Short Wave Broadcasting," Division of Electricity, National Museum of American History, Smithsonian Institution, n.d.; John H. Reyner, *Short Wave Radio* (London: Pitman and Sons, 1942); Albert Hoyt Taylor and Robert S. Kruse, "High Frequency Transmission and Reception," in *The Radio Engineering Handbook*, ed. Keith Henney (New York: McGraw-Hill, 1935).

6  "Germany Speaks," Princeton Listening Center, Report no. 11, October 21, 1940;
   Report no. 5, February 1–15, 1940, SD Records 811.76/510. Although the Italian
   international short-wave service was neither as harsh nor as insistent in its style
   as was its German model, Italian radio propaganda generally followed the German lead. See Thomas Grandin, *The Political Use of Radio* (New York: Arno,
   1971), 53; *Radio Guide,* June 1940, 15.

7  Mark Lincoln Chadwin, *The Hawks of World War II* (Chapel Hill: University
   of North Carolina Press, 1968), 44.

8  Conference minutes, Propaganda Committee, November 18, 1940, box 247,
   Ickes Papers.

9  Conference minutes, Propaganda Committee, November 28, 1940, box 247,
   Ickes Papers.

10 Memorandum, McCloy to George C. Marshall, February 8, 1941, box 18, Lilly
   Papers.

11 Ernst Kris and Nathan Leites, "Trends in Twentieth Century Propaganda,"
   in *A Reader in Public Opinion and Communication,* ed. Bernard Berelson and
   Morris Janowitz (Glencoe, Ill.: Free Press, 1953).

12 E. H. Gombrich, *Myth and Reality in German War-Time Broadcasts* (London:
   Athlone, 1970), 13.

13 Ibid., 19. See also Gombrich, *Art and Illusion: A Study in the Psychology of Pictorial Representation* (London: Phaidon, 1959).

14 John F. Sweets, *The Politics of Resistance in France, 1940–1944* (De Kalb: Northern Illinois University Press, 1976); M. R. D. Foot, *Resistance* (New York:
   McGraw-Hill, 1977).

15 Asa Briggs, *The History of Broadcasting in the United Kingdom,* vol. 3: *The War
   of Words* (London: Oxford University Press, 1970).

16 Norman D. Markowitz, *The Rise and Fall of the People's Century: Henry A. Wallace and American Liberalism, 1941–1948* (New York: Free Press, 1973), 48–57;
   James Edward Miller, *The United States and Italy, 1940–1950: The Politics and
   Diplomacy of Stabilization* (Chapel Hill: University of North Carolina Press,
   1986), 17–23.

17 For a contrasting argument see Allan M. Winkler, *The Politics of Propaganda:
   The Office of War Information, 1942–1945* (New Haven: Yale University Press,
   1978). In this excellent study, Winkler argues that by 1944 the leaders of the
   OWI increasingly served a coalition of conservatives composed of men from
   the Departments of State, War, and Navy and from Congress. After early 1944
   the liberal OWI leaders split between those who refused to accommodate their
   liberal views to administration policy and were fired, and those who were able
   to shelve their ideological commitments and remained to salvage what they
   could while working with conservatives outside the propaganda organization.
   But this argument does not take into account the effect of the war. What had
   been possible and reasonable in 1942 no longer remained so in 1944. The progress of the war destroyed the context of the original Voice of America and OWI,
   and in due time necessitated certain fundamental changes both in the propaganda and in the institutional structure of the OWI.

*Chapter 1.  Founding a Propaganda Agency*

1   Conference minutes, Propaganda Committee, November 18, 1940, box 247, Ickes Papers.

2   Richard W. Steele, "Preparing for the Public for War: Efforts to Establish a National Propaganda Agency, 1940–1941," *American Historical Review* 75 (October 1970): 1640–53; Louis Brownlow, Final Draft, November 28, 1940, Defense, Papers of Louis Brownlow, John F. Kennedy Library, Boston. Roosevelt may have considered using radio exchanges to implement foreign policy as early as 1934, when he suggested to Sir John Reith, director general of the British Broadcasting Corporation, that the BBC and American radio networks exchange programs. Roosevelt's goal was to explain his own administration's policies to the British. The idea was tried, but did not prove a success (David H. Culbert, *News for Everyman: Radio and Foreign Affairs in Thirties America* [Westport, Conn.: Greenwood, 1976], 102). No member of the State Department attended any of the three meeings Ickes called. The minutes of these meetings are contained in box 247, Ickes Papers.

3   For a more complete story see Holly C. Shulman, "The Voice of Victory: The Development of American Propaganda and the Voice of America" (Ph.D. diss., University of Maryland, 1985). The documentary sources for this early experiment are to be found in the BBC Written Archives Centre, Caversham Park, Reading, England. See also Andre J. E. Mostert, Jr., "A History of WRUL: The Walter S. Lemmon Years, 1931–1960" (M.A. thesis, Brigham Young University, 1969). There is also some correspondence in the records of the Ministry of Information and in the records of the Political Warfare Executive (PWE) filed as Records of the Foreign Office 898, Public Record Office, London; and in the records of the State Department, file 811.76, Record Group 59, National Archives.

4   Thomas F. Troy, *Donovan and the C.I.A.: A History of the Establishment of the Central Intelligence Agency* (Frederick, Md.: University Publications of America, Aletheia, 1981), 52–57; Bradley F. Smith, *The Shadow Warriors: O.S.S. and the Origins of the C.I.A.* (New York: Basic Books, 1983), 55–78; Kermit Roosevelt, *War Report: Office of Strategic Services* (Washington, D.C.: Government Printing Office, 1949), 5–9. In October 1940 the British Ministry of Information forwarded to Donovan a description of British propaganda activity (British Ministry of Information, October 19, 1940, box 1256, folder 2270-a-63, WD Records).

5   This discussion does not take into consideration the differences between "white" and "black" propaganda. White propaganda stuck to the truth and came from a known source such as the BBC or the Voice of America, whereas black propaganda was in and of itself a covert operation disguised as something it was not, such as a dissident German army officer's free radio station – which in reality was broadcast by the British from England. The British combined black and white propaganda within the aegis of the Political Warfare Executive. The Americans did so only under the Coordinator of Information. After

the breakup of the COI Donovan took black operations with him into the Office of Strategic Services, leaving the Overseas Branch of the Office of War Information with white propaganda only. See Sefton Delmar, *Black Boomerang* (New York: Viking, 1962).

6   Memorandum, William O. Hall to Bernard Gladieux, March 21, 1942, series 39.19, box 37, COI–General Administration, BOB Records.

7   Memorandum, Donovan to Roosevelt, March 4, 1942, as cited by Harold F. Gosnell, "Framing of the OWI Executive Order," n.d., box 15, unit 160, BOB Records.

8   Troy, *Donovan and the C.I.A.*, 74.

9   Smith, *The Shadow Warriors*, 18–19.

10  Asa Briggs, *The History of Broadcasting in the United Kingdom*, vol. 3: *The War of Words* (London: Oxford University Press, 1970).

11  Gabriel Kolko, *The Politics of War: The World and United States Foreign Policy, 1943–1945* (New York: Random House, 1968); Colin Gubbins, "Resistance Movements in the War," *Journal of the Royal United Service Institution* (May 1948): 210–23.

12  Bernard Gladieux, interview with author, August 20, 1984.

13  Harold Gosnell, "Organization of Information Activities, for Defense and War, 1940–1942," n.d., 286, series 41.3, unit 169, BOB Records; Robert W. Pirsein, *The Voice of America: An History of the International Broadcasting Activities of the United States Government, 1940–1962* (New York: Arno, 1979), n. 448.

14  Sherwood to Donovan, July 12, 1941, folder 1341, Sherwood Papers.

15  John Mason Brown, *The Worlds of Robert E. Sherwood–Mirror to His Times* (New York: Harper and Row, 1962), 364; Victor Samrock, interview with author, October 23, 1987.

16  Robert Bruce Lockhart, *Comes the Reckoning* (London: Putnam, 1947), 132; Brown, *The Worlds of Robert E. Sherwood*, 161. Tic douloureux is technically known as trigeminal neuralgia. It consists of severe brief tearing, or lancinating, pain in the distribution of one or more divisions of the fifth cranial nerve. Pain is intense, and although each bout may be brief, successive bouts may incapacitate the patient.

17  Wallace Carroll, interview with author, March 3, 1986; John Houseman, *Front and Center* (New York: Simon and Schuster, 1979), 45–46.

18  John Mason Brown, *The Ordeal of a Playwright: Robert E. Sherwood and the Challenge of War* (New York: Harper and Row, 1970), 132.

19  Sherwood defended the slowness with which he became actively anti-Nazi in the Preface to *There Shall Be No Night*. There he compared the events of the 1930s to those of the 1850s: "Lincoln knew that slavery was an evil, but considered war a greater evil. . . . It was when Lincoln saw that the spirit of acceptance of slavery was spreading–from Missouri into Kansas and Nebraska and on across the plains and mountains to Oregon and California–it was then that he turned from an appeaser into a fighter" (quoted in Brown, *The Ordeal of a Playwright*, 140–41).

20  Brown, *The Ordeal of a Playwright*, 105.

21  Robert E. Sherwood, *There Shall Be No Night* (New York: Scribner's, 1940), 153.

22  Quoted in John Houseman, *Front and Center* (New York: Simon and Schuster, 1979), 24.

23  Walter J. Meserve, *Robert E. Sherwood: Reluctant Moralist* (New York: Pegasus, 1970), 175.

24  Memorandum, Sherwood to Rosenman, n.d., box 10, Rosenman Papers.

25  Robert Lee Bishop, "The Overseas Branch of the Office of War Information" (Ph.D. diss., University of Wisconsin, 1966), 176, quoting from an interview with Joseph Barnes, July 26, 1965.

26  Joseph Barnes, "Reminiscences of Joseph Barnes" (1953), 209, Oral History Collection, Columbia University, New York.

27  Harold Gosnell, "Selected Personnel Problems," n.d., box 37, series 41.3, BOB Records, citing memorandum, Sherwood to Donovan, October 20, 1941.

28  Quoted in Richard Kluger, *The Paper: The Life and Death of the "New York Herald Tribune"* (New York: Knopf, 1986), 317.

29  Quoted in ibid., 300–301.

30  Betty Barnes, conversation with author, February 8, 1980.

31  Kluger, *The Paper,* 318.

32  Werner Michel, interview with author, April 26, 1983; Russell Page to Lucas, July 6, 1943, PRO, PWE Records, FO 898/137.

33  Barnes, "Reminiscences," 217.

34  Houseman, *Front and Center,* 34.

35  Interview with Aaron Bell, Control Office, Overseas Branch of OWI, as reported in Gosnell to Herring, July 1, 1943, box 14, unit 153(a), BOB Records.

36  Richard Crossman to David Bowes-Lyon, October 2, 1942, Miall Papers.

37  Sherwood hired several other notable journalists in 1941. Of these the most important were Nelson Poynter, publisher of the *St. Petersburg Times* and owner of a Florida radio station; Wallace Deuel, a foreign correspondent for the *Chicago News* who had published a book warning Americans against Hitler and calling them to action; and Edmond Taylor, also a foreign correspondent, who had worked for the *Chicago Tribune* and had written a book describing German psychological warfare. See memorandum, Poynter to Sherwood, July 25, 1942, box 36; Edward P. Lilly "Office of War Information History," n.d., ch. 4, "Developing Overseas Operations," 10, box 64, OWI Records; William L. Shirer, *Berlin Diary* (New York: Knopf, 1941), 4, 92–93; Wallace Carroll, *Persuade or Perish* (Boston: Houghton Mifflin, 1948), 27.

38  David Farrer, *The Warburgs: The Story of a Family* (New York: Stein and Day, 1975), 155–56.

39  James P. Warburg, *Hell Bent for Election* (New York: Doubleday, Doran, 1935); Warburg, *Still Hell Bent for Election* (New York: Doubleday, Doran, 1936).

40  Farrer, *The Warburgs,* 164.

41  Warburg, *Hell Bent for Election,* 29.

42  Ibid., 41.

43  Farrer, *The Warburgs,* 164–65. See James P. Warburg, *The Isolationist Illusion and World Peace* (New York: Farrar and Rinehart, 1941), Warburg, *Foreign Policy Begins at Home* (New York: Harcourt, Brace, 1944).

44 Warburg, *Foreign Policy Begins at Home*, 10.

45 Ibid., 181, 213.

46 Warburg, *The Isolationist Illusion*, 21.

47 Warburg, *Foreign Policy Begins at Home*, 35–36.

48 Edmond Taylor, *The Strategy of Terror* (Boston: Houghton Mifflin, 1942), 61.

49 Lilly, "Office of War Information History," ch. 3, "ONAF Sections," 10.

50 J. B. Priestley, *All England Listened: The Wartime Postscripts of J. B. Priestley* (New York: Chilmark, 1967), xiv.

51 Ivone Kirkpatrick, *The Inner Circle: Memoirs* (New York: St. Martin's, 1959).

52 Lilly, "Office of War Information History," ch. 4, "Developing Overseas Operations," 52.

53 Gosnell, "Organization of Information Activities," 105; Leonard Miall, interview with author, April 3, 1981.

54 Memorandum, Johnson to Barnes, April 21, 1942, box 10, PW Planning, Lilly Papers. A parallel conflict arose in Britain between the Political Warfare Executive planners in Woburn Abbey (known as "the country") and Whitehall in London. See Bruce Lockhart, *Comes the Reckoning*, 160–61.

55 Lilly, "Office of War Information History," ch. 4, "Developing Overseas Operations," 14.

56 Memorandum, Sherwood to Donovan, November 22, 1941, box 35, Coordinator of Information, OWI Records; Gosnell, "Organization of Information Activities," 164; *State Department Biographical Register, 1944* (Washington, D.C.: Government Printing Office, n.d.), 43.

57 Lilly, "Office of War Information History," ch. 4, "Developing Overseas Operations," 59.

58 Houseman, *Front and Center*, 20.

59 Houseman, ibid., 21.

60 Howard Koch, *The Panic Broadcast: Portrait of an Event* (Boston: Little, Brown, 1970), 12.

61 John Houseman, *Run-Through* (New York: Simon and Schuster, 1972), 173–281.

62 Sherwood to Auberjonois, February 1, 1942, box 35, Coordinator of Information, OWI Records.

63 Kirkpatrick, *Inner Circle*, 163; memorandum, Donovan to the President, February 4, 1942, box 164, OSS–Donovan Reports, PS Files; Irving Pflaum to Sherwood and Barnes, June 4, 1942; Barnes to London, June 6, 1942, box 10, PW Planning, Lilly Papers.

64 Kirkpatrick, *The Inner Circle*, 163; Michael Balfour, *Propaganda in War, 1939–1945: Organizations, Policies and Publics in Britain and Germany* (London: Routledge and Kegan Paul, 1979), 94; Robert Bruce Lockhart, Report on Political Warfare Mission to U.S., March 12, 1942, PRO, PWE Records, FO 898/106.

65 Memorandum, Loring B. Andrews to Paul West, Plans for Immediate Programming of WLWO by COI, February 5, 1942, box 35, Coordinator of Information, OWI Records.

66 Barnes to Sherwood, n.d., Barnes Papers. See also Felix Cole (American Consul General, Algiers) to the Secretary of State, July 24, 1942, SD Records 811.76; *Variety*, February 25, 1942, 27; *Broadcasting*, February 23, 1942, 10, 54; *Broadcast-*

*ing*, March 2, 1942, 54; James P. Warburg, *Unwritten Treaty* (New York: Harcourt, Brace, 1946), 80.

67   Use of these transmitters was also given to Nelson Rockefeller's Office of the Coordinator of Inter-American Affairs for broadcasts to Latin America.

68   "Draft of First Historical Report on Radio," 11–13, n.d.; "History of the Radio Program Bureau of the Overseas Branch of the OWI," n.d., box 24, OWI Records; Pirsein, *The Voice of America*, 56.

69   Harry Torczyner, interview with author, July 15, 1986.

70   Louis G. Cowan, "Reminiscences of Louis G. Cowan," 1967, Oral History Collection, Columbia University.

71   Michel Rapaport Gordey, interview with author, January 26, 1977.

72   Pierre Lazareff, *Deadline: The Behind-the-Scenes Story of the Last Decade in France* (New York: Random House, 1942), 9; Jean-Claude Lamy, *Pierre Lazareff* (Paris: Editions Stock, 1975), 194.

73   Lazareff, *Deadline*, 26.

74   Ibid.

75   Michel Rapaport Gordey, interview with author, November 6, 1985; Lazareff, *Deadline*, 48–49.

76   Gordey interview, November 6, 1985.

77   Lamy, *Pierre Lazareff*, 194.

78   Gordey interview, November 6, 1985.

79   Marie Pertchuk Whiteside, interview with author, April 3, 1986.

80   Whiteside interview; Lazareff, *Deadline*, 281.

81   Gordey interview, November 6, 1985.

82   Simon Michael Bessie, interview with author, April 2, 1986.

83   Houseman, *Front and Center*, 52–53.

84   Administrative Order, March 1942, box 4, Telecommunications, Lilly Papers. The core group of the original Planning Board included Donovan, Sherwood, Jay Allen, Hamilton Armstrong, Wallace Deuel, Francis Miller, Edmond Taylor, James Warburg, Joseph Barnes, and John Wiley.

85   Donovan, report to Roosevelt, November 14, 1941, box 141, PS Files.

86   Memorandum, George Fort Milton to Pendleton Herring, March 13, 1943, series 41.3, unit 152, BOB Records; Barnes to Sherwood, n.d., Barnes Papers.

87   Propaganda for Latin America remained under the direction of Nelson Rockefeller and the Office of the Coordinator of Inter-American Affairs. Troy, *Donovan and the C.I.A.*, 102. See also Smith, *The Shadow Warriors*, 68; Donald W. Rowland, *History of the Office of the Coordinator of Inter-American Affairs* (Washington, D.C.: Government Printing Office, 1947).

88   Troy, *Donovan and the C.I.A.*, 117–53.

89   By 1938 President Roosevelt had become convinced of the need for executive department reorganization to handle the coming crisis of war, but at the time he was constrained by his political defeat over the Supreme Court–packing controversy. In September 1939, however, Roosevelt issued his "limited national emergency" proclamation and an executive order transferring the Bureau of the Budget from the Treasury Department to the Executive Office.

In so doing, Roosevelt acquired an operational office with a large and well-organized department which would be solely responsible to him in seeing that overall policies were carried out. One of the tasks of the Bureau of the Budget became that of tracking all government agencies.

90  Rowland, *History;* Allan M. Winkler, *The Politics of Propaganda: The Office of War Information, 1942–1945* (New Haven: Yale University Press, 1978), 38–72.

91  Nelson Rockefeller's Office of the Coordinator of Inter-American Affairs was an exception; it escaped reorganization and remained independent. See Rowland, *History.*

92  Winkler, *The Politics of Propaganda,* passim.

## Chapter 2.  The Varied Context: Creating Propaganda Policy

1  Gregory D. Black and Clayton R. Koppes, *Hollywood Goes to War: How Politics, Profits and Propaganda Shaped World War II Movies* (New York: Free Press, 1987), 58; Roger Burlingame, *Don't Let Them Scare You: The Life and Times of Elmer Davis* (Philadelphia: Lippincott, 1961), 47–52; David H. Culbert, *News for Everyman: Radio and Foreign Affairs in Thirties America* (Westport, Conn.: Greenwood, 1976), 126–30; David Halberstam, *The Powers That Be* (New York: Knopf, 1979), 35.

2  Culbert, *News for Everyman,* 147; Allan M. Winkler, *The Politics of Propaganda: The Office of War Information, 1942–1945* (New Haven: Yale University Press, 1978), 32; Halberstam, *The Powers That Be,* 35–36; Robert Mertz, *CBS: Reflections in a Bloodshot Eye* (Chicago: Playboy, 1975), 90.

3  Quoted in Burlingame, *Don't Let Them Scare You,* 187.

4  *Time,* June 22, 1942, 21; *The New Republic,* June 22, 1942, 848.

5  Joseph Barnes, "Reminiscences of Joseph Barnes" (1953), 64, Oral History Project, Columbia University, New York. See also Winkler, *The Politics of Propaganda,* 31–34.

6  Telegram, Halifax to Foreign Office, June 17, 1942, PRO, FO 371/30688.

7  Alfred H. Jones, "The Making of an Interventionist on the Air: Elmer Davis and CBS News, 1939–1941," *Pacific Historical Review* 42 (February 1973), 92.

8  Extract from BPS Report 128, May 27, 1942, PRO, FO 371/30688.

9  Black and Koppes, *Hollywood Goes to War,* 64.

10  Simon Michael Bessie, interview with author, April 2, 1986.

11  Ibid. See also memorandum, Kehrli to Gladieux, July 17, 1942, series 39.19, box 82, OWI–General Administration, BOB Records; Bernard Gladieux, interview with author, August 20, 1984.

12  Statement by Elmer Davis in the *New York Sunday Mirror,* June 21, 1942, box 35, Coordinator of Information, OWI Records.

13  Michael Darrock and Joseph P. Dorn, "Davis and Goliath," *Harper's Magazine,* February 1943, 230.

14  Elmer Davis, "Aims and Functions of the Office of War Information," September 1942, 3, box 64, OWI Records.

15  Telegram, Halifax to Foreign Office, June 21, 1942, PRO, FO 371/30688.

16 Milton S. Eisenhower, *The President Is Calling* (New York: Doubleday, 1974), 128–29.
17 Ibid., 80–95, 128–49.
18 Gladieux interview.
19 Eisenhower, *The President Is Calling*, 128.
20 Ibid.
21 Joint American-British Plan of Psychological Warfare for France and the French Empire, September 23, 1942, PRO, PWE Records, FO 898/129.
22 For a discussion of American foreign policy toward Vichy see Raoul Aglion, *Roosevelt and de Gaulle: Allies in Conflict; A Personal Memoir* (New York: Free Press, 1988); Henry Blumenthal, *Illusion and Reality in Franco-American Diplomacy 1914–1945* (Baton Rouge: Louisiana State University Press, 1986); James J. Dougherty, *The Politics of Wartime Aid: American Economic Assistance to France and French Northwest Africa, 1940–1946* (Westport, Conn.: Greenwood, 1978); Louis Gottschalk, "Our Vichy Fumble," *Journal of Modern History* 20 (March 1948): 47–56; Julian G. Hurstfield, *America and the French Nation, 1939–1945* (Chapel Hill: University of North Carolina Press, 1986); William L. Langer, *Our Vichy Gamble* (New York: Knopf, 1947).
23 Hooper to Sykes, March 21, 1929, box 9, Papers of Stanford C. Hooper, Library of Congress, Washington, D.C.
24 Joao Carlos Muniz, "Address of His Excellency, Dr. Joao Carlos Muniz, Brazil," *Bulletin of the Pan American Union*, April 1947, 192. Rowe's papers are housed at the Columbia Memorial Library of the Organization of American States, Washington, D.C.
25 Gross to Southgate, November 2, 1933, PAU/1 1/2, SD Records 811.76.
26 Manning to Wilson, November 20, 1933, PAU/5, SD Records 811.76.
27 Ellis O. Briggs to Welles, November 18, 1941, SD Records 811.76/257 3/5.
28 Loy Henderson, quoted in Hugh DeSantis, *The Diplomacy of Silence: The American Foreign Service, the Soviet Union, and the Cold War, 1933–1947* (Chicago: University of Chicago Press, 1979), 19.
29 Forrest C. Pogue, conversation with author, November 18, 1983.
30 DeSantis, *Diplomacy of Silence*, 20. DeSantis goes even further, arguing that State Department officials were underpaid and undervalued, "professionally and socially alienated by the public and the government, unable to transfer their skills to other occupations in a depression-plagued economy, career officers retreated into their private institutional world. Collectively an enormous outgroup unified against the outside environment, on the eve of World War II, they languished in a state of 'diplomatic isolation,' a reflection of the political and psychological condition of the American people" (26).
31 Edward P. Lilly, "Office of War Information History," n.d., ch. 4, "Developing Overseas Operations," 56–57, box 64, OWI Records.
32 Vira B. Whitehouse, *A Year as a Government Agent* (New York: Harper and Brothers, 1920).
33 Joseph Barnes to Betty Barnes, July 31, 1942, Barnes Papers.
34 Charles A. H. Thomson, *Overseas Information Service of the United States Government* (Washington, D.C.: Brookings Institution, 1948), 24. Initially, OWI

freedom from the State Department was reinforced by the Bureau of the Budget. The bureau disliked the prudent and guarded State Department, which it felt was badly administered and overly cautious. When Executive Order 9182 was written, the bureau deliberately decided not to assign the State Department a clear policy role. Bernard Gladieux, "Reminiscences of Bernard Gladieux," 1951, Oral History Project, Columbia University, New York.

35  Memorandum, Kehrli to Gladieux, July 17, 1942, series 39.19, box 82, OWI–General Administration, BOB Records; Davis to Admiral King, July 14, 1942, box 2, OWI–Miscellaneous, ONI Records; Davis, report to the President, June 1945, 35, box 10, Davis Papers.

36  Minutes of the Operations Planning and Intelligence Board, 1942–1944, box 1, OWI–Planning and Operations, ONI Records.

37  Memorandum for heads of all branches and sections, September 23, 1942, box 1, ONI Records; memorandum, Edgar Mowrer to Sherwood, July 29, 1942, box 4, OWI Records.

38  Robert W. Pirsein, *The Voice of America: An History of the International Broadcasting Activities of the United States Government, 1940–1962* (New York: Arno, 1979), 61; Leonard Miall, interview with author, March 17, 1981; Gladieux interview.

39  Memorandum, Crossman to Bowes-Lyon, Note on Activities of September 30 and October 1, 1942, Miall Papers. Crossman described the single meeting he attended in derogatory terms. "I was irresistibly reminded of the palmy days of the Planning Committee at [Electra House]. . . . There was that same atmosphere of club chat and unconscious incompetence."

40  Memorandum, Sherwood to members of the Planning Board, bureau chiefs, and regional specialists to the Overseas Operation Branch, September 28, 1942, Warburg Papers.

41  Conversation with Captain Charles Thomson, Planning and Intelligence Board, OWI, as reported in memorandum, Gosnell to Herring, October 9, 1942, series 41.3, unit 153(d), BOB Records.

42  Werner Michel, interview with author, April 24, 1983.

43  Conversation with Harwood Childs, Regional Planning, as reported in Gosnell to McKee and Rosen, February 25, 1944, series 41.3, box 14, unit 153(d), BOB Records.

44  Michel interview.

45  Lord Ritchie-Calder, interview with author, March 23, 1981.

46  Memorandum, Crossman to Bowes-Lyon, Note on Activities of September 30 and October 1, 1942. See also James P. Warburg, *The Long Road Home: The Autobiography of a Maverick* (New York: Doubleday, 1964), 196.

47  Memorandum, Wellington (Ministry of Information) to Maurice Peterson (Director General, BBC), March 15, 1941, E2/17, BBC Archives.

48  Memorandum, "Reception of American Stations," January 1, 1941, E2/17, BBC Archives.

49  Russell Page, "French Rebroadcasts from the U.S.A.," January 23, 1941, E2/17, BBC Archives.

50  Cock to Rendall, March 5, 1941, E2/17, BBC Archives.

51   "French Commentaries from WRUL," April 8, 1941; K. Cockburn to O.N.E., "WRUL French Programme," April 9, 1941, E2/17, BBC Archives.

52   See reports filed in PRO, PWE Records, FO 898/103.

53   Foreign Information Service: Appendix B, n.d., PRO, PWE Records, FO 898/106.

54   H. Montgomery Hyde, *Room 3606: The Story of the British Intelligence Center in New York During World War II* (New York: Farrar, Straus, 1963), 157–59; Andre J. E. Mostert, Jr., "A History of WRUL: The Walter S. Lemmon Years, 1931–1960" (M.A. thesis, Brigham Young University, 1969), 65–67.

55   Ivone Kirkpatrick, *The Inner Circle: Memoirs* (New York: St. Martin's, 1959), 163. See also memorandum, Donovan to the President, February 4, 1942, box 164, OSS–Donovan Reports, PS Files.

56   Irving Pflaum to Sherwood and Barnes, June 4, 1942; Barnes to London, June 6, 1942, box 10, PW Planning, Lilly Papers.

57   Robert Bruce Lockhart, *Comes the Reckoning* (London: Putnam, 1947), 144.

58   Leonard Miall, interview with author, March 16, 1981. Sefton Delmar, director of British black radio operations, told a different version of this story in his memoirs. Delmar wrote that American military attaché reports began to cross his desk with tales of rising German army hostility to the Nazi party, and he knew immediately that these reports had to have been based not on accurate intelligence, but on monitored broadcasts of Gustav Siegfried Eins. Delmar therefore sent Bowes-Lyon to see Roosevelt and tell him the truth about the German freedom radio stations in general and Gustav Siegfried Eins in particular (*Black Boomerang* [New York: Viking, 1962], 36–80).

59   Wallace Carroll, *Persuade or Perish* (Boston: Houghton Mifflin, 1948), 235.

60   Kirkpatrick, *The Inner Circle*, 163. See also Leonard Miall, interview with author, March 18, 1981; Asa Briggs, *The History of Broadcasting in the United Kingdom*, vol. 3: *The War of Words* (London: Oxford University Press, 1970), 428–29; John Houseman, *Front and Center* (New York: Simon and Schuster, 1979), 63.

61   Russell Page, interview with author, June 9, 1981; Miall interview, March 18, 1981; Houseman, *Front and Center*, 64.

62   Miall interview, March 18, 1981.

63   Michael Balfour, *Propaganda in War, 1939–1945: Organizations, Policies and Publics in Britain and Germany* (London: Routledge and Kegan Paul, 1979); Anthony Howard, Introduction to Richard H. S. Crossman, *The Crossman Diaries* (London: Hamilton, 1979), 13–19; Richard H. S. Crossman, "Supplementary Essay," in Daniel Lerner, *Psychological Warfare Against Nazi Germany: The Skywar Campaign, D-Day to V-E Day* (Cambridge: M.I.T. Press, 1971), 324.

64   Walter Adams to Sherwood, September 30, 1942, folder 1314, Sherwood Papers; "Suggestions for Possible Lines of Propaganda," n.d., box 30, British Embassy, OWI Records.

65   Leonard Miall, Second Progress Report, October 2, 1942, Miall Papers.

66   Ibid.

67   Memorandum, Crossman to Wheeler-Bennett, Note on Activities of September 29, 1942, Miall Papers.

68   Ritchie-Calder interview, March 23, 1981.
69   Leonard Miall, Note on Meeting Held in Mr. Houseman's Office at the O.W.I., October 8, 1942, Miall Papers.
70   Ritchie-Calder interview, March 23, 1981.
71   Miall, Second Progress Report.
72   Pirsein, *The Voice of America*, 68; Leonard Miall, interview with author, April 7, 1981.
73   "Executive Order 9312: Defining the Foreign Information Activities of the Office of War Information," March 9, 1943, box 62, ABC 040.9 OWI WD Records; OSS Directive from Joint Chiefs of Staff, December 16, 1942, series 39.19, box 83, Gladieux File; Gladieux Notes, July 15, 1942, series 41.3, unit 151; memorandum, Hall to Gladieux, July 9, 1942, series 39.19, box 83, BOB Records. Donovan tried to control propaganda through the Joint Psychological Warfare Committee, but his position was undermined by international military opposition from General George V. Strong, and John J. McCloy.
74   Miall, Note on Meeting Held in Mr. Houseman's Office.
75   Miall interview, April 7, 1981.
76   Memorandum, Crossman to Wheeler-Bennett, Note on Activities of September 29, 1942.
77   Leonard Miall, "The Future Functions of the New York Office of the British Political Warfare Unit," December 7, 1943, Miall Papers.
78   Gosnell to Herring, June 19, 1943, box 14, unit 153(d), BOB Records.
79   Sherwood to Don [Hall], May 15, 1945, folder 1197, Sherwood Papers.
80   Memorandum, Kehrli to Gladieux, July 13, 1942, series 39.19, box 83, BOB Records; telegram, Sherwood to MacLeish, August 1942, SD Records 103.916602/117.
81   Telegram, Sherwood to Winant, June 24, 1942, SD Records 103.9166/20K; cable, Hull to Pflaum, July 10, 1942, SD Records 103.9166/117A.
82   Carroll, *Persuade or Perish*, 11; *Broadcasting*, August 31, 1942, 58; cable, Hull to American Embassy, London, September 9, 1942, SD Records 103.9166/420; cable, Winner to Sherwood, September 24, 1942, SD Records 103.9166/546.
83   Memorandum, McCloy to Strong, November 17, 1942, McCloy Papers.
84   Forrest C. Pogue, *George C. Marshall: Ordeal and Hope* (New York: Viking, 1966), 400; Russell F. Weigley, *The American Way of War* (New York: Macmillan, 1973), 320–22.
85   Carroll, *Persuade or Perish*, 12.
86   Cable, Carroll to Galantier and Bessie, January 12, 1945, box 107, France–Policy, OWI Records.
87   Cable, Warburg to MacLeish, August 28, 1942, SD Records 103.9166/212.
88   Winkler, *The Politics of Propaganda*, 75, 114; Michel interview; Carroll, *Persuade or Perish*, 27; Houseman, *Front and Center*, 81; *Variety*, March 30, 1938, 32; *Radio Guide*, November 6, 1937, 46.
89   Quoted in Houseman, *Front and Center*, 81.
90   Carroll, *Persuade or Perish*, 27–29; Memorandum for the Joint Psychological Warfare Committee, November 6, 1942, box 363, CCS 385; October 8, 1942,

box 374, CCS 385.7, Records of the U.S. Joint Chiefs of Staff, Record Group 218, National Archives, Washington, D.C.

91  Mark Abrams, interview with author, March 23, 1981.
92  Miall interview, April 7, 1981.
93  BBC European Service, *Output Report,* December 14–19, 1942, quoted in Briggs, *War of Words,* 445.

## Chapter 3. An Agent of Resistance:
### The Voice of America on the Air

1  "Overseas Operations," n.d. (1943), box 38 (notebook), OWI Records.
2  Leonard Miall, "Relations Between O.W.I., New York, and the Political Warfare Mission–A Six Months' Summary," August 20, 1943, Miall Papers.
3  MacLeish went on to become head of domestic information as director of the Office of Facts and Figures and later as director of the Domestic Branch of the OWI.
4  John Houseman, *Run-Through* (New York: Simon and Schuster, 1972), 398.
5  James B. Gilbert, "War of the Worlds," *Journal of Popular Culture* 10 (Fall 1976), 326–36; Max Wylie, ed., *Best Broadcasts of 1938–1939* (New York: Whittlesey House, 1939), 449. See also Howard Koch, *The Panic Broadcast: Portrait of an Event* (Boston: Little, Brown, 1970); Hadley Cantril, *The Invasion from Mars: A Study in the Psychology of Panic* (Princeton: Princeton University Press, 1940).
6  John Houseman, *Front and Center* (New York: Simon and Schuster, 1979), 35.
7  David H. Culbert, *News for Everyman: Radio and Foreign Affairs in Thirties America* (Westport, Conn.: Greenwood, 1976), 72; William L. Shirer, *The Nightmare Years, 1930–1940* (Boston: Little, Brown, 1984), 284–326; Erik Barnouw, *The Golden Web: A History of Broadcasting in the United States, 1933–1953* (New York: Oxford University Press, 1968), 74–83. For sound recordings of NBC international war news see material housed in the Division of Motion Pictures, Broadcasting and Recorded Sound, Library of Congress, Washington, D.C.
8  This style of news contrasted sharply with contemporary BBC news reporting. The BBC news readers remained nameless, and they were carefully chosen for their well-modulated "Oxbridge" accents, which gave no clue as to the speaker's regional origin. A single reader gave a careful report of the day's news, thus representing the voice of Britain's national radio authority.
9  "NBC International War News" (sound recording), March 4, 1942, LWO 16675, reel 106A4, Broadcasting Division, Library of Congress.
10  Sound recording, August 5, 1942, LWO 12487, reel 21A3, OWI Collection.
11  Herbert Spencer, "The Philosophy of Style," in *Essays in Rhetoric,* ed. Dudley Bailey (New York: Oxford University Press, 1965), 150.
12  Hugh Kenner, "The Politics of the Plain Style," *New York Book Review,* September 15, 1985, 1, 39–40.
13  Houseman, *Front and Center,* 35.

14  Douglas Cleverdon, interview with author, November 4, 1985. Cleverdon, a British radio producer, joined the BBC in 1939. He later produced Dylan Thomas's "Under Milk Wood" in 1953.

15  Peter Lewis, "Radio Drama and English Literature," in *Radio Drama*, ed. Peter Lewis (London: Longman, 1981), 179.

16  Howard Fink, "The Sponsor v. the Nation's Choice: North American Radio Drama," in *Radio Drama*, ed. Peter Lewis, 215; Peter Lewis, "'Under Milk Wood' as a Radio Poem," in *Papers of the Radio Literature Conference, 1977*, ed. Peter Lewis (Durham, N.C.: Durham University Printing Unit, 1978), 140.

17  Fink, "The Sponsor," 215.

18  Martin Esslin, *An Anatomy of Drama* (New York: Hill and Wang, 1976), 15.

19  Cleverdon interview.

20  Erik Barnouw, *Radio Drama in Action: Twenty-five Plays of a Changing World* (New York: Farrar and Rinehart, 1945), 204. See also R. LeRoy Bannerman, *Norman Corwin and Radio* (Tuscaloosa: University of Alabama Press, 1986).

21  Norman Corwin, "So This Is Radio" (sound recording), *Columbia Workshop*, September 7, 1939, LWO 16588-A, Broadcasting Division, Library of Congress.

22  David Lodge, *Working with Structuralism: Essays and Reviews on Nineteenth- and Twentieth-Century Literature* (London: Routledge and Kegan Paul, 1981), 8.

23  Paul Rotha, *Documentary Film* (London: Faber and Faber, 1952), 78–79; William Stott, *Documentary Expression and Thirties America* (New York: Oxford University Press, 1973), 12; Elkan and Dorotheen Allan, *Good Listening: A Survey of Broadcasting* (London: Hutchinson, n.d.), 124.

24  Wylie, ed., *Best Broadcasts of 1938–1939*, 138–40.

25  Fink, "The Sponsor," 209.

26  For a further description of "The March of Time" see Raymond Fielding, *"The March of Time," 1935–1951* (New York: Oxford University Press, 1978).

27  David Lodge, *Working with Structuralism*, 70; Robert Alter, *Partial Magic: The Novel as Self-Conscious Genre* (Berkeley and Los Angeles: University of California Press, 1978), 138–59.

28  Quoted in Mardi Valgemae, *Accelerated Grimace: Expressionism in the American Drama of the 1920's* (Carbondale: Southern Illinois University Press, 1972), 11–12; see also pp. 2–3; and Renate Benson, *German Expressionist Drama: Ernst Toller and Georg Kaiser* (New York: Grove, 1984), 3–4.

29  Valgemae, *Accelerated Grimace*, 12.

30  Benson, *German Expressionist Drama*, 9; Malcolm Goldstein, *The Political Stage: America Drama and Theater of the Great Depression* (New York: Oxford University Press, 1974), 8.

31  There were others within the Voice of America who had been influenced by agitprop and the Living Newspaper, such as the English desk writer Robert Newman and the English language announcer Norman Lloyd, who had been the star performer in several Living Newspapers. Robert Newman, interview with author, February 20, 1986; John Houseman, interview with author, March 26, 1986.

32  Jay Williams, *Stage Left* (New York: Scribner's, 1974), 3–4, 35–37; C. D. Innes,

*Irwin Piscator's Political Theatre: The Development of Modern German Drama* (Cambridge: Cambridge University Press, 1972), 26.

33   Goldstein, *The Political Stage,* 277–78.

34   Erwin Piscator, *The Political Theatre* (London: Eyre Methuen, 1980), 81; John Willett, *The Theatre of Erwin Piscator: Half a Century of Politics in the Theatre* (London: Eyre Methuen, 1978), 51; Innes, *Erwin Piscator's Political Theatre,* 187–90.

35   Piscator, *The Political Theatre,* 81.

36   Ibid., 47.

37   Houseman, *Front and Center,* 35.

38   French News Summary, April 15, 1942, box 6, Transcripts, OWI Records. For a discussion of the process by which the external setting of a text can impose on readers (or listeners) the way in which they understand that text see David Lodge, *The Modes of Modern Writing* (Ithaca: Cornell University Press, 1977), 9–17.

39   Sound recording, August 5, 1942, LWO 12487, reel 21A3, OWI Collection.

40   French News Summary, September 14, 1942, box 57, Transcripts, OWI Records. Compare this broadcast with the dialogue from a Living Newspaper play called *1935:*

VOICE OF THE LIVING NEWSPAPER:  Dutch Schultz beats the tax rap:
POLICEMAN:  Arthur Flegenheimer, alias Charles Harmon, alias Dutch Schultz . . . charged with grand larceny.
JUDGE:  Dismissed.
POLICEMAN:  Criminal assault.
JUDGE:  Dismissed.
POLICEMAN:  Disorderly conduct.
JUDGE:  Dismissed.
POLICEMAN:  Homicide.
JUDGE:  Dismissed.
POLICEMAN:  Robbery.
JUDGE:  Sentence suspended. . . .
POLICEMAN:  Income tax evasion.
JUDGE:  Discharged.

(quoted in Wilson Whitman, *Bread and Circuses: A Study of Federal Theater* [New York: Oxford University Press, 1937], 84).

41   Newman interview.

42   For an overview of reception theory see Susan Rubin Suleiman, Introduction to *The Reader in the Text,* ed. Susan Rubin Suleiman and Inge Crosman (Princeton: Princeton University Press, 1980).

43   For an extensive discussion on the relationship of literary form and content see Kenneth Burke, *The Philosophy of Literary Form: Studies in Symbolic Action* (Berkeley and Los Angeles: University of California Press, 1973). Burke argues that form follows problems of content—that content poses certain questions to which the forms then used are a strategy taken to answer those questions: "To guide our observations about the form itself we seek to discover the *functions* which the structure serves" (101; emphasis in original).

44  William L. Langer, *Our Vichy Gamble* (New York: Knopf, 1947), 80. See also Louis Gottschalk, "Our Vichy Fumble," *Journal of Modern History* 20 (March 1948): 47–56.

45  James J. Dougherty, *The Politics of Wartime Aid: American Economic Assistance to France and French Northwest Africa, 1940–1946* (Westport, Conn.: Greenwood, 1978), 19–20.

46  Robert O. Paxton, *Vichy France: Old Guard and New Order* (New York: Knopf, 1972), 27.

47  Ibid., 24. See also Alexander Werth, *France, 1940–1955* (Boston: Beacon Press, 1966), 18, 93; Gordon Wright, *France in Modern Times* (Chicago: Rand McNally, 1974), 399.

48  Langer, *Our Vichy Gamble*, 83.

49  Robert Aron, *The Vichy Regime, 1940–1944* (New York: Macmillan, 1958), 353.

50  Aron, *The Vichy Regime*, 352–53.

51  Paul Farmer, *Vichy: Political Dilemma* (New York: Octagon Books, 1977), 284.

52  Directive, France VII, April 20, 1942; France IX, May 4, 1942, box 339, FIS Directives, OWI Records.

53  Directive, France VI, March 28, 1942, box 339, Transcripts, OWI Records.

54  Memorandum, Donovan to Roosevelt, April 24, 1942, box 165, PS Files.

55  Ibid.

56  See, for example, cable, State Department to the Ambassador, April 16, 1942, confidential file, PS/RA, SD Records 851.00/2810A.

57  Cable, Leahy to Hull, April 17, 1942, confidential file, PS/BH, SD Records 851.00/2737; telegram, Matthews to Hull, April 23, 1942, confidential file, PS/EM, SD Records 851.00/2760.

58  "Canada," May 15, 1942, box 15, Transcripts, OWI Records.

59  French News Summary, March 15, 1942, box 4; "French Feature: Sabotage in Czechoslovakia," April 15, 1942, box 6, Transcripts, OWI Records.

60  "Canada," May 15, 1942, box 15, Transcripts, OWI Records.

61  The PWE had inaugurated a similar campaign a month before, in August, and the OWI echoed many initially British themes. See PWE Directives for BBC French Service, August 23–September 6, 1942, G-2 Regional Files, WD Records.

62  Directive, week of September 27, 1942, box 35, French Directives, OWI Records. See also directives for weeks of October 4, 11, 18, 1942, box 35, French Directives, OWI Records; guidance notes for OWI central directive, October 16–23, 1942, box 2, OWI – Miscellaneous, ONI Records.

63  Central Directive, October 10–16, 1942, box 818, OWI Records.

64  Ibid.

65  "French Solidarity Against German Plans," October 12, 1942, box 81, Transcripts, OWI Records. See also Labor Show, October 13, 1942, box 81, Transcripts, OWI Records.

66  Directive, week of October 4, 1942, box 35, French Directives, OWI Records.

67  Labor Show, October 13, 1942, box 81, Transcripts, OWI Records.

68  Gabriel Kolko, *The Politics of War: The World and United States Foreign Policy, 1943–1945* (New York: Random House, 1968); Warren F. Kimball, Introduc-

tion to Kimball, ed., *Churchill and Roosevelt: The Complete Correspondence*, vol. 1: *Alliance Emerging, October 1933–November 1942* (Princeton: Princeton University Press, 1984).

69  Quoted in Norman D. Markowitz, *The Rise and Fall of the People's Century: Henry A. Wallace and American Liberalism, 1941–1948* (New York: Free Press, 1973), 39.

70  Max Ascoli, quoted in James Edward Miller, *The United States and Italy, 1940–1950: The Politics and Diplomacy of Stabilization* (Chapel Hill: University of North Carolina Press, 1986), 21.

71  Ibid., 4.

72  Paul Seabury, *The Rise and Decline of the Cold War* (New York: Basic Books, 1967), 43.

73  James P. Warburg, *The Isolationist Illusion and World Peace* (New York: Farrar and Rinehart, 1941), 24.

74  "The Front of Resistance," Labor Show, September 11, 1942, box 57, Transcripts, OWI Records.

75  French News Summary, April 15, 1942, box 6, Transcripts, OWI Records.

76  Memorandum, Donovan to Roosevelt, April 2, 1942, box 165, OSS–Donovan Reports, Transcripts, PS Files.

77  Henri Michel, *The Second World War* (New York: Praeger, 1968), 329–415.

78  Directive, France XV, June 24, 1942, SD Records 103.9166/25H.

79  "Russian Front," July 16, 1942, box 34, Transcripts, OWI Records.

80  "On the Baltic Front," July 16, 1942, box 39, Transcripts, OWI Records.

81  Guidance Note, August 10, 1942, box 130, New York Guidance Notes, OWI Records.

82  Guidance Note, August 9–19, 1942, box 130, New York Guidance Notes, OWI Records.

83  Guidance Note, August 12, 1942, box 130, New York Guidance Notes, OWI Records.

84  Guidance Note, September 15, 1942, box 130, New York Guidance Notes, OWI Records.

85  Guidance Note, July 18, 1942, box 208, Daily Guidance Notes, OWI Records.

86  Guidance Note, August 27, 1942, box 130, New York Guidance Notes, OWI Records.

87  Guidance Note, August 4, 1942, box 130, New York Guidance Notes, OWI Records.

88  PWE Directives for BBC French Service, August 23–September 6, 1942, G-2 Regional Files, WD Records.

89  "Maneuvers for a Second Front," July 14, 1942; "Active Resistance in Europe," July 16, 1942, box 39, Transcripts, OWI Records.

90  Special Show B, October 14, 1942, box 81, Transcripts, OWI Records.

91  Directive, France II, March 11, 1942, box 39, FIS Directives, OWI Records.

92  Memorandum, Donovan to Roosevelt, March 7, 1942, box 165, OSS–Donovan Reports, PS Files.

93  French News Summary, May 15, 1942, box 15, Transcripts, OWI Records.

94  Memorandum, Donovan to Roosevelt, May 1, 1942, box 166, PS Files.
95  "The President and the Pilot," May 13, 1942, box 15, Transcripts, OWI Records.
96  Leonard Miall, interview with author, March 17, 1981.
97  Guidance note, June 26, 1942, box 38, Guidance Notes, OWI Records.
98  "Suggested Directive on Production for All Countries," September 9, 1942, box 10, Psychological Warfare Planning, Lilly Papers.
99  Ibid.
100  "The Quakers," Women's Show, September 11, 1942, box 57, Transcripts, OWI Records.
101  "Quoting Walter Lippmann," October 11, 1942, box 81, Transcripts, OWI Records.
102  Special Show B, October 14, 1942, box 81, Transcripts; guidance notes, September 5, 1942, box 130, New York Guidance Notes, OWI Records; central directive, October 30–November 6, 1942, box 2, ONI Records.
103  Central directive, October 2–9, 1942, box 2, ONI Records.
104  John Morton Blum, *"V" Was for Victory: Politics and American Culture During World War II* (New York: Harcourt Brace Jovanovich, 1976), 8.
105  U.S. News, November 10, 1942, box 89, Transcripts, OWI Records.
106  "General O'Ryan," November 9, 1942, box 89, Transcripts, OWI Records.
107  Stuart Davis, "Why an Artists' Congress?" in *Artists Against War and Fascism: Papers of the First American Artists' Congress,* ed. Matthew Baigell and Julia Williams (New Brunswick, N.J.: Rutgers University Press, 1986), 65.
108  Warren I. Sussman, *Culture as History: The Transformation of American Society in the Twentieth Century* (New York: Pantheon, 1984), 154–72, 205.
109  Paul Green, "Citizen for Tomorrow" (sound recording), "Columbia Workshop," December 14, 1941, LWO 17478, Broadcasting Division, Library of Congress.
110  "Le bombardier en pique," French Voice of America, November 10, 1942, box 89, Transcripts, OWI Records.
111  For an example of British drama as propaganda see "Le dix mai" (a dramatization of the invasion of Belgium), May 10, 1940, FB 5961; or "'V' for Victory," July 3, 1941, FB 5961-2, BBC Sound Archives, London.

## 4. After Torch: Propaganda and American Foreign Relations

1  Robert Beitzell, *The Uneasy Alliance: America, Britain and Russia, 1941–1943* (New York: Knopf, 1972), 42; William B. Breuer, *Operation Torch: The Allied Gamble to Invade North Africa* (New York: St. Martin's, 1985), 4–5; Stephen E. Ambrose, *Eisenhower: Soldier, General of the Army, President-Elect, 1890–1952* (New York: Simon and Schuster, 1983), 180–81; John McVane, *Journey into War: War and Diplomacy in North Africa* (New York: Appleton-Century, 1943), 37.
2  Wallace Carroll, *Persuade or Perish* (Boston: Houghton Mifflin, 1948), 48. See also Harold Macmillan, *The Blast of War, 1939–1945* (New York: Carroll and Graf, 1983), 165; Ambrose, *Eisenhower,* 215.
3  The president saw the political problems that Eisenhower's decision would, and did, present. Roosevelt wrote to Churchill that he had accepted Darlan,

but only as a temporary measure: "I thoroughly understand and approve the feeling in the United States and Great Britain and among all the other United Nations that in view of the history of the past two years no permanent arrangement should be made with Admiral Darlan." But he went on to say that "the present temporary arrangement in North and West Africa is only a temporary expedient, justified solely by the stress of battle" (personal from the President to the Former Naval Person, November 17, 1942, in Warren F. Kimball, ed., *Churchill and Roosevelt: The Complete Correspondence*, vol. 2: *Alliance Forged, November 1942–February 1944* [Princeton: Princeton University Press, 1984], 8–9).

4   Memorandum, Edmond Taylor to Colonel Hazeltine, December 1, 1942, POLAD-Algiers, box 1, General–1942, FSP Records.

5   Breuer, *Operation Torch*, 42.

6   Robert Bruce Lockhart, *Comes the Reckoning* (London: Putnam, 1947), 212.

7   Warburg and Sherwood are quoted in John Houseman, *Front and Center* (New York: Simon and Schuster, 1979), 82.

8   Carroll, *Persuade or Perish*, 46.

9   Memorandum, Ray Atherton to the President, May 10, 1943, SD Records 851.01/2138.

10  Carroll, *Persuade or Perish*, 83; Kimball, ed., *Churchill and Roosevelt* 2:104.

11  Harold Macmillan, *War Diaries: The Mediterranean 1943–1945* (New York: St. Martin's, 1984), 76. Although the British had supported de Gaulle since 1940 and therefore had an investment in continuing to do so, Macmillan's observations proved correct over the course of the year.

12  Quoted in Julian G. Hurstfield, *America and the French Nation, 1939–1945* (Chapel Hill: University of North Carolina Press, 1986), 197.

13  Quoted in François Kersaudy, *Churchill and de Gaulle* (London: Collins, 1981), 271.

14  Quoted in ibid., 319. See also Gaddis Smith, *American Diplomacy During the Second World War, 1941–1945* (New York: Wiley and Sons, 1965), 77.

15  Kersaudy, *Churchill and de Gaulle*, 319.

16  Hurstfield, *America and the French Nation*, 198.

17  Sidney Stahl Weinberg, "Wartime Propaganda and Democracy: America's Twentieth Century Information Agencies" (Ph.D. diss., Columbia University, 1969), 3.

18  Henry Blumenthal, *Illusion and Reality in Franco-American Diplomacy 1914–1945* (Baton Rouge: Louisiana State University Press, 1986), 303–304.

19  Telegram, Hull to Murphy, May 8, 1943, SD Records 851.01/2105.

20  Wallace Carroll, interview with author, March 3, 1986.

21  Houseman, *Front and Center*, 91.

22  Elmer Davis, "Specimen Day in Washington," January 5, 1943, box 10, OWI, Davis Papers; Hurstfield, *America and the French Nation*, 191–92.

23  Office of Public Information, State Department Reorganization Plan, January 1, 1944, main decimal file, SD Records 111/810A.

24  Interview with Harwood Childs, Regional Division, Overseas Branch–OWI,

as reported in memorandum, Gosnell to Herring, July 23, 1943, box 14, unit 153(d), BOB Records.

25  Interview with Nathan Leites, as reported in memorandum, Gosnell to Herring, July 31, 1943, series 41.3, unit 153(e), BOB Records.

26  Memorandum, C. A. H. Thomson to Paul Fredericksen, September 22, 1943, box 125, State Department, OWI Records.

27  Sherwood to Stettinius, January 22, 1944, box 97, main decimal file, SD Records 110.739166/12; interview with Mr. Pell, State Department Liaison with OWI on Policy, as reported in memorandum, Douglas W. Campbell to Richardson, January 12, 1944, series 39.19, box 82, BOB Records.

28  "Coordination of Political Warfare in the European Theatre," October 19, 1943, PRO, PWE Records, FO 898/372; Allan M. Winkler, *The Politics of Propaganda: The Office of War Information, 1942–1945* (New Haven: Yale University Press, 1978), 62–80; Carroll, *Persuade or Perish*, 13–61. Documents on the history of the PWB and PWD are to be found in the records of the British Foreign Office and the Political Warfare Executive, Public Record Office; OWI Records; Jackson Papers; the records of the U.S. Joint Chiefs of Staff, Record Group 218, National Archives, Washington, D.C.; WD Records; and the records of the Supreme Headquarters, Allied Expeditionary Forces.

29  Winkler, *The Politics of Propaganda*, 116.

30  Leonard Miall, "Relations Between O.W.I., New York, and the Political Warfare Mission—A Six Months' Summary," August 20, 1943, Miall Papers.

31  Winkler finds that "it was ironic that the propaganda effort, launched with such liberal and idealistic ends, made its greatest contributions in the military theaters of the war" (*The Politics of Propaganda*, 112). The irony was a function of the ambivalence I have described in the text. But it is important to remember that the OWI representatives who worked abroad in the PWB and PWD became members of a combined psychological warfare effort within the military. In this sense they lost their original identity, as did the British PWE team members. Thus when Winkler argues (p. 148) that the OWI came into its own within the military organizational framework, he is both right and wrong. He is correct in describing psychological warfare successes. But he is slightly off the mark in his assumption that the OWI segment of the PWB and PWD could be considered a simple extension of the OWI; it could not.

32  Memorandum, Sherwood to Winner, January 14, 1944, box 43, OWI Records.

33  Quoted in Sara Alpern, *Freda Kirchway: A Woman of "The Nation"* (Cambridge: Harvard University Press, 1987), 143.

34  Telegram, Glassford to Murphy, August 12, 1943, SD Records 851.01/2963.

35  John F. Sweets, *The Politics of Resistance in France, 1940–1944* (De Kalb: Northern Illinois University Press, 1976), x, 3–33, 187–228.

36  Harry Torczyner, interview with author, July 15, 1986.

37  Progress Report, October 15–November 15, 1943, box 358, OWI–Overseas Branch, New York Office of Control, OWI Records.

38  Kersaudy, *Churchill and de Gaulle*, 251.

39  Robert Dalleck, *Franklin Roosevelt and American Foreign Policy, 1932–1945* (New York: Oxford University Press, 1979), 380.
40  Smith, *American Diplomacy,* 8–9.
41  Ibid., 393–96; Ambrose, *Eisenhower,* 253.
42  Ambrose, *Eisenhower,* 253.
43  Dalleck, *Franklin Roosevelt,* 418.
44  Roosevelt had brought up the idea at the Quebec conference but had side-stepped it by referring to a permanent peace-keeping organization only as an institution that might be established "at the earliest possible [meeting] of a general international organization" (quoted in ibid., 420).
45  I. Berlin to Foreign Office, November 7, 1943, in H. G. Nicholas, ed., *Washington Despatches, 1941–1945: Weekly Reports from the British Embassy* (Chicago: University of Chicago Press, 1981), 269; See also James MacGregor Burns, *Roosevelt: The Soldier of Freedom, 1940–1945* (New York: Harcourt Brace Jovanovich, 1970), 358.
46  Dalleck, *Franklin Roosevelt,* 430–35; Daniel Yergin, *Shattered Peace: The Origins of the Cold War and the National Security State* (Boston: Houghton Mifflin, 1977), 53–54.
47  Central Directive, December 4–11, 1942, box 818, OWI Records.
48  Directive, January 24–31, 1943, box 35, French Directives, OWI Records.
49  Central Directive, April 9–16, 1943, box 2, OWI–Miscellaneous, ONI Records.
50  Directive, November 1, 1942, box 35, French Directives, OWI Records.
51  Central Directive, December 11–18, 1942, box 818, OWI Records.
52  Directive, November 8, 1942, box 35, French Directives, OWI Records.
53  A word of background discussion may be in order here on the size of the Voice of America's output in French. The Voice aired 220 French language broadcasts of fifteen minutes each per day over eighteen transmitters within the United States. These shows were based on forty-eight distinct scripts. Short-wave transmissions ran continuously from 6:30 in the morning until 10:15 at night (French time). From 10:15 P.M. until 6:30 A.M. there were two programs an hour, broadcast on the hour and the half hour. There were relayed programs as well. At 9:15 A.M. and 6:15 P.M. there were fifteen-minute rebroadcasts over eight medium- and long-wave transmitters from London. In addition, there were three thirty-minute programs and one fifteen-minute program broadcast over the North African stations, which included live material created on the spot. See Joint Staff Planners, "OWI Outline Plan of Propaganda for France–Basic," May 13, 1943, ABC 385 France, WD Records.
54  Central Directive, June 11–18, 1943, box 218, OWI Records.
55  Central Directive, May 21–28, 1943, box 218, OWI Records; Joint Staff Planners, "OWI Outline Plan of Propaganda for France–Basic."
56  Central Directive, July 9–16, 1943, box 218, OWI Records.
57  Central Directive, August 20–27, 1943, box 218, OWI Records.
58  Central Directive, November 5–12, 1943, box 218, OWI Records.
59  Central Directive, April 30–May 7, 1943, box 218, OWI Records.
60  Houseman, *Front and Center,* 81.

## Chapter 5. The Propagandists and the Federal Government: The Political Struggles of the Overseas Branch

1 Memorandum, Warburg to Carroll, August 28, 1942, box 704, London–1942, OWI Records; Harry C. Butcher, *My Three Years with Eisenhower* (New York: Simon and Schuster, 1946), 98–99.

2 Davis to General Deane, December 15, 1942, folder 1659; Sherwood to Hopkins, December 24, 1942, folder 1232, Sherwood Papers; Memorandum, Sherwood to Davis, December 24, 1942, box 12, Office of Strategic Services, OWI Records; cable, Bowes-Lyon to Bruce Lockhart, December 24, 1942, PRO, FO 371/30727. David Bowes-Lyon accompanied Sherwood and Davis to demonstrate British support for the OWI.

3 Stephen E. Ambrose, *Eisenhower: Soldier, General of the Army, President-Elect, 1890–1952* (New York: Simon and Schuster, 1983), 214–22. The new governor of Algeria was Marcel Peyrouton, who had been Vichy minister of the interior and was a noted Fascist. Eisenhower's diary entry elucidates the general's appreciation of the political maelstrom in which he operated: "Who'd they want?" he complained of the protesters. "He [Peyrouton] is an experienced administrator, and God knows it's hard to find many of them among the French in Africa" (quoted in Ambrose, *Eisenhower,* 217).

4 The Budget Bureau's concern with the inner workings of the OWI actually predated the conflict with the OSS. The bureau had continued to fret over the efficiency, budgeting, planning, and personnel of the OWI, which Budget officials thought too sloppy and excessively liberal. Operations within the OWI, they worried, were just as chaotic as they had been under the COI. Nevertheless, the Bureau of the Budget disliked Donovan and continued to support Davis and the OWI over him, regardless of other misgivings. See memorandum, Gosnell to Herring, December 15, 1942, reporting on a conference held with Davis, Sherwood, and Hamblett, series 41.3, unit 153(d); memorandum, Gosnell to Herring, January 26, 1943, reporting on a conference with Robert Pell, John K. Caldwell, and Cloyce Huston, series 39.19, box 82; Herring and Gosnell, notes on a conversation with Charles Hulton, December 14, 1942, series 39.19, box 83, BOB Records.

5 Quoted in Sidney Stahl Weinburg, "Wartime Propaganda in a Democracy: America's Twentieth Century Information Agencies" (Ph.D. diss., Columbia University, 1969), 433.

6 Staff Order 14 reorganized the OWI into seven regions with regional heads based in Washington, from which they were to develop regional policy directives, supervise regional production plans, and check New York's execution of these plans (Staff Order 14, February 19, 1943, box 2, OWI–Miscellaneous, ONI Records). Warburg too was to spend a greater part of his time in Washington, and be there when he drafted the Overseas Branch's weekly directive. See memorandum, Gosnell to Sydney Stem, Jr., February 27, 1943, box 14, unit 153(a), BOB Records; Ken Fry, "OWI: Past and Present; Its Organization," n.d., box 62, folder 13, OWI Records.

7   Conversation with Edd Johnson, as reported in memorandum, Gosnell to Herring, March 27, 1943, series 41.3, unit 153(d), BOB Records.

8   Miall to Calder, April 9, 1943, Miall Papers.

9   Sherwood to Davis, June 14, 1943, folder 1089, Sherwood Papers. See also interview with James Warburg, as reported in memorandum, Gosnell to Herring, July 1, 1943, series 41.3, unit 153(d), BOB Records.

10  Memorandum, Kehrli to McCandless, "OWI-OSS Relationships on Research and Analysis," August 9, 1943, series 39.19, box 83, BOB Records.

11  Miall to Crossman, May 5, 1943, Miall Papers. There was a certain truth to the allegation. Presidential advisers such as Archibald MacLeish and Lowell Mellett were also part of the Domestic Branch of the OWI. They would pass on to the president such tidbits of intelligence as the fact that morale was low in the Rocky Mountain states and the administration needed to take action. Roosevelt would then contact other leaders of the Domestic Branch, who in turn might send out lecturers or movies to that region. Such a tactic was used to preserve national support for the war effort, but no matter how necessary, it was a practice that lent itself to attack.

12  Joseph Barnes, "Reminiscences of Joseph Barnes" (1953), 239, Oral History Collection, Columbia University, New York.

13  Miall to Bowes-Lyon, June 2, 1943, Miall Papers; John Houseman, *Front and Center* (New York: Simon and Schuster, 1979), 74. Leo Lania was an Austrian playwright who had worked with both Bertolt Brecht and Erwin Piscator in Germany before the war.

14  John Houseman, *Front and Center* (New York: Simon and Schuster, 1979), 72.

15  Memorandum, Kehrli to Bryan, August 17, 1943, series 39.19, box 82, OWI–General Administration, BOB Records.

16  Quoted in Weinberg, "Wartime Propaganda in a Democracy," 271–72.

17  Quoted in ibid., 278.

18  Memorandum, Sherwood to Hopkins, June 23, 1943, folder 1232, Sherwood Papers. See also John Taber obituary, *New York Times*, November 23, 1965; interview with Milton Eisenhower, as reported in memorandum, Gosnell to Herring, July 23, 1943, series 41.3, unit 153(d), BOB Records; Allan M. Winkler, *The Politics of Propaganda: The Office of War Information, 1942–1945* (New Haven: Yale University Press, 1978), 70.

19  Richard Dunlop, *Donovan: America's Master Spy* (Chicago: Rand McNally, 1982), 473.

20  I. Berlin to Foreign Office, August 7, 1943, in H. G. Nicholas, ed., *Washington Despatches, 1941–1945: Weekly Reports from the British Embassy.* (Chicago: University of Chicago Press, 1981), 232.

21  David Halberstam, *The Powers That Be* (New York: Knopf, 1979), 223; Gaye Talese, *The Kingdom and the Power* (New York: New American Library, 1969), 186–92.

22  Leonard Miall, "The O.W.I. and the Fascist King," July 30, 1943, Miall Papers.

23  Arthur Krock, column in the *New York Times,* July 6, 1943.

24  Ambrose, *Eisenhower,* 253; Michael Balfour, *Propaganda in War, 1939–1945: Or-*

*ganizations, Policies and Publics in Britain and Germany* (London: Routledge and Kegan Paul, 1979), 350.

25 Wallace Carroll, interview with author, March 3, 1986.

26 James P. Warburg, *The Long Road Home* (New York: Doubleday, 1964), 202. It is interesting to note what the British PWE directive said on this subject. Like their American counterparts, the British immediately assumed that the resignation of Mussolini did not spell the end of the Fascist regime: "There is nothing in the proclamations which commits [the new Italian government] to the destruction of the Fascist regime or to the abandonment of the German war." The British anticipated no compromise with the revised Fascist regime. Nevertheless, unlike the Overseas Branch, the PWE did warn the propagandists to "reserve all comment on the King and his attitude." This was to prove an important distinction. See Political Warfare Executive Central Directive, "Special Directive on Resignation of Mussolini," July 26, 1943, PRO, FO 371/34387.

27 "Statement to Planning Board on the Incident of July 25, 1943," box 9, Propaganda Agency–Propaganda Committee, Lilly Papers.

28 Ibid.

29 Balfour, *Propaganda in War,* 214.

30 Quoted in Barnes, "Reminiscences," 46.

31 Quoted in ibid.

32 Quoted in ibid.

33 Jack Gould, telephone interview with author, June 2, 1986.

34 "OWI Says Fascists Remain in Power," *New York Times,* July 26, 1943.

35 *New York Times,* July 27, 1943.

36 Leonard Miall, "Relations Between O.W.I., New York, and the Political Warfare Mission–A Six Months' Summary," August 20, 1943, Miall Papers. See also Carroll interview. Forty-three years later Gould remembered this story quite differently. He recalled writing only the story that ran on page 1 on Tuesday, July 27, and he strongly refuted Barnes's assertion that Krock had urged Gould to criticize the OWI. But Miall was writing his report at the time of the events. For much of the time during the moronic little king crisis he was privileged to be sitting in Barnes's office. I have therefore trusted Miall's version and reconstructed the events as they seem to me most logical.

37 *New York Times,* July 27, 1943.

38 Miall, "The O.W.I. and the Fascist King."

39 Ibid.

40 Ibid.

41 Ibid.

42 I. Berlin to Foreign Office, August 7, 1943, in Nicholas, ed., *Washington Despatches,* 231.

43 Telegram, Washington to Foreign Office, August 30, September 26, October 3, 1943, PRO, FO 371/34161.

44 Interview with Mr. Pell, State Department Liaison with OWI on Policy, as reported in memorandum, Campbell to Richardson, January 12, 1944, series 39.19, box 92, BOB Records; memorandum, C. A. H. Thomson to Paul Fredericks, September 22, 1943, box 125, State Department, OWI Records.

45   Telegram, Washington to Foreign Office, Supplement to Weekly Political Summary, August 15, 1943, PRO, FO 371/34160.

46   Miall, "Relations Between O.W.I., New York, and the Political Warfare Mission–A Six Months' Summary."

47   Ibid.

48   Memorandum, Campbell to Richardson, "OWI Overseas Reorganization–Editorial Board in New York," September 9, 1943, series 39.19, box 92, BOB Records.

49   Miall, "Relations Between O.W.I., New York, and the Political Warfare Mission–A Six Months' Summary."

50   Memorandum, Gosnell to Herring, May 14, 1943, box 14, unit 153(a), BOB Records; *New York Times,* August 21, 1943; memorandum, Davis to Employees, September 2, 1943, box 29, OWI–Organization Papers, Warburg Papers.

51   Carroll interview.

52   Harrison E. Salisbury, *A Journey for Our Times: A Memoir* (New York: Harper and Row, 1983), 174.

53   Wallace Carroll, *Inside Warring Russia* (Winston-Salem, N.C.: United Press Associates, 1942), unpaginated.

54   Carroll interview.

55   Ibid.

56   Phil Hamblett to Sherwood, December 7, 1943, folder 1198, Sherwood Papers.

57   Warburg to Sherwood, December 12, 1943, box 29, OWI–Organization Papers, Warburg Papers.

58   Carroll interview.

59   Quoted in Halberstam, *The Powers That Be,* 35.

60   On Klauber's reputation see Robert Mertz, *CBS: Reflections in a Bloodshot Eye* (Chicago: Playboy, 1975), 39–48; Doris Klauber Wechsler, interview with author, March 13, 1986.

61   Memorandum to D.G, D.D.G, D. of P., (O)., C.A.O., February 7, 1944, PRO, PWE Records, FO 898/105.

62   Davis to Roosevelt, January 4, 1944, box 10, OWI, Davis Papers.

63   Sherwood to the President, January 13, 1944, box 172, OWI, PS Files.

64   Harold F. Gosnell, "Overhead Organization of the Office of War Information," n.d., 19, series 41.3, unit 170, BOB Records.

65   Elmer Davis, notes on a conversation with the President, February 2, 1944, box 10, OWI, Davis Papers.

66   Lord Ritchie-Calder, interview with author, March 23, 1981.

67   Warburg to Sherwood, February 6, 1944, box 29, OWI–Organization Papers, Warburg Papers.

68   Quoted in Leonard Miall, "Repercussions in New York of the OWI Shakeup," March 1944, Miall Papers.

69   Ibid.

70   Cowan, "Reminiscences," Oral History Collection, Columbia University; *Variety,* January 21, 1942, 22; April 15, 1942, 27; September 2, 1942, 38; *Broadcasting,* April 13, 1942, 52.

71   Harry Torczyner, interview with author, July 15, 1986.

72  Cowan, "Reminiscences."
73  Leonard Miall,"The Repercussions in New York of the OWI Shakeup," 1944, Miall Papers.
74  Ritchie-Calder interview, March 23, 1981.

## Chapter 6. Who's Listening? The Role of Changing Mass Communications Theories

1  Eisenhower had sought Houseman's services in order to improve the newly begun propaganda operations in North Africa, which were under the auspices of the Allied Forces Headquarters. Houseman assumed that the reason the State Department refused to let him go, despite several attempts to overturn the initial passport division order, was due to his background in the left-wing theater world of the thirties. His opinion was shared by many inside the OWI, who saw the decision as part of a general campaign against the OWI and its presumed radical elements. "The fact that Jack produced a show, the benefits of which went to the Spanish loyalists . . . cooked his goose for him," Leonard Miall wrote in April (Miall to Calder, April 9, 1943, Miall Papers). Houseman was too angry to let the matter rest there, and decided that he would rather leave the organization than live with the limitations henceforth surrounding him and the aspersions implicitly undermining him. See John Houseman, *Front and Center* (New York: Simon and Schuster, 1979), 86–91; Houseman, interview with author, March 26, 1986. For Eisenhower's interest in bringing Houseman to North Africa see telegram from Sumner Welles, March 5, 1943, POLAD–Allied Forces Headquarters, box 18, OWI, FSP Records; telegram, Washington to Ministry of Information, March 3, 1943, PRO, FO 371/3618.
2  Harry Torczyner, telephone conversation with author, July 23, 1986; Susan Dodson, telephone conversation with author, July 23, 1986; Harold Q. Masur, telephone conversation with author, July 23, 1986.
3  Wallace Carroll, telephone conversation with author, July 23, 1986.
4  Harry Torczyner, interview with author, July 15, 1986.
5  Werner Michel, interview with author, April 24, 1983.
6  Connie Ernst Bessie, interview with author, November 14, 1982; Michel, interview.
7  Michel Rapaport Gordey, interview with author, November 6, 1985.
8  Analysis Division Bulletin, October 2, 1943, box 121, New York Office, OWI Records.
9  Analysis Division Bulletin, January 20, 1944, box 121, New York Office, OWI Records.
10  On the Analysis Bureau see *Variety,* January 7, 1942, 111. These reports are variously filed in the records of the OWI, but see especially box 121, New York Office, and box 118, Bureau of Intelligence, OWI Records.
11  Harold D. Lasswell, *Propaganda Technique in the World War* (New York: Knopf, 1927), 9.
12  Daniel J. Czitrom, *Media and the American Mind: From Morse to McLuhan* (Chapel Hill: University of North Carolina Press, 1982), 122–46. Audience sam-

pling was a particularly American experience. In stark contrast, for example, the director general of the BBC, Lord Reith, cared little for audience program evaluations. Reith believed that the BBC should set the standards for what made good listening, not the public. "Only the authoritative guidance of a true elite could satisfy Reith where broadcasting to an unlimited audience was concerned," his biographer has written. "The masses, he believed, would learn in time to enjoy what was good. To offer them what *they* wanted would have turned the BBC into a spiritual whore-house, himself into a cultural pimp" (Andrew Boyle, *Only the Wind Will Listen: Reith of the BBC* [London: Hutchinson, 1972], 151).

13   Paul F. Lazarsfeld, "An Episode in the History of Social Research: A Memoir," in *The Intellectual Migration: Europe and America, 1920–1960*, ed. Donald Flemming and Bernard Bailyn (Cambridge: Harvard University Press, 1969), 270–337.

14   Harold D. Lasswell, "The Status of Research on International Propaganda and Opinion," *Papers and Proceedings of the American Sociological Society* 20 (December 1925): 198–209; Lasswell, *Propaganda Technique in the World War;* for Lasswell's later work on the potential influence of propaganda in the United States in the late 1930s see Harold D. Lasswell and Dorothy Blumenstock, *World Revolutionary Propaganda* (New York: Knopf, 1939).

15   Harold D. Lasswell, "Why Be Quantitative?" in *A Reader in Public Opinion and Communication,* ed. Bernard Berelson and Morris Janowitz (Glencoe, Ill.: Free Press, 1953), 269. It is worth noting that the Frankfurt school of sociology exerted very little influence on radio research and mass communications theories in the United States during the thirties and forties. Like Lazarsfeld, members of the Frankfurt school were émigrés from central Europe, and like Lazarsfeld, many were Jewish. Lazarsfeld, however, based his research on empirical studies rather than reasoned, philosophical analysis. Whatever the merits of the two approaches, Lazarsfeld's techniques proved translatable into the American academic and cultural idiom; those of the Frankfurt school did not. Furthermore, sociologists of the Frankfurt school wrote almost entirely in German, even when working in the United States, which made their theories all the more inaccessible to most American scholars. See Martin Jay, *The Dialectical Imagination* (Boston: Little, Brown, 1973), 190, 220–23.

16   Czitrom, *Media and the American Mind*, 132.

17   The problems faced by postwar researchers trying to measure the size of the listening audience in eastern Europe, by way of contrast, is distinctly different – and simpler – than were those of wartime workers. Since the war the Voice of America, Radio Free Europe, and Radio Liberty have continued to rely on interviews, but the range of those who can be interviewed, especially from eastern bloc countries excluding the Soviet Union, has expanded enormously. One Radio Free Europe report on listening habits in Poland during the late 1960s, for example, was based on a sample of 1,099 Poles. "Most of the respondents were visiting Western countries as tourists or guests of relatives or friends living there," the Radio Free Europe report explained. "A small minority were members of delegations, athletic teams, or artistic ensembles or

other organized groups." In direct contrast to wartime efforts, postwar research-ers have largely been freed from relying on refugees for evaluative data. "Only 4% were refugees or emigrants" (Radio Free Europe, Audience and Public Opinion Research Department, *Listening to Western Radio in Poland*, October 1968, 3).

18 Robert Silvey, *Who's Listening? The Story of BBC Audience Research* (London: Allen and Unwin, 1974), 46.

19 Ibid., 29.

20 Pierre Sorlin, "The Struggle for Control of French Minds, 1940–1944," in *Film and Radio Propaganda in World War II*, ed. K. R. M. Short (Knoxville: University of Tennessee Press, 1983), 268.

21 Paul F. Lazarsfeld and Robert K. Merton, "Studies in Radio and Film Propaganda," *Transactions of the New York Academy of Sciences*, ser. 2, vol. 6 (1942–43), 65.

22 BBC Bi-Monthly Survey: France, June 18, 1943, box 254, E9.2, BBC Bi-Monthly Surveys, OWI Records.

23 In this light it is interesting to note the observation made by Leonard Doob, the Yale social scientist who headed the Washington-based Bureau of Overseas Intelligence, which conducted policy research intended to help guide decisions about how best to direct daily, weekly, and long-range propaganda lines. "The problem of policy research," Doob wrote, was that to come up with answers to the question of what people were thinking and doing, or leaders plotting and planning, "required adequate data before any social science could be systematically employed. Such data were lacking" (Leonard W. Doob, "The Utilization of Social Scientists in the Overseas Branch of the Office of War Information," in *Propaganda in War and Crisis*, ed. Daniel Lerner [New York: Stewart, 1951], 297).

24 Ibid. There is an interesting parallel between the tension that existed between the creative side of the Overseas Branch of the Office of War Information/Voice of America and the OWI's social scientists, and the tension between the creators and the market researchers in the world of mass media advertising. On Madison Avenue copywriters are often hostile to those who conduct the copy tests. As one advertising executive argued, "Research is a tidy, scientific approach, which shouldn't even be applied to advertising—which, at its best, is an art form" (Michael Schudson, *Advertising, the Uneasy Persuasion: Its Dubious Impact on American Society* [New York: Basic Books, 1984], 82). This sentiment was largely felt, if rarely so clearly articulated, by wartime propagandists.

25 Torczyner interview.

26 Barrett to Sherwood and Barnes, September 28, 1943 box 50, folder 9, OWI Records.

27 Doob, "The Utilization of Social Scientists," 307.

28 Torczyner interview.

29 Report, Harry H. Schwartz (Chargé d'Affaires ad interim, Tangier) to the Secretary of State, March 31, 1943, box 3493, SD Records 811.76, shortwave/593.

30 BBC Bi-Monthly Survey: France, June 18, 1943, box 254, E9.2, BBC Bi-Monthly Surveys, OWI Records.
31 Cable, Winner to Sherwood, Barnes, and Warburg, September 3, 1943, box 107, France–Cables, OWI Records.
32 "Audience Reaction to OWI Radio Broadcast Report #3," November 6, 1943, box 118, Bureau of Intelligence, OWI Records.
33 Cable, Bern, Switzerland, to OWI, March 17, 1943, box 107, France–Cables, OWI Records.
34 W. C. Patterson (Chief Representative, OWI, Spain) to Sherwood, July 19, 1943, SD Records 103.9166/6050.
35 Guidance, September 26, 1943, box 123, Radio Program Bureau, Broadcasting Division, OWI Records.
36 Patterson to Sherwood, July 19, 1943, SD Records 103.9166/6050.
37 "Listeners' Reactions," n.d. (1943), box 29, OWI–Organization Papers, Warburg Papers. For a discussion of the continuing problems that have beset audience research since World War II see, for example, W. Phillips Davison, *International Political Communication* (New York: Praeger, 1965), 185–92; and Donald R. Browne, *International Radio Broadcasting: The Limits of the Limitless Medium* (New York: Praeger, 1982), 339–51.
38 The following discussion is indebted to Czitrom, *Media and the American Mind*, 136–39.
39 Leon Bramson, *The Political Context of Sociology* (Princeton: Princeton University Press, 1961), 32–33.
40 Eugene E. Leach, "Mastering the Crowd: Collective Behavior and Mass Society in American Social Thought, 1917–1939," *American Studies* 27 (Spring 1986): 106, 108–109.
41 Ibid., 110; Bramson, *The Political Context of Sociology*, 103.
42 Herbert Blumer, "Outline of Collective Behavior," in *Readings in Collective Behavior*, ed. Robert R. Evans (Chicago: Rand McNally, 1969), 78–80.
43 Harold D. Lasswell, "The Theory of Political Propaganda," *American Political Science Review* 21 (August 1927): 630. See also Herbert Blumer, "The Mass, The Public, and Public Opinion," in *A Reader in Public Opinion and Communication*, ed. Bernard Berelson and Morris Janowitz, 43–49.
44 Daniel Katz, "Three Criteria: Knowledge, Conviction and Significance," *Public Opinion Quarterly* 4 (June 1940): 281.
45 Hadley Cantril, "The Invasion of Mars," in *The Process and Effects of Mass Communication*, ed. Wilbur Schramm (Urbana: University of Illinois Press, 1954), 412.
46 For an early attack on the prevailing belief in the absolute power of propaganda see the essays contained in Harwood L. Childs, ed., *Propaganda and Dictatorship: A Collection of Papers* (Princeton: Princeton University Press, 1936).
47 Hans J. Speier, "Morale and Propaganda," in *War in Our Time*, ed. Hans J. Speier and Alfred Kahler (New York: Norton, 1939), 310.
48 Lazarsfeld and Merton, "Studies in Radio and Film Propaganda," 58–59. See also Bramson, *The Political Context of Sociology*, 100.

49  Lazarsfeld and Merton, "Studies in Radio and Film Propaganda," 69.

50  Parallel studies have been made on the effectiveness of advertising over the mass media which also challenge the idea that an advertisement can alter previously held beliefs about a product. For a discussion of what advertisers do and don't know and the influence of social science theory on Madison Avenue see Schudson, *Advertising, the Uneasy Persuasion*, 44–90.

51  Lazarsfeld and Merton, "Studies in Radio and Film Propaganda," 76.

52  Paul L. Lazarsfeld, Bernard Berelson, and Hazel Gaudet, *The People's Choice: How the Voter Makes up His Mind in a Presidential Campaign* (New York: Duell, Sloan and Pearce, 1944).

53  By the 1950s, doubts about the immediate effects of the mass media prevailed. American social scientists rejected the notion of an individual who was detached, isolated, and anonymous, the alienated man-in-the-street described by Blumer and others. They saw instead an America composed of individuals who still lived their lives set in solid social foundations, and who therefore heard and read the mass media within their own specific social contexts.

54  Hans J. Speier, "Psychological Warfare Reconsidered," in Schramm, ed., *The Process and Effects of Mass Communication*, 456.

55  Joseph T. Klapper, "What We Know About the Effects of Mass Communication: The Brink of Hope," in *Communications and Public Opinion*, ed. Robert O. Carlson (New York: Praeger, 1975), 366.

56  For a discussion of why these trends arose see Ernst Kris and Nathan Leites, "Trends in Twentieth Century Propaganda," in *A Reader in Public Opinion and Communication*, ed. Bernard Berelson and Morris Janowitz, 278–88.

57  "Overseas Operations," n.d. (1943), box 38 (notebook), OWI Records.

58  Guidance, September 26, 1943, box 123, Radio Program Bureau, Broadcasting Division, OWI Records.

59  "Listeners' Reactions," n.d. (1943), box 29, OWI–Organization Papers, Warburg Papers.

60  Paul Rotha, *Documentary Film* (London: Faber and Faber, 1952), 217–18.

61  Henry R. Luce, *The American Century* (New York: Farrar and Rinehart, 1941), 17, 19.

62  Ibid., 3, 27.

63  Ibid., 39.

64  C. Wright Mills, *The Sociological Imagination* (New York: Oxford University Press, 1959), 4.

65  Torczyner interview.

## *Chapter 7.* *Broadcasting the News:*
## *From Guidances to Programs*

1  Directive, January 31–February 7, 1943, box 35, French Directives, OWI Records.

2  Central directive, May 7–14, 1943, box 218, OWI Records.

3  Central directive, December 16–23, 1943, box 218, OWI Records.

4  A. Minor, French Section, August 15, 1943, box 116, Transcripts, OWI Records.

5  Guidance, March 17, 1943, box 128, Meeting Notes to Lattimore, OWI Records.

6  Robert O. Paxton, *Vichy France: Old Guard and New Order* (New York: Knopf, 1972), 280.

7  Directive, January 3, 1943, box 35, French Directives, OWI Records.

8  Directive, January 24–31, 1943, box 35, French Directives, OWI Records.

9  Directive, January 3, 1943, box 35, French Directives, OWI Records.

10  "France," August 10, 1943, box 201, Transcripts, OWI Records.

11  Directive, January 31–February 7, 1943, box 35, French Directives, OWI Records.

12  Cable, USINFO, March 15, 1943; cable, Carroll to Warburg, March 11, 1943, box 107, France–Policy, OWI Records.

13  Directive, January 8, 1944, box 212, French Directives, OWI Records.

14  Directive, July 31, 1943, box 35, French Directives, OWI Records.

15  "France," October 7, 1943, box 224, Transcripts, OWI Records.

16  "The Resistance Front," January 13, 1943, box 116, Transcripts, OWI Records.

17  "France," August 10, 1943, box 201, Transcripts, OWI Records.

18  M. R. D. Foot, *Resistance* (New York: McGraw-Hill, 1977), 240–41.

19  Central directive, June 18–25, 1943, box 218, OWI Records.

20  Directive, July 3, 1943, box 35, French Directives, OWI Records.

21  Directive, August 21, 1943, box 212, French Directives, OWI Records.

22  "PWE-OWI Plan for France for the Winter of 1943/44," November 16, 1943. See also memorandum, Jenkins to Scarlett, November 30, 1943, PRO, PWE Records, FO 898/379.

23  Directive, November 1, 1942, box 35, French Directives, OWI Records.

24  Guidance, November 9, 1942, box 35, French Directives, OWI Records.

25  Guidance, March 19, 1943, box 128, Meeting Notes to Lattimore, OWI Records.

26  Central Directive, June 25–July 2, 1943, box 218, OWI Records.

27  Central Directive, July 30–August 6, 1943, box 218, OWI Records.

28  Robert Dalleck, *Franklin Roosevelt and American Foreign Policy, 1932–1945* (New York: Oxford University Press, 1979), 380.

29  Central Directive, November 6, 1942, box 4, Directives; Guidance, November 9, 1943, box 3, Chronological, Lilly Papers; cable, New York to Colonel Solbert, November 23, 1942, box 130, Guidance Notes, OWI Records.

30  Central Directive, July 9–16, 1943, box 218, OWI Records.

31  Directive, August 28, 1943, box 35, French Directives, OWI Records.

32  Central Directive, October 23–November 3, 1943, box 218, OWI Records.

33  Directive, August 21, 1943, box 35, French Directives, OWI Records.

34  Directive, August 7, 1943, box 35, French Directives, OWI Records.

35  Quoted in Pierre Andler, "Occupied Countries #120," August 14, 1943, box 201, Transcripts, OWI Records.

36  "European Air Front," December 13, 1943, box 254, Transcripts, OWI Records.

37  Jean Rollin, Labor Show, May 10, 1943, box 169, Transcripts, OWI Records.

38  Michel Rapaport, European Show, December 15, 1943, box 254, Transcripts, OWI Records.

39  Central Directive, March 12–19, 1943, box 2, ONI Records.

40  Ibid.

41  Ibid.

42  Central Directive, January 15–22, 1943, box 2, ONI Records.

43  Central Directive, June 18–25, 1943, box 218, OWI Records.

44  Claude Day, "Day by Day: Portable Pipe-Lines on the Battle Fronts," October 9, 1943, box 224, Transcripts, OWI Records.

45  Jean Rollin, Labor Show, December 16, 1943, box 254, Transcripts, OWI Records.

46  Directive, January 17–24, 1943, box 35, French Directives, OWI Records.

47  Central Directive, September 3–10, 1943, box 218, OWI Records.

48  Directive, June 19, 1943, box 35, French Directives, OWI Records.

49  Central Directive, September 10–17, 1943, box 218, OWI Records; central directive, September 25–October 2, 1943, box 2, ONI Records.

50  The Connally resolution called for U.S. participation, through its constitutional process, in the "establishment and maintenance of international authority with power to prevent aggression and to preserve the peace of the world . . ." (James MacGregor Burns, *Roosevelt: The Soldier of Freedom, 1940–1945* [New York: Harcourt Brace Jovanovich, 1970], 428). See also I. Berlin to Foreign Office, October 22, 31, November 7, 14, 1943, in H. G. Nicholas, ed., *Washington Despatches, 1941–1945: Weekly Reports from the British Embassy* (Chicago: University of Chicago Press, 1981), 264, 267–68, 269, 272–73.

51  Directive, March 14, 1943, box 35, French Directives, OWI Records.

52  Julian G. Hurstfield, *America and the French Nation, 1939–1945* (Chapel Hill: University of North Carolina Press, 1986), 190.

53  Directive, June 19, 1943, box 35, French Directives, OWI Records.

54  Directive, July 31, 1943, box 35, French Directives, OWI Records.

55  Albert Guerard, "Franco-American Friendship," October 9, 1943, box 224, Transcripts, OWI Records.

56  "Radio Operations," April 24, 1943, box 24, Werner Michel Files, OWI Records; Leonard Miall, "Relations Between OWI, New York, and the Political Warfare Mission—A Six Months' Summary," July 20, 1943, Miall Papers.

57  Michel Rapaport Gordey to author, October 11, 1986.

58  Labor Show, November 10, 1942, box 89, Transcripts, OWI Records. Headlines tended to remain the same throughout the day, regardless of the program. Unlike features and many news bulletins, headlines were the same for each language, although their wording might differ from language to language (Gordey to author, October 11, 1986).

59  "News of the Day," October 9, 1943, box 224, Transcripts, OWI Records.

60  Guidance, September 19, 1943, box 123, Radio Program Bureau, Broadcasting Division, OWI Records. Michel addressed these guidances primarily to the producers because they were the ones responsible for each program. As he advised in another guidance, all such factors as timing, pace, volume, pauses, and so on were controlled by the producers. The announcer should devote his entire attention to the reading of the script and follow the directions of the producer. Guidance, October 17, 1943, box 123, Radio Program Bureau, Broadcasting Division, OWI Records.

61  "France at War," December 10, 1943, LWO 12608A, reel 1A4; French Morning Show, December 10, 1943, LWO 12608, reel 1B, OWI Collection.

62  Guidance, September 26, 1943, box 123, Radio Program Bureau, Broadcasting Division, OWI Records.

63  Peter J. Rabinowitz, "Audiences' Experience of Literary Borrowing," in *The Reader in the Text,* ed. Susan R. Suleiman and Inge Crosman (Princeton: Princeton University Press, 1980), 244.

64  "French North Africa," December 28, 1942, box 104, Transcripts, OWI Records.

65  "Mediterranean Front," January 15, 1943, box 116, Transcripts, OWI Records.

66  Wayne C. Booth, *The Rhetoric of Fiction* (Chicago: University of Chicago Press, 1983), 23–29, 67–77, 89–91, 119–25.

67  Lionel Durand, "Mediterranean Front," May 11, 1943, box 169, Transcripts, OWI Records.

68  Booth, *The Rhetoric of Fiction,* 422–23.

69  A. Minor, "France–Daladier–Jouhaux," October 9, 1943, box 224, Transcripts, OWI Records.

70  A. Minor, Military Show, October 9, 1943, box 224, Transcripts, OWI.

71  Memorandum, Lazareff to Barnes, Warburg, Carlton, Blochman, and Galantiere, October 12, 1943, box 29, OWI–Organization Papers, Warburg Papers.

72  Ibid.

73  Ibid.

74  Ibid.

75  Memorandum, Warburg to Davis and Sherwood, August 11, 1943, Miall Papers.

76  Leonard Miall, "The O.W.I. and the Fascist King," July 28, 1943, Miall Papers.

77  "Overseas Operations," n.d. (1943), box 38 (notebook), OWI Records.

78  Memorandum, Warburg to Davis, April 27, 1943, OWI–Organization Papers, Warburg Papers.

79  Edd Johnson to Warburg, September 18, 1944, box 29, OWI–General Correspondence, Warburg Papers.

## *Chapter 8. Sailing Between Wind and Water: Propaganda and American Foreign Relations, 1944*

1  Richard H. S. Crossman, "Psychological Warfare, Part I," *Journal of the Royal United Service Institution* 97 (August 1952): 320.

2  Wallace Carroll, interview with author, March 3, 1986.

3  Cable, Hamblett and Galantiere to Carroll, June 19, 1944, box 107, OWI Records.

4  Harry L. Coles and Albert K. Weinberger, *Civil Affairs: Soldiers Become Governors* (Washington, D.C.: Office of the Chief of Military History, Department of the Army, 1964), 94–95.

5  Stephen E. Ambrose, *Eisenhower: Soldier, General of the Army, President-Elect, 1890–1952* (New York: Simon and Schuster, 1983), 240–41.

6  Ibid., 279–80; Milton Viorst, *Hostile Allies: FDR and Charles de Gaulle* (New York: Macmillan, 1965), 174–75; Alexander Werth, *De Gaulle: A Political Biography* (New York: Simon and Schuster, 1965), 169; Arthur Layton Funk, *Charles de Gaulle: The Crucial Years, 1943–1944* (Norman: University of Oklahoma Press, 1959), 220.

7  Julian G. Hurstfield, *America and the French Nation, 1939–1945* (Chapel Hill: University of North Carolina Press, 1986), 210–11.

8  Ibid., 218.

9  Ibid., 215.

10  Ambrose, *Eisenhower,* 334–35.

11  Cable, Carroll to Hamblett and Galantiere, September 23, 1944, box 107, OWI Records; Funk, *Charles de Gaulle,* 290.

12  Funk, *Charles de Gaulle,* 336; Hurstfield, *America and the French Nation,* 223.

13  Hurstfield, *America and the French Nation,* represents the first view; for him Roosevelt is an example of the American imperial presidency. For the second view see Viorst, who wrote *Hostile Allies* during the second de Gaulle administration and was searching for an explanation for the French leader's intensely independent foreign policy. Funk, *Charles de Gaulle,* writing less than a decade after the events had taken place, takes a comprehensive and moderate view.

14  Henry L. Stimson and McGeorge Bundy, *On Active Service in Peace and War,* quoted in Funk, *Charles de Gaulle,* 270–71.

15  Funk, *Charles de Gaulle,* 199.

16  Dwight D. Eisenhower, *Crusade in Europe* (New York: Doubleday, 1948), 137.

17  Hurstfield, *America and the French Nation,* 240.

18  Funk, *Charles de Gaulle,* 198–99, 267; John F. Sweets, *The Politics of Resistance in France, 1940–1944* (De Kalb: Northern Illinois University Press, 1976), 187–89.

19  For a discussion of these ideas within the State Department see "The Treatment of France," May 4, 1944, CAC 188, roll 3; "The Treatment of France: Policy Recommendations," May 20, 1944, CAC 193, roll 3; "The Treatment of France: Policy Recommendations," May 30, 1944, CAC 193, roll 3 (microfilm, T 1221), Harvey Notter Files, Record Group 59, National Archives, Washington, D.C. See also "Policy Toward France," May 30, 1944, American Embassy, Paris, box 1560, FSP Records.

20  Viorst, *Hostile Allies,* 247; Funk, *Charles de Gaulle,* 88, 271.

21  Stettinius to Klauber, March 4, 1944, box 596, confidential decimal file, SD Records 811.20251R/18A.

22  Russell Barnes, "Outpost Service Bureau, North Africa," May 24, 1944, box 53, folder 2, OWI Records; C. D. Jackson to William Tyler, April 23, 1944, box 1, Army–Algiers-London, Jackson Papers. The PWD liaison to the French was Lt. Col. Joseph Fairlie.

23  Richard Hollander, "A Brief Account of the Activities of the European Theater of Operations Division," n.d., 109 box 64; Sherwood to Barrett and Barnard, July 30, 1944, box 75, folder 3; Tyler to Hamblett, box 59, folder 20, OWI Records; Carroll interview.

24  Simon Michael Bessie, interview with author, April 2, 1986. After the liberation of France Tyler moved to Paris, where he became deputy director of USIS-Paris in February 1945.

25  William R. Tyler, "Memorandum on the Role of the French Committee of National Liberation in Liberated France," December 31, 1943, box 1, Army–Algiers-London, Jackson Papers.

26  Tyler to Barrett, June 8, 1944, box 130, Algiers–Policy.

27  Quoted in Russell Barnes to Barrett, June 10, 1944, box 50, folder 8, OWI Records.
28  Bessie interview.
29  Jackson to McClure, March 27, 1944, box 51, folder 10, OWI Records.
30  Memorandum, Ed Olson to Sherwood, Hamblett, and Backer, June 9, 1944, box 74, Outpost–London, OWI Records.
31  Memorandum, Winner to Barrett, March 17, 1944, box 6, folder 9, OWI Records.
32  Bessie interview. See also Wallace Carroll, *Persuade or Perish* (Boston: Houghton Mifflin, 1948), 27.
33  Carroll interview, Sherwood to Sam Rosenman, March 5, 1944, box 4, Rosenman Papers.
34  Cable, Sherwood to Davis, June 9, 1944, box 107, FCNL–Policy, OWI Records.
35  Cable, Barrett to Sherwood, June 17, 1944; cable, Davis, Carroll and Barrett to Sherwood, June 22, 1944; cable, Sherwood to Davis, Carroll, and Barrett, June 24, 1944; cable, Barrett to Sherwood, June 26, 1944; cable, Barrett to Sherwood, June 28, 1944; cable, Sherwood to Barrett, June 30, 1944; cable, Barrett to Sherwood, July 1, 1944, box 107, FCNL–Policy, OWI Records.
36  Schneider to Barrett, June 26, 1944, box 107, FCNL–Miscellaneous, OWI Records.
37  Bessie interview.
38  Schneider to Barrett, June 26, 1944, box 107, FCNL–Miscellaneous, OWI Records.
39  Cable, Hamblett and Galantiere to Carroll, June 19, 1944, box 107, FCNL–Policy, OWI Records.
40  Schneider to Barrett, June 26, 1944, box 107, FCNL–Miscellaneous, OWI Records.
41  Carroll interview.
42  Central Directive, May 30–June 6, 1944, box 2, OWI–Miscellaneous, ONI Records.
43  Central Directive, May 2–9, 1944, box 2, OWI–Miscellaneous, ONI Records.
44  Central Directive, July 11–18, 1944, box 2, OWI–Miscellaneous, ONI Records.
45  "Long-Range Policy Guidance for France," October 28, 1944, box 107, OWI Records; central directive, July 18–25, 1944, box 2, OWI–Miscellaneous, ONI Records.
46  Central Directive, May 30–June 6, 1944, box 2, OWI–Miscellaneous, ONI Records.
47  Michel Rapaport Gordey to author, May 21, 1987.
48  Robert Newman, interview with author, February 20, 1986.
49  Conversation with Harwood Childs, Overseas Branch, Office of War Information, as reported in memorandum, Gosnell to Stoke, June 16, 1944, series 39.19, box 82, BOB Records.
50  Conversation with Harwood Childs, Office of Policy Coordination, Office of War Information, as reported in memorandum, Gosnell to File, January 25, 1945, series 39.19, box 82, BOB Records.
51  Notes of a telephone conversation between Barnard and Hamblett, Novem-

ber 1, 1944, box 131, London–General Correspondence, OWI Records. Hamblett had joined the OWI from the Office of Government Reports in 1942. At first he had acted as liaison with the advertising industry and then moved up the ladder of Overseas Branch administration. Russell Page considered Hamblett "the only administrator of any calibre in the Overseas Service" (Page to Lucas, July 6, 1943, PRO, PWE Records, FO 898/134), whereas C. D. Jackson wrote of Hamblett that he was so successful because "by his combination of business shrewdness and effervescent Americanism [he] is able to substitute for considerable rank; and, besides, he has the advantage of being an extremely able administrator . . ." (Jackson to Sherwood, October 28, 1943, box 74, Outpost–London, OWI Records). See also *Broadcasting,* July 13, 1942, 57; Charles A. H. Thomson, *Overseas Information Service of the United States Government* (Washington, D.C.: Brookings Institution, 1948), 34n; Lester G. Hawkins, Jr., and George S. Pettee, "OWI–Organization," February 12, 1943, box 62, folder 13, OWI Records; Robert Lee Bishop, "The Overseas Branch of the Office of War Information" (Ph.D. diss., University of Wisconsin, 1966), 219. Before the war Barnard had been vice president of the N. W. Ayer advertising agency. Once at the OWI he was put in charge of the flow of personnel, money, and equipment to the OWI's overseas offices, at which job he had, according to Carroll, "won universal respect" (*Persuade or Perish,* 201). After the overall reorganization of February 1944, Barnard became Barrett's right-hand man as assistant executive director and later, after Sherwood resigned on September 25, 1944, executive director. See Davis, Report to the President, June 1945, 33, box 10, Davis Papers; Staff Order 29, March 27, 1944, box 38, OWI–Internal Organization; Press Release, September 25, 1944, box 18, folder 9, OWI Records.

52  Carroll interview.
53  Carroll, *Persuade or Perish,* 193.
54  Carroll interview.
55  Hans J. Speier, "War Aims in Political Warfare," in *Propaganda in War and Crisis,* ed. Daniel Lerner (New York: Stewart, 1951), 70.
56  Paul M. A. Linebarger, *Psychological Warfare* (Washington, D.C.: Infantry Journal Press, 1948), 98–99.
57  Daniel Lerner, *Psychological Warfare Against Nazi Germany: The Skywar Campaign, D-Day to V-E Day* (Cambridge: M.I.T. Press, 1971), xvi.
58  Speier, "War Aims in Political Warfare," 70.
59  Memorandum, McCloy to Stimson, November 7, 1940, Propaganda, McCloy Papers. See also Conference minutes, Propaganda Committee, November 13, 1940, box 247, Ickes Papers.
60  Louis G. Cowan diary, June 6, 1944, Cowan Papers.

## Chapter 9. D-Day, Liberation and the End of the OWI: The Administrative Struggles of the Overseas Branch and the Voice of America, 1944–45

1  Louis G. Cowan, "Propaganda to the Enemy," 2nd revised version, March 23, 1944, Cowan Papers; "PWE–OWI Plan for France for the Spring of 1944,"

January 1, 1944, box 51, French Situation; "Propaganda Guidance for Use When 'Liberation' Starts," April 15, 1944, box 113, Special Documents, OWI Records; John L. Craven (?), "Study of OWI New York French Output During the Month Preceding D-day," June 1944, PRO, PWE Records, FO 898/108.

2   James P. McConnaughey, Report Prepared for Washington, June 13, 1944, box 75, Outpost–North Africa; Lawrence Blochman, Radio Program Bureau Progress Report, June 15, 1944, box 24, folder 4, OWI Records.

3   Memorandum, Edward W. Barrett to Staff of the Overseas Branch, n.d., box 8, Army–OWI–USA, Jackson Papers.

4   Sherwood to Samuel Rosenman, March 5, 1944, box 4, Rosenman Papers.

5   Leonard Miall, "Trend Away from Political Warfare in OWI New York," July 6, 1944, Miall Papers.

6   Quoted in ibid.

7   Doris Klauber Wechsler, interview with author, March 13, 1986. See also David Halberstam, *The Powers That Be* (New York: Knopf, 1979), 35.

8   This view has been most effectively argued by Allan M. Winkler, *The Politics of Propaganda: The Office of War Information, 1942–1945* (New Haven: Yale University Press, 1978). See also Sidney Stahl Weinberg, "Wartime Propaganda in a Democracy: America's Twentieth Century Information Agencies" (Ph.D. diss., Columbia University, 1969).

9   Louis G. Cowan diary, September 21, 1944, Cowan Papers.

10  Notes on a talk by Owen Lattimore, September 13, 1944, Cowan Papers.

11  "Draft Long Range Operational Plan for France," November 1, 1944, box 25, folder 8, OWI Records.

12  Walter Adams to Leslie Beck, April 21, 1944, PRO, PWE Records, FO 898/108.

13  Anne Allison, "Competition to OWI Broadcasts in French," May 23, 1944, box 441, OWI Records.

14  SHAEF/PWD Report, received June 20, 1944, box 28, Lt. Col. Hope File; memorandum, Lazareff to Paley, May 11, 1944, box 29, Lazareff File, OWI Records.

15  "BBC Special Studies of European Audiences," April 24, 1944, box 107, Miscellaneous, OWI Records.

16  Report of the General Board, "Psychological Warfare in the European Theater of Operations," box 1086, Records of the U.S. Interservice Agencies: National War College Library, Record Group 334, National Record Center, Suitland, Md.

17  William R. Tyler, "History of PWB Relations with the French Civilian Authorities in North Africa," September 1, 1944, box 2, folder 14, OWI Records. The AIS later came under the command of the PWD. For a discussion of the PWD see "The Psychological Warfare Division SHAEF: An Account of Its Operation in the Western European Campaign, 1944–1945," n.d., Records of the U.S. Occupation Headquarters, box 260, Record Group 260, National Archives, Washington, D.C. See also the discussion in Elmer Davis, Report to the President, June 1945, 78–80, box 10, Davis Papers.

18  The PWB ran United Nations Radio in Algiers (which was distinct from Radio Algiers, a Free French station) as a combined operation under the Allied Forces Headquarters. It was an instructive precedent for ABSIE, but it was

never as important a station: the pull was not as great, the damage to New York was not as severe, and the broadcasts themselves were not as important.

19  "OWI French Radio Section," box 30, ABSIE–French Policy, OWI Records; "The Voice of SHAEF: Revised Procedure," June 16, 1944, PRO, PWE Records, FO 898/391.

20  Pierre Lazareff, Progress Report, September 11, 1944, box 30, OWI Records.

21  Wendell Sether, "ABSIE," 1945, box 24, OWI Records; Robert Lee Bishop, "The Overseas Branch of the Office of War Information" (Ph.D. diss., University of Wisconsin, 1966), 218.

22  Lazareff, Progress Report, September 11, 1944, box 30, OWI Records.

23  Richard Hollander, "A Brief Account of the Activities of the European Theater of Operations Division," n.d. 28, box 64; "Final Broadcast," July 4, 1945, box 24, OWI Records; Charles A. H. Thomson, *Overseas Information Service of the United States Government* (Washington, D.C.: Brookings Institution, 1948), 69; Bishop, "The Overseas Branch," 222. Decisions about ABSIE programs were made in London at a daily meeting attended by representatives of the PWD, PWE, and OWI. This session was followed by a BBC meeting and then by an OWI guidance. Finally there was an ABSIE language desk conference on both the Nycast and the London daily guidance (Reports from London, April 15–May 15, 1944, box 74, Outposts–London, OWI Records).

24  Sether, "ABSIE," 1945, box 24, OWI Records.

25  Edward W. Barrett, interview with author, December 11, 1979; Leonard Miall, interview with author, March 17, 1981.

26  Leonard Miall, "Trend Away from Political Warfare in OWI New York," July 8, 1944, Miall Papers. See also memorandum, Adrian Berwick to John W. Jago, February 14, 1944, series 39.19, box 87, Budget Estimates, 1945, BOB Records.

27  Barrett interview.

28  François Auberjonois to Douglas Schneider, April 23, 1944, box 610, Algiers Operational Letters, OWI Records.

29  The French staff of ABSIE was concerned about the quality of programming from the beginning. This concern was not owing to any complaint about Lazareff, whose talents were both considerable and fully recognized, but from ABSIE's want of its own decent staff. As early as mid-April the ABSIE producers wrote in an interoffice memorandum that "our over-all impression of the records we heard yesterday is one of amazing triviality. We cannot find in them one real justification for opening a new radio station to carry the message they contain into France . . ." (April 12, 1944, box 29, Brewster Morgan File, OWI Records).

Lazareff himself complained of his lack of staff: they could not speak French well enough; he constantly had to give up his trained people to the PWD; the job of educating new recruits soaked up the time of experienced staff members; and the State Department was usually unwilling to support his obtaining French citizens for ABSIE. A rather typical complaint read: "We were sent a certain Mr. Clark, as announcer. He has a voice that is absolutely unsuitable for the radio and cannot read ten lines in French. (He had been an overseer on a sugar plantation.) We were sent a certain Miss Simone Rilleau, as secretary. She knows neither shorthand nor typing. We were sent a Mrs. Richards as translator. She has so far forgotten her French that in six lines of her first attempt she made several glaring errors" (Lazareff, Report Appendix: "Our Staff," n.d. (September 1944?), box 30, OWI Records). Lazareff reported that he did his best to improve output, but the task proved beyond his personal resources: "Since August 15 I have worked an average of 14 hours a day without a single day off. I am terribly tired. But until [another leader] arrives, I simply cannot leave the French section of ABSIE to get along." He despaired. During the first three months of operations, he stated, even the technical work was inadequate. ABSIE was often of more help to the Axis than America, Lazareff argued, for the United States was considered particularly advanced in radio production work, yet during these months the broadcasts were almost incomprehensible (Lazareff, Report, n.d. (September 1944?), box 30, OWI Records).

30   John L. Craven, "Notes on the Crisis in OWI French Section," July 18, 1944, PRO, PWE Records, FO 898/108. See also Michel Rapaport Gordey, interview with author, November 6, 1985. Craven, himself a French wartime exile, had been sent by the BBC to work with the French desk of the Voice after Russell Page moved on. Craven sent home an interesting series of reports, which are filed in the records of the Political Warfare Executive.

31   Craven, "Notes on the Crisis in OWI French Section."

32   Craven, "A Few Notes on OWI French Section – New York and Washington," October 4, 1944, PRO, PWE Records, FO 898/105.

33   Lazareff, Progress Report, September 11, 1944, box 30, OWI Records.

34   Interview with Gripsholm Arrival, May 10, 1944, box 306, OWI Records. See also interview with Gripsholm Arrival, June 9, 1944, box 156, OWI Records. There were dissenting opinions. One respondent told a British interviewer that he thought "our propaganda to France is very poor and that it lags far behind in what the Americans are doing in this respect" (BBC European Intelligence, interviews, April 11, 1944, box 441, OWI Records). But in general the trend ran against the Voice of America.

35   Anne Allison, "Listening Facilities in France for Receiving Shortwave Broadcasts Direct from the United States," September 27, 1944, box 286, France, OWI Records.

36   Hollander, "A Brief Account," 99; airgram, Jefferson Caffery to the Secretary of State, December 12, 1944, American Embassy, Paris, box 1560, FSP Records.

37   Guidance for European Information Program, October 30, 1944, box 42, Long Range Policy Directives; C. D. Jackson to Sherwood, October 28, 1943, box 74, Outposts – London, OWI Records.

38   Sherwood to Davis, September 20, 1944, folder 1089, Sherwood Papers.

39   Nor did the OWI representatives in France believe the OWI could compete with the British Ministry of Information. See C. D. Jackson to Drummond-Wolff, December 17, 1944, box 12, Army–War Files, Jackson Papers.

40   The British did not sanguinely accept the idea that the BBC would continue to attract a listening audience. For example, Walter Adams from the PWE mission in Washington worried about the BBC's future in France. "London can

no longer expect a continuous and mass listening public merely on the strength of its news service," he wrote. He posed the problem quite starkly: "How do we keep an audience in France? . . . how do you induce a French audience pre-occupied with its own rehabilitation to listen?" (Adams to Leslie Beck, August 30, 1944, PRO, PWE Records, FO 898/108). The problems that faced the Overseas Branch and the Voice of America, in other words, were not unique to America; but they were worse given the continual problem the Americans had had in attracting a wartime audience.

41 Cowan diary, June 22, 1944.

42 Ibid., August 3, 1944.

43 Ibid., September 2, 1944.

44 Louis G. Cowan, "Future Radio Programming: Draft Memo," ibid., August 30, 1944.

45 Ibid., July 13, 1944.

46 By May 1944, for example, the Voice broadcast a total of 1,370 quarter-hour programs in French. Of these, 1,081 were broadcast as regular short-wave programs, 10 were for BBC reserve, and 89 were broadcast by ABSIE. Of the total, 215 were produced by the Belgian desk and were therefore both in French and in Flemish. In comparison there was a total of 1,044 quarter-hour programs in German, 863 in English, 1,068 in Italian, 527 in Spanish, 223 in Polish, 102 in Danish, and 124 in Arabic (Report of Broadcast Division, May 1944, box 24, OWI Records).

47 Overseas Branch Radio Program Bureau Report, September 1945, box 24, folder 6, OWI Records.

48 "Report on European Listenership Reaction and Interest in 'Voice of America' Informational Broadcasts," September 11, 1945, box 123, Radio Program Bureau, Broadcasting Division, OWI Records. "L'Amèrique depuis 1939" was a half-hour program devoted to acquainting listeners with American wartime developments in music, literature, science, and medicine (memorandum, Stanley H. Silverman to Blochman, January 30, 1945, box 24, folder 3, OWI Records); "Echos d'Amèrique" was a variety program about which Michel Rapaport commented in May 1945 that "the balance achieved between gay and serious things is extremely effective" (Evaluations Division Bulletin, May 4, 1945, box 24, folder 2, OWI Records).

49 Overseas Branch Radio Program Bureau Report, September 1945, box 24, folder 6, OWI Records. The master radio desk began operations on May 25, 1944. The desk wrote "model scripts" to be adapted according to the needs of each language desk. By June 14, 1944, there were twelve writers on the desk. The master desk had the further function of creating an approved text of the most difficult stories; deviations from its text could be made only by special permission and in specified ways. It was also meant to handle European news from an American angle wherever possible. See memorandum, Blochman to all desks, May 25, 1944, box 123, Radio Program Bureau, Broadcasting Division; Blochman, Radio Program Bureau Progress Report, June 15, 1944, box 24, folder 4; Overseas Branch Radio Program Bureau Report, September 1945, box 24, folder 6, OWI Records; Thomson, *Overseas Information Service*, 57. For

an example of a master desk script see Claude Kirschen, News Reel, February 11, 1945, box 392, Transcripts, OWI Records.

50  Pierre Lazareff, "American Broadcasts for France After the Complete Liberation of French Territory," box 10, Army–Radio and Public Address Paris, Jackson Papers.

51  Memorandum from William Paley and Brewster Morgan, "The Future of OWI Radio in Europe," September 12, 1944, PWB–London, OWI Records.

52  Memorandum, Sherwood to Davis, September 20, 1944, folder 1089, Sherwood Papers; telegram, Chapin to Matthews, September 17, 1944, box 28, confidential decimal file, SD 103.9166/9-1744.

53  Memorandum, Sherwood to Davis, September 20, 1944, folder 1089, Sherwood Papers.

54  Lazareff laid out his thinking in three memos: "American Broadcasts for France After the Complete Liberation of French Territory," September 1, 1944; "Appendix to the Plan for American Radio in France in the Post-Liberation Period," September 11, 1944, box 10, Army–Radio and Public Address Paris, Jackson Papers; "Recent Arrival in London of an Official French Radio Mission," September 11, 1944, box 132, Algiers–French Operations, OWI Records.

55  Cowan diary, August 14, 1944.

56  Memorandum, Barrett to Davis, September 13, 1944, box 51, European Operations, OWI Records.

57  Memorandum, Eleanor Sontheimer to Lawrence Blochman, "Survey of NBC's and CBS's Shortwave Radio Output to Europe," December 11, 1945, box 120, Material Pending for London and Paris; Broadcasting Division Report, October 1945, box 123, Radio Program Bureau, Broadcasting Division, OWI Records.

58  C. D. Jackson to Clare Boothe Luce, August 21, 1945, box 8, Army–OWI-London, Jackson Papers.

59  Memorandum, Joseph C. Grew to the President, "Restoration of OWI Funds in Senate," June 11, 1945, box 900, OWI File, WD Records. See also Grew to Stimson, June 13, 1945; Stimson to Grew, June 16, 1945; Stimson to Truman, June 19, 1945, box 900, OWI File, WD Records.

60  Stimson to Truman, July 19, 1945, box 900, OWI File, WD Records.

61  Thomas F. Troy, *Donovan and the C.I.A.: A History of the Establishment of the Central Intelligence Agency* (Frederick, Md.: University Publications of America, Aletheia, 1981), 287.

62  Cowan, "Propaganda to the Enemy."

63  William Benton to Arthur Sulzburger, May 17, 1946, box 90, Unwritten Treaty Correspondence, Warburg Papers.

## Epilogue

1  John William Henderson, *The United States Information Agency* (New York: Praeger, 1969), 35–36.

2  Ronald I. Rubin, *The Objectives of the U.S. Information Agency: Controversies and Analysis* (New York: Praeger, 1966), 108.

3   Henderson, *The United States Information Agency*, 37.

4   Wilson P. Dizard, *The Strategy of Truth: The Story of the U.S. Information Service* (Washington, D.C.: Public Affairs Press, 1961), 37.

5   Rubin, *Objectives of the U.S. Information Agency*, 108–109.

6   Arthur E. Meyerhoff, *The Strategy of Persuasion: The Use of Advertising Skills in Fighting the Cold War* (New York: Coward-McCann, 1965), 85.

7   Maureen J. Nemecek, "Speaking of America: The Voice of America, Its Mission and Message, 1942–1982" (Ph.D. diss., University of Maryland, 1984), 88, 102; Henderson, *The United States Information Agency*, 46.

8   Dizard, *The Strategy of Truth*, 41; Meyerhoff, *The Strategy of Persuasion*, 88; Rubin, *Objectives of the U.S. Information Agency*, 127; Henderson, *The United States Information Agency*, 51–54.

9   Nemecek, "Speaking of America," 324.

10  Ibid., 358–69.

11  Henderson, *The United States Information Agency*, 225.

12  Nemecek, "Speaking of America," 122–37. Inside the Voice, Russian émigrés largely sided with McCarthy and created a groundswell for him. The Russian desk, although intended by the State Department to build up an anti-Soviet position gradually, flung itself into a violent anticommunist campaign that spilled over into domestic politics, tearing the Voice apart and further demoralizing the whole of the Voice's staff.

13  Quoted in Meyerhoff, *The Strategy of Persuasion*, 94.

14  Quoted in A. M. Sperber, *Murrow, His Life and Times* (New York: Freundlich, 1986), 655.

15  Quoted in ibid.

16  Nemecek, "Speaking of America," 280; Paul Grimes, "Three Crippling Factors," in *The Case for Reappraisal of U.S. Overseas Information Policies and Programs*, ed. Edward L. Bernays and Burnet Hershey (New York: Praeger, 1970), 56.

17  Meyerhoff, *The Strategy of Persuasion*, 93.

18  Quoted in ibid., 87.

19  Quoted in Henderson, *The United States Information Agency*, 170.

20  Quoted in ibid.

21  Ibid., 166–68.

22  Spyridon Granitsas, "The Voice of America in Greece," in *The Case for Reappraisal*, ed. Edward L. Bernays and Burnet Hershey, 64–67.

23  Frederick T. C. Yu, "The Voice of America in Communist China," in *The Case for Reappraisal*, ed. Edward L. Bernays and Burnet Hershey, 53.

24  Henderson, *The United States Information Agency*, 220–21.

25  Harry Torczyner, interview with author, July 15, 1986.

26  Quoted in Houseman, *Front and Center* (New York: Simon and Schuster, 1979), 80–81.

27  Ibid.

28  James P. Warburg, *Unwritten Treaty* (New York: Harcourt, Brace, 1946), 56.

29  See Daniel Lerner, *Psychological Warfare Against Nazi Germany: The Skywar Campaign, D-Day to V-E Day* (Cambridge: M.I.T. Press, 1971); Wallace Carroll, *Persuade or Perish* (Boston: Houghton Mifflin, 1948).

30  Richard H. S. Crossman, "Psychological Warfare, Part I," *Journal of the Royal United Service Institution* 97 (August 1952): 320.

31  Ibid., 325, 327.

32  Lerner, *Psychological Warfare,* 15.

33  For a discussion of Murrow's years in government see biographies of Murrow: Alexander Kendrick, *Prime Time: The Life of Edward R. Murrow* (Boston: Little, Brown, 1969); Sperber, *Murrow;* Joseph E. Persico, *Edward R. Murrow: An American Original* (New York: McGraw-Hill, 1988).

34  Quoted in Nemecek, "Speaking of America," 135.

35  Quoted in ibid., 42.

36  Quoted in ibid., 102.

37  Quoted in ibid., 142.

38  For a more complete description of how the Voice of America operated in the 1980s see Robin Grey, "Inside the Voice of America," *Columbia Journalism Review,* 21 (May/June 1982): 23–30.

# Bibliography

## A Note on Interviews

Like many historians, it was only reluctantly that I began talking to the men and women who people this book. The value of interviews seemed to me dubious, especially since I was working on events that had taken place more than forty years ago. Whose memory, I asked myself, stretches back so far with any clarity? How could I evaluate their reports, I worried, without knowing what personal battles these men and women had fought: might they now use me and this book to launch a final attack? But I decided to go ahead. I met with people; I asked them to rummage through their memories; and I encouraged them to analyze events. As I worked my way through these interviews, I defined and redefined what I could gain from each of these conversations.

Interviews have a special role to play for the contemporary historian. To begin with, through my interviews I met some of the participants. The historian must continually assess not only the relative significance of each person about whom he or she writes, but the more general consequence of individuals, weighing out the balance of the actors' importance against such larger motivating factors as ideology or economics. Nevertheless, regardless of broad theoretical conclusions, the people I wrote about and the propagandists I interviewed were for me the vehicles of the story. They gave to the past its color and texture and much of its drama. Occasionally I would remind myself of the importance of individuals by considering how different the Voice of America would have been had President Roosevelt chosen Edward R. Murrow, newscaster and master of the style of plain prose, to head it in 1942, rather than John Houseman, dramatist and proponent of the forms of experimental theater.

Furthermore, oral testimony has certain advantages over the kind of bureaucratic written record on which I was otherwise dependent. Propaganda directives, for example, might look like a straightforward source on paper, but what I had in these memos more often than not proved a kind of bureaucratic flow chart that set forth someone's idealization of what ought to happen rather than an accurate picture of what did happen. To follow the process of propaganda policy I relied on letters, diaries, and reports; but the majority of the men and women who worked in the

OWI during World War II found themselves too busy to sit down and write a personal letter, let alone take the time to keep a journal. I therefore supplemented the bureaucratic record with interviews in which I could ask such questions as who got what directives, how the French desk worked from day to day, or how a Voice of America script writer went about his job.

Having said all this, I must confess that as an interviewer I enjoyed a distinct advantage. Many of those to whom I talked had known my father, Louis G. Cowan, who was director of the Radio Program Bureau until February 1944, when he took over Joseph Barnes's job and became head of the New York office of the Overseas Branch of the OWI. My name was my calling card. The importance of my filial connection became clear to me one day as I sat in a hotel in downtown Washington, interviewing one of the British representatives from the BBC who had gone to New York to assist the developing Voice of America. I had written to this man months before I actually saw him, detailing not only the general questions I wanted to ask but setting forth my personal connection to the OWI. He may never have read the letter; I am certain that he saw me only because a mutual friend asked him to do so. As we sat in the hotel lounge I found him stiff, hard to wring answers from, and opaque. After close to an hour of hard work I asked him how many Americans in the early days of the Voice of America had radio production experience. Well, first and foremost there was Lou Cowan, he told me. But he was my father, I exclaimed. That broke the ice; this formal man relaxed as he recalled the pleasant evenings he had spent at my parents' New York apartment. He had met with Holly C. Shulman, historian, only as a favor to a friend of his; he trusted Holly Cowan Shulman and looked on her in an entirely different light.

Oral testimony has its pitfalls, however, as well as its benefits. These are, after all, memories that stretch across a chasm of forty-odd years. Our minds play tricks on us: how many of us have gone back to some spot we thought we remembered as children, only to find ourselves lost and bewildered? I decided early on that I should never rely on an individual's recollection of details, and indeed, most of those I interviewed quite honestly admitted that the fine points of the past had long escaped them. Often, for example, they could not remember when they left the OWI except by association: I left only to go work on President Roosevelt's election campaign, they would say, or I stayed until a bit after D-Day.

Meeting the participants can also pose special problems that the written record does not present. I worried that my emotional instincts—whether or not I had liked a certain person—would intrude on my objectivity and distort the interviewing process. I was concerned that exactly where I was in my research and my momentary concerns would distort the questions I asked, and the answers I received. I knew that the way I phrased my questions would determine the responses I got. As one British propagandist wrote, contemplating the extent to which the English should allow the Americans to control the process of interviewing the citizens of occupied nations, "It would be unfortunate if [the interviews] were conducted exclusively by the Americans, since the answers you get depend upon the questions you ask. . . ."*

*Memorandum, Director of Plans to D.P.W.I., September 25, 1943, PRO, PWE Records, FO 898/390.

One wintry day, as I neared the end of my researches, I sat in a bright, cheerful apartment on the Upper West Side of New York, asking a Voice of America script writer what he had been doing on D-Day. The Voice of America had decided that it wanted man-on-the-street interviews, he told me. He and some of the other writers therefore walked around the city and quite literally nabbed people off the street, bringing them up to the recording studios of the Voice of America. Do you remember any of the people you interviewed, I asked, eager to hear this bit of color. Not anymore, the writer replied. Do you remember what you asked them, I pushed. Not any longer, he said. I pressed on, but got nothing further. After the interview was over I explained why I had asked so many questions about D-Day: it might prove a good place to begin the book, I said, and so I had hoped you could dredge up something concrete. It sounds to me like quite a good idea, he responded enthusiastically. Why don't you just make it up?

## *Manuscript Collections and Archival Records*

Barnes, Joseph. Papers. In the possession of Elizabeth Barnes, New York, N.Y.

Brownlow, Louis. Papers. John F. Kennedy Library, Boston, Mass.

Celler, Emmanuel. Papers. Library of Congress, Washington, D.C.

Clark, George. Papers. National Museum of American History, Smithsonian Institution, Washington, D.C.

Cowan, Louis G. Papers. Columbia University Library, New York, N.Y.

Davis, Elmer. Papers. Library of Congress, Washington, D.C.

Espenscheid, Lloyd. Papers. National Museum of American History, Smithsonian Institution, Washington, D.C.

Fly, James L. Papers. Columbia University, New York, N.Y.

Great Britain. British Broadcasting Corporation. Written Archives Centre, Caversham Park, Reading, England.

Great Britain. British Broadcasting Corporation. Sound Archives, London.

Great Britain. Foreign Office. Records of the Political Warfare Executive. FO 898. Public Record Office, London.

Great Britain. Ministry of Information. Records. Public Record Office, London.

Gross, Gerald. Papers. National Museum of American History, Smithsonian Institution, Washington, D.C.

Hooper, Stanford C. Papers. Library of Congress, Washington, D.C.

Hopkins, Harry. Papers. Franklin D. Roosevelt Library, Hyde Park, N.Y.

Ickes, Harold L. Papers. Library of Congress, Washington, D.C.

MacLeish, Archibald. Papers. Library of Congress, Washington, D.C.

McCloy, John J. Office of the Assistant Secretary of War. Correspondence of John J. McCloy, 1941–1945. Record Group 107. National Archives, Washington, D.C.

Paglin, Max D. Papers. In the possession of Max D. Paglin, Washington, D.C.

Roosevelt, Franklin D. Papers. Franklin D. Roosevelt Library, Hyde Park, N.Y.

Rosenman, Samuel I. Papers. Franklin D. Roosevelt Library, Hyde Park, N.Y.

Rowe, Leo S. Papers. Columbia Memorial Library, Organization of American States, Washington, D.C.

Sherwood, Robert E. Papers. Houghton Library, Harvard University, Cambridge, Mass.

United States. Army. Intelligence Decimal File, 1941–1948. Record Group 319. National Records Center, Suitland, Md.

United States. Bureau of the Budget. Record Group 51. National Archives, Washington, D.C.

United States. Defense Communications Board. Record Group 259. National Archives, Washington, D.C.

United States. Department of State. Record Group 59. National Archives, Washington, D.C.

United States. Federal Communications Commission. Record Groups 60-a-625, 173. National Records Center, Archives Division, Suitland, Md.

United States. Foreign Service Posts of the Department of State. Record Group 84. National Records Center, Suitland, Md.

United States. Information Agency. Records. United States Information Agency, Washington, D.C.

United States. Interservice Agencies. National War College Library. Record Group 334. National Records Center, Suitland, Md.

United States. Joint Chiefs of Staff. Record Group 218. National Archives, Washington, D.C.

United States. Office of Naval Intelligence. USDIA Records 737-001725. National Records Center, Suitland, Md.

United States. Office of Strategic Services. Record Group 226. National Archives, Washington, D.C.

United States. Office of War Information. Record Group 208. National Records Center, Suitland, Md.

United States. War Department General and Special Staff. Record Group 165. National Archives, Washington, D.C.

Warburg, James. Papers. John F. Kennedy Library, Boston, Mass.

## Public Documents

United States. Congress. House of Representatives. Committee on Naval Affairs. *Hearings Authorizing the Secretary of the Navy to Construct and Maintain a Government Radio Broadcasting Station, H.R. 4281.* 75th Cong., 2d sess., 1937.

United States. Congress. Senate. Interstate Commerce Committee. Subcommittee. *Hearings: A Bill to Authorize the Construction and Operation of a Radio-Broadcasting Station Designed to Promote Friendly Relations Among the Nations of the Western Hemisphere, S.3342.* 75th Cong., 3d sess., 1938.

United States. Department of State. *Report of the Interdepartmental Committee to Study International Broadcasting: Report of Subcommittee on Programs.* Washington, D.C.: Government Printing Office, 1939.

United States. Federal Communications Commission. *Report on Chain Broadcasting.* Washington, D.C.: Government Printing Office, 1941.

## Personal Interviews with Author (in Author's Files)

Abrams, Mark. London, March 23, 1981.
Barrett, Edward W. New York City, December 11, 1979.
Bessie, Connie Ernst. New York City, November 14, 1982.
Bessie, Simon Michael. New York City, March 24, April 2, 1986.
Bird, Jean. London, March 23, 1981.
Carroll, Wallace. Winston-Salem, N.C., March 3, 1986.
Cleverdon, Douglas. London, November 4, 1985.
Ehrenreich, Dolores Vanneti. New York City, April 4, 1986.
Gladieux, Bernard. Washington, D.C., August 20, 1984.
Gordey, Michel Rapaport. New York City, January 26, 1977; Paris, November 6, 7, 1985.
Gould, Jack. Telephone interview, June 2, 1986.
Houseman, John. New York City, March 26, 1986.
Hyde, Rosel. Washington, D.C., February 17, 1982.
McNaughten, Neal. Washington, D.C., February 9, 1982.
Miall, Leonard. London, March 16, 17, 18, April 7, 1981; August 9, 1985.
Michel, Werner. Los Angeles, April 24, 1983.
Newman, Robert. New York City, February 20, 21, 1986.
Page, Russell. Washington, D.C., June 9, 1981.
Pogue, Forrest C. Washington, D.C., February 5, 24, 1981; February 18, 1984.
Riegel, Oscar W. Glasgow, Va., December 2, 1985.
Ritchie-Calder, Lord. London, March 23, 24, 1981.
Samrock, Victor. New York City, October 23, 1987.
Siepmann, Charles. London, April 6, 1981.
Torczyner, Harry. New York City, July 15, 1986.
Van Doren, Dorothy. Cornwall, Conn., July 7, 1986.
Wechsler, Doris Klauber. New York City, March 13, 1986.
Whiteside, Marie Pertchuk. New York City, April 3, 1986.

## Oral Histories

Barnes, Joseph. "Reminiscences of Joseph Barnes." 1953. Oral History Collection, Columbia University, New York, N.Y.
Blankenhorn, Heber. "Reminiscences of Heber Blankenhorn." 1955. Oral History Collection, Columbia University, New York, N.Y.
Cowan, Louis G. "Reminiscences of Louis G. Cowan." 1967. Oral History Collection, Columbia University, New York, N.Y.
Fly, Sally Connell. "The Fly Project: Collected Interviews About L. Fly." 1967. Oral History Project, Columbia University, New York, N.Y.
Gladieux, Bernard. "Reminiscences of Bernard Gladieux." 1951. Oral History Collection, Columbia University, New York, N.Y.
Warburg, James P. "Reminiscences of James P. Warburg." 1935. Papers of James P. Warburg. John F. Kennedy Library, Boston, Mass.

## Sound Recordings

The following sound recordings are among those housed in the Division of Motion Pictures, Broadcasting and Recorded Sound, Library of Congress, Washington, D.C.:

Anderson, Sherwood. "Mercury Theatre on the Air: I'm a Fool." August 8, 1936.
Corwin, Norman. "Columbia Workshop: So This Is Radio." September 7, 1939.
Corwin, Norman. "This Is War: Yours Received and Contents Noted." May 9, 1942.
Corwin, Norman, and Earl Robinson. "The People Yes." ABC. May 18, 1941.
Green, Paul. "Columbia Workshop: Citizen for Tomorrow." December 14, 1941.
Langen, Tom. "This Is Radio." NBC. November 13, 1938.
Lagerman, John K. "Columbia Workshop: So Wake Up and Die." October 12, 1939.
"The March of Time: War Comes." May 17, 1942.
"Mercury Theatre on the Air: Abraham Lincoln." August 15, 1938.
NBC International War News. March 4, 1942.
NBC International War News–Comments. January 6, 1941.
Obeler, Arch. "Arch Oberler's Plays: Johnny Got His Gun." March 9, 1940.
Office of War Information. Collection of the Office of War Information.
"The Pursuit of Happiness" (variety show). CBS. November 5, 1939.
Welles, Orson. "Mercury Theatre on the Air: Dracula." July 11, 1938.
Werner, Michel. "Columbia Workshop: Man Without a Shadow." January 25, 1942.

## Unpublished Manuscripts

Aiken, William. "Official History of the Propaganda Branch, Military Intelligence Division, 1945." N.d. Records of the United States Army Intelligence Decimal File, 1941–1948. Record Group 319. National Records Center, Suitland, Md.
Auxier, George W. "Historical Manuscript File: Material on the History of Military Intelligence in the United States, 1885–1944." N.d. Center of Military History, Washington, D.C.
Baudino, Joseph. "A History of Short Wave Broadcasting." N.d. Division of Electricity, National Museum of American History, Smithsonian Institution, Washington, D.C.
Bidwell, Bruce W. "History of the Military Intelligence Division, Department of the Army General Staff." N.d. Center of Military History, Washington, D.C.
Birn, Donald S. "The War of Words: The British Council and British Propaganda Efforts in the 1930's." Paper presented at a meeting of the Society of Historians of American Foreign Relations, Washington, D.C., August 1984.
Bishop, Robert Lee. "The Overseas Branch of the Office of War Information." Ph.D. diss., University of Wisconsin, 1966.
Cohen, Phyllis. "Representative Emmanuel Celler–A Case Study in Legislative Behavior, 1923–1950." M.A. thesis, New York University, 1952.
Craft, Ray K. (Maj.). "Report to the General Board, United States Forces, European Theater: Psychological War in the European Theater of Operations." July 1947. Records of the United States Interservice Agencies, National War College Library. Record Group 334. National Records Center, Suitland, Md.

Davis, Vernon E. "The History of the Joint Chiefs of Staff in World War II: Organizational Development." 2 vols. 1972. Historical Division, Joint Secretariat, Joint Chiefs of Staff. Record Group 218. National Archives, Washington, D.C.

Fejes, Fred Allan. "Imperialism, Media, and the Good Neighbor: New Deal Foreign Policy and United States Shortwave Broadcasting to Latin America." Ph.D. diss., University of Illinois, 1982.

Feldman, Mildred Bos. "Participation by the United States in Selected International Telegraph and Radio Conferences Prior to the Affiliation of the International Communications Union with the United Nations." Ph.D. diss., Louisiana State University, 1973.

Fodor, Marcel W. "History of the Voice of America." Records, United States Information Agency, Washington, D.C.

Gillie, Cecilia. "BBC French Service Wartime Broadcasts, 1940–1944." 1977. BBC Written Archives Centre, Caversham Park, Reading, England.

Gosnell, Harold F. "The Framing of the OWI Executive Order." N.d. Records of the Bureau of the Budget. Record Group 51. National Archives, Washington, D.C.

Gosnell, Harold F. "Organization of Information Activities for Defense and War, 1940–1942." N.d. Records of the Bureau of the Budget. Record Group 51. National Archives, Washington, D.C.

Gosnell, Harold F. "Overhead Organization of the Office of War Information." N.d. Records of the Bureau of the Budget. Record Group 51. National Archives, Washington, D.C.

Gosnell, Harold F. "Selected Personnel Problems in the War Information Field." N.d. Records of the Bureau of the Budget. Record Group 51. National Archives, Washington, D.C.

Hojem, Phyllis M. "A Study of Propaganda and of the Analysis of the Institute for Propaganda Analysis, Incorporated." M.A. thesis, University of Colorado, 1950.

Huebner, Lee W. "The Discovery of Propaganda: Changing Attitudes Toward Public Communication in America, 1900–1930." Ph.D. diss., Harvard University, 1968.

Lilly, Edward P. "Early Psychological Warfare Planning." N.d. Records of the United States Joint Chiefs of Staff. Record Group 218. National Archives, Washington, D.C.

Lilly, Edward P. "Initial Wartime Planning." N.d. Records of the United States Joint Chiefs of Staff. Record Group 218. National Archives, Washington, D.C.

Lilly, Edward P. "Office of War Information History." N.d. Records of the Office of War Information. Record Group 208. National Records Center, Suitland, Md.

Marks, Barry Alan. "The Idea of Propaganda in America." Ph.D. diss., University of Minnesota, 1957.

Mostert, Andre J. E., Jr. "A History of WRUL: The Walter S. Lemmon Years, 1931–1960." M.A. thesis, Brigham Young University, 1969.

Myers, Larry Ross. "The Idea of Propaganda in America, 1917–1941." M.A. thesis, University of Maryland, 1975.

Nemecek, Maureen J. "Speaking of America: The Voice of America, Mission and Message, 1942–1982." Ph.D. diss., University of Maryland, 1984.

Reeves, Byron, and James L. Baughman. "Fraught with Such Great Possibilities: The Historical Relationship of Mass Communication Research to Mass Media Regulation." Paper presented at the Telecommunications Policy Research Conference, Annapolis, Md., April 1982.

Sidel, Michael Kent. "A Historical Analysis of American Shortwave Broadcasting, 1916–1942." Ph.D. diss., Northwestern University, 1976.

Shulman, Holly C. "The Voice of Victory: The Development of American Propaganda and the Voice of America." Ph.D. diss., University of Maryland, 1984.

Smulyan, Susan R. "'And Now a Word from Our Sponsors . . .': The Commercialism of American Broadcast Radio, 1920–1934." Ph.D. diss., Yale University, 1985.

United States. Military Intelligence Division, G-2. "A History of the Military Intelligence Division: 7 December 1941–2 September 1945." Records of the War Department General and Special Staff. Record Group 165. National Archives, Washington, D.C.

Weinberg, Sidney Stahl. "Wartime Propaganda in a Democracy: America's Twentieth Century Information Agencies." Ph.D. diss., Columbia University, 1969.

## Books

Ades, Dawn, ed. *Posters.* New York: Abbeville, 1984.

Aglion, Raoul. *Roosevelt and de Gaulle: Allies in Conflict; A Personal Memoir.* New York: Free Press, 1988.

Albig, William. *Public Opinion.* New York: McGraw-Hill, 1939.

Allan, Elkan, and Dorotheen. *Good Listening: A Survey of Broadcasting.* London: Hutchinson, n.d.

Alpern, Sara. *Freda Kirchway: A Woman of "The Nation."* Cambridge: Harvard University Press, 1987.

Alter, Robert. *Partial Magic: The Novel as Self-Conscious Genre.* Berkeley and Los Angeles: University of California Press, 1978.

Ambrose, Stephen E. *Eisenhower: Soldier, General of the Army, President-Elect, 1890–1952.* New York: Simon and Schuster, 1983.

Ambrose, Stephen E. *Rise to Globalism: American Foreign Policy Since 1938.* 3rd ed. New York: Penguin, 1984.

Anderson, Karen. *Wartime Women: Sex Roles, Family Relations and the Status of Women During World War II.* Westport, Conn.: Greenwood, 1981.

Arnheim, Rudolph. *Radio.* London: Faber and Faber, 1936.

Aron, Robert. *The Vichy Regime, 1940–1944.* New York: Macmillan, 1958.

Baigell, Matthew, and Julia Williams, eds. *Artists Against War & Fascism: American Artists' Congress.* New Brunswick, N.J.: Rutgers University Press, 1986.

Balfour, Michael. *Propaganda in War, 1939–1945: Organizations, Policies and Publics in Britain and Germany.* London: Routledge and Kegan Paul, 1979.

Bannerman, R. LeRoy. *Norman Corwin and Radio.* Tuscaloosa: University of Alabama Press, 1986.

Barnouw, Erik. *The Golden Web: A History of Broadcasting in the United States, 1933–1953.* New York: Oxford University Press, 1968.

Barnouw, Erik. *Handbook of Radio Production*. Boston: Little, Brown, 1949.

Barnouw, Erik. *Radio Drama in Action: Twenty-five Plays of a Changing World*. New York: Farrar and Rinehart, 1945.

Barnouw, Erik. *A Tower in Babel: A History of Broadcasting in the United States to 1933*. New York: Oxford University Press, 1966.

Barrett, Edward W. *Truth Is Our Weapon*. New York: Funk and Wagnall, 1953.

Beitzell, Robert. *The Uneasy Alliance: America, Britain and Russia, 1941–1943*. New York: Knopf, 1972.

Bennett, Jeremy. *British Broadcasting and the Danish Resistance Movement, 1940–1945*. Cambridge: Cambridge University Press, 1966.

Benson, Renate. *German Expressionist Drama: Ernst Toller and George Kaiser*. New York: Grove, 1984.

Berelson, Bernard, and Morris Janowitz, eds. *A Reader in Public Opinion and Communication*. Glencoe, Ill.: Free Press, 1953.

Bernays, Edward L. *Biography of an Idea: Memoirs of Public Relations Counsel Edward L. Bernays*. New York: Simon and Schuster, 1965.

Bernays, Edward L. and Burnet Hershey, eds. *The Case for Reappraisal of U.S. Overseas Information Policies and Programs*. New York: Praeger, 1970.

Black, Edwin. *Rhetorical Criticism: A Study in Method*. Madison: University of Wisconsin Press, 1978.

Black, Gregory D., and Clayton R. Koppes. *Hollywood Goes to War: How Politics, Profits and Propaganda Shaped World War II Movies*. New York: Free Press, 1987.

Blankenhorn, Heber. *Adventures in Propaganda: Letters from an Intelligence Officer in France*. Boston: Houghton Mifflin, 1915.

Blewett, David. *Defoe's Art of Fiction*. Toronto: University of Toronto Press, 1979.

Blum, John Morton. *"V" Was for Victory: Politics and American Culture During World War II*. New York: Harcourt Brace Jovanovich, 1976.

Blumenthal, Henry. *Illusion and Reality in Franco-American Diplomacy 1914–1945*. Baton Rouge: Louisiana State University Press, 1986.

Bogart, Leo. *Premises for Propaganda: The United States Information Agency's Operating Assumptions in the Cold War*. New York: Free Press, 1976.

Booth, Wayne C. *The Rhetoric of Fiction*. Chicago: University of Chicago Press, 1983.

Boyle, Andrew. *Only the Wind Will Listen: Reith of the BBC*. London: Hutchinson, 1972.

Bramson, Leon. *The Political Context of Sociology*. Princeton: Princeton University Press, 1961.

Breuer, William B. *Operation Torch: The Allied Gamble to Invade North Africa*. New York: St. Martin's, 1985.

Briggs, Asa. *The History of Broadcasting in the United Kingdom*. Vol. 2: *The Golden Age of Wireless*. London: Oxford University Press, 1965.

Briggs, Asa. *The History of Broadcasting in the United Kingdom*. Vol. 3: *The War of Words*. London: Oxford University Press, 1970.

Brown, Cecil. *Suez to Singapore*. New York: Random House, 1942.

Brown, John Mason. *The Ordeal of a Playwright: Robert E. Sherwood and the Challenge of War*. New York: Harper and Row, 1970.

Brown, John Mason. *The Worlds of Robert E. Sherwood—Mirror to His Times.* New York: Harper and Row, 1962.

Browne, Donald R. *International Radio Broadcasting: The Limits of the Limitless Medium.* New York: Praeger, 1982.

Brownlow, Louis. *A Passion for Anonymity: The Autobiography of Louis Brownlow, Second Half.* Chicago: University of Chicago Press, 1958.

Bruce Lockhart, Robert. *Comes the Reckoning.* London: Putnam, 1947.

Bruntz, George C. *Allied Propaganda and the Collapse of the German Empire in 1918.* Stanford: Stanford University Press, 1938.

Burke, Kenneth. *The Philosophy of Literary Form: Studies in Symbolic Action.* Berkeley and Los Angeles: University of California Press, 1973.

Burlingame, Roger. *Don't Let Them Scare You: The Life and Times of Elmer Davis.* Philadelphia: Lippincott, 1961.

Burns, James MacGregor. *Roosevelt: The Soldier of Freedom, 1940–1945.* New York: Harcourt Brace Jovanovich, 1970.

Butcher, Harry C. *My Three Years with Eisenhower.* New York: Simon and Schuster, 1946.

Buttitta, Tony, and Barry Witham. *Uncle Sam Presents: Memoir of the Federal Theatre, 1935–1939.* Philadelphia: University of Pennsylvania Press, 1982.

Cantril, Hadley. *The Invasion from Mars: A Study in the Psychology of Panic.* Princeton: Princeton University Press, 1940.

Carlson, Robert O., ed. *Communications and Public Opinion.* New York: Praeger, 1975.

Carroll, Wallace. *Inside Warring Russia.* Winston-Salem, N.C.: United Press Associates, 1942.

Carroll, Wallace. *Persuade or Perish.* Boston: Houghton Mifflin, 1948.

Chandler, Frank M. *Aspects of Modern Drama.* New York: Macmillan, 1914.

Chadwin, Mark Lincoln. *The Hawks of World War II.* Chapel Hill: University of North Carolina Press, 1968.

Chafe, William H. *The American Woman: Her Changing Social, Economic and Political Roles, 1920–1970.* New York: Oxford University Press, 1972.

Childs, Harwood L., ed. *Propaganda and Dictatorship: A Collection of Papers.* Princeton: Princeton University Press, 1936.

Childs, Harwood L., and J. B. Whiton, eds. *Propaganda by Short Wave.* Princeton: Princeton University Press, 1942.

Clark, Keith. *International Communications: The American Attitude.* New York: Columbia University Press, 1931.

Clurman, Harold. *All People Are Famous.* New York: Harcourt Brace Jovanovich, 1974.

Clurman, Harold. *The Fervent Years: The Group Theatre and the Thirties.* New York: Da Capo, 1975.

Clurman, Harold, ed. Introduction to *Famous American Plays of the 1930's.* New York: Dell, 1959.

Codding, George A., Jr. *Broadcasting Without Barriers.* The Hague, the Netherlands: UNESCO, 1959.

Codding, George A., and Anthony M. Rutkowski. *The International Telecommunications Union in a Changing World.* Dedham, Mass.: Artech House, 1982.

Codel, Martin, ed. *Radio and Its Future*. New York: Harper and Brothers, 1930.

Cole, Wayne S. *Roosevelt and the Isolationists, 1932–1945*. Lincoln: University of Nebraska Press, 1983.

Coles, Harry L., and Albert K. Weinberg. *Civil Affairs: Soldiers Become Governors*. Washington, D.C.: Office of the Chief of Military History, Department of the Army, 1964.

Columbia Broadcasting System. *A Resume of CBS Broadcasting Activities During 1937*. New York: CBS, 1938.

Corwin, Norman. *This Is War: A Collection of Plays About America on the March*. New York: Dodd, Mead, 1942.

Corwin, Norman. *Holes in a Stained Glass Window*. Secaucus, N.J.: Stuart, 1978.

Creel, George. *How We Advertised America*. New York: Harper and Brothers, 1920.

Culbert, David H. *News for Everyman: Radio and Foreign Affairs in Thirties America*. Westport, Conn.: Greenwood, 1976.

Czitrom, Daniel J. *Media and the American Mind: From Morse to McLuhan*. Chapel Hill: University of North Carolina Press, 1982.

Dalleck, Robert. *Franklin Roosevelt and American Foreign Policy, 1932–1945*. New York: Oxford University Press, 1979.

Dalton, Hugh. *The Fateful Years: Memoirs, 1931–1945*. London: Muller, 1952.

Davis, Elmer. *By Elmer Davis*. Edited by Robert Lloyd Davis. Indianapolis: Bobbs-Merrill, 1964.

Davis, Elmer. *Two Minutes Till Midnight*. Indianapolis: Bobbs-Merrill, 1955.

Davis, H. O. *The Empire of the Air: The Story of the Exploitation of Radio for Private Profit, with a Plan for the Reorganization of Broadcasting*. Ventura, Calif.: Ventura Free Press, 1932.

Davis, Lennard J. *Factual Fictions: The Origins of the English Novel*. New York: Columbia University Press, 1983.

Davison, W. Phillips. *International Political Communication*. New York: Praeger, 1965.

Davison, W. Phillips. *Mass Communication and Conflict Resolution: The Role of the Information Media in the Advancement of International Understanding*. New York: Praeger, 1974.

Delmar, Sefton. *Black Boomerang*. New York: Viking, 1962.

DeSantis, Hugh. *The Diplomacy of Silence: The American Foreign Service, the Soviet Union, and the Cold War, 1933–1947*. Chicago: University of Chicago Press, 1979.

Dizard, Wilson P. *The Strategy of Truth: The Story of the U.S. Information Service*. Washington, D.C.: Public Affairs Press, 1961.

Dobb, Leonard W. *Propaganda: Its Psychology and Technique*. New York: Holt, 1935.

Dougherty, James J. *The Politics of Wartime Aid: American Economic Assistance to France and French Northwest Africa, 1940–1946*. Westport, Conn.: Greenwood, 1978.

Douglass, Susan. *Inventing American Broadcasting, 1899–1922*. Baltimore: Johns Hopkins University Press, 1987.

Drakakis, John, ed. *British Radio Drama*. Cambridge: Cambridge University Press, 1981.

Dubois-Jallais. *La Tzarine: Helene Lazareff et l'aventure de "Elle."* Paris: Laffont, 1984.

Dunaway, John M. *The Metamorphoses of the Self*. Lexington: University Press of Kentucky, 1978.

Dunlop, Richard. *Donovan: America's Master Spy*. Chicago: Rand McNally, 1982.

Eisenhower, Dwight D. *Crusade in Europe.* New York: Doubleday, 1948.

Eisenhower, Milton S. *The President Is Calling.* New York: Doubleday, 1974.

Elder, Robert E. *The Information Machine: The USIA and American Foreign Policy.* Syracuse, N.Y.: Syracuse University Press, 1968.

Eliot, T. S. *The American of Poetic Drama.* London: Folcroft Library, 1976.

Esslin, Martin. *An Anatomy of Drama.* New York: Hill and Wang, 1976.

Ettlinger, Harold. *The Axis on the Air.* Indianapolis: Bobbs-Merrill, 1943.

Evans, Robert R., ed. *Readings in Collective Behavior.* Chicago: Rand McNally, 1969.

Farmer, Paul. *Vichy: Political Dilemma.* New York: Octagon Books, 1977.

Farrer, David. *The Warburgs: The Story of a Family.* New York: Stein and Day, 1975.

Fielding, Raymond. *"The March of Time," 1935–1951.* New York: Oxford University Press, 1978.

Foot, M. R. D. *Resistance.* New York: McGraw-Hill, 1977.

Funk, Arthur Layton. *Charles de Gaulle: The Crucial Years, 1943–1944.* Norman: University of Oklahoma Press, 1959.

Gamlin, Lionel. *You're on the Air: A Book About Broadcasting.* London: Chapman and Hall, 1947.

Galantiere, Lewis. *America and the Mind of Europe.* London: Hamilton, 1951.

Gleason, Archer. *Big Business and Radio.* New York: American Historical Company, 1939.

Goldstein, Malcolm. *The Political Stage: American Drama and Theater of the Great Depression.* New York: Oxford University Press, 1974.

Gombrich, E. H. *Art and Illusion: A Study in the Psychology of Pictorial Representation.* London: Phaidon, 1959.

Gombrich, E. H. *Myth and Reality in German War-Time Broadcasts.* London: Athlone, 1970.

Graebner, Norman A. *The Age of Global Power: The United States Since 1939.* New York: Wiley and Sons, 1979.

Graebner, Norman A. *America as a World Power: A Realist Appraisal from Wilson to Reagan.* Wilmington, Del.: Scholarly Resources, 1984.

Graebner, Norman A. *Cold War Diplomacy: American Foreign Policy, 1945–1975.* 2nd ed. New York: Van Nostrand Reinhold, 1977.

Grandin, Thomas. *The Political Use of Radio.* New York: Arno, 1971.

Graves, Harold N., Jr. *War on the Short Wave.* New York: Foreign Policy Association, 1941.

Green, Julien. *Diary, 1928–1957.* New York: Carroll and Graf, 1985.

Greene, Sir Hugh. *The Third Floor Front: A View of Broadcasting in the Sixties.* London: Bodley Head, 1969.

Halberstam, David. *The Powers That Be.* New York: Knopf, 1979.

Halperin, Morton. *Bureaucratic Politics and Foreign Policy.* Washington, D.C.: Brookings Institution, 1974.

Head, Sydney W. *Broadcasting in America.* Boston: Houghton Mifflin, 1976.

Henderson, John W. *The United States Information Agency.* New York: Praeger, 1969.

Hill, Frank Ernest, and W. E. Williams. *Radio's Listening Groups: The United States and Great Britain.* New York: Columbia University Press, 1941.

Hirsch, E. D., Jr. *Validity in Interpretation.* New Haven: Yale University Press, 1967.

Hodgson, Godfrey. *America in Our Time.* New York: Doubleday, 1976.

Hollingworth, H. L. *The Psychology of the Audience.* New York: American Book Company, 1935.

Honey, Maureen. *Creating Rosie the Riveter: Class, Gender and Propaganda During World War II.* Amherst: University of Massachusetts Press, 1984.

Houseman, John. *Front and Center.* New York: Simon and Schuster, 1979.

Houseman, John. *Run-Through.* New York: Simon and Schuster, 1972.

Howes, Raymond F. *Historical Studies of Rhetoric and Rhetoricians.* Ithaca: Cornell University Press, 1961.

Hughes, H. Stuart. *The Obstructed Path: French Social Thought in the Years of Desperation, 1930–1960.* New York: Harper and Row, 1966.

Hurstfield, Julian G. *America and the French Nation, 1939–1945.* Chapel Hill: University of North Carolina Press, 1986.

Hyde, H. Montgomery. *Room 3603: The Story of the British Intelligence Center in New York During World War II.* New York: Farrar, Straus, 1963.

Ickes, Harold L. *The Secret Diary of Harold Ickes.* New York: Simon and Schuster, 1954.

Innes, C. D. *Erwin Piscator's Political Theatre: The Development of Modern German Drama.* Cambridge: Cambridge University Press, 1972.

International Telecommunications Union. *Liste des fréquences.* Berne: Bureau de l'Union Internationale des Telecommunications, 1933.

Irons, Peter. *Justice at War.* New York: Oxford University Press, 1983.

Iser, Wolfgang. *The Act of Reading: A Theory of Aesthetic Response.* Baltimore: Johns Hopkins University Press, 1978.

Iswolsky, Helen. *Light Before Dusk: A Russian Catholic in France, 1923–1941.* New York: Longmans, Green, 1942.

Jablon, Howard. *Crossroad of Decision: The State Department and Foreign Policy, 1933–1937.* Lexington: University Press of Kentucky, 1983.

James, D. Clayton. *The Years of MacArthur, 1880–1941.* Boston: Houghton Mifflin, 1970.

Jay, Martin. *The Dialectical Imagination.* Boston: Little, Brown, 1973.

Kaplan, Milton Allen. *Radio and Poetry.* New York: Columbia University Press, 1949.

Kendrick, Alexander. *Prime Time: The Life of Edward R. Murrow.* Boston: Little, Brown, 1969.

Kennan, George F. *Memoirs, 1925–1950.* Boston: Little, Brown, 1967.

Kenny, V. *Paul Green.* New York: Twayne, 1971.

Kernau, Julie. *Our Friend Jacques Maritain: A Personal Memoir.* New York: Doubleday, 1975.

Kersaudy, François. *Churchill and de Gaulle.* London: Collins, 1981.

Kerwin, Jerome. *The Control of Radio: Public Policy Pamphlet No. 10.* Chicago: University of Chicago Press, 1934.

Kimball, Warren, ed. *Churchill and Roosevelt: The Complete Correspondence.* 3 vols. Princeton: Princeton University Press, 1984.

Kirby, Edward M., and Jack W. Harris. *Star Spangled Radio.* Chicago: Ziff-Davis, 1948.

Kirkpatrick, Ivone. *The Inner Circle: Memoirs.* New York: St. Martin's, 1959.

Kluger, Richard. *The Paper: The Life and Death of the "New York Herald Tribune."* New York: Knopf, 1986.

Koch, Howard. *The Panic Broadcast: Portrait of an Event.* Boston: Little, Brown, 1970.

Kochnitsky, Leon. *Negro Art in the Belgian Congo.* New York: Belgian Government Information Center, 1948.

Kolko, Gabriel. *The Politics of War: The World and United States Foreign Policy, 1943–1945.* New York: Random House, 1968.

Ladner, Alan W., and C. R. Stoner. *Short Wave Wireless Communication.* New York: Wiley and Sons, 1936.

Lamy, Jean-Claude. *Pierre Lazareff.* Paris: Editions Stock, 1975.

Langer, William L. *Our Vichy Gamble.* New York: Knopf, 1947.

Lasswell, Harold D. *Propaganda Technique in the World War.* New York: Knopf, 1927.

Lasswell, Harold D., and Dorothy Blumenstock. *World Revolutionary Propaganda.* New York: Knopf, 1939.

Lazareff, Pierre. *Deadline: The Behind-the-Scenes Story of the Last Decade in France.* New York: Random House, 1942.

Lazarsfeld, Paul F., Bernard Berelson, and Hazel Gaudet. *The People's Choice: How the Voter Makes Up His Mind in a Presidential Campaign.* New York: Duell, Sloan and Pearce, 1944.

Lazarsfeld, Paul F., and Frank N. Stanton, eds. *Radio Research, 1942–1943.* New York: Duell, Sloan and Pearce, 1944.

Lean, Edward Tangye. *Voices in the Darkness.* London: Secker and Warburg, 1943.

Lee, Raymond E. *The London Journal of General Raymond E. Lee, 1940–1941.* Boston: Little, Brown, 1971.

Leinwoll, Stanley. *From Spark to Satellite: A History of Radio Communication.* New York: Scribner's, 1979.

Leopold, Richard. *The Growth of American Foreign Policy.* New York: Alfred A. Knopf, 1962.

Lerner, Daniel. *Psychological Warfare Against Nazi Germany: The Skywar Campaign, D-Day to V-E Day.* Cambridge: M.I.T. Press, 1971.

Lerner, Daniel, ed. *Propaganda in War and Crisis.* New York: Stewart, 1951.

Lerner, Max. *Ideas Are Weapons.* New York: Viking, 1940.

Lessing, Lawrence. *Man of High Fidelity: Edwin Howard Armstrong.* Philadelphia: Bantam, 1956.

Lewis, Peter, ed. *Papers of the Radio Literature Conference, 1977.* Durham, N.C.: Durham University Printing Unit, 1978.

Lewis, Peter, ed. *Radio Drama.* London: Longman, 1981.

Linebarger, Paul M. A. *Psychological Warfare.* Washington, D.C.: Infantry Journal Press, 1948.

Lodge, David. *The Modes of Modern Writing.* Ithaca: Cornell University Press, 1977.

Lodge, David. *Working with Structuralism: Essays and Reviews on Nineteenth- and Twentieth-Century Literature.* London: Routledge and Kegan Paul, 1981.

Luce, Henry R. *The American Century.* New York: Farrar and Rinehart, 1941.

Lumley, Frederick E. *Means of Social Control.* New York: Century, 1925.

MacDonald, J. Fred. *Don't Touch That Dial: Radio Programming in American Life from 1920 to 1960.* Chicago: Nelson-Hall, 1979.

MacLatchy, Josephine M., ed. *Education on the Air: Eleventh Yearbook of the Institute for Education by Radio.* Columbus: Ohio State University, 1940.

Macmillan, Harold. *The Blast of War, 1939–1945.* New York: Carroll and Graf, 1983.

Macmillan, Harold. *War Diaries: The Mediterranean 1943–1945.* New York: St. Martin's, 1984.

Mance, Harry Osborne. *International Telecommunications.* London: Oxford University Press, 1944.

Margolin, Leo Jay. *Paper Bullets: A Brief Story of Psychological Warfare in World War II.* New York: Froben, 1946.

Markel, Lester, ed. *Public Opinion and Foreign Policy.* New York: Harper and Brothers, 1949.

Markowitz, Norman D. *The Rise and Fall of the People's Century: Henry A. Wallace and American Liberalism, 1941–1948.* New York: Free Press, 1973.

McLeod, Stuart. *Modern Verse Drama.* Salzburg: University of Salzburg, 1972.

McLuhan, Marshall. *Understanding Media.* New York: McGraw-Hill, 1964.

McVane, John. *Journey into War: War and Diplomacy in North Africa.* New York: Appleton-Century, 1943.

Meerloo, A.M. *Total War and the Human Mind: A Psychologist's Experiences in Occupied Holland.* London: Allen and Unwin, 1944.

Merton, Robert K. *Mass Persuasion: The Social Psychology of a War Bond Drive.* New York: Harper and Brothers, 1946.

Mertz, Robert. *CBS: Reflections in a Bloodshot Eye.* Chicago: Playboy, 1975.

Meserve, Walter J. *Robert E. Sherwood: Reluctant Moralist.* New York: Pegasus, 1970.

Meyerhoff, Arthur E. *The Strategy of Persuasion: The Use of Advertising Skills in Fighting the Cold War.* New York: Coward-McCann, 1965.

Michel, Henri. *The Second World War.* New York: Praeger, 1968.

Miller, Douglas. *You Can't Do Business with Hitler.* Boston: Little, Brown, 1941.

Miller, James Edward. *The United States and Italy, 1940–1950: The Politics and Diplomacy of Stabilization.* Chapel Hill: University of North Carolina Press, 1986.

Millett, Allan R., and Peter Maslowski. *For the Common Defense: A Military History of the United States of America.* New York: Free Press, 1984.

Mills, C. Wright. *The Sociological Imagination.* New York: Oxford University Press, 1959.

Mock, James R., and Cedric Larson. *Words That Won the War: The Story of the Committee on Public Information, 1917–1919.* New York: Russell and Russell, 1939.

Mohrmann, G. P., Charles J. Stewart, and Donovan J. Ochs, eds. *Explorations in Rhetorical Criticism.* University Park: Pennsylvania State University Press, 1973.

Morse, Arthur. *While Six Million Died: A Chronicle of American Apathy.* New York: Random House, 1967.

Mosher, Frederick C., ed. *Basic Documents of American Public Administration, 1776–1950.* New York: Holmes and Meier, 1976.

Mosher, Frederick C., ed. *Basic Literature of American Public Administration, 1787–1950.* New York: Holmes and Meier, 1981.

Natanson, Maurice, and Henry W. Johnstone, Jr. *Philosophy, Rhetoric and Argumentation.* University Park: Pennsylvania State University Press, 1965.

Nicholas, H. G., ed. *Washington Despatches, 1941–1945: Weekly Reports from the British Embassy.* Chicago: University of Chicago Press, 1981.

Nilsen, Thomas R., ed. *Essays on Rhetorical Criticism.* New York: Random House, 1968.

O'Neill, Neville. *The Advertising Agency Looks at Radio.* New York: Appleton, 1932.

Paley, William S. *As It Happened: A Memoir.* Garden City, N.Y.: Doubleday, 1979.

Paxton, Robert O. *Vichy France: Old Guard and New Order.* New York: Knopf, 1972.

Persico, Joseph E. *Edward R. Murrow: An American Original.* New York: McGraw-Hill, 1988.

Pierson, Ruth R. *"They're Still Women After All": The Second World War and Canadian Womanhood.* Toronto: McClelland and Stewart, 1986.

Pirsein, Robert W. *The Voice of America: An History of the International Broadcasting Activities of the United States Government, 1940–1962.* New York: Arno, 1979.

Piscator, Erwin, *The Political Theatre.* London: Eyre Methuen, 1980.

Pogue, Forrest C. *George C. Marshall: Ordeal and Hope.* New York: Viking, 1966.

Powe, Marc B. *The Emergence of the War Department Intelligence Agency, 1885–1918.* Manhattan, Kans.: Military Affairs, 1975.

Priestley, J. B. *All England Listened: The Wartime Postscripts of J. B. Priestley.* New York: Chilmark, 1967.

Reyner, John H. *Short Wave Radio.* London: Pitman and Sons, 1942.

Riegel, Oscar W. *Mobilizing for Chaos: The Story of the New Propaganda.* New Haven: Yale University Press, 1934.

Rigby, Charles A. *The War on the Short Waves.* London: Cole, 1943.

Robinson, Thomas P. *Radio Networks and the Federal Government.* New York: Arno, 1979.

Rolo, Charles J. *Radio Goes to War: The "Fourth Front."* New York: Putnam's, 1942.

Roosevelt, Kermit. *War Report: Office of Strategic Services.* Washington, D.C.: Government Printing Office, 1949.

Rosen, Philip T. *The Modern Stentors.* Westport, Conn.: Greenwood, 1980.

Rosenbaum, Edward, and A. J. Sherman. *M. M. Warburg and Co., 1798–1938: Merchant Bankers of Hamburg.* New York: Holmes and Meier, 1979.

Rotha, Paul. *Documentary Film.* London: Faber and Faber, 1952.

Rowland, Donald W. *History of the Office of the Coordinator of Inter-American Affairs.* Washington, D.C.: Government Printing Office, 1947.

Rubin, Ronald I. *The Objectives of the U.S. Information Agency: Controversies and Analysis.* New York: Praeger, 1966.

Rupp, Leila J. *Mobilizing Women for War: German and American Propaganda, 1939–1945.* Princeton: Princeton University Press, 1978.

Saerchinger, Cesar. *Hello America: Radio Adventures in Europe.* Boston: Houghton Mifflin, 1938.

Saint-Jean, Robert de. *Julien Green par lui-même.* Paris: Editions du Seuil, 1968.

Sales, Raoul de Roussy de. *The Making of Yesterday: The Diaries of Raoul de Roussy de Sales.* New York: Reynal and Hitchcock, 1947.

Salisbury, Harrison E. *A Journey for Our Times: A Memoir.* New York: Harper and Row, 1983.

Samuel, Richard H., and R. Hinton Thomas. *Expressionism in German Life, Literature and the Theatre 1910–1940.*

Schlesinger, Arthur M., Jr. *The Coming of the New Deal*. Boston: Houghton Mifflin, 1958.

Schramm, Wilbur, ed. *The Process and Effects of Mass Communication*. Urbana: University of Illinois Press, 1954.

Schudson, Michael. *Advertising, The Uneasy Persuasion: Its Dubious Impact on American Society*. New York: Basic Books, 1984.

Seabury, Paul. *The Rise and Decline of the Cold War*. New York: Basic Books, 1967.

Seldes, Gilbert. *The Great Audience*. New York: Viking, 1950.

Severeid, Eric. *Not So Wild a Dream: A Personal Story of Youth and War and the American Faith*. New York: Atheneum, 1979.

Sherwood, Robert E. *There Shall Be No Night*. New York: Scribner's, 1940.

Shirer, William L. *Berlin Diary*. New York: Knopf, 1941.

Shirer, William L. *The Nightmare Years, 1930–1940*. Boston: Little, Brown, 1984.

Shuman, R. Baird. *Robert E. Sherwood*. New York: Twayne, 1964.

Sill, Geoffrey M. *Defoe and the Idea of Fiction, 1713–1719*. Newark: University of Delaware Press, 1983.

Silvey, Robert. *Who's Listening? The Story of BBC Audience Research*. London: Allen and Unwin, 1974.

Skornia, Harry J., and Jack William Kitson, eds. *Problems and Controversies in Television and Radio*. Palo Alto, Calif.: Pacific, 1968.

Smith, Bradley F. *The Shadow Warriors: O.S.S. and the Origins of the C.I.A.* New York: Basic Books, 1983.

Smith, Gaddis. *American Diplomacy During the Second World War, 1941–1945*. New York: Wiley and Sons, 1965.

Sorensen, Thomas C. *The Word War: The Story of American Propaganda*. New York: Harper and Row, 1968.

Speier, Hans J., and Alfred Kahler, eds. *War in Our Time*. New York: Norton, 1939.

Sperber, A. M. *Murrow, His Life and Times*. New York: Freundlich, 1986.

Steele, Richard W. *Propaganda in a Open Society: The Roosevelt Administration and the Media, 1933–1941*. Westport, Conn.: Greenwood, 1985.

Stephens, Oren. *Facts to a Candid World: America's Overseas Information Program*. Stanford: Stanford University Press, 1955.

Sterling, George. *The Radio Manual*. New York: Van Nostrand, 1928.

Stimson, Henry L., and McGeorge Bundy. *On Active Service in Peace and War*. New York: Putnam's, 1948.

Stott, William. *Documentary Expression and Thirties America*. New York: Oxford University Press, 1973.

Suleiman, Susan Rubin. *The Ideological Novel as a Literary Genre*. New York: Columbia University Press, 1983.

Suleiman, Susan Rubin, and Inge Crosman, eds. *The Reader in the Text*. Princeton: Princeton University Press, 1980.

Sussman, Warren I. *Culture as History: The Transformation of American Society in the Twentieth Century*. New York: Pantheon, 1984.

Sweets, John F. *The Politics of Resistance in France, 1940–1944*. De Kalb: Northern Illinois University Press, 1976.

Talese, Gay. *The Kingdom and the Power.* New York: New American Library. 1969.

Taylor, Edmond. *The Strategy of Terror.* Boston: Houghton Mifflin, 1942.

Taylor, Karen Malped. *People's Theatre in Amerika.* New York: Drama Book Specialists, 1972.

Thomson, Charles A. H. *Overseas Information Service of the United States Government.* Washington, D.C.: Brookings Institution, 1948.

Thomas, Hugh. *Armed Truce: The Beginnings of the Cold War, 1945–1946.* New York: Atheneum, 1987.

Tomlinson, John D. *The International Control of Radiocommunications.* Ann Arbor, Mich.: Edwards, 1945.

Troy, Thomas F. *Donovan and the C.I.A.: A History of the Establishment of the Central Intelligence Agency.* Frederick, Md.: University Publications of America, Aletheia, 1981.

Valgemae, Mardi. *Accelerated Grimace: Expressionism in the American Drama of the 1920's.* Carbondale: Southern Illinois University Press, 1972.

Van Laan, Thomas. *The Idiom of Drama.* Ithaca: Cornell University Press, 1970.

Vaughn, Stephen. *Holding Fast the Inner Lines: Democracy, Nationalism, and the Committee on Public Information.* Chapel Hill: University of North Carolina Press, 1980.

Viorst, Milton. *Hostile Allies: FDR and Charles de Gaulle.* New York: Macmillan, 1965.

Waldron, Gloria. *The Information Film.* New York: Columbia University Press, 1949.

Warburg, James P. *And Then What? Poems by Paul James.* New York: Knopf, 1920.

Warburg, James P. *Foreign Policy Begins at Home.* New York: Harcourt, Brace, 1944.

Warburg, James P. *Hell Bent for Election.* New York: Doubleday, Doran, 1935.

Warburg, James P. *The Isolationist Illusion and World Peace.* New York: Farrar and Rinehart, 1941.

Warburg, James P. *The Long Road Home: The Autobiography of a Maverick.* New York: Doubleday, 1964.

Warburg, James P. *Man's Enemy and Man.* New York: Farrar and Rinehart, 1942.

Warburg, James P. *Peace in Our Time.* New York: Harper and Brothers, 1940.

Warburg, James P. *Shoes and Ships and Sealing Wax: Poems by Paul James.* New York: Knopf, 1932.

Warburg, James P. *Still Hell Bent for Election.* New York: Doubleday, Doran, 1936.

Warburg, James P. *Unwritten Treaty.* New York: Harcourt, Brace, 1946.

Weigley, Russell F., ed. *The American Military: Readings in the History of the Military in American Society.* Reading, Mass.: Addison-Wesley, 1969.

Weigley, Russell F. *The American Way of War.* New York: Macmillan, 1973.

Weigley, Russell F. *History of the United States Army.* New York: Macmillan, 1967.

Weil, Martin. *A Pretty Good Club: The Founding Fathers of the U.S. Foreign Service.* New York: Norton, 1978.

Werth, Alexander. *De Gaulle: A Political Biography.* New York: Simon and Schuster, 1965.

Werth, Alexander. *France, 1940–1955.* Boston: Beacon Press, 1966.

White, Eugene E., ed. *Rhetoric in Transition: Studies in the Nature and Uses of Rhetoric.* University Park: Pennsylvania State University Press, 1980.

White, Llewellyn. *The American Radio*. Chicago: University of Chicago Press, 1947.

Whitehouse, Vira B. *A Year as a Government Agent*. New York: Harper and Brothers, 1920.

Whitman, Willson. *Bread and Circuses: A Study of Federal Theatre*. New York: Oxford University Press, 1937.

Willett, John. *The Theatre of Bertolt Brecht: A Study for Eight Aspects*. Norfolk, Conn.: New Directions, 1959.

Willett, John. *The Theatre of Erwin Piscator: Half a Century of Politics in the Theatre*. London: Eyre Methuen, 1978.

Williams, Jay. *Stage Left*. New York: Scribner's, 1974.

Winkler, Allan M. *The Politics of Propaganda: The Office of War Information, 1942–1945*. New Haven: Yale University Press, 1978.

Wright, Gordon. *France in Modern Times*. Chicago: Rand McNally, 1974.

Wylie, Max, ed. *Best Broadcasts of 1938–1939*. New York: Whittlesey House, 1939.

Wylie, Max, ed. *Best Broadcasts of 1939–1940*. New York: Whittlesey House, 1940.

Wylie, Max, ed. *Best Broadcasts of 1940–1941*. New York: Whittlesey House, 1941.

Yergin, Daniel. *Shattered Peace: The Origins of the Cold War and the National Security State*. Boston: Houghton Mifflin, 1977.

Zeman, Z. A. B. *Nazi Propaganda*. London: Oxford University Press, 1964.

## Articles

Allport, Gordon W. Review of Frederick C. Bartlett, *Political Propaganda*. *Saturday Review*, March 7, 1942, 18.

Almond, Gabriel A. "The Resistance and the Political Parties of Western Europe." *Political Science Quarterly* 62 (March 1947): 27–61.

Barbour, Philip L. "Open Questions in Inter-American Broadcasting." *The Annals of the American Academy of Political and Social Science* 213 (January 1941): 116–24.

Barbour, Philip L. "Short Wave Broadcasting and Latin America." *Bulletin of the Pan American Union* 10 (October 1937): 739–51.

Bechtold, William E. "The World Propaganda War." *North American Review*, November 1934, 421–31.

"Behind the Radio Battle on the Austrian Front." *Literary Digest*, September 2, 1933, 11.

Behrman, S. N. "Old Monotonous." *The New Yorker*, June 1, 8, 1940, 33–40; 23–36.

Bent, Silas. "Propaganda Rules the Waves." *Review of Reviews*, February 1937, 38–41.

Bernays, Edward L., ed. "Censorship and Propaganda." *Saturday Review of Literature* March 7, 1942, 183–87.

Bernays, Edward L. "War Against Words." *Coast Artillery Journal* 83 (September–October 1940): 458–62.

Biro, Sidney. "The International Aspects of Radio Control." *Journal of Radio Law* 2 (January 1932): 45–66.

Blankenhorn, Heber. "The Battle of Radio Armaments: Broadcasting and International Friction." *Harper's*, December 1931, 83–90.

Blumer, Herbert. "The Mass, the Public, and Public Opinion." In *A Reader in Pub-*

*lic Opinion and Communication,* edited by Bernard Berelson and Morris Jano-
    witz. Glencoe, Ill.: Free Press, 1950: 43–49.
Blumer, Herbert. "Outline of Collective Behavior." In *Readings in Collective Behavior,*
    edited by Robert R. Evans. Chicago: Rand McNally, 1969.
Brinkley, Alan. "Minister Without Portfolio." *Harper's,* February 1983, 29–33.
Brinton, Crane. "Letter from Liberated France." *French Historical Studies* 2 (Spring
    1961): 1–27.
Burdick, Eugene. Introduction to Arthur E. Meyerhoff, *The Strategy of Persuasion:
    The Use of Advertising Skills in Fighting the Cold War.* New York: Coward-McCann,
    1965.
Callender, Harold. "Europe's Propaganda Mills Keep Busy." *New York Times,* April 9,
    1933.
Cantril, Hadley. "The Invasion of Mars." In *The Process and Effects of Mass Commu-
    nication,* edited by Wilbur Schramm. Urbana: University of Illinois Press, 1954.
Church, George F. "Short Waves and Propaganda." *Public Opinion Quarterly* 3 (April
    1939): 209–22.
"Communications: The Fourth Front." *Fortune,* November 1939, 90–97.
Crossman, Richard H. S. "Psychological Warfare, Part I." *Journal of the Royal United
    Service Institution* 97 (August 1952): 319–32.
Crossman, Richard H. S. "Psychological Warfare, Part II." *Journal of the Royal United
    Service Institution* 98 (August 1953): 351–61.
Crossman, Richard H. S. "Supplementary Essay." In Daniel Lerner, *Psychological War-
    fare Against Nazi Germany: The Skywar Campaign, D-Day to V-E Day.* Cambridge:
    M.I.T. Press, 1971.
Darrock, MDavis, Elmer. "Broadcasting the Outbreak of War." *Harper's,* November
    1939, 579–88.
Davis, Elmer. "OWI Has a Job." *Public Opinion Quarterly* 7 (Spring 1943): 5–12.
Davis, Robert Lloyd. Introduction to *By Elmer Davis,* edited by Robert Lloyd Davis.
    Indianapolis: Bobbs-Merrill, 1964.
Davis, Stuart. "Why an Artists' Congress?" In *Artists Against War and Fascism: Papers
    of the First American Artists' Congress,* edited by Matthew Baigell and Julia Wil-
    liams. New Brunswick, N.J.: Rutgers University Press, 1986.
Denny, Reuel. "The Discovery of the Popular Culture." In *American Perspectives:
    The National Self-Image in the Twentieth Century.* Cambridge: Harvard University
    Press, 1961.
Doob, Leonard W. "The Utilization of Social Scientists in the Overseas Branch of
    the Office of War Information." In *Propaganda in War and Crisis,* edited by Daniel
    Lerner. New York: Stewart, 1951.
Drummond, Donald F. "Cordell Hull." In *An Uncertain Tradition: American Secre-
    taries of State in the Twentieth Century,* edited by Norman A. Graebner. New York:
    McGraw-Hill, 1961.
The Literary Digest, "Europe's Wireless Towers of Babel." *Literary Digest,* June 26,
    1937, 24–26.
Fellows, Otis, and Harry Torczyner. "Triangles on the Air." *Belgium* 4 (June 1943):
    212–13.

Fenwick, C. G. "The Use of Radio as an Instrument of Foreign Propaganda." *American Journal of International Law* 32 (April 1938): 339.

Fink, Howard. "The Sponsor v. the Nation's Choice: North American Radio Drama." In *Radio Drama,* edited by Peter Lewis. London: Longman, 1981.

Foster, H. Schuyler, Jr. "The Official Propaganda of Great Britain." *Public Opinion Quarterly* 3 (April 1939): 261–70.

Frantz, Harry W. "Dr. Leo Rowe and His Office." *Bulletin of the Pan American Union* (April 1947): 231–33.

Friederich, Carl J., and Evelyn Sternberg. "Congress and the Control of Radio-Broadcasting." In *Problems and Controversies in Television and Radio,* edited by Harry J. Skornia and Jack William Kitson. Palo Alto, Calif.: Pacific, 1968.

Friedson, Eliot. "Communications Research and the Concept of Mass." In *The Process and Effects of Mass Communication,* edited by Wilbur Schramm. Urbana: University of Illinois Press, 1954.

Galantiere, Lewis. Introduction to *America and the Mind of Europe,* edited by Lewis Galantiere. London: Hamilton, 1951.

"German Defiance of Britain and France." *Literary Digest,* August 19, 1933, 13.

Giddens, Jackson A. Introduction to Harold Lasswell, *Propaganda Technique in World War I.* Cambridge: M.I.T. Press, 1971.

Gilbert, James B. "War of the Worlds." *Journal of Popular Culture* 10 (Fall 1976): 326–36.

Gombrich, E. H. "The Mask and the Face: The Perception of Physiognomic Likeness in Life and in Art." In *Art, Perception, and Reality,* edited by Maurice Mandelbaum. Baltimore: Johns Hopkins University Press, 1972.

Gottschalk, Louis. "Our Vichy Fumble." *Journal of Modern History* 20 (March 1948): 47–56.

Granitsas, Spyridon. "The Voice of America in Greece." In *The Case for Reappraisal of U.S. Overseas Information Policies and Programs,* edited by Edward L. Bernays and Burnet Hershey. New York: Praeger, 1970.

Greene, Fred. "The Military View of American National Policy, 1904–1940." *American Historical Review* 66 (January 1961): 354–77.

Grey, Robin. "Inside the Voice of America." *Columbia Journalism Review* 21 (May/ June 1982): 23–30.

Grimes, Paul. "Reshaping the Image of the United States." In *The Case for Reappraisal of U.S. Overseas Information Policies and Programs,* edited by Edward L. Bernays and Burnet Hershey. New York: Praeger, 1970.

Grimes, Paul. "Three Crippling Factors." In *The Case for Reappraisal of U.S. Overseas Information Policies and Programs,* edited by Edward Bernays and Burnet Hershey. New York: Praeger, 1970.

Gubbins, Colin (Maj.-Gen.). "Resistance Movements in the War." *Journal of the Royal United Service Institution* (May 1948): 210–23.

Guttman, Allen. "Conservatism and the Military Establishment." In *The American Military: Readings in the History of the Military in American Society,* edited by Russell F. Weigley. Reading, Mass.: Addison-Wesley, 1969.

Guy, Raymond F. "An International Broadcasting System." *RCA Review,* July 1938, 20–36.

Habord, James G. *Radio and Its Future*. New York: Harper and Brothers, 1930.

Hallborg, H. E., L. A. Briggs, and C. W. Hansell. "Short Wave Commercial Long Distance Communication." *Proceedings of the Institute of Radio Engineers* 15 (June 1927): 467–501.

Hanighen, Frank C. "Propaganda on the Air: The International Problem of Radio Censorship." *Current History* 44 (June 1936): 45–51.

Hardy, Barbara. Introduction to George Eliot, *Daniel Deronda*. Harmondsworth, Middlesex: Penguin, 1967.

Hawkins, Lester G., Jr., and George S. Pettee. "OWI – Organization and Problems." *Public Opinion Quarterly* 7 (Spring 1943): 13–52.

Hickock, Guy C. "Developments in International Broadcasting." In *Education on the Air: Eleventh Yearbook of the Institute for Education by Radio*, edited by Josephine M. MacLatchy. Columbus: Ohio State University, 1940.

Houseman, John. "The Men from Mars." In *Gentlemen, Schools and Scoundrels*, edited by Horace Knowles. New York: Books for Libraries, 1972.

Howard, Anthony. Introduction to Richard H. S. Crossman, *The Crossman Diaries*. London: Hamilton, 1979.

Huntington, Samuel P. "The Making of the American Military." In *The American Military: Readings in the History of the Military in American Society*, edited by Russell F. Weigley. Reading, Mass.: Addison-Wesley, 1969.

Horn, C. W. "International Broadcasting." In *Radio and Its Future*, edited by Martin Codel. New York: Harper and Brothers, 1930.

Janowitz, Morris. "Military Career Patterns and the Military Mind." In *The American Military: Readings in the History of the Military in American Society*, edited by Russell F. Weigley. Reading, Mass.: Addison-Wesley, 1969.

Jones, Alfred H. "The Making of an Interventionist on the Air: Elmer Davis and CBS News, 1939–1941." *Pacific Historical Review* 42 (February 1973): 74–93.

Katz, Daniel. "Three Criteria: Knowledge, Conviction and Significance." *Public Opinion Quarterly* 4 (June 1940): 277–84.

Kenner, Hugh. "The Politics of the Plain Style." *New York Book Review*, September 15, 1985, 1, 39–40.

Kessler-Harris, Alice. "Rosie the Riveter: Who Was She?" *Labor History* 24 (Spring 1983): 249–53.

Klapper, Joseph T. "Mass Media and Persuasion. In *The Process and Effects of Mass Communication*, edited by Wilbur Schramm. Urbana: University of Illinois Press, 1954.

Klapper, Joseph T. "What We Know About the Effects of Mass Communication: The Brink of Hope." In *Communications and Public Opinion*, edited by Robert O. Carlson. New York: Praeger, 1975.

Kostelanetz, Richard. "On the New Arts in America." In *The New America Arts*, edited by Richard Kostelanetz. New York: Horizon, 1965.

Kris, Ernst, and Nathan Leites. "Trends in Twentieth Century Propaganda." In *A Reader in Public Opinion and Communication*, edited by Bernard Berelson and Morris Janowitz. Glencoe, Ill.: Free Press, 1953.

Landry, Robert J. "Radio and Government." *Public Opinion Quarterly* 2 (October 1938): 557–69.

Lasswell, Harold D. Foreword to George C. Bruntz, *Allied Propaganda and the Collapse of the German Empire in 1918.* Stanford: Stanford University Press, 1938.

Lasswell, Harold D. "The Status of Research on International Propaganda and Opinion." *Papers and Proceedings of the American Sociological Society* 20 (December 1925): 198–209.

Lasswell, Harold D. "The Theory of Political Propaganda." *American Political Science Review* 21 (August 1927): 627–31.

Lasswell, Harold D. "Why Be Quantitative?" In *A Reader in Public Opinion and Communication,* edited by Bernard Berelson and Morris Janowitz. Glencoe, Ill.: Free Press, 1953.

Lazarsfeld, Paul. "An Episode in the History of Social Research: A Memoir." In *The Intellectual Migration: Europe and America,* edited by Donald Flemming and Bernard Bailyn. Cambridge: Harvard University Press, 1969.

Lazarsfeld, Paul, and Robert K. Merton. "Requisite Conditions for Propaganda Success." In *Voice of the People: Readings in Public Opinion and Propaganda,* edited by Reo M. Christenson and Robert O. McWilliams. New York: McGraw-Hill, 1962.

Leach, Eugene E. "Mastering the Crowd: Collective Behavior and Mass Society in American Social Thought, 1917–1939. " *American Studies* 27 (Spring 1986): 99–114.

LeRoy, Howard S. "Treaty Regulation and Short Wave Broadcasting." *American Journal of International Law* 32 (October 1938): 719–37.

Lewis, Peter. "Radio Drama and English Literature." In *Radio Drama,* edited by Peter Lewis. London: Longman, 1981.

Lewis, Peter. "'Under Milk Wood' as a Radio Poem." In *Papers of the Radio Literature Conference, 1977,* edited by Peter Lewis. Durham, N.C.: Durham University Printing Unit, 1978.

Lutz, Ralph H. "Studies of World War Propaganda, 1914–1933." *Journal of Modern History* 5 (September/October 1933): 496–516.

Makin, W. J. "Short Wave Warfare." *Reader's Digest,* May 1938, 42.

Mathews, Joseph J. "The Radio and International Relations." *Southwestern Social Science Quarterly* 20 (September 1939): 140–50.

Miller, Clyde R. "Radio Propaganda." *Annals of the American Academy of Political and Social Science* 213 (January 1941): 69–74.

"More About Short Wave Transmission." *Radio Broadcast,* December 4, 1923, 103–105.

Morecroft, J. B. "The March of Radio." *Radio Broadcast,* August 1924, 296–97.

Muniz, Joao Carlos. "Address of His Excellency, Dr. Joao Carlos Muniz, Brazil." *Bulletin of the Pan American Union* 6 (April 1947): 192.

Nelson, Roger B. "Hitler's Propaganda Machine." *Current History* 38 (June 1933): 287–94.

Odegard, Peter H. Review of Philip Davidson, *Propaganda and the American Revolution. Saturday Review,* March 7, 1942, 5–6.

Otterman, Harvey G. "Inter-American Radio Conferences." *American Journal of International Law* 32 (July 1938): 569–74.

Peyre, Henri. "Literature and Philosophy in Contemporary France." In *Ideological Differences and World Order,* edited by F. S. C. Northrop. New Haven: Yale University Press, 1949.

Price, Claire. "Europe Wages War on the Radio." *New York Times Magazine*, September 10, 1933, 6, 14.

Quick, Paddy. "Rosie the Riveter." *Radical America* 9 (July–October 1975): 115–31.

Rabinowitz, Peter J. "Audiences' Experience of Literary Borrowing." In *The Reader in the Text*, edited by Susan Rubin Suleiman and Inge Crosman. Princeton: Princeton University Press, 1980.

Rabkin, Gerald. "The Federal Theatre Project." In *The Thirties*, edited by Warren French. Deland, Fla.: Everett/Edwards, 1967.

Riegel, Oscar W. "Press, Radio and the Spanish Civil War." *Public Opinion Quarterly* 1 (January 1937): 131–36.

Rodgers, W. W. "Is Short-Wave Relaying a Step Toward National Broadcasting Stations?" *Radio Broadcast*, June 1923, 119–22.

Rolo, Charles J. "The Strategy of War by Radio." *Harper's*, November 1940, 640–50.

Rolo, Charles J., and R. Strausz-Hupe. "U.S. International Broadcasting: What We Are Doing, What We Must Do." *Harper's*, 3 August 1941, 301–13.

Rowe, Leo S. "Address Delivered to the University of San Marcos." *Bulletin of the Pan American Union* 3 (January 1925): 15.

Rowe, Leo S. "Pan American Union." In *Encyclopedia Britannica*. 14th ed. London: Encyclopedia Britannica, 1937.

Saerchinger, Cesar. "Radio as a Political Instrument." *Foreign Affairs* 16 (January 1938): 244–59.

Sawyer, John E. "The Reestablishment of the Republic in France: The de Gaulle Era, 1944–1945." *Political Science Quarterly* 62 (September 1947): 354–67.

Scanlan, Ross. "The Nazi Rhetorician." In *Historical Studies of Rhetoric and Rhetoricians*, edited by Raymond F. Howes. Ithaca: Cornell University Press, 1961.

Seldes, George. "The New Propaganda for War." *Harper's*, October 1934, 540–53.

Sharp, John. "Propaganda on the Airwaves." *Christian Science Monitor Magazine*, 27 (October 1937), 5, 14.

Shover, Michele. "Roles and Images of Women in World War I Propaganda." *Politics and Society* 5, no. 4 (1975): 469–86.

Sorlin, Pierre. "The Struggle for Control of French Minds, 1940–1944." In *Film and Radio Propaganda in World War II*, edited by K. R. M. Short. Knoxville: University of Tennessee Press, 1983.

Speier, Hans J. "Morale and Propaganda." In *War in Our Time*, edited by Hans J. Speier and Alfred Kahler. New York: Norton, 1939.

Speier, Hans J. "Psychological Warfare Reconsidered." In *The Process and Effects of Mass Communication*, edited by Wilbur Schramm. Urbana: University of Illinois Press, 1954.

Speier, Hans J. "War Aims in Political Warfare." In *Propaganda in War and Crisis*, edited by Daniel Lerner. New York: Stewart, 1951.

Speier, Hans J., and Margaret Otis. "German Radio Propaganda to France During the Battle of France." In *Radio Research, 1942–1943*, edited by Paul F. Lazarsfeld and Frank N. Stanton. New York: Duell, Sloan and Pearce, 1944.

Steele, Richard W. "American Popular Opinion and the War Against Germany: The Issue of Negotiated Peace, 1942." *Journal of American History* 65 (December 1978): 704–23.

Steele, Richard W. "The Great Debate: Roosevelt, the Media and the Coming of the War, 1940–1941." *Journal of American History* 71 (June 1984): 69–92.

Steele, Richard W. "Preparing the Public for War: Efforts to Establish a National Propaganda Agency, 1940–1941." *American Historical Review* 75 (October 1970): 1640–53.

Stowe, Leland. "Propaganda over Europe." *Scribner's*, August 1934, 99–101.

Sullivan, Harry Stack. "Conceptions of Modern Psychology." *Psychiatry* 3 (February 1940): 1–117.

Taylor, Albert Hoyt, and Robert S. Kruse. "High Frequency Transmission and Reception." In *The Radio Engineering Handbook*, edited by Keith Henney. New York: McGraw-Hill, 1935.

"The Transatlantic Broadcasting Tests and What They Prove." *Radio Broadcast* January 4, 1924, 183–95.

Trey, J. E. "Women in the War Economy—World War II." *Review of Radical Political Economics* 4 (July 1972): 40–57.

Van Gelderland, Karl. "The War in the Ether." *The Nation*, March 12, 1938, 300–301.

White, Ralph K. "Hitler, Roosevelt and the Native of War Propaganda." *Journal of Abnormal and Social Psychology* 44 (April 1949): 157–74.

Whitton, John. "War by Radio." *Foreign Affairs* 19 (April 1941): 584–96.

Wilson, J. S. "Short Wave War in Latin America." *Radio News*, September 1938, 10.

Wright, Gordon. "Reflections on the French Resistance (1940–1944)." *Political Science Quarterly* 77 (September 1962): 336–49.

Yandell, Lunsford P. "How to Build Good Will and Sales by Short-Wave Broadcast." *Export Trade and Shipper*, May 13, 1940, 3–5.

Yandell, Lunsford P. "Radio Programs and Listeners in Latin America." *Export Trade and Shipper*, October 21, 1940, 7–8.

Yu, Frederick T. C. "The Voice of America in Communist China." In *The Case for Reappraisal of U.S. Overseas Information Policies and Programs*, edited by Edward L. Bernays and Burnet Hershey. New York: Praeger, 1970.

## Newspapers and Magazines

*Broadcasting*, 1937–42.
*New York Times*, 1942–45.
*Radio Guide*, 1935–40.
*Variety*, 1935–42.

# Index

033474

3  5282  00675  8901